SEMIOTEXT(E) FOREIGN AGENTS SERIES

Originally published as *Sphären I. Blasen* by Editions Suhrkamp, Frankfurt.
© Suhrkamp Verlag Frankfurt am Main 1998. All rights reserved

Published by Semiotext(e)
PO BOX 629, South Pasadena, CA 91031
www.semiotexte.com

Special thanks to Marc Lowenthal and John Ebert.

Cover art by Eva Schlegel. Draft for Installation, MAK Vienna, 2010.
Design: Hedi El Kholti

ISBN: 978-1-58435-104-7
Distributed by The MIT Press, Cambridge, Mass. and London, England
Printed in the United States of America
10 9 8 7 6 5

SPHERES

VOLUME I: BUBBLES

MICROSPHEROLOGY

Peter Sloterdijk

Translated by Wieland Hoban

Contents

The difficulty that had to be overcome [...] was to avoid all geometrical evidence. In other words, I had to start with a sort of intimacy of roundness.

— Gaston Bachelard, *The Poetics of Space*

Tradition has it that Plato put an inscription at the entrance to his academy, reading: "Let no one enter who is not a geometrician." Were these arrogant words? A declaration of war on the vulgar mind? Undoubtedly; for it was not without reason that a new form of elitism was invented at the academy. For one amazing moment, the school and the avant-garde were identical. Avant-gardism is the skill of forcing all members of a society to make a decision about a suggestion that has not come from them. It was Socrates who first went about this game seriously, and Plato escalated the philosophical provocation by elevating the compulsion to choose between knowledge and nonknowledge to a higher authority. In shutting out the ageometric rabble and only admitting candidates equipped with the appropriate knowledge, he challenged all mortals to qualify themselves for access to his research community by showing the necessary credentials. Here one must bear in mind: what are humans in the academic age but forgetful mammals that have, in most cases, merely forgotten that they are geometricians at heart? A geometrician—what is that? An intelligence coming from the world of the dead, bringing vague memories with it of a stay in a perfect sphere. Exoterically effective philosophy begins by splitting society into those who remember and those who do not—and, furthermore, into those who remember a particular thing and those who remember something else. That has remained its business to this day, even if the criteria for the division have become a little more complicated.

Like any author who has come a little way since his magical beginnings, I am aware that it is impossible to restrict the uses to which the literate community puts published writings to one single perspective in advance. Nonetheless, it strikes me as useful to point out that the following reflections, in their general outlines, are probably best read as a radicalization of Plato's motto. I would not only set Plato's statement above the gate to an academy, but above the gate to life itself—were it not such an inappropriate idea to adorn the doorway to the light of the world, which is already too narrow, with warning signs… We appeared in life with no prior geometric schooling, and no philosophy can subject us to an entrance examination after the fact. This does not alter the exclusive mandate of philosophy in the slightest, however, because the assumption that we are given the world only through innate geometric prejudices cannot simply be dismissed. Could one not hold the view that life is a constant *a posteriori* testing of our knowledge about the space from which everything emanates? And the splitting of society into those who know something about this and those who know nothing—does it not extend deeper in the present than ever before?

Life is a matter of form—that is the hypothesis we associate with the venerable philosophical and geometric term "sphere."

It suggests that life, the formation of spheres and thinking are different expressions for the same thing. Referring to a vital spheric geometry is only productive, however, if one concedes the existence of a form of theory that knows more about life than life itself does—and that wherever human life is found, whether nomadic or settled, inhabited orbs appear, wandering or stationary orbs which, in a sense, are rounder than anything that can be drawn with compasses. The following books are devoted to the attempt to probe the possibilities and boundaries of geometric vitalism.

A rather extravagant configuration of theory and life, one must admit. The hubris of this angle may become more bearable, or at least understandable, if one remembers that there was a second inscription above the entrance to the academy, occult and humorous, stating that whoever was unwilling to become entangled in love affairs with other visitors in the garden of theory should keep away. One can already sense it: this motto too must be applied to life as a whole. Whoever has no interest in sphere formation must naturally avoid amorous dramas, and whoever steers clear of eros excludes themselves from the efforts to understand the vital form. And so the hubris changes camps: the exclusivity of philosophy is expressed not in its own presumptuousness, but in the self-gratification of those who are certain of being able to dispense with philosophical thought. If philosophy is exclusive, it mirrors most people's self-exclusion from the best—in exaggerating the existing division in society, however, it creates an awareness of these exclusions and puts them to the vote again. Philosophical exaggeration provides an opportunity to revise completed options and decide against exclusion. Hence philosophy, if it is sufficiently focused on its task, is always also self-advertisement. If others see something else as the best, and achieve something convincing as a result, then so much the better.

The present attempt, as one can see, declares its concern with reference to a Platonic problem; it does not view itself as part of Platonism, however, assuming the latter means the sum of misguided readings that have made the founder of the Athenian academy an object of debate throughout the ages—including the anti-Platonism extending from Kant to Heidegger and their successors. I will only remain on the trail of Platonic references in the sense that I will develop, more obstinately than usual, the hypothesis that love stories are stories of form, and that every act of solidarity is an act of sphere formation, that is to say the creation of an interior.

The surpluses of first love, once it breaks away from its origins to make its own fresh starts elsewhere, also feed philosophical thought—which, we must above all remember, is a case of transference love for the whole. Unfortunately, many of those active in the current intellectual discourse have contented themselves with characterizing the phenomenon of transference love as a neurotic mechanism that is to blame for genuine passions being felt in the wrong places most of the time. Nothing has harmed philosophical thought more than this pitiful reduction of motives, which has sought to validate itself—rightly and wrongly—through psychoanalytical models. Rather, one must insist that transference is the formal source of the creative processes that inspire the exodus of humans into the open. We do not so much transfer incorrigible affects onto unknown persons as early spatial experiences to new places, and primary movements onto remote locations.

The limits of my capacity for transference are the limits of my world.

If I had to place a sign of my own at the entrance to this trilogy, it would be this: let no one enter who is unwilling to praise transference and to refute loneliness.

SPHERES

VOLUME 1: BUBBLES

MICROSPHEROLOGY

Bubbles, mezzotint by G. H. Every, 1887, after Sir John Everett Millais (1829–1896)

The Allies;
Or, The Breathed Commune

The child stands enraptured on the balcony, holding its new present and watching the soap bubbles float into the sky as it blows them out of the little loop in front of his mouth. Now a swarm of bubbles erupts upwards, as chaotically vivacious as a throw of shimmering blue marbles. Then, at a subsequent attempt, a large oval balloon, filled with timid life, quivers off the loop and floats down to the street, carried along by the breeze. It is followed by the hopes of the delighted child, floating out into the space in its own magic bubble as if, for a few seconds, its fate depended on that of the nervous entity. When the bubble finally bursts after a trembling, drawn-out flight, the soap bubble artist on the balcony emits a sound that is at once a sigh and a cheer. For the duration of the bubble's life the blower was outside himself, as if the little orb's survival depended on remaining encased in an attention that floated out with it. Any lack of accompaniment, any waning of that solidary hope and anxiety would have damned the iridescent object to premature failure. But even when, immersed in the eager supervision of its creator, it was allowed to drift through space for a wonderful while, it still had to vanish into nothingness in the end. In the place where the orb burst, the blower's excorporated soul was left alone for a moment, as if it had embarked on a shared expedition only to lose its partner halfway. But the melancholy lasts no more than a second before the joy of playing returns with its time-honored cruel momentum. What are broken hopes but opportunities for new attempts? The game continues tirelessly, once again the orbs float from on high, and once again the blower assists his works of art with attentive joy in their flight through the delicate space. At the climax, when the blower is as infatuated with his orbs as if they were self-worked miracles, the erupting and departing soap bubbles are in no danger of perishing prematurely for lack of rapturous accompaniment. The little wizard's attention follows their trail and flies out into the open, supporting the thin walls of the breathed bodies with its eager presence. There is a solidarity between the soap bubble and its blower that excludes the rest of the world. And each time the shimmering entities drift into the distance, the little artist exits his body on the balcony to be entirely with the objects he has called into existence. In the ecstasy of attentiveness, the child's consciousness has virtually left its corporeal source. While exhaled air usually vanishes without a trace, the breath encased in these orbs is granted a momentary afterlife. While the bubbles move through space, their creator is truly outside himself—with them and in them. In the orbs, his exhaled air has separated from him and is now preserved and carried further; at the same time, the child is transported away from itself by losing itself in the breathless co-flight of its attention through the animated space. For its creator, the soap bubble thus becomes the medium of a surprising soul expansion. The bubble and its blower coexist in a field spread out through attentive involvement. The child that follows its soap bubbles into the open is no Cartesian sub-ject, remaining planted on its extensionless thought-point while observing an extended thing on its course through space. In enthusiastic solidarity with his iridescent globes, the experi-menting player plunges into the open space and transforms the zone between the eye and the object into an animated sphere. All eyes and attention, the child's face opens itself up to the space in front of it. Now the playing child imperceptibly gains an insight in the midst of its joyful entertainment that it will later forget under the strain of school: that the spirit, in its own way, is in space. Or perhaps one should say that when people referred in former times to "spirit," what they meant was always inspired spatial communities? As soon as one begins making concessions to such suspicions, it becomes natural to investigate further in the same direction: if the child breathes its air into the soap bubbles and remains loyal by following them with its ecstatic gaze—who previously placed their breath into the child? Who remains loyal to the child upon its own exodus from the nursery? In what attentions, what spaces of animation will the children remain contained if their lives on ascending paths succeed? Who will accompany the young ones on their way to things and their epitome, the divided world? Is there someone, under all those circumstances, whose ecstasy the children will be when they float out into the space of possibility—and what will happen to those who are nobody's exhalation? Indeed, does all life that emerges and goes its own separate way remain contained in an accompanying breath? Is it legitimate to imagine that every-thing which exists and becomes relevant is someone's concern? The need is a familiar one, in fact—Schopenhauer called it the metaphysical one—the need for all things belonging to the world or being as a whole to be contained in a breath like an indelible purpose. Can this need be satisfied? Can it be justified? Who first had the thought that the world is nothing but the soap bubble of an all-encompassing breath? Whose being-outside-oneself would everything that is the case then be?

The thought of the Modern Age, which presented itself for so long under the naïve name of "Enlightenment" and the even more naïve programmatic word "progress," is characterized by an innate movement: wherever it follows its typical forward motion, it achieves the breakthrough of the intellect out of the caves of human illusion into the nonhuman world outside. It is no coincidence that the cosmological turn named after Copernicus marks the start of the newer history of knowledge and disappointment. It brought the people of the First World the loss of the cosmological center, and subsequently set off an age of progressive decentralizations. From that point on, earth's citizens, the old mortals, could bid farewell to all illusions about their position in the lap of the cosmos, even if such ideas cling to us like inborn illusions. Copernicus' heliocentric theory initiated a series of research eruptions into the deserted outer reaches, extending to the inhumanly remote galaxies and the most ghostly components of matter. The cold new breath from outside was sensed early on, and a number of the pioneers of the revolutionarily changed knowledge about the position of the earth in space did not conceal their unease in the infinity now imposed on them; thus even Kepler objected to Bruno's doctrine of the endless universe with the words that "this very cogitation carries with it I don't know what secret, hidden horror; indeed one finds oneself wandering in this immensity, to which are

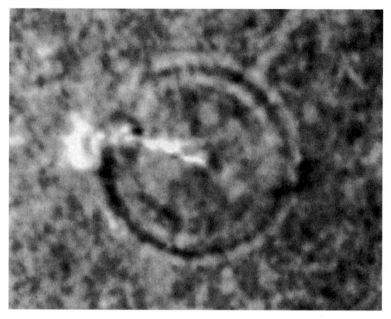

Circle without Constructor I, solar quake: the spreading waves reach a size corresponding to ten times the earth's diameter, photographed by the space probe SOHO

denied limits and center and therefore all determinate places."[1] Evasions to the outermost realms were followed by irruptions of coldness from the cosmic and technical ice worlds into the human inner sphere. Since the start of the Modern Age, the human world has constantly—every century, every decade, every year and every day—had to learn to accept and integrate new truths about an outside not related to humans. From the seventeenth century on, starting with the European educated classes and increasingly affecting the informed masses of the First World, the new psycho-cosmologically relevant sentiment spread that humans were not the concern of evolution, the indifferent goddess of becoming. Every view into the earthly

Circle without Constructor II, cartwheel galaxy in the Sculptor constellation, photographed by the Hubble Space Telescope

factory and the extraterrestrial spaces provided increasing evidence that mankind is towered above on all sides by monstrous externalities that breathe on it with stellar coldness and extra-human complexity. The old nature of *homo sapiens* is not up to these provocations by the outside. Research and the raising of consciousness have turned man into the idiot of the cosmos; he has sent himself into exile and expatriated himself from his immemorial security in self-blown bubbles of illusions into a senseless, unrelated realm that functions on its own. With the help of its relentlessly probing intelligence, the open animal tore down the roof of its old house from the inside. Taking part in modernity means putting evolved immune systems at risk. Since the English physicist and cosmographer Thomas Digges proved in the 1670s that the two-thousand-year doctrine of the celestial domes was both physically unfounded and thought-economically superfluous, the citizens of the Modern Age inevitably found themselves in a new situation that not only shattered the illusion of their home's central position in space, but also deprived them of the comforting notion that the earth is enclosed by spherical forms like warming heavenly mantles. Since then, modern people have had to learn how one goes about existing as a core without a shell; Pascal's pious and observant statement "the eternal silence of these infinite spaces fills me with dread" formulates the intimate confession of an epoch.[2] Since the times became new in the precise sense, being-in-the-world has meant having to cling to the earth's crust and praying to gravity—beyond any womb or shell. It cannot be mere coincidence: since the 1490s, those Europeans who sensed what had to be done have built and examined ball-shaped images of earth, globes, like possessed members of some undefined cult, as if the sight of these fetishes was to console them for the fact that they would exist for all eternity only on a ball, but no longer inside a ball. We will show that everything referred to as "globalization" today comes from this play with the eccentric ball. Friedrich Nietzsche, the master formulator of the truths one cannot live with, but cannot ignore without intellectual dishonesty, finally articulated what the world as a whole had to accept becoming for the modern entrepreneurs: "a gate to a thousand deserts, empty and cold."[3] Living in the Modern Age means paying the price for shellessness. The peeled human being acts out its epochal psychosis by replying to external cooling with warming technologies and climate policies—or with climate technologies and warming policies. But now that God's shimmering bubbles, the celestial domes, have burst, who could have the power to create prosthetic husks around those who have been exposed?

To oppose the cosmic frost infiltrating the human sphere through the open windows of the Enlightenment, modern humanity makes use of a deliberate greenhouse effect: it attempts to balance out its shellessness in space, following the shattering of the celestial domes, through an artificial civilizatory world. This is the final horizon of Euro-American technological titanism. From this perspective, the Modern Age appears as the age of an oath sworn in offensive desperation: that a comprehensive house-building operation for the species and a policy of global warming must be successful faced with the open, cold and silent sky. It is above all the entrepreneurial nations of the First World that have translated their acquired psycho-cosmological restlessness into offensive constructivism. They protect themselves from the terror of the bottomless, of the infinitely expanded space, through the utopian yet pragmatic erection of a global greenhouse intended to offer modern living in the open. That is why the further the process of globalization proceeds, the more one ultimately finds people looking at the sky—by day or by night—indifferently and distractedly; in fact, it has almost become a sign of naïveté to continue pursuing cosmological questions with existential pathos. By contrast, the certainty that there is nothing more to look for up there is in keeping with the spirit of advanced circumstances. For it is not cosmology that tells people today where they stand, but rather the general theory of immune systems. What makes the Modern Age special is that after the turn to the Copernican world, the sky as an immune system was suddenly useless.[4] Modernity is characterized by the technical production of its immunities and the increasing removal of its safety structures from the traditional theological and cosmological narratives. Industrial-scale civilization, the welfare state, the world market and the media sphere: all these large-scale projects aim, in a shelless time, for an imitation of the now impossible, imaginary spheric security. Now networks and insurance policies are meant to replace the celestial domes; telecommunication has to reenact the all-encompassing. The body of humanity seeks to create a new immune constitution in an electronic medial skin. Because the old all-encompassing and containing structure, the heavenly *continens* firmament, is irretrievably lost, that which is no longer encompassed and no longer contained, the former *contentum*, must now create its own satisfaction on artificial continents under artificial skies and domes.[5] Those who help to build the global civilization greenhouse, however, become entangled in thermo-political paradoxes: to achieve its creation—and this spatial fantasy underlies the globalization project—enormous populations, at the center as well as the margins, must be evacuated from their old casing of temperate regional illusion and exposed to the frosts of freedom. Here total constructivism unbendingly demands its price. To free up ground for the artificial surrogate sphere, the leftovers of faith in inner worlds and the fiction of security are being destroyed in all old countries in the name of a thoroughgoing market enlightenment that promises a better life, yet initially lowers the immune standards of the proletariats and marginal peoples to a devastating degree. Dumbfounded masses soon find themselves in the open, without ever receiving a proper explanation of their evacuation's purpose. Disappointed, cold and abandoned, they wrap themselves in surrogates of older conceptions of the world, as long as these still seem to hold a trace of the warmth of old human illusions of encompassedness.

> Who gave us the sponge to wipe away the entire horizon? What were we doing when we unchained this earth from its sun? Where is it moving to now? Where are we moving to? Away from all suns? Are we not continually falling? And backwards, sidewards, forwards, in all directions? Is there still an up and a down? Aren't we straying as though through an infinite nothing? Isn't empty space breathing at us? Hasn't it got colder?[6]

These questions open up the yawning abyss that current discourses on globalization ignore in their industrious hysteria. In shelless times, without spatial orientation and overwhelmed by their own progress, those living in modernity suddenly had to become splendid people by the masses. One can view technological civilization, in particular its accelerations in the twentieth century, as an attempt to drown the questions of Nietzsche's chief witness, the tragic Diogenes, in comfort. By making technical living tools of unknown perfection available to individuals, the modern world aims thus to silence their uneasy inquiries about the space in which they live, or from which they constantly fall. And yet it was precisely existentialist modernity that identified the reasons why it is less important for people to know *who* they are than *where* they are. As long as intelligence is sealed up by banality, people are not interested in their place, which seems given; they fix their imaginations on the ghost lights that appear to them in the form of names, identities and business. What recent philosophers have termed forgetfulness of being [*Seinsvergessenheit*] is most evident as an obstinate willful ignorance of the mysterious place of existence. The popular plan to forget both oneself and being is realized through a deliberate nonawareness of the ontological situation. This willfulness is currently fuelling all forms of rapid living, civil disinterestedness and anorganic eroticism. It drives its agents to limit themselves to small, malicious arithmetic units; the greedy of recent days no longer ask where they are as long as they are allowed to be someone, anyone. If, by contrast, we are here attempting to pose the question of "where?" anew in a radical fashion, that means restoring to contemporary thought its feeling for absolute localization, and with it the feeling for the basis of the difference between small and large.

It is possible to give a competent contemporary reply to the Gnostically inspired question "where are we if we are in the world?" We are in an outside that carries inner worlds. With the hypothesis of the priorness of the outside in mind, we no longer need to undertake any naïve investigations into mankind's position in the cosmos. It is too late to dream ourselves back to a place under celestial domes whose interiors would permit domestic feelings of order. That security in the largest circle has been destroyed for those in the know, along with the old homely, immunizing cosmos itself. Whoever still wished to look outwards and upwards would find themselves in a space devoid of humans and remote from the earth, with no relevant boundaries. Even on the smallest material level, complexities have been revealed in which we are the ones who are excluded and remote. Thus an inquiry into our location is more productive than ever, as it examines the place that humans create in order to have somewhere they can appear as those who they are. Here, following a venerable tradition, this place bears the name "sphere." The sphere is the interior, disclosed, shared realm inhabited by humans—in so far as they succeed in becoming humans. Because living always means building spheres, both on a small and a large scale, humans are the beings that establish globes and look out into horizons. Living in spheres means creating the dimension in which humans can be contained. Spheres are immune-systemically effective space creations for ecstatic beings that are operated upon by the outside.

The vessels thus filled with You do not render You any support: for though they perished utterly, You would not be spilt out. And in pouring Yourself out upon us, You do not come down to us but rather elevate us to You: You are not scattered over us, but we are gathered into one by You.

— Saint Augustine, *Confessions*, Book I, III[7]

Among the outdated and valuable expressions that metaphysics used, in its time, to build subtle bridges between heaven and earth, there is one that still comes to the aid of some contemporaries—and not only artists and their imitators—when faced with the problem of finding a respectable name for the source of their ideas and inventions: inspiration. Even if the word seems antiquated, and sooner earns its users a smile than recognition, it has not entirely lost its symbolic radiance. It is still vaguely suitable for marking the unclearly different, heterotopic origin of those ideas and works which cannot simply be attributed to the application of rules and the technical repetition of familiar searching and finding patterns. Whoever invokes inspiration admits that creative ideas are nontrivial events whose occurrence cannot be forced. Its medium is not its master, and its recipient is not its producer. Whether it is genius that whispers the idea to its executor or chance that makes the dice fall as they do, whether it is a rupture in the usual conceptual fabric that leads to the articulation of thoughts never thought before, or whether a productive error results in the new: whatever powers are considered possible transmitters of the inspired idea, the receiver always knows that in a sense, beyond their own efforts, they have housed visitors from elsewhere in their thought. Inspiration—breathing life into something, intuition, the instantaneous appearance of the idea or a gaping open of the new: in former times, when it could still be used without irony, the concept referred to the fact that an informing power superior in nature makes a human consciousness its mouthpiece or sounding board. Heaven, metaphysicians would say, appears as the earth's informant and gives its sign; something foreign passes through the door of the own and acquires validity. And although the foreign no longer bears any lofty, concisely metaphysical name today—not Apollo, not Yahwe, not Gabriel, not Krishna and not Xango—the phenomenon of the inspired idea has not disappeared entirely from enlightened fields of view. Whoever experiences inspired ideas can, even in post-metaphysical or hetero-metaphysical times, understand themselves as a host or matrix for the non-own. It is only with reference to such passings-through by the foreign that a tenable concept of what subjectivity could mean can be articulated in our times. Certainly the entering visitors have become anonymous today. Even if, as the joke goes, one is often surprised to which people the ideas choose to occur: no one who is familiar with the process need doubt their sudden arrival. Where they appear, one acknowledges their presence without any closer concern for their provenance. Whatever enters the imagination is not supposed to come from anywhere except somewhere over there, from without, from an open field that is not necessarily a yonder realm. People no longer want to receive their inspired ideas from some embarrassing heavens; they are supposed to come from the no man's land of ownerless, precise thoughts. Through their lack of a sender, they permit the free use of their gift. The inspired idea that delivers something for you remains a discreet visitor at the door. It makes no religion of itself, in so far as such a religion always involves fealty to its founder's name. Its antonym, which many rightly find beneficial, creates one of the preconditions for finally asking today, in general terms, about the nature of what we call media. Media theory: what is it, practiced *lege artis*,[8] other than the conceptual work to supplement regular visits both discreet and indiscreet? Messages, senders, channels, languages—these are the basic concepts, frequently misunderstood, of a general science of visitability of something by something in something. We will show that media theory and sphere theory converge; this is a hypothesis for whose proof three books cannot be excessive. In spheres, shared inspirations become the reason for the possibility of humans existing together in communes and peoples. The first thing that develops within them is that strong relationship between humans and their motives of animation—and animations are visits that remain—which provide the reason for solidarity.

The primal scene for what, in the Judeo-Christian tradition, deserves to be called inspiration, is the creation of humans—an event that appears in the Genesis account in two versions: once as the final act of the six-day work of creation, though it passes over the life-breathing scene in silence, and once as the initiatory act for all further creation, but now with an explicit emphasis on creation through breath and with the characteristic distinction of clay modeling in the first case and breathing in the second. Here the reader of Genesis encounters the inspirator, the Lord of Creation, as a figure with a sharp ontological profile: He is the first producer with complete authority. The creature into which He breathes life, for its part, appears on the stage of existence as the first human being, the prototype of a species that can experience inspired ideas. The biblical account of the first breath reproduces the original visit of the spirit to a host medium.

> When the Lord God made the earth and the heavens—and no shrub of the field had yet appeared on the earth and no plant of the field had yet sprung up, for the Lord God had not sent rain on the earth and there was no man to work the ground, but streams came up from the earth and watered the whole surface of the ground—the Lord God formed the man from the dust of the ground and breathed into his nostrils the breath of life, and the man became a living being. (Genesis 2:4–7)[9]

Would it be possible to speak of this breath in a language not yet molded into formulas by theologians' routines and pious subordinations to its supposed and prescribed meaning? If one takes seriously these lines that have been parroted, interpreted, translated and exploited ten thousand times as a statement about a production process, the explicit succession they describe reveals above all a procedural insight: man is an artificial entity that could only be created in two installments. In the first stage of the work process, as we read, the creator forms Adam—the clay creature taken from the soil, *adama*—and molds him into a work of art unlike any other that, like all products of artifice, owes its existence to the combination of artistic knowledge and raw material. Craft and earth are equally necessary to erect the image of man in the form of the first statue. Hence, in His initial access, the creator is no more than a potter who enjoys using suitable starting material to form a figure that resembles Himself, the producing master. Whoever wishes to imagine humans as primitive machines finds here an early model of how to create statues, human dolls, golems, robots, android illusions and the like according to the rules of art. The God of the first phase of human creation embodies a representative of the oldest technological culture, whose main emphasis is on ceramic skills. It was the potters who first discovered that earth is more than simply farmland to be cultivated. The ceramist as an early creator of works or demiurge has the experience to know that the ground which bears fruit can also be raw material for clay vessels to which *form*, clarity in conjunction with stability, is lent in workshops and ovens. If the Lord of Genesis began the creation of humans as a potter, it was because this creation succeeds most plausibly when it begins as the production of vessels. Being able to make android creatures according to ceramic routines: at the time of the biblical Genesis, this marked the state of art. Hence there is nothing unusual about Adam's body being manufactured from clay. It is initially no more than a hollow-bodied sculpture awaiting significant further use. Only then does the

Neolithic reconstruction of a head through the application of dyed plaster, which gave the skull the form of the layers of tissue that had once existed

extraordinary element come into play, for if the clay creature is made hollow in its original modeling, it is only because it is henceforth to serve as a jug of life. It is formed as a semi-solid figure from the start, as its creator has a special sort of filling in mind. Metaphysics begins as metaceramics, for the substance to be filled into this singular vessel will be no merely physical content. Though liquids can be taken up by the vase android in

Life-size clay figures from the burial complex of Qin Shi Huang (259–210 BC), first Emperor of China

limited amounts, its hollow space is of a more sublime nature, not suitable for being lined with sensual fluids. The Adamic vessel is created with cavities that only awaken to their true purpose in a second, initially very mysterious phase of creation: "…and breathed into his nostrils the breath of life, and the man became a living being."

With this act of inspiration, the second phase of the production of humans asserts its rights. Without the completion of the clay body through breath, Adam would forever have remained merely a bizarre work of earthen art; he would be no more than a willful installation on the untended earth. Such a statue would perhaps have been adequate as a burial gift for its producer, comparable to clay figures in the graves of ancient Chinese aristocrats; from a craftsman's perspective this Adam, at least in his upper parts, may have resembled his presumed technical models: the ancient Palestinian head sculptures produced through the application of a lifelike clay or plaster finish to skulls of the dead.[10] The account in Genesis, read outside of theological conventions, suggests that the semi-finished Adamitic products were given their decisive pneumatic value in a second operation. The implicit lesson is that man is a vascular creature, and only awakens to its destiny of being an "image" through a specific supplement. The Hebrew text refers to the living being with the word *nefesh*, which means something like "that which is animated by a living breath"; according to Hebrew scholars, this is largely synonymous with *ruach*, meaning "moving air, breath, breath of life, spirit, feeling and passion, thought." A two-phase process in procedural terms, this anthropopoiesis escalates from the creation of vessels to the creation of spirit beings, with this climax intended from the start; the breathing-in of life is not simply an ornamental supplement to an autonomous bodily massif. That is why each phase of the creation act has its own individual, resolutely *technical* character: if Adam, as the Genesis account purports, is to be understood in every respect as the creature or work of a creator—as a *factum* or *ens creatum*, the Latin *patres* would say—

then the divine power of creation must expressly encompass the task of producing beings that are fully animated, ontologically complete, intelligently active, equipped with subjectivity and, by virtue of all this, *godlike*.

Thus the Genesis account breaks open the horizon of the technical question with the last possible radicality: what technology is can henceforth only be understood by measuring the distance between what God was capable of *in illo tempore* and what humans will, in time, themselves be capable of. The first part of producing the human image is, as we have seen, no mystery with regard to humanity's divine maker, and humans have successfully repeated it under suitable conditions. The belief that the production of human images can be learned and mastered forms the basis for all master classes in nature studies at traditional art academies. The artificer from the first phase of creation would be no more than an art student noted for his talent in a nude painting class; he would simply be an applier of learnable arts. The second part, on the other hand, requires a thoroughly postgraduate trick that none but the God of Genesis have performed thus far: this addition tears the divide between human technology and theotechnology wide open. For, from a demiurgic perspective—and the tale of Adam is above all the myth of a supreme royal craftsman—the inner human spirit itself now purports to be the work of a manufacturer. How to awaken statues to animated life: this is something that, until recently, had simply been unknown to the human productive capacity. Breath was the epitome of a divine technology capable of closing the ontological gap between the clay idol and the animated human with a pneumatic sleight of hand. Consequently, the title "God" denotes an expertise whose art extends to the creation of living beings similar to oneself. As the creator of all things, the God of Genesis is lord of both the dissimilar and the similar. One can easily establish the significance of this hypothesis by looking at the simplest and highest creatures and, in the face of their givenness, reminding oneself that all of these, without exception, are meant to be understood as products of a single, continually active creative potency! Theologians tend to deny, on the other hand, that crystals, amoebas, trees or dragonflies are godlike. Nature, from a theological perspective, is the name for God's self-realization in the dissimilar. As far as realization in the similar is concerned, however, the most eminent text states with authority that Adam resembled his creator. One need therefore only take due notice of the factual existence of the animated clay creature to ask almost automatically: who was capable of that? Who was in a position to *make* man? By what method was he, the similar one, the subject, the spirited being who observes and handles the world as world, installed? In so far as we are concerned with the ceramic Adam, as stated earlier, we are sufficiently informed to lift the secret of his existence, as we know the rules of working with clay that reliably enable us to arrive at android figures. For a further treatment of the statue to yield a living human, on the other hand, we must introduce a pneumatic or noogenic bonus that, it would seem, we have so far lacked any procedural rules to imitate. The breathing in of life was a technical-hypertechnical procedure that had to be honored as God's exclusive patent throughout the entire period of religious-metaphysical thought. Nonetheless, in attributing Adam's spirit to the skilled act of a craftsman (or breathsman), the narrators of Genesis stretch out their hands for this bonus.

Since then, one part of high-cultural theology has always been the theology of the utmost skill and the interpretation of the world's totality in the light of a fabrication principle. God is an ecstasy of that idea of competence which encompasses the production of the world and its native subjectivities. With the advent of theo-technical thought, the European obsession with the ability to manufacture set in. One could yield to the suspicion that history itself, as a technological process, obeys the rule: where there was once God's secret technology, there must now be public human techniques. Perhaps what we call historicity is nothing but the time required for the attempt to repeat God's trick through human ability? This would urge us to conclude that even the breath of life must one day become a thoroughly formulated skill that can be brought down to earth from heaven. But can we dare to imagine a technology that makes the pneumatic rhythm of creation its own business? Should, with sufficiently precise formulable artistic and procedural rules, even the phenomenon once known as animation become something amenable to serial production? Should it transpire that breath sciences lie in the realm of possibility, and that the humanities have already embarked on repeating the divine breath through the higher mechanism?[11]

With these questions, we are drawing a veiled theme of the Jewish Genesis account to belated light: the issue here is Adam's chosen hollowness. What gives us food for thought is his vascular nature, his resonant constitution, his preferred aptness as a *canal* for breathing by an inspirator. From a conventional point of view, the historically established preconception that there must be an unbridgeable hierarchical divide—an ontological difference—between creator and creature could re-establish itself today. Is it not inevitable that the creature, even if we are dealing with man in relation to the maker of man, is so distant from its creator as to verge on meaninglessness? In this light, even the first man ever created will always appear primarily as the ceramic object shaped at will from an earthen nothing by the hands of a master craftsman, only to fall back some day—earth to earth—into the clay from which he originated.

It is only at second glance that a less hierarchical image of the connection between the creator-subject and his breathed-on piece of work suggests itself. Now we realize that there cannot possibly be such a sharp ontological asymmetry between the inspirator and the inspired as there is between an animated lord and his inanimate tool. Where the pneumatic pact between the giver and the taker of breath comes into effect—that is, where the communicative or communional alliance builds up—this results in a bipolar intimacy that cannot have anything in common with a merely dominating control of a subject over a manipulable object mass. Even if the breather and the one breathed on face each other as first and second in temporal terms, a reciprocal, synchronously interchanging relationship between the two breath poles comes into effect as soon as the infusion of the breath of life into the android form is complete. The main part of God's trick, it would seem, is to reckon with a counter-breath immediately after the initial one: one could almost say that the originator does not preexist the pneumatic work, but creates himself synchronously with it as the intimate counterpart of one like himself. Indeed, perhaps the notion of an originator is simply a misleading, conventional figure to describe the phenomenon of the resonance that originally developed. Once set up, the canal of animation between Adam and his Lord, filled with endless double echo games, can only be understood as a two-way system. The lord of all that lives would not also be the God of answers in whose guise he appears in His early invocations if confirmations of his breath impulses did not immediately flow back to Him from the animated figure. This breath is hence conspiratory, respiratory and inspiratory from the outset; as soon as breath exists, there are two breathing. With the number two at the start, it would be misguided to force any statement about which pole began in the interior of this dual. Naturally the myth must seek to describe how everything started and what came first—in this case as in most others. In attempting to do so in earnest, however, it must now also speak of an original exchange in which there can be no first pole. That is the meaning of the biblical reference to God's image: not that the Creator was some mystical solo android who was one day seized by the whim to trace His appearance—appearing to whom?—onto earthly bodies. This would be as absurd as the notion that God could have longed for the company of non-equal, formally similar clay figures. The creation of subjectivity and mutual animation does not refer to the hollow human puppet; the image of God is simply a rigidly visualizing term from the jargon of the artist's workshop for a relationship of pneumatic reciprocity. The intimate ability to communicate in a primary dual is God's patent. It suggests not so much a visually experienceable similarity between an original image and the replica as the original augmentation of God through his Adam, and of Adam through his God. Breath science can only get underway as a theory of pairs.

With this phrase—original augmentation—we have named a basic figure of the subsequent reflections in the spheromorphological field. It states that in the spiritual space—under the as yet unconsolidated assumption that "spirit" refers to a spatiality of its own kind—the simplest fact is automatically at least a two-part or bipolar quantity. Isolated points are only possible in the homogenized space of geometry and intercourse; true spirit, however, is by definition spirit in and in relation to spirit, and true soul is by definition soul in and in relation to soul. In the present case, the elemental, initial and simple already appears as a resonance between polar authorities; the original expresses itself as a correlative duality from the start. The addition of the second to the first occurs not in an external and *a posteriori* supplementation—in the way that, in classical logic, attributes join substances as latecomers of a sort, as suppliers of properties. Certainly, if one thinks in substances, the attributes arrive later, just as blackness is added to the horse and redness to the rose. In the intimate sharing of subjectivity by a pair inhabiting a spiritual space open for both, second and first only appear together. Where the second does not enter, the first was not given either. This means that whoever says "Creator" without emphasizing Adam's prior coexistence with Him has already strayed into an origin-monarchical error—just as anyone who presumes to speak of humans without mentioning their inspirators and intensifiers, or their media, which amount to the same, has missed the topic through their very approach. A Platonic horse or a heavenly rose: they could, if necessary, still remain what they are without blackness or redness. As far as God and Adam are concerned, however, they form—if the bond of breath between them is indeed as the wording and sense of the Genesis convey—a dyadic union from the start, a union that can only last on the basis of a developed bipolarity. The primary pair floats in an atmospheric biunity, mutual referentiality and intertwined freedom from which neither of the primal partners can be removed without canceling the total relationship.

If this strong relation inevitably seems asymmetrical in theological tradition—characterized by a powerful leaning towards God's side—it is primarily because, aside from his engagement with Adam, his co-subject, God is always assigned the indivisible burden of cosmogonic responsibilities. God appears as the absolute adult, indeed the only one in the universe—Adam and his ilk, on the other hand, remain children to the end in a sense. Only against this background was Augustine able to say to his God: "But You, Lord, know all of him, for You made him."[12] For the church father, the joy of being understood depends on the notion that only he who made you can also understand and restore you. This provides the basic impulse for all disciplines of the spirit and its healing, in so far as it marks the advent of the idea that understanding means having made, and, more importantly in religious terms, that having been made means being able to be understood and repaired—an idea on which all priesthood and all psychotherapeutic structures are based to this day. The main purpose of this demiurgic interpretation of human creatureliness was to make the pact between the producing God and the produced soul unbreakable. The damaged but prudent soul should constantly think of its originator or representative, the therapist, because only this thought can save it from ontological isolation and from losing its way amid the incomprehensible, the unmade, the fortuitous and the external. It was to Adam before the Fall of Man, and to him and his kind alone, that Saint Teresa of Ávila's rule applied: the soul must view all things as if the world consisted only of God and the soul—an idea still quoted approvingly by Leibniz[13]—whereas it pleases God to express Himself not only in Adam and his species, but in the entire household of the creation. In this respect the biblical God resembled a husband who has the conventional expectation that his wife should be there for him alone, while he must keep himself available not only for her, but also for a world of business. But He also resembled a mother who is good enough to give her child the secure sense that she is wholly there for it whenever necessary, even though she also has a house and hearth to look after when she is not attending to the little being. These asymmetries initially thwart the equality in the image; but this does not change the incomparable particularity of the pneumatic pact. The one breathed on is by necessity an ontological twin of the breather. The two are bonded by an intimate complicity such as can only exist between beings that originally share the placenta of subjectivity. Adam and his Lord live off the same ego-forming placenta—they nourish themselves with the same I-am-who-I-am substance that spreads between them like a subtle shared scent of intimacy and synchronous desire. The thorn bush in the desert burns not for itself alone, but always for itself and Moses, its agent and representative. That is why he is not meant to gaze at the flames in admiration when it burns, but form a chain of messengers: we, this fire and my testimony to it, belong together like the message and its immediate recipient. Flame and speech are original accomplices. The open secret of the historical world is that the power to belong together, which is experienced in exemplary fashion by select couples—and, why not, by burning bushes and prophets on fire—can be extended to communes, teams, project groups, and perhaps even entire peoples.

We refer to this connecting force, using a creaky word from the nineteenth century, as solidarity. The nature of this force, which allies people with their own kind or a superhuman other in shared vibrations, has never been examined sufficiently seriously in the history of thought. So far one has always presupposed and demanded solidarity, has attempted to raise it, politicize it and sabotage it; people have sung its praises and lamented its fragility; but never has anyone inquired far enough back into its origin. At this point we have at least realized that solidarity between people must be a transference phenomenon outside of primary couple relationships and primal hordes. But what is transferred here? The strong reason for being together is still awaiting an adequate interpretation.[14]

Let us translate these rhapsodic reflections on an Old European and Middle Eastern theological motif into the language of the present investigation: when the Jewish God and the prototypical human each turn their contact side towards the other, they form a shared interior sphere. What is here termed a sphere is, in a first and provisional understanding, an orb in two halves, polarized and differentiated from the start, yet nonetheless intimately joined, subjective and subject to experience—a biune shared space of present and past experience. What is known in tradition as spirit is thus originally, through sphere formation, spatially spread. In its basic form the sphere appears as a twin bubble, an ellipsoid space of spirit and experience with at least two inhabitants facing one another in polar kinship. Living in spheres thus means inhabiting a shared subtlety. The aim of this three-part book is to show that, for humans, being-in-spheres constitutes the basic relationship—admittedly, one that is infringed upon from the start by the non-interior world, and must perpetually assert itself against the provocation of the outside, restore itself and increase. In this sense, spheres are by definition also morpho-immunological constructs. Only in immune structures that form interiors can humans continue their generational processes and advance their individuations. Humans have never lived in a direct relationship with "nature," and their cultures have certainly never set foot in the realm of what we call the bare facts; their existence has always been exclusively in the breathed, divided, torn-open and restored space. They are the life forms designed to be floating beings—if floating means depending on divided moods and shared assumptions. Humans are thus fundamentally and exclusively the creations of their interior and the products of their work on the form of immanence that belongs inseparably to them. They flourish only in the greenhouse of their autogenous atmosphere.

What recent philosophers referred to as "being-in-the-world" first of all, and in most cases, means being-in-spheres. If humans are *there*,[15] it is initially in spaces that have opened for them because, by inhabiting them, humans have given them form, content, extension and relative duration. As spheres are the original product of human coexistence, however—something of which no theory of work has ever taken notice—these atmospheric-symbolic places for humans are dependent on constant renewal. Spheres are air conditioning systems in whose construction and calibration, for those living in real coexistence, it is out of the question not to participate. The symbolic air conditioning of the shared space is the primal production of every society. Indeed—humans create their own

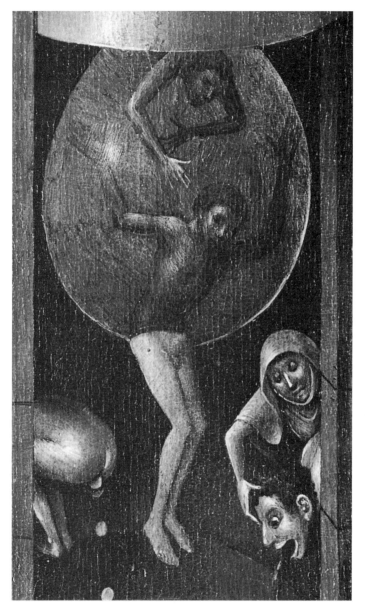

Hieronymus Bosch, *The Garden of Earthly Delights*, couple in bubble, detail

climate; not according to free choice, however, but under preexisting, given and handed-down conditions.[16]

Spheres are constantly disquieted by their inevitable instability: like happiness and glass, they bear the risks native to everything that shatters easily. They would not be constructs of vital geometry if they could not implode; even less so, however, if they were not also capable of expanding into richer structures under the pressure of group growth. Where implosion occurs, the shared space as such is cancelled out. What Heidegger called being-toward-death means not so much the individual's long march into a final solitude anticipated with panic-stricken resolve; it is rather the circumstance that all individuals will one day leave the space in which they were allied with others in a current, strong relationship. That is why death ultimately concerns the survivors more than the deceased.[17] Human death thus always has two faces: one that leaves behind a rigid body and one that shows sphere residues—those that are sublated into higher spaces and re-animated and those that, as the waste products of things, fallen out of former spaces of animation, are left lying there. In structural terms, what we call the end of the world is the death of a sphere. This small-scale emergency is the separation of the lovers, the empty apartment, the torn-up photograph; its comprehensive form manifests itself as the death of a culture, the burnt-out city, the extinct language. Human and historical experience at least shows that spheres can continue to exist even beyond mortal separation, and that things lost can remain present in memories—as a memorial, a specter, a mission or as knowledge. It is only because of this that not every separation of lovers need become the end of the world, and not every change undergone by language a culture's demise.[18]

The fact that the internally differentiated bubble of those in intimate coexistence can initially seem to be resolutely closed and secure in itself is due to the tendency of the communicating poles to be consumed fully in their care for the other half. This is also manifest in the Jewish creation myth: in passing on His breath to Adam, the God of Genesis in fact places His utmost stake in the pneumatic relation. Adam and his companion, for their part, remain in their exclusive partnership with God for as long as they manage to allow nothing to grow inside themselves other than what was originally breathed into them: the awareness of their original counterpart's glory and its demand for an answer. I am the one closest to you and your inspirator; you shall have no other inspirator but me—the first commandment of dyadic communication. Initially, there is nothing within them but the breathed, back-and-forth double rejoicing of the pact against externality. Adam and his God form an oscillatory circuit of generosity that celebrates and elevates itself *in dulci iubilo*. Through God's communication with Adam, this mirroring of His being radiates unanimously back to Him from Adam. Perhaps it is appropriate to image the music of angels and sirens as the sonic miracle of such an untainted bi-unanimity.

Unscathed spheres carry their destruction within themselves: this too is taught with merciless stringency by the Jewish paradise account. There is nothing to impair the perfection of the first pneumatic bubble until the disturbance of a sphere leads to the primal catastrophe. The distractable Adam falls prey to a second inspiration through the secondary voices of the serpent and the woman; as a result he discovers what theologians called his freedom. Initially, however, this consists only in

Masaccio, *The Expulsion from Paradise*, fresco, 1427,
Capella Brancacci, Florence, detail

a certain willing openness to seduction by outside elements. The phenomenon of freedom subsequently takes on its full, unnerving magnitude by installing radicalized independence of will and the desire for other things than those prescribed, indeed for many kinds of things—all declensions of a metaphysically interpreted evil will. From the very first whim of individual freedom, however, humans lost the ability to stay in their place within the purely sounding biunity of the God-self space, devoid of all secondary voices. The "expulsion from paradise" is a mythical title for the spherological primal catastrophe—in psychological terminology it would be paraphrased as a general weaning trauma. Only an event of this kind—the withdrawal of the first completer—could give rise to what would later be termed the "psyche": the semblance of a soul that, almost like a private spark or an isolated vital principle, inhabits a single desirous body. The mythical process outlines the inevitable corruption of the original interior-forming biunity through the emergence of a third, a fourth and a fifth, which led to the advent of frolicking. The biune world had known neither number nor resistance, for even the mere awareness that there were other things, countable and third options, would have corrupted the initial homeostasis. The expulsion from paradise means the fall from the blissful inability to count. In the dyad, the united two even have the power to deny their twoness in unison; in their breathed retreat they form an alliance against numbers and interstices. *Secundum, tertium, quartum, quintum—non dantur.* We are what we are, without separations and joints: this space of happiness, this vibration, this animated echo chamber. We live, as intertwined beings, in the land of We. But this measureless, numberless happiness with closed eyes cannot ever last anywhere; in post-paradise times—and does the count not always start "after paradise lost"?—the sublime biune bubble is damned to burst.

The modalities of bursting set the conditions for cultural histories. Transitional objects, new themes, secondary themes, multiplicities and new media step between the two partners; the symbiotic space, once intimate and filled with a single motif, opens up into a multiple neutrality, where freedom is only granted along with foreignness, indifference and plurality. It is torn open by non-symbiotic urgencies; for the new is always born as something that disturbs earlier symbioses. It intervenes in the individual interior as an alarm and a compulsion. Now the adult cosmos becomes clear as the epitome of work, struggle, diversion and coercion. What was God becomes a lonely, transcendent pole. He survives in the only way he can: as a distant delusional address for scattered quests for salvation. What was Adam's symbiotically hollow interior now opens itself up to more and less spiritless occupants known as worries, entertainments or discourses; these fill out the space that, in the intimate state of coexistence, would have wanted to remain for free for the one, the initial breath partner. The adult has now understood that he has no right to happiness; at most, a call to remember that other state. Who would be allowed to follow it? The utmost that a consciousness filled with worry and violence can allow itself in the way of symbolic nurturances are backward-looking, yet also future-summoning phantasms of the reinstated dyad. Such dreams belong to the stuff of which the visionary religions are made; Plato's magic trail through the course of the European spirit also follows these dream lines. In countless encodings these phantasms, partly in public and partly concealed, call up witching images from the perfect globe of sheltering, sheltered mutual inspiration. Stirred up or sucked in by mysterious memories and regressions, sunken notions of a prehistoric breath community of the double soul on the sixth day of creation.

All history is the history of animation relationships. Its nucleus, as certain anticipatory formulations hinted, is the biune bond of radical inspiration communities. It may initially be unimportant whether this bond is addressed in the terms of the creation myth as the alliance of divine image between Yahwe and Adam, or under the psychoanalytical concept of the early mother-child dyad, or the poetic-existential figures of the inseparable lovers, the twins, the Great Couple and the conspiring two. In all these models, spheric liaisons are brought up in which reciprocal animations generate themselves through radical resonance; each of them demonstrates that real subjectivity consists of two or more parties. Where two of these are exclusively opened towards each other in intimate spatial division, a livable mode of subjectness develops in each; this is initially no more or less than a participation in spheric resonances.

In earlier times, it was almost exclusively religious traditions, with special considerations, that bore witness to this enigma of subjectivity as participation in a bipolar and pluripolar field.[19] Only with the incipient Modern Age did individual complexes step out of these vague constructs and move towards worldly views—especially in psychological, medical and aesthetic discourses. In premodern worlds, the only way for phenomena of biune and communitarian inspiration to articulate themselves was in religious languages—monovalent-animistic and bivalent-metaphysical ones. It will therefore be inevitable in the following reflections on the establishment of a general spherology also to open up the religious fields of European and non-European cultures in free traversals for an open discourse of intimacy. In doing so, this anthropology beyond humans identifies itself perhaps not as the servant-girl of theology, but certainly as its pupil. It would not, admittedly, be the first to outgrow its teacher. Worldly spherology is the attempt to free the pearl from the theological oyster.

The spherological drama of development—the emergence into history—begins at the moment when individuals step out into the multipolar worlds of adults as poles of a biunity field. They inevitably suffer a form of mental resettlement shock when the first bubble bursts, an existential uprooting: they come out of their infantile state by ceasing to live completely under the shadow of the united other and thus starting to become inhabitants of an expanded psycho-sociosphere. For them, this is where the birth of the outside takes place: upon emerging into the open, humans discover what they initially think can never become part of their own, inner, co-animated realm. There are, as humans learn fascinatedly and painfully, more dead and outer things between heaven and earth than any worldling can dream of appropriating. When the youths bid farewell to their maternal kitchens-cum-living rooms, they are confronted with subjectless, external, excitingly uncontrollable phenomena. They would not be viable human individuals, however, if they did not bring a dowry of memories of the symbiotic field and its enclosing power with them into the strange new land. It is this power to transfer the integral space that ultimately also overcomes the intruder trauma, the law of the disruptive third, fourth and fifth parties, for it integrates the disrupter like a new sibling—as if, in fact, it were a necessary element in its own system.

Piero della Francesca, *Brera Madonna*, detail

> Leopards break into the temple and drink to the dregs what is
> in the sacrificial pitchers; this is repeated over and over again;
> finally it can be calculated in advance, and it becomes part of
> the ceremony. (Franz Kafka)[20]

Time and again, the literature of the interior deprives the fortuitous and the senseless of its destructive sting. From the outset,

there is a process of world literature competing with the rise of the external, the foreign, the fortuitous and those forces that threaten to burst the sphere; its aim is to settle every outside, no matter how cruel and unfitting, all demons of the negative and monsters of foreignness, within an expanded inside. Context turns into text—as often and as long as the external is worked away or reduced to tolerable formats. In this sense, order is above all the effect of a transference from interior to exterior. What we know as the metaphysical worldviews of Old Europe and Asia are the tensest ascetic drawings-in of the foreign, the dead and the external into the circle of soul-animated, text-woven large-scale interiors. Until yesterday, their poets were the thinkers. They taught the citizens of being how to achieve symbiosis with the stars and the stones; they interpreted the outside as an educator. Hegel's great synthesis is the last European monument to this will to draw all negativity and externality into the inside of a logically sealed dome. But philosophy could not have erected its sublime constructions without the mandate of its carrier culture, and logical syntheses presuppose the political and military situations that demand such symbolic vaulting; their exoteric mission—living on a large scale, ruling over palaces and distant borders—requires consolidation through metaphysical knowledge. The first philosophy is the last transference. Novalis would go on to lift the secret when he interpreted thought allied with writing as a general homecoming: "Where are we going? Always home." The total parental home does not want to lose even the most foreign elements. On all paths to high culture, sphere extension and growing inclusivity dictate the law by which consciousness develops.

What we call growing up consists of these strenuous resettlings of smaller subjectivities in larger world forms; often, it simultaneously means the reformatting of the tribal consciousness to suit imperial and text-supported circumstances. For the child we were, the expanded space of interaction may be the large family for a while; as soon as the familial horizon is exceeded, however, the more developed social forms stake their claims to form and animate the individuals. As far as prehistoric times are concerned, the decisive social form manifests itself as the horde, with a tendency towards forming clan communities and tribes; in historical times, it appears as the people, with a tendency towards founding cities, nations and kingdoms. In both regimes, the prehistoric and the historical, human existence never simply adjusts itself to fit into what, using a modern and overly smooth term, we call its "environment"; rather, this existence creates its own surrounding space through which and in which it appears. Every social form has its own world house, a bell jar of purpose, under which human beings first of all gather, understand themselves, defend themselves, grow and dissolve boundaries. The hordes, tribes and peoples, and the empires all the more, are—in their respective formats—psycho-sociospheric quantities that arrange themselves, climatize themselves and contain themselves. At every moment of their existence, they are forced to place above themselves, by their typical means, their own semiotic heavens from which character-forming collective inspirations can flow to them.

No people can last in its own process of generations and in competition with other peoples unless it succeeds in keeping up its process of self-inspiration. What is referred to here as autogenous inspiration is, more dispassionately expressed, the continuum of ethnospheric climate techniques. Through ethnotechniques spanning generations, tens and hundreds of thousands, perhaps even millions of individuals are attuned to superior collective spirits and particular rhythms, melodies, projects, rituals and fragrances. By virtue of such formal games, which produce a shared and productive sensuality, the collected many keep finding the proof of their destiny to be together, even under adverse conditions; where this proof becomes powerless, discouraged people dissolve within stronger cultures or decline into rioting bands and childless leftover groups.[21] Because of its exaggerated aim, the task of enclosing such absurdly large numbers of people in unifying systems of delusion sounds like an impossible demand. Mastering precisely such difficulties, however, was obviously part of the logic of the way in which peoples were actually formed. In the historical world, it seems, the more improbable option develops an inclination to assert itself as the realer one. How implausible and impossible the mere existence of a united mass like a people seems from the perspective of the primal hordes—the cultural synthesis of a thousand or ten thousand hordes—yet it is the peoples who made history, sucked up the hordes and demoted them to mere families or houses. To us, the concept of empire—in terms of the swarming of tribes and peoples—seems all the more of an impossibility; it is precisely the polyethnic empires, however, that called the tune of volatile history during the last four millennia and translated their expectations of order into reality. Anyone who studies the course of the past ten millennia with regard to the creation of peoples must conclude from the evidence that wherever there are peoples, divine heavens to form these peoples cannot be far away. The native gods stand, like ethnotechnic universals, for communality instead of diverse segments—they are the unbelievable that demanded belief, and did so with the greatest historical success. Almost everywhere, brute force had a catalytic role in ethnopoietic processes. It is only the language games of the gods, however, that prove to be effective guarantees of longer-lasting ethnospheric animation effects; one could say that they ensure syntheses of peoples *a priori*.

The case of the Jewish Yahwe, the spirit God who blows over the desert, is an especially striking example of a supreme inspirator carrying out His ethnopoietic office for His chosen people. Not only does he remain the intimate God of Adam and Abraham, and offer himself to human souls in the monotheistic cultures as the eternal super-thou; He is, above all, the transcendent integrator who unites the twelve tribes to form the people of Israel. He is the one who stabilizes his people not only as bearers of the law, but also as a military stress community,[22] enabling them to assert themselves at the ever-changing battlefronts of innumerable conflicts. He commits Himself to His people in the most remarkable manner by binding it to Him through the pneumatic legal form of the covenant. Friedrich Heer once observed that the sheer physical existence of the Jewish people in the present essentially amounts to a proof of God from history; in less effusive terms, one could say that the historical persistence of Judaism through the last three thousand years at least constitutes the most concrete of all spheric proofs based on survival.[23]

In spherological terms, peoples appear above all as communities of cult, arousal, effort and inspiration. As autogenous vessels, they live and survive only under their own atmospheric, semiospheric bell jar. Through their gods, their stories and their arts, they supply themselves with the breath—and thus the stimuli—that make them possible. In this sense, they are successful pneumotechnic and auto-stressory constructs. By lasting, peoples prove their ethnotechnic genius *ipso facto*. And although the individuals within peoples pursue their own concerns in relative obliviousness, overarching myths, rituals and self-stimulations still create social fabrics of sufficient ethnic coherence, even from the most resistant material. Such endogenously stressed collective bodies are spheric alliances that drift in the current of the ages. That is why the most successful sphere-forming communities, the religion-based folk traditions or cultures, have survived for centuries with impressive ethnospiritual constancy. The prime example, alongside Judaism, is Indo-Aryan Brahmanism, which has been symbolically air-conditioning the Hindu world for millennia. The Chinese continuum likewise confirms the law that sphere politics is fate: was China not one great artistic exercise on the theme "existence in an exteriorless, self-immured space" until the turn of our decade? We shall attempt, especially in the second volume, to explain how this imperial enclosure reflected the characteristic spatial understanding of the metaphysical epoch.

Speaking of spheres, then, does not only mean developing a theory of symbiotic intimacy and couple-surrealism; though sphere theory by its nature begins as a psychology of inner spatial formation from biune correspondences, it inevitably develops further into a *general theory of autogenous vessels*. This theory provides the abstract form for all immunologies. Under the sign of the spheres, finally, the question is posed as to the *form* of political outer space creations as such.

In our account, then, sphere psychology will go before sphere politics; the philosophy of intimacy must be used to support political morphology, open it up, accompany it and circle it. This order has an obvious dramaturgical reason, but ultimately stems from the matter itself. At its beginning, every life goes through a phase in which a mild two-person illusion defines the world. Caring ecstasies enclose mothers and children in an amorous bell whose resonances remain, under all circumstances, a precondition for a successful life. Early on, however, the unified two become related to third, fourth and fifth elements; as the singular life ventures out of its initial shell, additional poles and larger spatial dimensions open up, each defining the extent of the developing and developed connections, worries and participation. In fully-grown spheres, forces are at work that draw the individual into an illusion shared by millions. It seems impossible to live in large societies without yielding in some measure to the delirium of one's own tribe. From the outset, therefore, spherology examines the risks involved in transference processes from micro- to macropsychoses. What it considers above all else, however, is the exodus of the living from the real and the virtual mother's womb into the dense cosmoses of the regional advanced civilizations, and beyond these into the non-round, non-dense foam worlds of modern global culture. In this, our account follows the Romanesque idea of describing the world as a glass bead game, even if, conditioned by its subject, it will take away the weightlessness of this motif. Spheres are forms as forces of destiny—from the fetal marble in its private, dark waters to the cosmic-imperial ball that appears before us with the supremely confident aim of containing and rolling over us.

Once spheres are elevated to a theme as effective forms of the real, the perspective of the world's *form* reveals the key to its symbolic and pragmatic order. We can explicate why, wherever people think in large round forms, the idea of self-sacrifice inevitably gains power. From time immemorial, the massive globes that present mortals with their comforting roundness have demanded that whatever does not fit into the smooth curvature of the whole should be subordinated to them: first of all the stubborn, cumbersome, private ego, which has always resisted complete absorption into the great round self. The forces of empire and salvation find their obligatory aesthetic in the circle. Hence our phenomenology of spheres is forced by the obstinacy of its theme to overturn the morphological altar on which, in imperial times, the non-round was always sacrificed to the round. On the largest scale, the theory of spheres leads into a critique of round reason.

The first book of this sphere trilogy speaks of microspheric units that will be referred to here as *bubbles*. They constitute the intimate forms of the rounded being-in-form and the basic molecule of the strong relationship. Our analysis sets about the task, never undertaken before, of narrating the epic of those biunities that have always been lost to the adult intelligence, yet never fully eradicated. We shall dive into a lost history that tells of the blossoming and sinking of the intimate Atlantis; we will explore a breathed continent in the matriarchal sea that we inhabited in a subjectively prehistoric time, and abandoned with the start of what we believe to be our own histories. In this distinctive world, elusive quantities flash at the edge of conventional logic. Recognizing our inevitable conceptual helplessness as our only sure companion, we traverse landscapes of pre-objective existence and prior relationships. If it were appropriate to speak of penetrating,

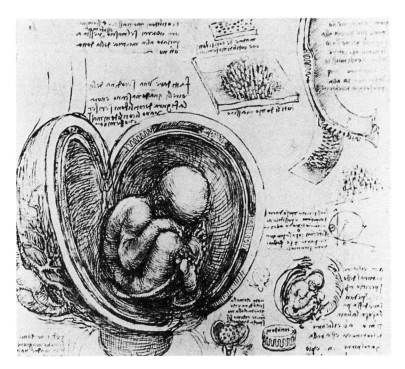

Leonardo da Vinci, drawing with uterus, embryo and placenta, c. 1520, detail

one might say that we will penetrate into the realm of intimate absurdities.[24] The things themselves, however, as becomes apparent, will only tolerate non-invasive invasions; in this area one must entrust oneself, more permissively than in one's usual methodical explorations and goal-directed thought tasks, to a drift that pulls us forwards on the lymphatic currents of pre-subjectively primitive self-awareness. On the way through the evasive underworld of the inner world, the schematic image of a fluid and auratic universe unfolds like a map in sound, woven entirely from resonances and suspended matter; it is there that we must seek the prehistory of all things pertaining to the soul.

By its very nature, this search has the form of an impossible problem that can neither be solved nor left alone.

These journeys along the edges to the source regions of the soul, self-sense and entwinement bring to light just how far the prehistory of the intimate has always proceeded as a history of mental catastrophe. One cannot speak of the intimate spheres without mentioning how their bursting and expanded regeneration take place. All amniotic sacs,[25] organic models of autogenous vessels, live towards their bursting; with the turbulent waters of birth, every life is washed up on the coast of harder facts. Those who reach it can use those facts to explain what drives the intimate, all too intimate bubbles to failure and forces their inhabitants into transformations.

The second book of *Spheres* will open up a historico-political world whose models are the geometrically exact orb and the globe. Here we enter the Parmenidean dimension: a universe whose boundaries are drawn with a compass and whose center is occupied by a specifically philosophical, circumspect and overflowing joviality. In the era of metaphysics and classical empires, not so much overcome as simply forgotten, God and the world seemingly made a pact to present everything intrinsically being thing as an inclusive orb. Theology and ontology have, as far as we can see, always been teachings on the round container form; only from this perspective do the shapes of the empire and the cosmos become conceivable in a binding fashion. Not without reason was Nicholas of Cusa able to write: "And so, the whole of theology is said to be circular."[26] Theologians may continue under the illusion that their God is deeper than the God of the philosophers; but the God of the morphologists

Mosaic showing a group of philosophers from the Villa Albani, Rome, 1st century BC

is deeper than the God of the theologians.[27] On such expeditions into worlds now almost entirely lost, where the idea of a necessary roundness of the whole predominated, we gain insights into the function and construction of political ontologies in premodern empires. There is no traditional empire that failed to secure its borders by cosmological means, and no ruling body that did not discover the instruments of political immunology for itself. What is world history if not also the war history of immune systems? And the early immune systems—were they not always militant geometries too?

The recollection of the venerable doctrines of orb-shaped being uncovers the philosophical origins of a process that, under the name of "globalization," is on everyone's lips today. Its true story needs to be told—from the geometrization of the heavens in Plato and Aristotle to the circumnavigation of the final orb, the earth, through ships, capitals and signals. It will transpire how the Uranian globalization of ancient physics had to change into terrestrial globalization upon its modern failure. Underlying this is the decision to give the *globe* back the significance that is assigned to it nominally in the usual talk of globalization, but never in a conceptually serious fashion, namely as the true icon of heaven and earth. Once one has gained an idea of terrestrial globalization as the basic process of the Modern Age, it can be made clear why a third globalization, triggered by the rapid images in the networks, is currently leading to a general space crisis. This is indicated by the concept, as familiar as it is opaque, of *virtuality*. The virtual space of cybernetic media is the modernized outside that can no longer be presented as one form of the divine interior; it is made feasible in the shape of technological exteriority—and hence as an outside that lacks any inside counterpart from the outset. Cybernetic virtuality was preceded by philosophical virtuality, admittedly, which had been founded with the Platonic exposition of the world of ideas. Classical metaphysics already cast vulgar spatial thought into a crisis, for Plato made the virtual sun known as "good" rise over the sensual world, and it is only from this that everything that is "real" about the three-dimensionally sensual gains being at all. The current writings about virtual space are just in time to participate in the 2,400-year anniversary of the discovery of the virtual.

The concept of the sphere—both as an enlivened space and as the imagined and virtual orb of being—is ideally suited to recapitulating the transition from the most intimate to the most encompassing, from the closed to the burst-open concept of space. That the space-spawning extraversions of the spheres show a touch of the weird and even the monstrous was hinted at by Rilke, who did more for the poetics of space than any contemporary thinker, in a decisive verse:

And how perplexed must any womb-born creature feel, who is obliged to fly thin air.[28]

The theory of spheres is a morphological tool that allows us to grasp the exodus of the human being, from the primitive symbiosis to world-historical action in empires and global systems, as an almost coherent history of extraversion. It reconstructs the phenomenon of advanced civilization as the novel of sphere transference from the intimate minimum, the dual bubble, to the imperial maximum, which one should imagine as a monadic round cosmos. If the exclusivity of the bubble is a lyric motif, the inclusivity of the orb is an epic one.

It is in the nature of the matter that the phenomenology of imperial roundnesses must turn into a critical gynecology of the state and the large-scale church; in the course of our account, we will in fact show that peoples, empires, churches and, above all, modern nation states, are not least space-political attempts to recreate fantastic wombs for infantilized mass populations by imaginary and institutional means. Because the greatest of all possible container figures had to be envisaged as the one God in the age of patriarchal metaphysics, however, the theory of the orb leads directly to a morphological reconstruction of Western ontotheology: this doctrine conceptualizes God Himself, in Himself and for Himself, as an all-encompassing orb of which esoteric doctrines circulating since the High Middle Ages would claim that its center was everywhere and its perimeter nowhere.[29] Was the process of the Modern Age not identical, in its deep structure, to the attempts of European intellectuals to find their bearings in this unstable super-orb?

From the early Middle Ages, Catholic infernologists considered that humans are beings which could fall out of the divine round space. It was only with Dante that hell was cleared up geometrically: in his vision, even those who are excommunicated from the divine orb after judgment will remain contained in the immanences of hell's circles—we shall refer to these, with the rings of the *Commedia* in mind, as the anti-spheres. Their description, as remains to be shown, anticipates the modern phenomenology of depression and the psychoanalytical separation of analyzable and non-analyzable spirits.[30]

In examinations of the metaphysics of telecommunication in large-scale social bodies, we will show how the classical empires and *ecclesiae* managed to present themselves as sun-like orbs whose rays break forth from a monarchic center to illuminate even the periphery of all that is.[31] Here it becomes apparent why the attempts of classical metaphysics to conceive of all that is as a concentrically organized monosphere were doomed to failure, for more reasons than immanent construction errors—why, in fact, such a hyper-orb, because of its forced abstractness, was a flawed immunological design to begin with. The widespread homesickness for the Aristotelian world that is seeing a particular revival today, and which recognizes its goal in the word "cosmos" and its longing in the phrase "world soul," exists not least because we do not practice any historical immunology, and draw the dangerously false conclusion from the evident immunodeficiencies of contemporary cultures that earlier world systems were constructed better in this respect. The livability of the classically totalistic systems of former times is a peculiar matter, however. One need only recall the Gnostic claustrophobia under the tyrannical walls of heaven, or the early Christian unease about encompassing the world at all, to judge how far the world of late antiquity already saw reasons to revolt against the flawed immunological design of its official cosmology. We will explain how the Christian epoch was only able to discover the formula for its success in a historic compromise of its immune systems, both the personalistic-religious and the imperial-constructivistic— and why their decline had to result in the technization of immunity that characterizes modernity.

Finally, it will have to be shown how the delayed failure of the European dream of universal monarchy supplied the driving forces for the terrestrial globalization process, in whose course the scattered cultures on the last orb will be drawn together into an ecological stress commune.[32]

The third book will address the modern catastrophe of the round world. Using morphological terms, it will describe the rise of an age in which the form of the whole can no longer be imagined in terms of imperial panoramas and circular panopticons. From a morphological perspective, modernity appears primarily

Planetarium under construction in Jena in the 1920s

as a form-revolutionary process. It is not by chance that its conservative critics decried it as a loss of the center and rejected it as a rebellion against the divine circle—to this day. For Catholic Old Europeans, the essence of the Modern Age can still be expressed in a single phrase: spheric blasphemy. Much less nostalgically, though taking an untimely non-Catholic path, our spherological approach supplies the means to characterize the catastrophes of world form in modernity—that is, terrestrial and virtual globalization—in terms of non-round sphere formations.

This *contradictio in adiecto* mirrors the formal dilemma of the current contemporary state of the world, in which global markets and media have ignited an acute world war of ways of life and informational commodities. When everything has become the center, there is no longer any valid center; when everything is transmitting, the allegedly central transmitter is lost in the tangle of messages. We see how and why the age of the one, the greatest all-encompassing circle of unity and its bowed exegetes has irrevocably passed. The guiding morphological principle of the polyspheric world we inhabit is no longer the orb, but rather *foam*. The structural implication of the current earth-encompassing network—with all its eversions into the virtual realm—is thus not so much a globalization as a foaming. In foam worlds, the individual bubbles are not absorbed into a single, integrative hyper-orb, as in the metaphysical conception of the world, but rather drawn together to form irregular hills. With a phenomenology of foams, we shall attempt to advance—in concepts and images—towards a political amorphology that gets to the bottom(less)[33] of the metamorphoses and paradoxes of the solidary space in the age of multifarious media and mobile world markets. Only a theory of the amorphous and non-round could, by examining the current fame of sphere destructions and sphere regenerations, offer the most intimate and general theory of the present age. Foams, heaps, sponges, clouds and vortexes serve as the first amorphological metaphors, and will help to investigate the formation of inner worlds, the creation of contexts and the architectures of immunity in the age of unfettered technical complexity. What is currently being confusedly proclaimed in all the media as *the* globalization of the world is, in morphological terms, the universalized war of foams.

The Eiffel Tower

As an inevitable result of the subject itself, we shall also encounter perspectives on sphere pathology in the modern-postmodern process. Referring to a pathology of spheres displays a threefold focus: a politicological one, in so far as foams tend to be ungovernable structures with an inclination towards morphological anarchy; a cognitive one, in so far as the individuals and associations of subjects can no longer produce any complete world, as the idea of the whole world itself, in its characteristically holistic emphasis, unmistakably belongs to the expired age of metaphysical total-inclusion-circles, or monospheres; and a psychological one, in so far as single individuals in foams tend to lose the power to form mental-emotional spaces, and shrink to isolated depressive points transplanted into random surroundings (correctly referred to systemically as their environment). They suffer from the immunodeficiency caused by the deterioration of solidarities—to say nothing, for the moment, of the new immunizations acquired through participation in regenerated sphere creations. For sphere-deficient private persons, their lifespan becomes a sentence of solitary confinement; egos that are extensionless, scarcely active and lacking in participation stare out through the media window into moving landscapes of images. It is typical of the acute mass cultures that the moving images have become far livelier than most of their observers: a reproduction of animism in step with modernity.

In fact, the soul in the non-round age must, even under the most favorable conditions, be prepared for the fact that for the single bubbles, the self-completing, released individuals who furnish their personal spaces medially, the hybrid global foam will remain something impenetrable; at least navigability can partially replace transparency. Certainly, as long as the world

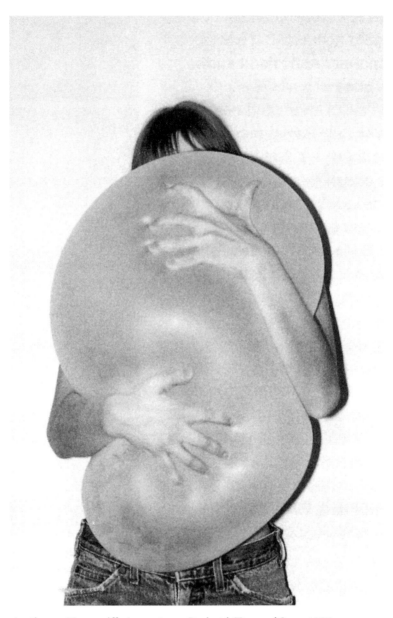

Annika von Hausswolff, *Attempting to Deal with Time and Space*, 1997

could still be panoptically overviewed as a whole from a single ruling point, it seemed intelligible through the self-transparency with which the divine orb illuminated itself in order to possess itself completely at every point. The notion of human participation in such a provision of transparency released imperial and monologic forms of reason; the world as a whole was illuminated by the circumspection that ruled from the center. God Himself was nothing but the center and the perimeter of the orb of being that was projected and viewed by Him, and all thought that based itself on Him shared analogously in the sublimity of His central view. In the foam worlds, however, no bubble can be expanded into an absolutely centered, all-encompassing, amphiscopic orb; no central light penetrates the entire foam in its dynamic murkiness. Hence the ethics of the decentered, small and middle-sized bubbles in the world foam includes the effort to move about in an unprecedentedly spacious world with an unprecedentedly modest circumspection; in the foam, discrete and polyvalent games of reason must develop that learn to live with a shimmering diversity of perspectives, and dispense with the illusion of the one lordly point of view. Most roads do not lead to Rome—that is the situation, European: recognize it. Thinking in the foam means navigating on unstable currents—others would say that it changes, under the impression of the thought tasks of the time, into a plural and transversal practice of reason.[34]

With this neither gay nor sad science of foams, the third book of *Spheres* presents a theory of the current age whose main tenor is that deanimation has an insurmountable lead over reanimation. It is the inanimable outside that gives food for thought in intrinsically modern times. This conclusion will inevitably drive the nostalgic yearning for a conception of the world, which still aims for a livable whole in the education-holistic sense, into resignation. For whatever asserts itself as the inner realm, it is increasingly exposed as the inner side of an outside. No happiness is safe from endoscopy; every blissful, intimate, vibrating cell is surrounded by swarms of professional disillusioners, and we drift among them—thought paparazzi, deconstructivists, interior deniers and cognitive scientists, accomplices in an unlimited plundering of Lethe. The rabble of observers, who want to take everything from without and no longer understand any rhythm—have we not long since become part of them, in most matters and at most moments? And how could it be any different? Who could inhabit in such a way that they inhabit everything? Or in such a way that they do not interfere in anything exterior? The world, it seems, has grown much too large for people of an older type, who strove for true community with things both near and far. The hospitality of the *sapiens* beings towards what arose behind the horizon has long been strained beyond the critical level. No institution, not even a church that thought *kata holon* and loved universally—let alone an individual who reads on bravely—can imagine that it is sufficiently open for everything that infiltrates, speaks and encounters it; viewed from any point in our lifeworld, the vast majority of individuals, languages, works of art, commodities and galaxies remain an unassimilable outside world, by necessity and forever. All "systems," whether households, communes, churches or states—and especially couples and individuals—are damned to their specific exclusivity; the zeitgeist celebrates its responsibility-free connivance in the external multiplicity with increasing openness. Intellectual history today: the endgames of external observation.

From C. V. Boys, *Soap-Bubbles, and the Forces which Mould Them,* London, 1902

Whether these diagnoses lead to disturbing and restrictive conclusions or to beneficial openings and syntheses is an open question. In all three parts, this treatise on spheres as world-creating formal potencies is an attempt to speak about the contemporary world without innocence. Anyone who relates experiences of the Modern Age to themselves must stand by the loss of innocence in three respects: psychologically, politologically and technologically. What makes this more difficult is that a complicated difference between losing innocence and attaining adulthood reveals itself. Be that as it may—it is nothing new that thinking means breaking with harmlessness.

The present account of the rise and the changes in the shape of the spheres is, as far as we know, the first attempt since the failure of Oswald Spengler's "morphology of world history" to restore the highest priority in an anthropological and culture-theoretical investigation to a concept of form. Spengler's morphological pretensions, despite his invocation of Goethe as a patron, were doomed to failure, because they applied to their objects a concept of form that could not possibly do justice to their willfulness and history. It was already a brilliant act of force to isolate cultures in general as "life forms of the highest order," declaring them windowless units that grow and decline purely according to immanent laws, and force was even more necessary for Spengler to interpret his cultures as thousand-year empires of a regional soul disposition—as soap bubbles of the highest order, so to speak, that would be kept in their shape through internal tensions of an occult nature. The descriptions of life presented under the sign of morphology for the eight cultures he acknowledged may have their place of honor in the history of cultural philosophy as the monument to a great, perhaps incomparable speculative and deductive energy; it is, however, a monument best placed in one of the quieter corners. As far as the application of morphological concepts in the cultural sciences is concerned, Spengler's example has so far had rather discouraging effects. Our own attempt can therefore not be overly indebted to such a model—except as an impressive demonstration of what should be avoided in future.

If we speak here of spheres as self-realizing forms, we do so in the conviction that we are not imposing concepts—and if they were imposed in a certain sense, it would be in a manner encouraged by the objects themselves. The theory of the spheres: that means gaining access to something that is the most real, yet also the most elusive and least tangible of things. Even to speak of gaining access is misleading, for the discovery of the spheric is less a matter of access than of a slowed-down circumspection amid the most obvious. We are always ecstatically involved in spheric circumstances from the start, even if, for deep-seated and culturally specific reasons, we have learned to overlook them, think past them and exclude them from our discussions. Because of its orientation towards objectivity, European scientific culture is an undertaking that aims to de-thematize spheric ecstasy. The animated interiority we shall attempt to show in all basic circumstances of human culture and existence is indeed a *realissimum* that initially eludes any verbal or geometric depiction—any representation at all, in fact—and yet, at every point of existence, forces something resembling original circle and orb formations—thanks to a potency of rounding that takes effect prior to all formal and technical constructions of circles.

The inherent morphological dynamic of the worlds shared by those who live together in reality is that of *arrondissements*, which form as they please without any contribution from the geometricians. The self-organization of the psychocosmic and political spaces lead to those metamorphoses of the circle in which existence gives itself its spheric-atmospheric constitution. The word "self-organization"—which is used here without the usual scientistic hysteria—is meant to draw attention to the fact that the circle holding humanity is neither purely made nor purely found, instead rounding itself spontaneously on the threshold between construction and self-realization. Or, more accurately put: it realizes itself in rounding events—just as those gathered around a hearth group freely *and* decidedly around the fireplace and its immediate advantages of warmth.[35] Hence the spherological analysis initiated with this first volume, beginning with the micro-forms, is neither a purely constructivist projection of rounded-off spaces in which people imagine they are leading a shared existence, nor a purely ontological meditation on the circle in which mortals are captured through an inaccessible transcendent order.

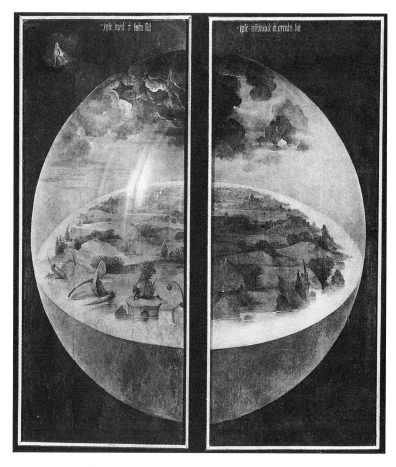

Hieronymus Bosch, *The Garden of Earthly Delights*, outside view with closed wings

As an introduction to a medial poetics of existence, the initial aim of spherology is simply to retrace the formations of shapes among simple immanences that appear in human (and extra-human) systems of order—whether as organizations of archaic intimacy, as the spatial design of primitive peoples, or as the theological-cosmological self-interpretation of traditional empires. At first glance, the present study, especially in its second part, could thus have the appearance of a cultural history defamiliarized with the aid of morphological, immunological and transference-theoretical concepts. This view, though it does not yet lead to our central concerns, would be neither entirely false nor entirely unwelcome—provided one is willing to admit that only from philosophy can the intelligence learn how its passions find concepts.

Thinking the Interior

I put an apple on my table. Then I put myself inside this apple. What tranquility!

> — Henri Michaux, "Magic"

Humans are beings that participate in spaces unknown to physics: the formulation of this axiom enabled the development of a modern psychological typology that scattered humans— without regard for their first self-localizations—among radically different places, conscious and unconscious, day-like and nightly, honorable and scandalous, places that belong to the ego and places where inner others have set up camp. What lends modern psychological knowledge its strength and autonomy is that it has shifted the human position beyond the reach of geometry and registration offices. Psychological investigations have responded to the question of *where* a subject is located with answers that belie physical and civil appearances. Only the bodies of the dead can be localized unambiguously; the anatomist, standing before his granite table, will not have any doubts about the location of his object: for the bodies in the outer space, the observer's coordinates alone are of interest. With beings that are *alive* in a humanly ecstatic manner, the question of place is fundamentally different, as the primary productivity of human beings lies in working on their accommodation in wayward, surreal spatial conditions.

In reaching this insight, psychology is initially assured the agreement of cultural anthropology: only through secession from their old nature have humans become an ontological fringe group that disconcerts itself. They cannot be adequately explained by what is natural, or rather old-natural, about them—despite the abundance of attempts to portray cultures as emerging continuously from natural processes. In the midst of outer nature and above their inner nature, humans lead the lives of islanders, at first constantly confusing their symbolic actions, their acclimatizations, their pamperings and their breakings-away from instinct-guided patterns with what is self-evident, and in this sense with the natural of old. Upon closer inspection, however, they live initially only in constructs that have grown from within themselves like second natures—in their languages, their systems of ritual and meaning, and in their constitutive deleria, which are admittedly propped up somewhere on the earth's surface. (The political is the product of group delusion and territory.)

The revolution of modern psychology does not stop at explaining that all humans live constructivistically, and that every one of them practices the profession of the wild interior designer, continually working on their accommodation in imaginary, sonorous, semiotic, ritual and technical shells. The specific radicality of the sciences of human psychology only becomes manifest when they interpret the subject as something that not only arranges itself within symbolic orders, but is also taken up ecstatically into the shared activity of arranging the world with others. It is not only the designer of its own interior, filled with relevant objects; it must also, constantly and inevitably, allow itself to be placed as a friendly furnishing in the container of the close and closest inner parties. Consequently, the relationship between human subjects sharing a field of proximity can be described as one between restless containers that contain and exclude one another. How can one conceive of this bizarre relationship? In the physical space, it is impossible for something within a container simultaneously to contain its container. It is equally inconceivable to imagine a body in a container as something that is excluded from that very container. It is precisely with relationships of this type, however, that the doctrine of psychological space deals from the start. This notion, an insurmountable paradox in geometric and physical terms, is the point of departure for the doctrine of psychological or human locators: individuals are subjects only to the extent that they are partners in a divided and assigned subjectivity. If one wished to take this to its precarious limits and revive Platonic intuitions in contemporary formulations, one could say: every subject is the restless remainder of a couple whose missing half never ceases to make demands on the one left behind.

With the very first lines it draws, then, modern psychology dissolves the individualistic semblance, which attempts to understand individuals as substantial ego units that voluntarily interact with others like members of a liberal club—after the fact, arbitrarily and revocably, as befits the ideology of the individualistic contract society. Where such individualisms appear, there is considerable psychological evidence pointing to a liberty-neurotic starting position; it is characteristic of this position that a subject cannot conceive of itself as contained, restricted, encompassed or occupied. It is the basic neurosis of Western culture to have to dream of a subject that watches, names and owns everything, without letting anything contain, appoint or own it, not even if the discreetest God offered himself as an observer, container and client. The dream persistently returns of an all-inclusive, monadic ego orb whose radius is its own thought—a thought that would easily pass through its spaces up to the outermost periphery, gifted with a wonderfully effortless discursivity that no real external thing could resist.

The other side of this masterful panoptic egotism shows itself in the Jonah complex, whose subject would have created a happy exile for himself in the belly of a whale, like the thirteen-year-old whose phantasms the psychoanalyst Wilhelm Stekel described: in his daydreams, the young man longed to set foot in the monstrous inside of a giantess whose abdominal cavity presented itself as a vault ten meters high. In the center of her stomach there was supposed to be a swing on which the blissful Jonah would propel himself aloft, safe in the knowledge that even the wildest vigor would never carry him out of there.[36] The first, fixed ego, which contains everything in its view around itself, and the second ego, the swinging one that allows itself to be contained fully by its cavity, are related in character insofar as both attempt to withdraw from the folded, interlaced, participatory structure of the real human space. Both have annulled the original dramatic difference between inside and outside by placing themselves, in a fantastic manner, in the middle of a homogeneous sphere not challenged by any real outside or unappropriated

Federico Fellini, *Casanova*: the great Muna

other. Clearly, the thesis that everything is outside is no less delirious than the longing to have everything on the inside. The two extreme postulates, which are probably tempting for all Western individuals in one way or another, tend away from the ecstatic entwinement of the subject in the shared interior, where those who actually live together wear one another out.

The truth and wisdom of modern psychology with regard to such phantasms of impregnable inwardness or sovereign outwardness lies in its description of the human space as an intertwining of several interior spaces; here the surreal becomes the real. Every subject in the real consubjective space is containing, in so far as it absorbs and grasps other subjective elements, and contained, in so far as it is encompassed and devoured by the

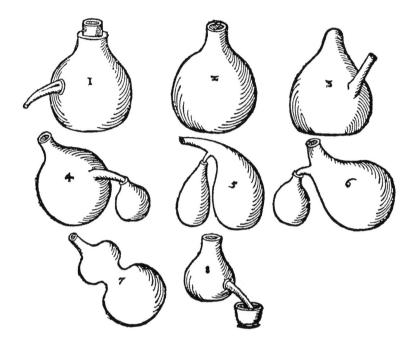

Collecting vessels: 1. large bottle for spirits with tube, 2. single-bellied bottle, 3. collecting vessel closed at top, 4. bellied twin collecting vessel, 5. elongated twin collecting vessel, 6. the same in bottle form, 7. double-bellied bottle, 8. connecting vessel

circumspections and arrangements of others. The real human proximity field is thus more than a simple system of communicating vessels; if your fluid rises in my tubes and vice versa, this is only the first indication of what allows humans to affect one another at close range through their joins and overflows. As a system of hybrid communicating vessels, the human interior consists of paradoxical or autogenous hollow bodies that are at once tight and leaky, that must alternate between the roles of container and content, and which simultaneously have properties of inner and outer walls. Intimacy is the realm of surreal autogenous containers.

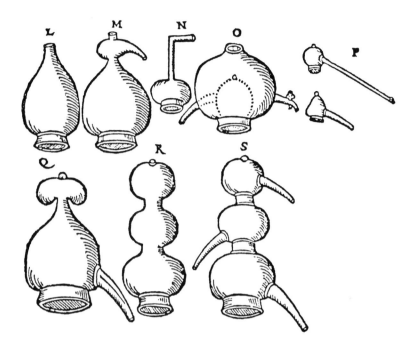

Receiving and connecting vessels: L. "tiara" for connecting coils, M. cydaris, N. alembic with connecting tube, O. alembic for cooling, P. small alembics for flasks and vials, Q. combination of blind and beak alembic, R. triple blind alembic, S. triple beak alembic

Intimacy: with this much-abused keyword, for want of any better and less prostituted one, we shall attempt in the following investigations to get closer to the secrets of human displacement, which always begins as inward displacement (before becoming conspicuous as outward displacement). Perhaps it is useful, as far as the challenge of the idea is concerned, to approach the most unusual relationship with the most worn-out of terms. It would be premature at this point to address Heidegger's remark that Dasein means "suspendedness in nothingness"—for we are not yet far enough to say with refreshed explicitness what *Dasein*, suspendedness, nothingness, and above all *in* actually mean.[37] It would be equally inappropriate now to discuss the theorem put forward by Deleuze and Foucault, namely that the subject is a *fold* of the outside; for we are still absolutely ignorant of any surface or outwardness whose folding could produce something resembling an interior or a self. We shall make just one anticipatory observation: intimacy, beyond its first sugary experience, can only be understood as an inscrutability within the most obvious. The theory of the intimate set in motion with the following microsphere analysis is dedicated to showing that all human sciences have always collected contributions to a topological surrealism, because it was never possible to speak of humans without having to deal with the various aimlessly wandering poetics of the inhabited interior. The spaces that humans allow to contain them have their own history—albeit a history that has never been told, and whose heroes are *eo ipso* not humans themselves, but rather the topoi and spheres as whose function humans flourish, and from which they fall if their unfolding fails.

For many intelligences, the thought of homely intimacies is associated with a spontaneous disgust at too much sweetness—which is why there is neither a philosophy of sweetness nor an elaborated ontology of the intimate. One must assess the nature of this resistance if one is to get past typical initial aversions. From a distance, the subject appears so unattractive and inconsequential that for the time being, only suckers for harmony or theophilic eunuchs would get stuck on it. An intellect that spends its energy on worthy objects usually prefers the sharp to the sweet; one does not offer candy to heroes. In the light of this disposition towards intellectual and existential sharpness, what

Mathematical knots

could seem more cloying, sticky and unheroic than the demand to participate in an investigation of the doughy, vague and humble-matriarchal space in which humans—at first and in most cases—have settled as seekers of security, good-natured inhabitants of normality and inmates of contentment institutions? What would be subject to greater *a priori* contempt than the devotion of individuals to their parochial habitat, which seems to offer them a certain drowsy convenience among themselves? The reason why strong minds usually despise sweetness can be partly explained by the subversive effects that sweet things, and sticky things even more, arouse in the proud subject. In an artful phenomenological micro-drama, Friedrich W. Heubach made explicit a candy experience that reveals the motives for the rejection of sweetness. Let us see how this oral drama, after the core-removing foreplay, the unwrapping of the "sweet-pregnant oval" from its delightful paper shell, moves towards its climax with the object's insertion into the mouth of the hero:

> The pursed lips seize the candy and release it laboriously into the oral cavity, where it is finally received by the tongue with expectant twists. Sweetness unfolds, opens out into a small, flattering O, and has soon transformed the mouth into a sweet, stickily and greedily pulsating ball that absorbs more and more as it expands. One is encircled oneself, and ultimately exists only as the fine, ever tauter periphery of this ball of sweetness; one closes one's eyes and finally implodes: taking on the characteristics of a ball oneself, one forms *one* object with the world that has now become round in sweetness.
>
> We now find "outer" events running in parallel with these "inner" ones: the empty candy wrapper is smoothed out more

and more until it is a flat rectangle, which is then rolled around the finger to form a cylindrical tube and finally folded into ever smaller surfaces. And when the ball of sweetness begins to lose its tension, flattens out and falls apart, the paper between the fingers takes on increasingly disordered and lumpy shapes; and when the sweetness forms no more than a fine, weakening line of deprivation, it is finally pressed into a hard little ball and flicked with relish far into the distance.[38]

This reveals a reason for aversions to sweetness. Even the most harmless oral enjoyment causes something that will remain unacceptable for the freedom hero: the sweetness-in-me experience casts the enjoying subject out of the center and places it, for a few precarious yet welcome moments, on the fringe of an autocratic taste sphere. Wanting to resist this small overpowering would not be a sublime sentiment so much as a laughable one, not least because, according to the heroic postulate, allowing oneself to be infiltrated through the consumption of confectionery is shameful to begin with. The lesson of this incorporation has lasting effects: intimacy is experienced here as the inside of my body being broken through by the presence of a taste whose strength in pleasantness opens me up and forces me into submission—that sweeps me out of the way, in fact, because I can only truly enjoy it by allowing it to make me the fortunate spectator of its triumphal march through my oral cavity. The most basic luxury food is suitable to convince me that an incorporated object, far from coming unambiguously under my control, can take possession of me and dictate its topic to me. If a banal case of sugar consumption already hollows out the subject through the flaring up of an aroma presence, however, and makes it the

Béla Vizi, *Koordination*

scene of invasive sensualities, what is to become of the subject's conviction that its destiny is self-determination on all fronts? What remains of the dream of human autonomy once the subject has experienced itself as a penetrable hollow body?

It would seem that, in such questions, the roles of self-will and rapture are inverted, and that the weakling insists on his own power while the strong one abandons himself. Should we not precisely understand the strongest subject as the most successful metabolic agent—the person who makes the least secret of his hollowness, penetrability and mediality? Should not the most decentered individual accordingly be understood as potentially the most powerful? And did the central psychological model of modernity, the ego-strong self-realizer, not step on the scene as a polyvalent metabolism-maximizer who surrenders himself to multifarious invasions, seductions and appropriations under the mask of controlled consumer power? Does not the entire universe of human intimacy, the web of divided interiors in the literal and metaphorical sense, grow from such inversions of appropriative-incorporative gestures? Do we, as phenomenologists, psychologists and topologists, not have to start from the observation that from the outset, subjects always form themselves through the experience of being "taken at their taking"? The constitutive candy, which epi-Freudian psychoanalysts have both viewed with suspicion and deified since the time of Melanie Klein, is none other than "the mother's breast," that alleged first "object" (note the singular) which the child (which is no more able to count to two than an object-relationship theorist) cannot accept and incorporate without reaching, in its way, the limits of the milky ball of sweetness within it. The early subject—should one deem it merely a gleeful observer on the periphery of a euphoric gulp?

Such considerations have troubling consequences for the doctrine of the human being, as they break with the illusion of circulating ego-delimitation systems. The point of this game on the I-you and I-it boundaries[39] can be clarified via a mythological thought experiment. If candies and portions of mother's milk were subjects, not mere things—if they were benign demons, for example—it would not be extravagant to claim that they take possession of their consumers, settling inside them like occupiers who plan to stay for good. This would undoubtedly be a sound method to deduce the animation of the *infans* from its interaction with demons; then receiving a soul would simply mean becoming involved in a profitable obsession through spirit contact and productive incorporations. The notion of demonic possession is not available to a modern psychological theory, of course, although the circumstances themselves—the opening and population of a divided intimate space—are such that a discreet demonology would probably be its most fruitful interpretation.[40] Is it not, in fact, the whispering of nymphs' voices to the subject from its earliest states that unlocks its inner dimensions?[41] Does not every unneglected child realize the advantage of being born only thanks to eudemonic nipples, good candy spirits, conspiratorial bottles and drinkable fairies that watch discreetly by its bed, occasionally entering the interior to nurse it? Does a sum of advantageous invasions not hollow out a love grotto within the individual, with enough space to house the self and its associated spirits for life? Does not every subjectification, then, presuppose multiple successful penetrations, formative invasions and interested devotions to life-enriching intruders? And is not every feeling of offensive self-positing injected with anger over missing the chance at being taken?

In the eight chapters of this book, we will begin a slow journey through the vaults of consubjective intimacy. Here we shall

From Evandro Salles, *Ten Dreams of Oedipus*

discuss, in sequence: the spaces of hysterical heartiness and the interfacial field; magnetopathic rapport in hypnosis and the fetal position of amniotic enclosure; placental doubling and the cultural manifestations of the dual soul; the psychoacoustic evocation of the self; and finally also theological attempts to give the liaison between God and the soul an intimo-topological foundation. The character of the observations made in all these layers and twists of the shared interior is not, however, merely that of metaphorical constructs. The interior we shall examine here has a different structure from that "hall of memory" that caused Augustine to marvel at how the human spirit contains a dimension large enough to preserve the trifles of one's own life story as well as the immeasurable knowledge of God and the world accumulated by the generations before us. Nor is it like the submerged part of the iceberg, the tip of which the schools of depth psychology so like to use when characterizing the human conscious. The intimate spaces of microspherology are neither the majestic auditoriums nor the cave-like hiding places of the individual conscious, which interacts with itself to create spatial images suitable for understanding the nature of its own position, spread out between the largest and the smallest.

The category of the intimate discussed here deals exclusively with divided, consubjective and inter-intelligent interiors in which only dyadic or multi-poled groups are involved—and which, in fact, can only exist to the extent that human individuals create these particular spatial forms as autogenous vessels through great closeness, through incorporations, invasions, intersections, interfoldings and resonances (and, in psychoanalytical terms, also identifications). This intimate vault system as a whole in no way corresponds to the unconscious as understood in depth psychology, for access to it is gained neither through a particular listening technique nor the insinuation of a latent meaning that manifests itself in halting speech, nor through the assumption of unconscious wish production. Readers can easily convince themselves that the dimensions of interiority spread out in this microspherology are, in their structure, worlds apart from the serial three-room-apartments of the Freudian soul apparatus. Philosophical interior research and the psychology of the unconscious only overlap in a few places, as we shall see; if we occasionally borrow from psychoanalytical notions in the following, it is only because the material permits and suggests it, not because we view the school as an authority. If we were to invoke a genius for this first part of the *Spheres* enterprise, one of the foremost candidates would be Gaston Bachelard, who, with his phenomenology of material imagination, especially his studies on the psychoanalysis of the elements, created a valuable store of brilliant insights to which we shall return on several occasions. In his idea-laden 1948 book *La terre et les rêveries du repos* [The Earth and Reveries of Rest], the author gathered together diverse material concerning the dreams of material intimacy: birth houses and dream houses, grottos, labyrinths, snakes, and above all the aforementioned Jonah complex, which places every human being who knows freedom simultaneously into an unmistakable relationship with an enabling interior darkness. In this work, Bachelard notes that simply by looking inwards, every person becomes a Jonah—or, more precisely, becomes prophet and whale in a single body. The great phenomenologist of the experienced space did not forget to name the reason for this:

> The unconscious is as sure of the closure of the circle as the most skilled geometrician: if one lets the reveries of intimacy take their course, [...] the dreaming hand will draw the *original circle*. It seems, then, as if the unconscious itself knew a Parmenidean sphere as the symbol of being. This sphere does not possess the rational beauties of geometric volume, but it offers the great securities of a belly.[42]

We shall attempt in the following to develop these indispensable intuitions further. But we will also have to exceed their boundaries for the purpose of unfolding them, as we need to explain why the consubjective, intimate sphere can initially by no means possess a eucyclic or Parmenidean structure: the primitive mental orb, unlike the beautifully rounded philosophical one, does not have a center of its own that radiates and collects everything, but rather two epicenters that evoke each other through resonance. Furthermore, it transpires that the inside of the soul grottos will not always remain exclusively a place of quiet happiness. The innermost access to your living cell is often reserved, as we can see, for a voice that wishes to reduce or deny the possibility of your existence. It characterizes the basic risk of all intimacy that our destroyer sometimes gets closer to us than our ally.

CHAPTER 1

Heart Operation;
Or, On the Eucharistic Excess

The heart was hailed as the sun, indeed as the king, yet closer
inspection reveals no more than a muscle.

— Niels Stensen, *Opera philosophica*[1]

For Europeans who, even at the turn of the third millennium,
still count their years *post Christum natum*, it is natural to begin
an inquiry into the basis of the intimate—assuming it is appropriate to the structure of intimacy to speak of any basis—with a
recollection of the human heart. The heart, even in the age of its
transplantability, is still viewed as the central organ of internalized humanity in the dominant language games of our
civilization. For the primary European intuitions, it is still barely
conceivable how humanity and cordiality could not converge. A
quick glance at ancient and non-European cultures is enough to
teach us that the association of the heart and the innermost self
is no anthropological universal; the heart has by no means been
equated with the deepest interior of humans—one could also call
it the source of their sense of self and their capacity for relationships—in all places at all times. The views of different peoples on

the corporeal seat of the soul diverge to a degree that remains astounding to European cardiocentrists. They could probably still communicate with tradition-conscious Chinese and ancient Egyptians with a degree of consonance; they would find it rather more laborious to converse with Japanese, who articulate their notions of the central emotional sphere using two complex terms: *kokoro*, meaning "heart," "soul," "spirit" or "sense," and *hara*, meaning "belly" or "center of the body."[2] It would be even more difficult to reach an understanding with peoples like the Inuit, who distinguish between three types of soul: the sleep soul, located at the side of the body under the diaphragm, which separates from the body when it awakens (this is why one should begin the morning slowly), the life soul, which resides at the base of the neck between the torso and the head, and the smaller life spirits that inhabit the joints.[3] In the domain of Christianity, however, the personal religion *par excellence*, the search for the focus of animation has unwaveringly directed itself at the "organ" of the heart. Christian language games and emotional disciplines have spawned a universe of subtle physiologies whose only aim is to deepen and emphasize the equation of the heart and the center of the sense of self; among Christianized Europeans, especially in the Middle Ages and early Modern Age, heartiness is the epitome of affective core subjectivity. Cordial subjectivity is characterized by its declaration that holding onto its own heart is an impossibility, or a pathological confinement at best. Heartiness as such automatically creates complicity and community, and is consequently interested in *concordia*, the coordination of heart rhythms. This suggests, then, that we should begin our investigation of the twin intimate space with reflections on heart-historical motifs that cannot deny their roots in Christian models of bodily-spiritual communion. Passing through a sequence of episodes in which communicating hearts act as the heroes, the horizon of a radicalized, interpersonal intimate spatiality as formulated by European theologians, philosophers and storytellers will be made visible in suggestive glances ahead.

First of all we shall give an abbreviating paraphrase of Konrad of Würzburg's well-known *Herzmaere* [Heart Fable] from the thirteenth century; this will be followed by an episode from the life of the Italian mystic Catherine of Siena from the second half of the fourteenth century—we shall quote the legend of her mysterious heart exchange with Christ in the version handed down by her confessor, Raymond of Capua, in his lives of the saints. As a third example we will present a passage from Marsilio Ficino's epoch-making commentary on Plato's *Symposium*, *De amore* (1469), on the mechanical basis of sensual infatuation. These metaphysically, religiously and psychologically oriented models for bipolar cardial relationships will be contrasted with a passage from La Mettrie's 1748 treatise on the machine man, which displays the most pronounced break with the tradition of religious languages of intimacy. Synoptically viewed, this sequence offers a provisional indication of the proportions, tasks and breaking points of a theory of biune intimacy.

Herzmaere, a verse novella by the poet Konrad of Würzburg, who died in Basel at the age of sixty-two, is a piece of erotic-romantic light literature generally thought to date from the 1360s. It deals with the heroically doomed, noble love between a knight and his lady, both of whom remain nameless and typical characters in Konrad's tale. Konrad's novellistic idea of the eaten heart probably stems from ancient Indian motifs that return in the Greek myth of Pelops and the fairy tale about the Juniper Tree. The story itself, according to medievalists, was widely distributed in medieval France, from where it conquered the whole of Europe; Boccaccio's *Decameron* alone presents two variations on it.[4] In Konrad's version, the story of the cannibalistic heart communion is turned into an instrument for achieving a restoration of courtly love. The poet takes up the motif in order to glorify high courtly-religious attitudes nostalgically, in a time when citizens and knights had long been signaling to one another in a mediocre consensus that the demands placed by the love of noble souls were too great for them.

A knight and his lady are enamored of each other according to the laws of high courtly love [*Minne*]; their lives and souls (*muot*), we are told in lines 30–32, are so intertwined that their innermost parts have fully become one (*ein dinc*). The legal bond between the lady and her lawful husband, however, damns all the lovers' hopes of fulfillment to failure. Thus, as the script of the romantic drama prescribes, their intimate connection itself becomes a cause of torment and downfall: when the jealous husband becomes aware of their relationship, he plans to go with his wife on a pilgrimage to the Holy Sepulcher in order to estrange the lovers from each other. The lady convinces her knight to travel to the orient in her stead. Obedient to the lady he calls his mistress, the knight agrees to the bitter task; as a pledge of love, she takes a ring from her hand and gives it to him to accompany him on his journey. Having reached the distant land, the melancholy knight seals his terrible suffering in his heart (lines 244–45) and, after spending a while wasting away with yearning, he dies abroad. Before his

"Amour" places the king's heart in the hands of "Vif-Désir," from the treatise by King René, *Livre du Cuer d'Amours espris* (Book of the Love-Struck Heart), miniature by an unknown illustrator, 1457

death, the knight had entrusted his squire with the task of cutting the heart "bloody and sorrow-colored" from the knight's body, embalming it thoroughly and preserving it carefully in a shrine, and then bringing it back to the lady in the distant occident together with the ring as a mark of identification. When the squire arrives at the lady's castle bearing the embalmed heart, he is confronted by the lord—her husband—and asked what the precious box contains. After seeing the heart and the ring and realizing their significance, the man orders his cook to prepare a dish with it and has it served to his wife. "My wife, he spoke to her in a sweet voice, this is a delicious (*cleine*) meal; you should eat it by yourself, for you cannot share it" (lines 426–29). When the lady, having finished her meal, declares that she has never eaten anything so delicious, her husband reveals the recipe's secret. At these words, the woman's heart freezes in her chest, blood spills from her mouth, and she swears that after this noblest of all meals she will never touch food again. Her heart breaks immediately, and in dying, the poet tells us, she amply compensates for everything her lover had done in advance. The poem ends with a culture-critical word of warning in a time lacking in love: by recalling the ideals of high courtly love, Konrad praises the two lovers as an example of perfect mutual devotion.

The novella shows how the classical metaphysical schema of union out of duality permeated the worldly narrative culture of the age of chivalry. That the most demanding thought figure in mystical theology could appear in the profane realm in such a drastic transposition, that amorous relationships between man and woman could be modeled on the monastic and mystical union of God and the soul: this was the dangerously great achievement of the Arab- and Provençal-inspired medieval culture of courtly love. One of its daring aspects was the parallel between erotic and Christological language games and the super-elevation of sexual desire through the metaphysical idea of union. What takes place here between the lovers as the courtly love of the heart from a distance and the consumption of the heart up close transposes the act of communion into a dimension of hybridized intersubjectivity; the knight's cooked heart forms a precise equivalent to the host over which the transforming words *hoc est corpus meum* are spoken. Instead of the altar, the kitchen becomes a place of transubstantiation. With the gift of his heart the knight, seconded by his poet, creates a heretical variation of the Eucharist. With this act he supports the hypothesis that to love means to offer oneself up for consumption by others as a self-wafer. Oblation is not part of eros as such, however, but of the imperial and feudal idea of service; and only when, as in medieval Europe, serving and loving had been radically combined as primal acts of devotion could the surrender of the heart be noted as a valid erotic record. In the courtly game—and the court is first and foremost a collection of staff—the donation of one's own heart to the only communicant can present itself as an admirably chivalrous act that aligns itself with a new, boldly literatized hyper-orthodoxy of erotic devotion. The law of courtly love neutralized the blasphemous daring of the eucharistic and union-mystical alliance of man and woman, surrounding it with the tolerable nimbus of noblest courtesy. If the ceremonial words of communion state of the bread that "this is my body," the novella says of the embalmed, cooked and eaten heart: "this is my love." Consequently the woman's husband does not wrong her with his cynical culinary ruse. On the contrary: even as an unworthy priest, the jealous husband can have the heart-host prepared and served to her without any lack of sacramental validity. Consumption by the woman is the most suitable thing that could happen to a heart devoted to perfect service. Why else did it travel all the way from the Holy Sepulcher back to the European castle in its host shrine if not to be with HER—naturally not without the accompaniment of the evidential ring that testifies to the lovers' union in the shared field of animation.

In its day, the story of the devoured heart came at exactly the right time to respond to a quandary just discovered by the players in the game of courtly love: that for perfect love, as is already established at the start of the tale, no higher level or future is possible—only fatigue through physical fulfillment. There are two options for escaping the inhuman sterility of erotic idealism; one leads to monstrous exaltation, the other to the licensing of base courtly love. Late medieval literature proves, in a wealth of variations, that both paths were taken. Anyone who relies on a heightening of events, like the neoconservative poet, who seeks to combine entertainment through fascination with moral conversion, must accept the cannibalistic communion as a valid procedure for elevating the lovers' unification to a wild Eucharist. It is not out of the question that this excess recalls a forgotten birth of the human awareness of the interior from anthropophagy. In the opinion of some anthropologists, the notion of a secret, sinister interior in the human body points back to an archaic "cannibalistic order," now all but vanished, where evil, which manifested itself especially in the guise of the bothersome fellow human, was supposedly "interned" in the bellies of the primal horde's members at a shared anthropophagous meal.[5] The Christian sacrament did not, at any rate, eschew everything that resembled such terrifying archaisms: for the Christian world, the community-forming consumption of God opens up a possibility to practice the impermissible without remorse in sublimated forms. Among Christians, the spiritual ingestion of the one God has always been unabashedly underlined by an act of physical ingestion: they devour that by which they themselves wish to be devoured and collected. Whatever one thinks about the latent connections of *Herzmaere* to eucharistic, theophagous and anthropophagous practices, one can make out a heterodox voice in history itself that contradicts the tale's manifest edifying intentions. Suffering and death as the fair reward for true love, and a heart-devouring communion for the couple in place of amorous days and nights together—in its pre-arranged discrepancy, this scenario would more likely have given the courtly audience of the time a morbid thrill than inspired analogous sublimations. The listeners would sooner have concentrated on the tale's evocative horror than yielded to its overly lofty edifyingness. When the heart of the beloved, instead of finding its counterpart in the woman's bosom while still alive, reaches a *unio mystica* with her innards, the worldly ear hears in such movements not only the subversive Christological parallelisms, but most of all revels in the novellistic monstrosity of such a gastric theology. Here it is precisely love that appears as the religion of a world standing on its head. The didactically monstrous aspect indicates how the path to biune intimacy in advanced civilization is hampered by mistaken embraces. Is it not part of being erotically experienced, however, to know that the desire to enter the other can lead one to the wrong entrance?

In the following account, the intimate transaction is heightened into a direct exchange of heart for heart. Catherine of Siena, the stigmatized *Patrona Italiae*, was born in 1347 as the twenty-fifth child of a poor dyer couple in Siena, and died in 1380 at the ideal Jesuan age of thirty-eight. When the Dominican Tertiary receives the heart of the revealed Christ from him to replace her own, this exchange mirrors more than simply the heart-to-heart conversation of religious friendship books. The scene described seeks to testify to an existential hysterectomy that is inconceivable without the delighted horror of a literal mystico-physiological transformation. We shall quote the decisive passage from Raymond of Capua's *La vita di Santa Caterina da Siena*:

> Once, when she was praying to the Lord with the utmost fervour, saying to Him as the Prophet had done, "Create a clean heart within me, O God, and renew a right spirit within my bowels," and asking Him again and again to take her own heart and will from her, He comforted her with this vision. It appeared to her that her Heavenly Bridegroom came to her as usual, opened her left side, took out her heart, and then went away. This vision was so effective and agreed so well with what she felt inside herself that in confession she told her confessor that she no longer had a heart in her breast. He shook his head a little at this way of putting it, and in a joking way reproved her; but she repeated it and insisted that she meant what she said. "Truly, Father," she said, "in so far as I feel anything at all, it seems to me that my heart has been taken away altogether. The Lord did indeed appear to me, opened my left side, took my heart out and went away." Her confessor then pointed out that it is impossible to live without a heart, but the virgin replied that nothing is impossible to God, and that she was convinced that she no longer had a heart. And for some time she went on repeating this, that she was living without a heart.
>
> One day she was in the church of the Preaching Friars, which the Sisters of Penance of Saint Dominic in Siena used to attend. The others had gone out, but she went on praying.

Anonymous (15th century): *Lo scambio dei cuori* [The Exchange of Hearts], pen and ink drawing from *Libellus de Supplemento*, Siena City Library

Finally she came out of her ecstasy and got up to go home. All at once a light from heaven encircled her, and in the light appeared the Lord, holding in His holy hands a human heart, bright red and shining. At the appearance of the Author of

Light she had fallen to the ground, trembling all over, but He came up to her, opened her left side once again and put the heart He was holding in His hands inside her, saying, "Dearest daughter, as I took your heart away from you the other day, now, you see, I am giving you mine, so that you can go on living with it for ever."[6]

Here too, in keeping with the law of similarity, two intimate elements are made equal in a daring exchange. Compared to *Herzmaere*, the stakes have been noticeably raised: the exchange is not of one human life for another, but of a human heart for God's heart. In this exceptional mystical situation, the metaphysical asymmetry between the two poles seems almost to have been removed. Man is no longer simply God's work or vassal; the distance that the individual soul lags behind its transcendent foundation seems mysteriously to have been caught up. Through a scarcely analyzable immersion in inward—here the comparative is important: *more* inward—relationships, man suddenly becomes the comrade, co-subject, ecstatic accomplice and same-aged partner in crime of the absolute. The prerequisite for this rise to equality is that the human subject feels an excessive longing for the absolute I-ness of the other, a longing that cannot fail to be fulfilled. The desire must be excessive, for without insatiability, it is impossible to break through the fetishistic object notions of the desired *summum bonum*—crude and subtle ones alike—to the fullest extent. Edifying literature treats this matter formally: only those who are able to "imagine" God as the purest subjectivity can reach the crucial zone of utterly de-reified, unimagined subject-being. Consequently the highest subject, God, can only be "experienced" by adopting His manner of being without imagining anything external. Catherine's cardio-mystical liaison with her Lord at least approaches such objectless mysteries; at the same time, the drastic heart operation displays a grotesque physiologism closer to surges of hysteria than to non-objective immersion.

Clinically speaking, hysteria is—not only among the religious—the ability to somatize figures of speech; from a philosophical perspective, one could say that hysterics are individuals who delay their coming-into-the-world until they can exit into overheated language games; their manner of existence is the epitome of metaphysical neurosis. The hysterics move without any interlude, as it were, or after a long period of latency somewhere inconspicuous, from the womb into the house of language—or the hall of sounds and grand acoustic gestures. Through language and gesture, they hope to skip the phase of pre-linguistic forlornness, the infant trauma, and make it never have happened. Hence, perhaps, their ability to make verbal expressions glow in their own bodies. In Catherine's case, the linguistic figure intended to become a physical one was a prayer, with massive theological preconditions, to be emptied of everything that was her own: very conventionally, yet at once in an arousedly personal fashion, the young Sienese nun had requested that her Lord take away everything in her inner being that belonged to her. She longed, in keeping with the oldest language games of Neoplatonic and monastic asceticism, to renounce her own innards, as it were, in order to become empty in the physical and the psychological sense. Her prayer amounts to the wish to be emptied of all reality that is not successful symbiosis. Since time immemorial, mysticism has sought to clear out the crammed intimate zone[7] of the self, whose content can calm, yet

Scambio del cuore, altarpiece, c. 1463, Brussels, Stocklet collection

never satisfy the hysterical hunger. Catherine's devotion thus has the purpose of creating a vacuum within her to enable a deep invasion by the mystical bridegroom.

It would be misguided here to follow the oft-traveled arterial roads of psychoanalytical sexual theory, which heads for the genital even in the archaic; the Lord's infiltration of the nun's left side is simply not coitus via the ribs. Nor, then, is Catherine's great inner other the penetrator who has contrived unusual entrances to female cavities. Catherine, for her part, is not a pervert tempting a heavenly lover into cardial intercourse. The Lord who takes her heart is—at least in the first phase of the drama—simply responding to the nun's irresistible urge to empty herself so that she can better enter her other. Once emptied, hollowed out, gutted, de-hearted, her cavity exerts a suction that even—no, especially—the God in her does not resist.[8]

As soon as Christ's heart is implanted in Catherine, it becomes clear that her own intimate zone had never been the point; she wants not so much to absorb the other into herself as to immerse herself in the aura of the other. The inside of the nun's body serves as a physiological stage on which her wish to bathe inside the other enacts itself. Her desire is to enter the cave of a shared selfness. To achieve this, she must somatize that which is hollow in herself; in her own body, she creates a space whose suction resolutely forces the life of life, the highest subject.

Catherine's case also involves an obvious parody of the Eucharist, in that she induces Christ to give his worshipper a special sacrament: *Hoc est cor meum*. One should also note that the blessed Raymond of Capua, the saint's confessor and biographer, who was assigned to her as spiritual supervisor, seems to have been the supporting accomplice and stimulating accessory to Catherine's excesses on the interpersonal or inter-delirious level. The Catholic monastic milieu has always been a breeding ground for the *folie à plusieurs*—this also includes the whispering of the other nuns, who supposedly saw the scar on Catherine's left side while bathing. In guarding, envying, deifying and describing the ailing, hyperactive ecstatic, he became a silent participant in her ascension to Jesuan symbiosis. Like all biographers of saints, who watch their partners with concern while they are alive and idealize them *post mortem*, he derived profit for his own desire to achieve the utmost intensification from Catherine's struggle for unification. It is to his participation in Catherine's participation in the lord of the inner world that posterity owes one of the most revealing documents on the phenomenology of the saint in the late Middle Ages. In his biography he records, among other things, a remarkable breast-feeding phantasm in which the Lord's wounded heart was supposedly transformed into an overflowing mamma. In an earlier vision, Christ is said to have pulled Catherine towards himself so that she could drink from his pierced side:

> And she, finding herself thus near to the source of the fountain of life, put the lips of her body, but much more those of the soul, over the most holy wound, and long and eagerly and abundantly drank that indescribable and unfathomable liquid.[9]

The suggestive image of the nun being nursed at the bubbling fountain of blood may remind us that every deeper penetration of the intimate world presupposes the transformation of separate solids into miscible and incorporable liquids.

The notion of the inner world as a mixing jar for liquefied selves can be further developed using the third example in our course on the exploration of bipolar intimate spatiality. It takes us—a century after Catherine of Siena—to the center of the Platonic revival in Florence, whose key figures were Cosimo de' Medici (1389–1464) and his young protégé Marsilio Ficino (1433–1499). Cosimo had given Ficino a house in Careggi, near Florence, in 1462, together with the task of translating the hermetic writings and the *Corpus Platonicum* from Greek. This alliance between a prince and his philosopher not only provided Western culture with the first modern edition of Plato's dialogues; in 1469, at the same time as completing his translation work, Ficino also published the first of his influential commentaries on Plato, *Commentarium in convivium Platonis de amore*, a work of inestimable significance for the modern view of Socratic or Platonic love. In his dedications, Ficino expressed the hope that he had written a loving theory of love with this text, and that, like a theoretical amulet, the book itself might ensure that no one who read it hastily or reluctantly would ever understand it:

> For one cannot understand the fervor of love with presumptuous superficiality, and love itself cannot be grasped with hatred.

The work aimed to create by its own means the narrow circle in which it could be received and appropriated by kindred spirits. That is why Ficino's book *On Love* gained an early place of honor in the literary history of sympathetic magic. It brings to bear the insight that great books and their sympathizers exist in their own circle of resonance which the rest of the public, though seemingly equally able to read them, passes by disinterestedly. The great book, like the eminent work of art later on, forges its path through the modern public space and proves itself a sphere-forming power of a caliber all its own. Where eminent works open themselves up generously, those who are unsuited ill-temperedly exclude themselves.

What Ficino calls commentary is undoubtedly the opposite of what philologists have wanted the term to mean since the nineteenth century. Ficino does not offer an obliging word-for-word explanation of the old text, but rather an unabashed rewriting of the original that takes the liberty of overlaying the seven speeches of the Platonic symposium with the same number of counter-speeches by modern participants at a contemporary symposium. This takes place on Plato's birthday, November 7th, in Careggi, with the aim of reviving an ancient academic custom after a twelve-hundred-year interruption. Commentary here transpires as a method for pouring the wine of the Modern Age into ancient wineskins. In the seventh speech, given by Cristo-foro Marsupini, who is assigned the role of Alcibiades, Plato's final speaker, we find the passage that will enrich our cardio-mythological investigations with a sensational model. Here, language encounters physical love as toxicosis and enchantment from afar:

> Put before your eyes, I beg of you, Phaedrus the Myrrhinu-sian, and that Theban who was seized by love of him, Lysias the orator. Lysias gapes at the face of Phaedrus. Phaedrus aims into the eyes of Lysias sparks of his own eyes, and along with those sparks transmits also a spirit. The ray of Phaedrus is easily joined to the ray of Lysias, and spirit is easily joined

to spirit. This vapor produced by the heart of Phaedrus immediately seeks the heart of Lysias, through the hardness of which it is condensed and turns back into the blood of Phaedrus as before, so that now the blood of Phaedrus, amazing though it seems, is in the heart of Lysias. Hence each immediately breaks out into shouting: Lysias to Phaedrus: "O, my heart, Phaedrus, dearest viscera." Phaedrus to Lysias: "O, my spirit, my blood, Lysias." Phaedrus pursues Lysias because his heart demands its humor back. Lysias pursues Phaedrus because the sanguine humor requests its proper vessel, demands its own seat. But Lysias pursues Phaedrus more ardently. For the heart can more easily do without a very small particle of its humor than the humor itself can do without its proper heart.[10]

It is easy to see in this passage how the model of the neighborly-intimate two-heart-space is overlaid with a quasi-telepathic component; this component employs the Platonic concept of the active light and visual rays to establish an equally bizarre and concrete enchantment, referred to by the author as *fascinatio*, between the hearts of the lovers. According to Ficino, infatuation appears as the acute form of a malign fascination; this is no apparition in a vacuum, but the result of a long-distance effect thoroughly conditioned by a subtle physiology.

To make this telepathic transport plausible, Ficino bases his arguments on Platonic radiology—that first theoretical formulation of the idea of causation through radiation, which refers back to the famous solar parable in *The Republic*.[11] The view of the heart as the sun of the internal organs is equally conventional: it transfers the Platonic image of the sun's kingship in

Telepathic radiation causality: Albrecht Altdorfer, *The Stigmatization of Saint Francis*, 1507, Prussian Cultural Heritage Foundation

the world of astral bodies to the heart as the monarch in the world of animal-human bodies. Platonic kings are naturally sun kings; *de facto*, they rule as heart kings who tie even the most distant points to the center of cardial emanation. In this semi-mythical physics, both the sun and the heart rule in the mode of radiation; all forms of emanationism—models of the discharging of archetypal forces into empty spaces or those filled with amorphously dark bodies—can be traced back to Plato's concept of solar monarchy. In the image of the sun's kingly rule, the thinker set about rendering imaginable the causation of the sensually experienceable real through the super-sensual most real, that is, the good that pours out. Where the solar model is transferred onto the heart, the latter has emanative properties bestowed upon it.

This radiocracy of the heart defines Ficino's erotic theory; it inspires the incomparable phantasm of telepathic blood transfusion through the eyes of Phaedrus into the heart of Lysias. In fact, Ficino imagines the eyes of the beloved like an active radio signal that transmits a small, real quantum of blood into the eye of the lover. This blood transmission is made possible by the notable circumstance that on the way from the heart to the eye of the transmitter, the blood is subtilized into steam or fine *vapor*, as it were, so the notion that it could be transported outside the body by a visual ray filled with the spirit of life (*spiritus*) can only seem utterly absurd. What makes this path from the blood to the gaseous form and back again plausible is the well-known pattern of evaporation and its reversal through distillation. In the recipient's eye, the haze of vapor between the eye and the heart can collect again like condensate, enabling authentic Phaedrus blood finally to reach Lysias' heart. Having arrived there, the blood triggers participation-mystical effects: in its foreign location, it develops a form of longing for its origin, for it longs to return to the heart from which it came, and through this striving it magically draws the entire person of Lysias with it towards Phaedrus.

It is this suction drawing the blood taker to the blood giver that we call infatuation or enchantment. Base erotic affection therefore means that a subject is caught up in the atmosphere, and hence the blood circulation, of another—as if it were once more a fetus, enclosed in a shared circulation with its mother through the umbilical cord. It is characteristic of Ficino's time that he was only able to reproduce one half of this blood symbiosis, namely the blood's way from the sender's heart to the susceptible periphery, which is represented here by the second, receiving eye-heart-system. In the fifteenth century, two significant discoveries concerning the secret of blood circulation had not yet been made; the organ-theoretical and blood vessel-theoretical image of the complete circulation, the circulation closed through the system of veins, was still unknown, and the reconstruction of the placenta-mediated exchange of blood between the mother and the fetus was even more remote from what was physiologically and anatomically conceivable in Ficino's time. In fact, more than a century and a half would pass from 1469 to the first description of the blood's complete path as a circulation to and from the heart by the English anatomist Harvey; it was only in 1628 that he published his groundbreaking treatise *Exercitatio anatomica de motu cordis et sanguinis in animalibus*, which took modern anatomy into the mechanics of inner liquid movements. Until then—in spite of all physiological probabilities—the model based on the heart as the king of all organs, wastefully giving his blood to the extremities, remained so dominant that the seemingly logical notion that the blood sent forth could circuitously return to the sender was unable to develop. In the age of strong monarchic ideas, this would have amounted to insulting the sovereign; for if the circulatory system were complete, one could no longer have imagined the king and the heart as absolute givers, but also as takers of gifts that flow towards them from the periphery. The center would then no longer be able to rule as the heart by the grace of God, only as the constitutional heart, which would have to swear an oath on the constitution of the circulation.

That explains why Ficino can ascribe a form of homesickness for the origin to the blood of Phaedrus in Lysias' heart, yet does not outline any effective way for the spent blood to return to its source; to explain this, he would indeed have had to postulate the complete circulation. Hence the sensational blood transfusion to the lover in Ficino's treatise is only carried out as a semi-circulation; but it does cause the passionate magnetic pull that chains Lysias to Phaedrus, as well as making it plausible that Phaedrus should also find something attractive about Lysias. Here, infatuation is in fact no more or less than the magical action of telepathically spent blood. Above all, however, this long-distance transfusion offers a new explanation for the asymmetry between the lover (*erastes*) and the beloved (*eromenos*), which had formed the subject of inexhaustible discussions since the days of the Old Academy. It attributes the inevitable inequality of the erotic interrelation to the fact that the enchanter and the enchanted cannot be exact mirror images of each other. According to academic tradition, the lover is usually an older man of great spiritual qualities who is enchanted by the captivating appearance of perfection exuded by the attractive exterior of a noble, vitally superior youth. In Ficino's exemplary scene, the respected rhetorician Lysias does indeed love the inexperienced, irresistibly charming youth Phaedrus, to whose beauty, according to Plato, even Socrates had to pay tribute on their famous joint excursion before the gates of Athens.

As far as our probings in the space of bipolar intimacy are concerned, the passage from *De amore* offers a decisive analytical step beyond the sacramental model underlying both *Herzmaere* and the episode with Saint Catherine. It describes the shared inner sphere between the two mutually attracted hearts in a quasi-anatomical, rudimentarily biotechnical language as the effect of a depth-psychological exchange. This proves the hypothesis that the erotology of the Renaissance progressed more than halfway to a modern theory of things concerning the soul; the protagonists of Renaissance psychology had already realized that the soul cannot be anything other than a studio for transactions with inspiring others. These achievements of Renaissance knowledge have, admittedly, been almost entirely forgotten in our century, and overlaid with scientistically stylized and usually also individualistically shallowed new versions of the psychological space. Anyone wishing to overcome the founder legends surrounding Freud, Jung and their ilk and counter with a valid image of the real history of psychodynamic knowledge in the Modern Age cannot avoid confronting at least two major formations of European depth psychology with the teaching systems of the twentieth century. First of all the Platonically inspired magological theories of fascination, which inquired as to the conditions of love, influence, enchantment and disenchantment using subtle physiological and memory-theoretical means;[12] bold conceptions of a general magic of intersubjectivity emerged from the fifteenth century on,[13] but these were destined to be embarrassed and eradicated by later systems. Secondly, the mesmerist-magnetopathic universe, which expanded between 1780 and 1850 into a fully-fledged depth-psychological classicism; the positivistic zeitgeist in the later nineteenth century and the organized forgetfulness of the Freudian school in the twentieth were its undoing.[14]

With a few observations concerning heart-theoretically relevant thought motifs from the sixteenth and seventeenth centuries, we can perhaps place this exemplary course through the motivic world of religio-metaphysically coded inwardnesses of the heart into a perspective that already takes into account the caesura of modernity. It is said of the Roman priest Filippo Neri (1515–1595), the "humorous saint" mentioned favorably by Goethe in his *Italian Journey*, that when his body was dissected after death a hand-sized gap was discovered between the ribs close to the heart, as well as a significant enlargement of the heart and the coronary artery. Contemporaries attributed these physical anomalies to Neri's frequent states of rapture, which, with outward indications of congestive crises, supposedly caused a heightened flow of blood to the heart and a swelling of the heart and ribcage; it has been confirmed that Neri suffered severe tumor-like eversions of the chest near the heart during prayer, in addition to swellings of the mouth and cheeks when receiving the host, which gave the impression that he had a gag in his mouth. Based on these findings, Neri too belongs to the long line of scriptural somatizers, for whom the mystical text is translated directly into a baroque dialect of the organs. Pentecostal motifs and figures of speech conveying Christian great-heartedness in particular were transported, in Neri's case, into bodily demands for expansion and reaching out.

Such abnormalities could only be handed down in the internal world of Catholic spiritual physiologies; they found their place in a well-organized, thousand-year stream of words about the

Allegory of the Imitatio Christi: Christ offers the soul his open heart for reproduction, 1578 copperplate from Anvers, Paris, Cabinet des Estampes

supernatural bodily effects of pious intensities. The realm of Catholic heart theologies forms a procession of deliria that formed in late medieval mysticism and grew into a large cultic movement in post-Reformation times, especially under the influence of the Sacred Heart mystic Marguerite Marie Alacoque (1647–1690); in the end, it also forced liturgical concessions and determined formulations in the teaching profession. Also drifting in the current of these ecclesiastically administered phantasms of intimacy, one finds the work of the Normandy-born Oratorian priest and popular missionary Johannes Eudes (1601–1680), who went down in the Catholic annals as the founder of a liturgically significant two-hearts cult. Running through his extensive output is one of the underlying notions in modern active mysticism, namely that the Christian life, both in contemplation and works, must be completely absorbed in God. Eudes' inner mission was a battle against the un-Catholic outer being as the non-interior of God. According to Eudes, the life of the saints can only be described as a constant floating in the amniotic sac of the absolute. Eudes introduced a far-reaching innovation into the repertoire of Catholic heart phantasms when he augmented the established cult of the Sacred Heart with the cult of the Heart of Mary. The essence of his commitment to the Heart of Mary was, in our language, to create a bipolar cardial heaven in which the heart of the son could fuse with the mother's in mystical union. From a psychodynamic perspective, Eudes thus satisfied the long-acute need for a fetalization of post-Copernican Catholic heaven; according to this doctrine, the *anima naturaliter christiana* was allowed to live as a sharing third party under the canopy of the dual son-mother heart. This corresponded to the move in post-Reformation Catholic psychopolitics to keep individuals fixed not only in the withered bosom of Mother Church, but also to show them their place in a metaphysically superelevated, inter-cordial small family.

While the mysticism of the Counter-Reformation became entangled in increasingly frenetic cardio-theological language games, medical research at European universities had set in motion an inexorable anatomical disenchantment of the heart. Between the sixteenth and seventeenth centuries, the once

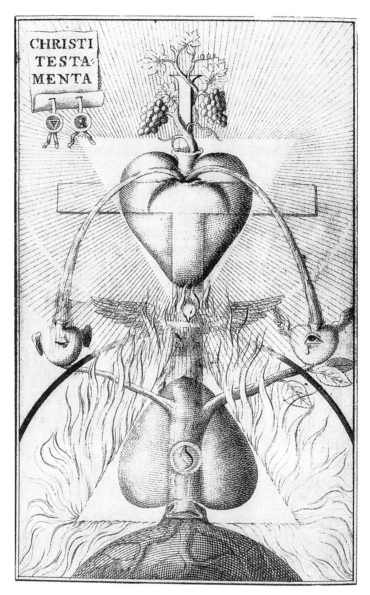

The heart of nature, burning in the fire of wrath, touches the radiant heart of love in the world above. Illustration from Jakob Böhme, *Theosophische Wercke*, Amsterdam, 1682

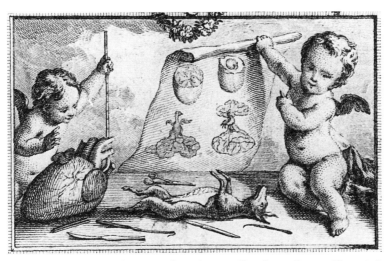

Frontispiece from Albrecht von Haller, *Elementa Physiologiae Corporis Humani*, 8 vols, Lausanne, 1757–1766, copperplate by P. F. Tardieu after Charles Eisen

frowned-on science of postmortem dissection brought forth a new conception of the human being as a wondrous manufacture of the organs. Alongside theologians, doctors now also raised their voices unmistakably, demanding a public teaching discipline in matters of human nature. The dissecting tables of the anatomists were transformed into the altars of the new science of humans; the corpses graduated as assistant lecturers in anthropology. They taught authoritatively that humans, above all relationships to others of their kind, were firstly and ultimately single, unrelated bodies—bodies that exist in original functional unity and organismic individuality, only secondarily being integrated into social groups. Thus one should also consider an influential anatomical factor among the sources of modern individualism. The absolutizing of single beings is predicated not only on modern subject-philosophical motifs and property-bourgeois interests, but also on that anatomical individualism in which the human corpse was viewed as an unrelated body. To the analytical eye of the anatomist, the individual human body presented itself as an autonomous workshop of life, as it were, the physiological thing-in-itself. For there is nothing in the opened-up innards of the corpse that allows a tendency towards existence in intimate connection with others to come to light.

While Baroque churches filled up with cultic images of burning hearts in reactionary Catholic countries, anatomists were putting the feudal heart on trial at a different location. They launched a cardiological discourse tantamount to pure subversion by turning the heart from a sun to a machine, demoting it from a king of the organs to a leading functionary in the blood circulation. Even if priests like Johannes Eudes were bringing their cult of the most sacred hearts of Christ and Mary into early modern masses, this did not prevent his contemporary William Harvey from finding out the trade secrets of the desanctified heart. One hundred and fifty years after Harvey's breakthrough, the process of cardiological disenchantment had progressed sufficiently far for Romantic rehabilitations of the lost cardio-magical world to appear on the horizon; by the early nineteenth century, the general cooling-off process had reached such a precarious level that it had to bring about the cordial restoration, shaped in Germany primarily by Wilhelm Hauff with his period-critical fairy tales of the cold heart.[15] Since then, the struggle for the calibration of the world's temperature has been one of the dramaturgical constants of literary and mass-medial modernity. After the shift from the absolutist to the bourgeois age, a willing-ness to interpret the world and life as a whole in the central terms of physiology and mechanics grew among a broad range of middle-class intellectuals, not least doctors, engineers, opportunists and men of letters, and, in the course of an inevitable counter-differentiation, minds of a synthetic-holistic orientation asserted the thermal rights of cooled-down and over-publicized inner worlds.

Among the exponents of the new anti-metaphysical mentality, the doctor, philosopher and satirist Julien Offray de La Mettrie (1709–1751) stands out for the ironic radicality and aggressiveness of his mechanistic concept of the world and human beings. Even among the more liberal of his contemporaries, La Mettrie's anarcho-skeptic temperament made him an outsider accused of fostering physical and moral excesses. When his position became unsustainable even in free-thinking Holland following the anonymous publication of his scandalous text *L'homme machine* by the Leiden publisher Elie Luzac in autumn 1747, he took refuge at the court of Frederick II of Prussia, where he adopted the role of an Epicurean-atheistic court jester. According to the salacious legend, he died after excessive consumption of truffle pâté. His treatise on the human machine—which many considered the most loathsome book of its century—offers samples of the new style of thought, which has no inhibitions about translating matters of the soul into the language of mechanism without any noteworthy residue. Here anatomical naturalism forged ahead as the central anthropological and psychological discourse. According to this new science, the first thing one needs to know about the soul is that the word "soul" is an empty one. La Mettrie's book is full of cardiological and gynecological motifs that all break with the traditional mystery language of inwardness. We shall quote a passage from a longer argument which the author uses to show

First blood transfusion from an animal (lamb) to a human by the Parisian doctor Jean-Baptiste Denis

that one should by no means cite spiritual, non-physical phenomena to explain the independent movements of muscles and organs; a long list of empirical observations is presented to support his thesis that the organs and fibres of human and animal bodies have motivating forces—*ressorts*—which are responsible for their autonomous movements.

> 5. A frog's heart moves for an hour or more after it has been removed from the body, especially when exposed to the sun or better still when placed on a hot table or chair. If this movement seems totally lost, one has only to stimulate the heart, and that hollow muscle beats again. Hervey made this same observation on toads.
>
> 6. Bacon of Verulam in his treatise "Sylva Sylvarum" cites the case of a man convicted of treason, who was opened alive, and whose heart thrown into hot water, leaped several times, each time less high, to the perpendicular height of two feet.
>
> 7. Take a tiny chicken still in the egg, cut out the heart and you will observe the same phenomena as before, under almost the same conditions. The warmth of the breath alone reanimates an animal about to perish in the air pump.
>
> The same experiments, which we owe to Boyle and to Stenon, are made on pigeons, dogs and rabbits. Pieces of their hearts beat as their whole hearts would. The same movements can be seen in paws that have been cut off from moles.[16]

It is immediately clear that, with this text, we have left the zone of bipolar intimacies in general and the religious heartland in particular, both in the content and the style of the passage. It is especially the content of argument 6 that recalls the theater of terror which the territorial states in the Europe of the early Modern Age often employed to stage their punitive power.[17] The removal of the living heart was in fact carried out frequently on traitors and rebels, for example during the execution of the aristocratic conspirator Grumbach in Gotha in 1567; his heart was not burned, however, but used to strike him in the face.[18] As these acts of public cruelty were not Aztec sacrifical rituals,[19] but rather gestures to demonstrate the jurisdiction of Christian regimes, the desire for a closer decription of the punitive ritual has adequate motives. It undoubtedly offered an answer to a form of injustice that was understood as a violation of the life-world itself—a crime against the sacred public sphere of the state. The fact that perpetrators of high treason in particular were punished in this way shows how the attack on the heart of the political order was responded to with a counter-attack on the heart of the attacker. This most of expressive of all punishments casts the delinquent out of the cardial space of society; not by falling back on the archaic method of banishment, but rather by removing the evildoer by turning him into a sacrificial victim on the inside of the political sphere. This shows that the political sphere, unlike the intimate, cannot be a space of mere biune intimacies. But because, in times of absolutist monarchy and the rule of landed nobles, each subject is nonetheless called upon to enter a personally tinged relationship with the lord of the political sphere, treason can be experienced and punished as a crime of the heart against the authorities; to the lords of the manor in the early Modern Age, it was an attack on the personal life secret of the political space—the expectation of *concordia*. That is why the spheric felon is theatrically drawn into the center and expelled from the middle of the political sphere into a shameful outside.

The gesture of banishment from the circle of the living and the saved is certainly a general implication of executions and excommunications; in this hysterical form of capital punishment, the act of expulsion from the cardial space of shared life is displayed especially garishly. It expresses that death and the outside mean the same thing in this world of sentiments.

If the punitive ritual mentioned by La Mettrie with reference to Bacon brings an expressive outside into play, the philosopher's argumentation itself contains a methodical or conceptual outside that extends further than the cruel rite. The author envisages the muscular and vascular system that is the heart in anatomical abstraction; taken as an organ per se, it is essentially no more for him than an isolable piece of organic tissue. This tissue does not in itself possess any intersubjective dimension, but only an automatic potential for motion, a bundle of *departments* that realize themselves, depending on the favorable or unfavorable nature of circumstances. Understood in this way, a heart—whether cut out or in its natural place—is automatically located in an externality that does not belong to any intimate self-field and cannot be reached by any breath from a human sphere. Its existence in accordance with its own mode of being as an organismic machine in a context of cooperating machines of the same kind. Because La Mettrie is not a follower of metaphysical dualism, however, he does not make his enlightened subject spook about like a Cartesian ghost inside a bodily apparatus; it *is* itself a function of the machine that it is—a machine that produces an experienced inside at the same time as unexperienced physiological processes. Through this radical machine theory, intimacy is declared an effect of that outside in which all "machines," whether mechanisms or organisms, have always resided. The imagined body is not an element within either an interior or an experienced space of proximity, but rather a place within a homogenized, geometric position spatiality.[20] For what is anatomy but the enforcement of position-spatial physical concepts in the former corporeal darkness, an enforcement that first of all turns every living body into a black box for every other? What we call intimate relationships are undoubtedly possible between such machine men, but these do not initially change the fact that the radical-materialistic theory of the being-isolated of bodies must allow their relationships amongst themselves to precede it. Relationships between machine men are, for their part, mechanical processes; these may have an experienced side, but in terms of their imagined nature they belong entirely to the outer realm.

La Mettrie's outside, however, does not—as the humanistic interpretation claims with horror—want to be the door through which we exit to the realm of the dead and the foreign, but should rather be grasped as the field of a human freedom that must be conquered anew and understood in a different way. In his writings, the philosopher celebrated the joy of being an enlightened machine because he thought he had found—in the particular nature of the machine—a possibility to satisfy the interest in well-understood human freedom. He placed emancipatory hope in the vision that machines which sufficiently understand themselves would emerge from the fog of imaginary, religiously veiled slavery, which from a sensualistic point of view means: into a life full of pleasures, unsuppressed by any conventional religious morality. This marked the advent of an ethic of intensity. "The soul is clearly an enlightened machine (*Voilà une Machine bien éclairée*)."[21] For La Mettrie, reaching this outside was the precondition for all emancipation; while the inwardness born of theology simply shows how we are supposed to entrap ourselves through inhibitions, fears and privations, exteriority opens up before us as a field on which we can expect the truly living, the intense, the event-like other that transforms and releases us. This motif has survived to this day in the radical, non-dialectical materialisms of French philosophy, especially in the philosophical project of Gilles Deleuze.[22] To rescue his happy machine, La Mettrie abandoned the concepts of God and the soul and set about re-dissecting their sultry accretions.

In the course of this operation, the philosopher lost sight of a central question, namely whether his anarchically cheerful machines should not be structured differently from solitary automata; even after suppressing the metaphysical ideas of God and the soul, it could have become a problem for the author that machines, if they are humans, always function in relation to others—and not only in the phase of initial adjustment conventionally known as socialization or upbringing. For personal machines too, it would make sense to suppose that they can only be successfully kept going in bipolar, multipolar coexistence and an inter-intelligent parallel circuit. La Mettrie could have noticed that human machines consistently function in ensembles, and that only those which succeed in replacing interaction with present social machines through non-human augmentative media—such as mirrors, books, cards, musical instruments or pets—are capable of separation. De Sade at least put together lust machines from several individuals in his erotic arrangements, albeit only in mechanical copulations where humans are no more than prefabricated parts capable of pleasure.

Modern mechanistics are not alone, however, in their difficulty to conceive of beings for whom entanglement with their own kind forms the central motivation. When, in the early phase of the theological process that elevated Christianity to intellectual supremacy, the concern was to formulate the incarnation of God conceptually, theologians also faced the problem of correctly defining how far God's descent to the human level extended. It took centuries for the second nature of Christ, his human gravity and psychosomatic capacity for suffering, to win out over the docetic or spiritistic temptation to understand the God-man simply as a manifestation from above. Only after dogma battles with heavy losses was it officially agreed that for God, the way into flesh involved birth by a genuine mother—or, extended in modern terms, also via early symbiosis, the unconditional dependence on ego formation in successful interactions with others and, in the event of their factual failure, via religious psychosis. If God desires to become human, He can only realize His second nature in a defective human being or a madman who declares himself the Son of God. As the machine's transformation into a human being has been a task for thinkers since the seventeenth century, one should also demand that machines take up the cross of human nature. The machine can only realize its second nature in the madmen who reveal themselves as incarnated machines capable of suffering, and hence defective. Today it is humans, as non-trivial ontological machines, who have to meet the standards of a dual nature doctrine. *Homo totus, tota machina*. Mysteries of a kind all their own grow in a technological culture: is it not reasonable to admit that *l'homme machine* and *la femme machine*, by embracing and letting each other go, pose more riddles for each other than inter-intelligent machines can, for the time being, solve? Machine from machine, man from man.

CHAPTER 2

Between Faces

On the Appearance of the Interfacial Intimate Sphere

And that behind Orpheus' laments shines the glory of having seen, however fleetingly, the unattainable face at the very instant it turned away...

— Michel Foucault, "The Thought of the Outside"[1]

The Theban Lysias stares open-mouthed into the face of Phaedrus, while the latter, the beautiful youth, turns his eyes against those of Lysias, sending out a gaze pregnant with bloody vapor.[2] In the scene described by Marsilio Ficino, the mutual infatuation of the two model Greeks begins with an optical encounter, an infectious face-to-face. What will create a visceral alliance—or, more precisely, an erotic toxemia—between the two protagonists must begin with an exchange of glances in a space of openness. The one-to-one space must already be open before the radically intimized two-heart sphere can be lifted out of it. The two poisoned and enamored parties have left the interfacial public space in order, devouring each other face to face, to immerse themselves in each other in a magically symbiotic fashion. If one wanted to restrict one's view to the exceptional erotic situation in order to explore the nature of the intimate, however, one would be distracted by the normal forms of intersubjectivity in which individuals see and hear one another while in full possession of their delimiting powers; for pre-bourgeois times, one should probably also assume a mutual perception of odor as an unavoidable indication of presences within the space of encounters. Where the paths of individuals cross in everyday interaction, the sight of the other offers them an opportunity to note that they do not normally lose their composure merely through a glance at the individual. It is more likely that this act of seeing will assure the seer of his secure position in the middle of his own surrounding space; it affirms him in his distantial, non-merging forms of intercourse with the protagonists and opponents who populate his human environment. "I am I and you are you; I am not in the world to meet the expectations of others; and if we meet by chance, that is fine; if not, there is nothing to be done about it." Our first model analyses have detached themselves forcefully from this brutal orthodoxy concerning the normal distance between Me and You on the open market of chance contact in order to plunge directly into intersubjective states of emergency. The suspicion might arise that we have broken through to the fusionary-ecstatic level much too quickly while approaching the dyadic sphere. The anthropophagous communion, the mystical exchange of hearts, the telepathic transfusion in an erogenous two-person blood circulation—these were models for encounter excesses beyond the personal melting point; our intercardial scenes describe the final stages of relationships in which individuals are already sharing their innards with each other. In the fusionary-dyadic models described, the level of everyday distanced relationships between Me and Them was broken through in sudden excesses; without any preparation, a sultry cosmos opened up that refused to allow any distances or free spaces between persons. Without uncovering premises, we dived into a cavernous world for two whose protagonists hum along with the melodies of the others with their eyes closed, on this side of the handshake, the conversation and eye contact. Each time, the fusion between the two connected parties turned out so intense that it initially remained impossible to say from which primal scenes of communion such participations in one another could have been transferred to the current scenes. Hence, in the following, we must step back from such eyeless interaction in fantastic, shared abdominal cavities so that the encounter between two parties in the standard situation of mutual perception—seeing each other in the public light—can begin. Here we can discover that even the seemingly distanced and distance-affirming optical encounter with the other can contribute something to producing a bipolar world of intimacy. (We shall speak of the acoustically intimate in a later chapter.)[3] For the human faces, as remains to be shown, are themselves creations of a unique field of intimacy in which the regarding is modeled by the regard.

Lysias, the Theban rhetorician, stares open-mouthed (*inhiat*) into the face of his lover Phaedrus: the beauty of his young friend places the lover in a state of painful intoxication. He feels the urge to be close to his beloved, even if he does not understand himself what exactly he desires of the youth. As the names reveal, Ficino based the models used in the relationship theater of his analysis on Platonic examples. According to Plato, the sight of the beautiful causes a memory shock that propels the beholder beyond his normal views of the trivial world of things and people. In select moments, amidst a thousand everyday sights of objects, human bodies and circumstances, shapes flare up and enchant the soul. In the disquiet over such sights, the seer feels transposed to a different stage. He senses that in the current manifestation, whether a human face or a work of art, a primal sight is reaching for him and taking him out of the everyday. "Whoever has fully gazed at beauty / is already marked for death" (August von Platen, "Tristan"). Plato seems to have been certain that the unease caused by the sight of beauty breaks open a memory store hidden in everyday life: erotic fear points to an elsewhere from which the subject originally comes, and which places it in a painful state of homesick tension when it re-encounters beauty. Where this longing is clear with itself about its nature, it transpires as a trace of the memory of prenatal visions. This is what Plato makes his Socrates explain in the dialogue *Phaedrus*:

> But he whose initiation is recent, and who has been the spectator of many glories in the other world, is amazed when he sees any one having a godlike face or form, which is the expression or imitation of divine beauty; and at first a shudder runs through him, and some "misgiving" of a former world steals over him; then looking upon the face of his beloved as of a god he reverences him, and if he were not afraid of being thought a downright madman, he would sacrifice to his beloved as to the image of a god; then as he gazes on him there is a sort of reaction, and the shudder naturally passes into an unusual heat and perspiration; for, as he receives the effluence of beauty through the eyes, the wing moistens and he warms.[4]

Plato's achievement lies in providing, at the same time as his aesthetic theory of the beautiful body, a speech on the shock caused by the beautiful face. Socrates' reference to the "godlike face" (*theoeidés prósopon*) is the earliest trace of a philosophical reflection that develops in the court of human faciality. For Plato, the face of the beautiful beloved does not represent the person himself or the inner part of the fair-faced youth; the beautiful one is simply a medium for the beauty that illuminates him, the privileged or truthful body. We learn from Plato that in the beautiful human, as in other beautiful things of the body and beautiful sights, a prehuman radiance of perfection reveals itself in the desired purity before our melting eyes. The most beautiful human body, then, is the most transparent, the one with the least will and darkness of its own, the one most pervaded and illuminated by goodness. Where something like the young Phaedrus appears, a sunrise is repeated in facial translation in the world of the senses. The lucency of his face is thus not his *proprium*; it remains the property of the sun-like first and good from which, according to Plato, everything which seems well formed and accomplished in the sensory world lights up and flows forth. Falling in love with Phaedrus means yielding to a *truth*. This intelligent re-rapprochement with the prenatally observed metaphysical sun corresponds to the erotic heat wave that melts the darkened, chilled human body and releases a pathos-laden recollection of ancient blisses. For the philosopher, the shock of the beautiful face equals the emergency situation of nuclear radiation. For in the noble visage, as with all well-formed bodies, the form-creating light that shines in from the other side is not fully absorbed by the dark matter. Projected through a transparent screen of flesh, as it were, the transcendent light falls into the dulling material world to which our intelligence is temporarily confined. Hence, for Plato, beauty is always epiphanic and diaphonous, revelatory and full of radiant power. A *godlike face* such as that of Phaedrus is the diapositive of an invisible sun that, following the idealistic reform, is no longer called Helios but rather Agathon. Whoever exposes their naked eye to this illuminating perfection is thrown into an erotic daze that constitutes a form of clairvoyance.

Admittedly, if Plato had not connected the real facial appearance to a soul-shaking look on the part of the observer, his suggestion for a philosophical cult of the beautiful human face would, precisely by assigning the beautiful as such to a transcendent source of light, stop in a fatal manner at the abstract semblance, having to cover the individual face completely with the impersonal facial ideal. In grasping the facial appearance and the deep opening of the eye under the spell of the face opposite as elements that belong together, Plato becomes the discoverer of the drama, unrepresentable and scarcely ever considered before or since, that has always taken place between human faces. The discovery that faces can do something to each other which brings questions of truth and participation into play is taken up by Ficino; his account of the fascinogenic eye contact between Lysias and Phaedrus constitutes the first attempt in modern philosophy to describe the interfacial space in such a way that it no longer appears as a vacuum, or as something neutrally intermediate. Following Plato's trail, Ficino presents the space between the faces as a force field filled with turbulent radiations. In this field, each of the facial surfaces turned towards each other works on its opposite number in such a way that it can only open itself up to a human-historical faciality through its being-for-the-other-face.

As early as a century and a half before the Platonic revival in Florence, painters of the early Modern Age had begun to elevate the interfacial space to observation as a reality in its own right. Nowhere did this pictorial discovery of human faces turned towards each other take place as resolutely and completely as in the Cappella degli Scrovegni, the Arena Chapel in Padua. In these frescoes, which were probably completed before 1306, Giotto wrote down an alphabet of interfacial configurations. In dozens of scenes from sacred history, he unfolds a screen for pictorial events that is covered in mutually illuminating human faces as the firmament is covered in constellations. Giotto's two most profound studies on the biblical face-to-face motif are in the cycle of scenes on the birth of Mary and in the passion cycle: Saint Anne's greeting of Joachim at the Golden Gate of Jerusalem and the kiss of Judas. In these two kiss scenes, Giotto presents the most sublime pictorial attempts towards a metaphysics of the facial encounter.

According to art historians, the painter based his scenes from Marian history on the Protoevangelium of James,[5] as well as the group of tales *On the Birth of Mary* from the *Legenda aurea*. Jacobus de Voragine, the Archbishop of Genoa who died in 1298, relates in his collection of myths about Christian saints that Mary's parents, Joachim and Anne, were still childless after twenty years of marriage despite being God-fearing people. One day, Joachim decided to travel to Jerusalem for Hanukkah in order to make a sacrifice before the altar of Yahwe and ask for the child they so desired. There he was recognized by the priest, who expelled him from the temple in a fit of rage because he was cursed by the law, which made no provision "for a sterile man, who made no increase to the people of God, to stand among men

Giotto, *Legend of Saint Joachim, Meeting at the Golden Gate*, fresco

who begot sons."[6] Marked by shame, Joachim henceforth avoids the company of the zealots and seeks refuge in the desert among shepherds. One day, an angel of the Lord appears to him and announces that his wife Anne will bear a child, which they are to call Mary—the later mother of the Messiah; Joachim should return to Jerusalem, the angel continues, where his wife will meet him. Anne is immediately visited by an angel who tells her what he has revealed to Joachim. Giotto's painting reproduces the moment when Anne, already expecting Mary, welcomes her returning husband at the Golden Gate of Jerusalem:

So they met as the angel had predicted, and were happy to see each other and be sure they were to have a child.[7]

Giotto set this legendarily idealized and novellistically animated scene on a small bridge in front of the Golden Gate. Joachim and Anne lean towards each other and kiss in a delicate embrace, each knowing the secret of the other. Atop their heads is a golden double halo, placed around the chosen couple like an exact painterly explication of their spheric communion. From the observer's perspective, Joachim's face is a little in front of Saint Anne's, so that the male contribution to this extraordinary kiss overshadows the female by a trace. It is no coincidence that this is the kiss with which Joachim accepts his unconceived daughter Mary as his own coming child; it is a kiss that, in paternal resignation, replaces conception with greeting. Joachim embraces a mother who carries a child of unknown, that is to say divine origin within her; Anne, for her part, greets a man who has abandoned his own pretensions as a begetter for the sake of the future—it goes without saying that these parents have the function of prefiguring the later alliance of Joseph and Mary. Their faces form a shared circle of happiness: they float in a bipolar sphere of intimate mutual recognition based on shared hope and a joint plan for a fulfilled time. Their faces convey the respective knowledge of two human beings about the merit of the other. With their kiss, Anne and Joachim acknowledge each other as communicating vessels with eminent fates and tasks.

Giotto captured the fruitful moment of this encounter like a quick-witted observer. The partners in his chosen couple do not greet each other in a world devoid of people: there are six witnesses standing around the highlighted scene, storing the image internally

Giotto, *Legend of Saint Joachim, Meeting at the Golden Gate*, detail

as they gaze upon it with profane eyes. It is not only the beholder who perceives what the painter wants to be seen; the picture itself is full of eyes that are present at the event depicted and draw it into an image-immanent public domain. As a painter, Giotto is thus more of a novella writer than a teller of legends; his salvation history is more reminiscent of a newspaper from the Holy Land than a monastic tome. His scenes unfold not before the eyes of mystery theologians and hermits, but those of an urban and courtly society that scarcely pays attention to the differences between sacred and profane history in its choice of conversational matter. The novella, like modern society, lives off what is interesting. What the picture's viewers observe is thus also seen by the bystanders in the picture. Forty years before Boccaccio, Giotto rediscovered the eye's human right to entertaining sights; in the spirit of the novella, he anticipates the modern, convivial division of knowledge about events that stimulate our affective and participatory intelligence. The frescoes manifest a narrative vitality that exceeds the horizon of their written sources, especially simplistic legend literature, and moves towards a world set in motion by the advent of the Modern Age. One is tempted to claim that even Giotto already placed the principle of entertainment for the eye above the law of religious contemplation. This is especially clear at the hot spot of the greeting painting; for where the faces of the holy couple meet, the painter creates a third face through a sleight of hand. One can perceive it by withdrawing one's gaze from the two main figures and focusing, from a decentered perspective, on the area between the two faces. Once one has recognized them, the features of this visible-invisible third figure keep appearing when one looks at the picture again—they are certainly eerie and slightly deformed, yet nonetheless clear in their presence, like an allusion to the new life that is starting to awaken in Anne's body. It is not a child's face that results from the union of the parents' faces, and one is more inclined to think of their grandchild Jesus than their child Mary. From a hermeneutical perspective, this emergent third face could be read as the climax of an artistic effort to translate didactic scenes of popular Marian theology into speaking images. In aesthetic terms, the new face breaks its pious mold and reclaims an originally pictorial prerogative: making the invisible visible. This testifies to a birth of the wonderful from the interfacial space. In this and only this space it is true, as Lévinas said, that encountering a person means being kept awake by a riddle. The painters of the early Modern Age were, it would seem, the first to take note of this keeping-awake of humans through the face that is turned towards them.

In the scene of the kiss of Judas, the viewer encounters a painting in which the space between two human faces is charged with extreme, antithetical spheric tensions—it is the fourth painting in the twelve-part series of passion scenes, following the betrayal, the Last Supper and the anointing of feet. In this fresco, which presents both figures in profile, Giotto developed a threefold difference between Christ and Judas. The rupture between them concerns not only the distance separating each individual in the mass of mortals from every other; rather, it tears open the anthropological continuum between the persons in three ways and assigns them to radically divergent ranks and places of being. As the simultaneous portraitist of Christ and Judas, Giotto becomes the painter of anthropological difference.

On the first level, the God-man and the mere man are standing face to face. Here, as in all frescoes from the Scrovegni cycle, Giotto uses haloes resembling golden helmets to set the saints and Christ Himself apart from the non-luminous, common mortals. The painter uses this conventional stylistic device to comment on the metaphysical reason for the inequality between the figures: he depicts the saints in the world like divine actors in an earthly comedy. He thus creates a pictorial manifestation of the theological idea of the secret of injustice, which posits the impenetrable distinction between the elect and the profane; through the aureoles, he gives the *mysterium iniquitatis*

Giotto, *Kiss of Judas*

a place in the visible realm. On the second level, Judas and Christ stand facing each other in real presence as the noble and the vulgar human. To underline this difference, Giotto fell back on common physiognomic traditions; his Christ surpasses Judas not only in height and in the well-balanced beauty of his head, in which the noble proportions of the forehead and the middle and lower portions of the face serve to maintain equilibrium, but also through his aristocratic posture, which displays a hint of condescension towards Judas, who is stooped in an almost bestial manner and looking up deviously. In a physiognomic interpretation of this facial constellation, Rudolf Kassner pointed out the menacing indentation in Judas' profile between the forehead and nose: "This evil angle indeed has a terrible meaning: that the mental faculties are separated from those of the soul."[8] Giotto undoubtedly apollonized his Christ, presenting him in the light of Western European ideas of *aristeia*; Judas, by contrast, faces him as a sly Eastern plebeian with base drives and disharmonic features.

The decisive difference between Christ and Judas in Giotto's painting, however, is neither the metaphysical difference between the God-man and the unblessed mortal nor the physiognomic difference between the noble and the common man. In his depiction of the eye contact between the two figures, Giotto renders a third, spherologically relevant difference visible, and only here does it become clear why an intimate alliance between the two protagonists is impossible. Christ's gaze, questioning and knowing at once, shows an open, sphereforming power that would even reintegrate the traitor into its space if he were able to enter it; in Judas, however, he sees the embodiment of a greedy isolation that, even in close physical proximity to the other, cannot become part of the shared space. Thus Judas kisses what he cannot attain, and his kiss becomes the obscene gesture of one who infiltrates the space of love with the attitude of one who does not belong. Saint Augustine would have said: he is curled up like a thief who steals what he has already been given, and what would belong to him if he knew how to take what he has. Even up close he is always apart from the rest, an agent of egotism who has crept into the center of an ecstatic community. His gaze grates against the nobly open aura

Giotto, *Kiss of Judas*, detail

of the God-man with a skulking, evilly stupid expression; even in the closest bodily proximity to the masterful subject, Judas' behavior is that of an actor who is stuck in his calculating greed and has lost all distance from his role. If one wanted to use Sartre's terminology, one could say that Judas is the embodiment of *mauvaise foi*, which follows the renunciation of the free distance from the pantomime of one's own life. Even while face to face with the teacher of freedom, the epitome of inspiring reciprocity and participatory animation, Judas displays a degraded selfishness that knows things only in the context of greedy possession and people only as parts of manipulative transactions. The latent heading for the scene of the *kiss of Judas* is unmistakably "The Sold God." Giotto shows how the twelvefold biune love sphere between Christ and His disciples is torn at this point. It falls prey to a debasing interest that posits itself as the higher one. In Giotto's painting, this spherological rip opens up dramatically between the two faces confronting each other eye to eye. Between the two protagonists' profiles, a narrow cavity opens up with a shape reminiscent of a chalice. Christ and Judas exchange a glance from which no shared life can grow any longer. From the perspective of the figure of Christ, it is a glance through the burst biune sphere into the realm of the deanimated, a mere two hands' breadth before one's own eyes. For the traitor Judas, the sphere-forming man is standing there like an unattainable, impenetrable, alien thing. Now it is death that marks the face of the God-man.

Giotto's explorations in the interfacial space were not to be without consequence; already among his immediate successors, painters emerged who dared to portray the Madonna and the baby Jesus looking at each other, even kissing, as if they wanted to make the viewer a witness, albeit one who could only catch sideways glimpses of the intimacies shared by the holiest persons. In *Madonna Enthroned with Child and Saints*, displayed inside Massa Marittima Cathedral, Ambrogio Lorenzetti placed precisely such a mother-child tête-à-tête in the middle of a public realm comprising angels and holy adorers. Between 1360 and 1370, a master from Bologna painted a Madonna and child triptych, with pairs of angel musicians on either side, in which the boy and his mother sit cheek to cheek, looking into each other's eyes. Here the

Ambrogio Lorenzetti, *Madonna Enthroned with Child and Saints*

cultic image, which seeks to draw viewers into its sensual sphere by addressing them head-on, changes into the painted novella of a simultaneously holy and private eros. This is no longer the Baby Jesus who has always been the savior, anticipating the passion enthroned on his mother's lap; instead, He has almost entirely become the natural child of a natural mother, without any sideways glance at the believers who crowd around Him, demanding acts of salvation and sucking at the aura of the suckling child. As a childlike child, the *infans* Jesus, relieved for a second of His representational duties, can immerse Himself in tender embrace with His mother. There is no holy script here transporting the infant into cosmic contexts; for a precarious moment, the designated savior can enjoy a breather from salvation history.

It is no coincidence that spiritualists of varying complexions have taken offense at such Italianizations of the Gospel. The Russian Orthodox priest and icon painter Pavel Florensky, a defender of the Old Eastern European iconic concept, took a belated swing at them when he posited the following thesis in 1922:

> From the Renaissance on, the religious art of the West has been based upon aesthetic delusion. The Western religious artists have loudly proclaimed the nearness and truth of the spiritual reality they claim to represent in their art; but, lacking any genuine relation to the spiritual reality, they think it completely unnecessary to heed even those few scanty instructions about icon painting (hence, about spiritual reality) that the Roman Church gives them.[9]

Like all thinkers taken over by Christianized Platonic furor, Florensky misses the fact that the philosophical basis of Renaissance painting was a radical shift in its truth model: in a world-historical act of sensualizing and dramatizing its truth relation, the European West exchanged primal images for primal scenes. As a result of this fundamental semio-political decision, European painters regained sights of the moving, lively world for representation as scenes capable of expressing truth, while the Platonizing East—including Islam[10]—continued to base its image concept on the statuesque elevation and immobilization of the ideas shining in. Part of the revolutionary truth-theoretical commitment of the burgeoning Modern Age in Europe was the attempt to unite the principles of research and revelation, while Eastern orthodoxy, faithfully

Ambrogio Lorenzetti, *Madonna Enthroned with Child and Saints*, detail

Joos van Cleve, *The Holy Family*, after 1511, detail

Platonic, monarchist and hierarchist, insisted that the striving for truth could only ever be interpreted as the homeward journey from the image to the archetype. For the pictorial culture and the politics of the European East, the shift to the individual never took place in the way that had become second nature for the Italians and their successors in the West. Even the art of socialist realism in Soviet Russia remained stuck in Platonizing protest against the Western liaison between the novella and the primal scene: it glorified, in decidedly anti-Italian ways, the eternal icons of the saints of production. Florensky's polemic against Western painting thus has its factual basis in the image-typological opposition between the *eidos* and the novella scene: someone who is looking for prototypes and instead encounters proto-scenes can easily be tempted to speak of aesthetic delusion or untruth, when he should actually be speaking of an altered pictorial and visual truth model. Consequently, Florensky cannot do justice to the image-producing elan of Western painting since the Renaissance, as he fails to understand that it has been taken over by a post-Platonic, scenic idea of truth. Along its own line, the history of the Modern Age's great art became a torch relay of vitalization for our views of the existent through the medium of elevated scenes. Only subsequently, at the turn of the twentieth century, did that second shift towards free pictoriality in the visual arts become possible to which we refer, with a term that has still scarcely been philosophically fulfilled, as the "art of modernity." It constituted no less than an overcoming of the common European dogma of the object and the liberation of perception from the age-old service of concreteness; at the same time, it freed artists from the meanwhile unbearable expectation to prove their brilliance while bound by the shackles of nature imitation.[11]

Art historiography has only recently developed an adequately complex notion of the long way European pictorial culture had to travel before arriving at the representation of the individualized human face.[12] Overall, this path can be described as an artistic process from the Christogram to the anthropogram. In this retelling of the ascending path to the portrait face, the Western European culture of religious devotion appears as a hothouse of vision that, after waiting for centuries before the *imagines Christi*, has finally learned to meditate on the profane human face in its indefensible uniqueness and to read it like a worldly sacred text. This means that the germinal forms of all later portrait optics should be sought in pictures of Christ whose typological extremes are marked by the Catholic passion face and the Orthodox transfiguration face. The typological threshold values of Christography are the Western European crucifix and the Eastern European true icon. In their respective regions, these form the basis of an immeasurably rich pictorial practice whose consequences have sedimented themselves to the very eyeground of European viewers. These cultic image seeds were grown in a virtual thousand-year hotbed before finally being planted out into the open—that is, into the unabashedly profane world of aristocratic and bourgeois self-descriptions. In the countless portrait paintings of European individuals since the Renaissance, then, one does not merely find the artistic co-founding of "modern" individualism; the precise readings in the faces of humans of all temperaments, all moods and almost all social classes also show unmistakably that for the painters and societies

Joel-Peter Witkin, *Venus Preferred to Christ*

of the Modern Age, an epoch of newly animating transactions on a liberated physiognomic market had dawned. Even in the isolated portrait, which affords a single face an entire visual space, the Neoplatonic pictorial order is now suspended; the portraits of the Modern Age are not character icons testifying to the participation of an individual face in an eternal facial *eidos*, but rather scenic variations on a dramatic facial presence. In the portrait as a genre, the great change of model likewise replaces the icon with the primal scene, even if it appears that the individual face depicted in isolation has been removed from all manifest contexts of actions and events. In fact, it was now permitted to set apart single faces in pictures of their own because, under the new seeing conditions, they could still be recognized as latently dramatic presences even in quiet, apparently static visualization. Each individual image of a person realizes a facial event that has leaped across from pictorial Christology to the profane dimension. Behind every portrait of the Modern Age lies the *ecce homo* face—the primal scene of human exposure with which Jesus, standing next to Pilate, made his debut as the bringer of the historically new perceptual imperative: recognize the mortal God in the face of this man![13] After the transition to the Modern Age, the eye-opening power of this scene was beneficial for every profane individual who appeared in paintings as an *uomo singulare*, and perhaps even everyone in the twentieth century in their most informal private photos. In the Christian school of eye training, any face painted using newer techniques or reproduced by other means can potentially become a novella, a notable visual incident, because every portrait presents a human being to whom, in however diluted a form, the words "Behold the Man" still apply. Every portrait shows a face whose purpose is to challenge others to acknowledge its singularity. If every individual soul is interesting for God, then its face—under the given conditions—is permitted to appeal to the attention of its kind. The portrait as an artistic act is part of a protracting procedure—that is, one that draws out aspects of the characteristic and individual—which connects scenes back to primal scenes and embeds events in primal events. Through this rooting of the special scenes and sights in primal scenes of eventful life, the modern space of visibilities began to explode. A new seeing technique, a refined art of face reading and a physiognomic semiotics now emancipated the facial scenes from iconic repose. Thus, as a result of the novellistic cultural revolution, even the face of the profane individual was able to advance to the space of things that are elevated to the dignity of representation; faces become visual dignitaries through their ascent to the artistically recreatable and pre-creatable world.

This ascent merits a discussion of its own. By no means can it be understood as an event that is only of concern for art history; nor, however, could an expanded cultural and media history of the image adequately describe the birth of the face from the interfacial space, as this involves a process that points back to long before all questions of representation. The elevation of the profane face to portrait-worthy status is itself a very late and precarious operation in the interfacial space, and cannot manifest itself as such in any one portrait. Portrait art, as a protracting procedure that emphasizes or draws out individuality, is part of a comprehensive face-producing movement that, beyond all art- and image-historical manifestations, possesses genre-historical status. The possibility of *faciality*[14] is connected to the process of anthropogenesis itself. The drawing out of human faces from the snouts of mammals: this points to a facial and interfacial drama whose beginnings extend back into the early history of the species. A glance at the facial forms of those apes most closely related to humans shows that they too, from afar, are on the way to a quasi-human faciality, even though they have scarcely covered half of the evolutionary distance between the mammal's head and the human face. We refer to this biologically and culturally motivated setting apart of human faces from animal faces as *protraction*. It is not the portrait that enables the face to be highlighted to the point of recognizability; rather, it is protraction that elevates faces to the threshold of portrayability in an open-ended facio-genetic process. Protraction is the clearing[15] of being in the face; it invites us to conceive of the history of being as a somatic event. The opening up of the face—even more than cerebralization and the creation of the hand—enabled people to become animals open to the world, or, more significantly, to their fellow humans. Its purpose, expressed in anthropological terms, is an evolution of luxury within an insulating hothouse; its agent and medium is above all, among other elements, the interfacial space or sphere. Anyone seeking proof of the reality and effectiveness of intimate spheric processes can practically touch this subtle *realissimum* here. It is sufficient to call to mind that human faces have pulled themselves out of their animal form simply by looking at one another, so to speak, in the course of a long-term evolutionary drama. Naturally, sight and selection are positively connected. That means: this turning of faces towards other faces among humans became face-creating and face-opening, because the welcome qualities of faces for the eyes of the potential sexual partner inform generic processes via selection-effective preferences. One could thus say that in a certain sense, human faces produce one another; they blossom within an oscillatory circuit of luxuriant reciprocal opening. Even the ancient faces from the age of hordes were already sculptures of the attentiveness showed by the *sapiens* specimens as they regarded one another. The evolutionarily successful type *Homo sapiens sapiens*, who advanced to Southwest Asia and the Mediterranean from the edges of the African deserts sixty or seventy thousand years ago in the third exodus wave (after *Homo erectus* one million years ago and the

Albrecht Dürer, *Self-Portrait in a Fur Coat*, oil on wood panel, 1500, Alte
Pinakothek, Munich

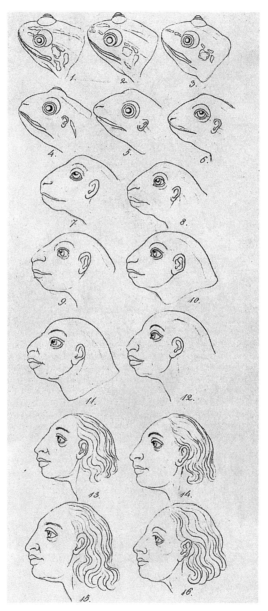

From Frog to Poet, from the collection of Johann Caspar Lavater. The original includes further drawings

Neanderthal two hundred thousand years ago), embodied a slightly more graceful branch of the *Homo* species; this type, named Cro-Magnon man after one of the main places of archaeological discovery in Southwest France, developed into *Homo sapiens aestheticus*, with whom elegance was connected to selection advantages. The more recent facial genesis—with its fair and foul monsters—has taken place in an interfacial hothouse where human faces grow like physiognomic orchids. This facialization, admittedly, is a species-wide, acute noetic-facial drama. Gilles Deleuze and Félix Guattari, who, along with Thomas Macho, presented the most original theory of facial development, fall prey to their own de-generalizing elan when, in their reflections on the creation of the face among Europeans, they claim:

> "Primitives" may have the most human of heads, the most beautiful and most spiritual [sic!], but they have no face and need none. The reason is simple. The face is not a universal. It is not even that of the white man; it is White man himself, with his broad white cheeks and the black hole of his eyes. The face is Christ. The face is the typical European […]. Thus the face is by nature an entirely specific idea […].[16]

It is clear enough that these emphatic statements are only possible because the authors have failed to make a necessary and fundamental distinction, namely between the protraction of the *Homo sapiens* face as such and the characterological "writing" on the facial slate. As a result, they were prone to confusing the species-wide, open *sapiens* face with the culture-specifically molded physiognomic or semantic face. In their fruitful methodic aversion to the deceptively universal, the case-specific thinkers Deleuze and Guattari make themselves unnecessarily blind to the overarching case of faciality, the long-term facio-genetic drama, which encompasses the entire human race without exceptions, and always takes place in two acts via the primary stage of facial opening and the secondary stage of cultural and character inscription.[17] The primal interfacial process is a genetic-aesthetic movement characteristic of all *sapientes* whose course can be made clear through a simple comparison of human children's faces and those of young chimpanzees; this process extends back at least a million years, and its result is the Cro-Magnon type in the bio-aesthetic and racial branches that are scattered worldwide. The facial genesis sums up a universal history of luxuriant participations of humans in the facial creation of their fellows. Whoever wishes to know what defines the content of this history need only seek the basis of the difference between an ape's face and a human's. Once these poles of protraction have been marked and the course of the facio-genetic movement thus mapped out, one can ask as to the motives or motors that drive or pull along the process leading to the human face.

One can grasp the efficient motor or protractor of human facial genesis by becoming sure of the hothouse character of all prehistoric and historical hominid life forms, in which the interfacial warmth field forms a decisive cell. To gain an idea of the affective temperatures in the horde hothouses of early history, it is sufficient to recall how, throughout our species, many adult women—as well as those men capable of paternal feelings—are still delighted by the beautiful faces of babies and infants. What requires explanation about this spontaneous inclination to adopt a charmed and friendly posture towards children's faces is not its universality, but rather its occasional absence among individuals who, through specializations of affectivity or emotional barriers, are excluded from the tender microclimate that normally ensues spontaneously between adult and infant faces. The species-wide interfacial greenhouse effect—which manifests itself above all in the joy at the visible joy of the encountered face—is itself embedded in the emotional density of the primary sociospheres. In these, horde and family members are affectively transparent for one another to a high degree; their participative patterns are synchronized in bipolar and multipolar fashion *a priori*. In the innermost ring of those bell jars of social participation which emotionally rhythmicize and air-condition group life, one almost universally finds an especially protected and charged field with a highly refined character akin to the nest and the incubator: the mother-child space. One could, with very good reason, attempt to describe the entire process of anthropogenesis in terms of this primary rooming-in. What we refer to with the unfortunate modernist term "society" is, from an evolutionary perspective, essentially a shell system composed of more dispensable persons—later known as fathers—whose function is to protect the indispensable and fragile core sphere of the mother-child field. It is in these mother-child symbioses that the interfacial incubator has its warmest, most open, and normally also its most jovial points; and it is with the facial interaction of mothers and children in the transitional field between animal and human that the true facioplastic operation on humans begins. It does not simply inscribe some aesthetic moods into the facial features of individuals as modern plastic surgeons do for their customers, who reject their own natural faces; it is what gives human faces their open, slate-like character in the first place, and this character is

the adhesive that sticks the gold leaf of facial beauty and particularity to a person. There must have been high evolutionary
prizes attached over long periods to the production of facial
profiles that were more delicate, more open, more delightful and
more capable of joy. In this case, Darwin's theorem must be
modified into a law of the survival of the more attractive.
Increasing the attractiveness of humans for humans, however, is
the opposite of environmental adaptation in the sense of improving
fitness: it shows the early tendency of evolution towards free
flower formation in the erotic-aesthetic hothouse of humanization.
How else could the primitives mentioned by Deleuze and
Guattari have attained such human, beautiful and spiritualized
"heads"? The major groups of the *sapiens* family are probably
separated by divergent ethno-aesthetics; hence there is no guarantee
that all of them would appeal sensually to all others. But all those
specific and singular aspects noted in the face as character traits,
or as letters and lines of regional temperaments and acquired
qualities, can only enter the facial slate once this latter has been
opened up, through protraction, as a clearing for physiognomic
entries and fortuitous properties. The most accurate illustration
of this protraction's modus operandi is the reciprocal, delicately
enlivened radiance of the mother's and the child's faces in the
period of postnatal bonding. Its back-and-forth motion is rooted
in old tribal-historical synchronizations between the protagonists
in primal-scenic games of affection; it belongs to an ensemble of
inborn schemata for careful bipersonal participation.[18]

More than 95 precent of *Homo sapiens*' long way to his present
faciality probably lies in prehistoric times. Throughout this
entire period, the face of the respective other cannot yet—
aside from vague hints of familiarity and relatedness—have

functioned as an identifying mark or living signal element, as it did in the time of later peoples and kingdoms. The question of the face as proof of identity would not have become significant until the formations of peoples in the early classical period, the time in which human groups were exceeding their critical size for the first time and having to develop new means of cognitive orientation in an environment of mostly unrelated, unknown people. From this point on, the eyes of humans within peoples became attuned to reading faces with a view to tracing family resemblances and individual character traits. The eyes of earlier humans would have lacked this combination of facial curiosity and identificatory interest entirely; their concern for the faces of the others must largely have been of a bio-aesthetic nature. Before the time of Neolithic villages and the first towns, close faces were more a comfort than a signal connected to identification. This is why cultural historians and philosophers, especially Leroi-Gourhan and Thomas Macho, have rightly pointed out that depictions of human faces are completely absent from the pictorial world of the Stone Age—as if, for early humans, not only their own faces were invisible, but also those of their fellow men and women.

The absence of faces from the oldest pictures only proves one thing unequivocally, however: the concern for the faces of the others belongs in an area that neither permits nor demands representation. The early interfacial perceptions are not interested in meanings and character traits, but in qualities of familiarity and cheer; they are geared towards facial light. Mothers and children do not paint each another; they beam at each other. Evolution and its heightened form in anthropological self-breeding have evidently rewarded facial formations that portray the ability to express joy. Just as the genitals are the organic creations of an inter-genital pleasure principle, human faces are the expressive forms of an interfacial joy principle. Facial magic has a clear formula: the original separation of joy. This is what made the accommodation of faces by other faces a fundamental possibility in the human field. The reference in *Phaedrus* to the "godlike face" contains the first attempt in philosophical thought to approach protractive facial resonance as a point of contact with happiness. Platonic semantics cannot quite do justice to this facial brightening, however, because it only inter-prets facial beauty in the individual as the shining through of a light from the transcendent world. A Spinozist semantics, on the other hand, would have the advantage of understanding facial opening as the expression of a force that does not—like the idea—still remain transcendent while shining into the realm of images, but completely fulfills and exhausts itself in expres-sion.[19] The opening of the face thus extends as far as there is joy that communicates itself to the other's face. (By analogy, there is only as much real sexuality as there is actual genital perfor-mance.) These resonance relationships belong to entirely pre-personal and field-like circumstances, as this joy can neither be appropriated by individuals nor occupied by meaningful representations. For as soon as representation reaches for the faces, it generally no longer portrays the face of the joy principle, but rather the faces of the representative power and their expres-sions of meaningfulness. Only the countenance of Buddha and the smiling angels of Gothic art have succeeded in evading this subordination to meaningfulness; their pictorial appearance displays the facial clearing itself. Who could overlook the fact that part of the Mona Lisa's appeal comes from being allowed

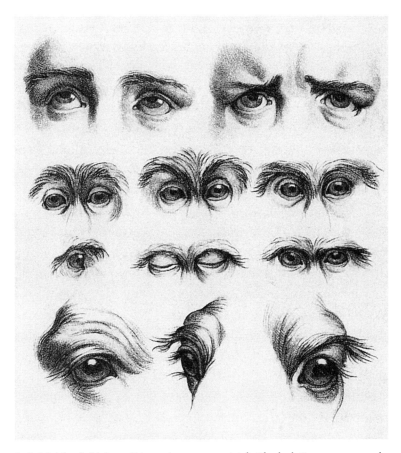

L. J. M. Morel d'Arleux, *Dissertation sur un traité de Charles le Brun, concernant les rapports de la physionomie humaine avec celle des animaux,* Paris, 1806

to show a face which has eluded, in the most mysterious and subversive manner, the compulsion to express meaning rather than joy?

When Deleuze and Guattari write in good epigrammatic cheer that "The face is Christ. The face is the typical European," they touch—starting from the exceptional case of the prototypical

European face—on a fundamental aspect of the history-creating process in the age of empires and advanced religions. In fact, wherever advanced civilizations have established themselves— that is, by no means only in Europe—protraction reaches a stage in which meaningfully standardizing central icons of historicity push the older bio-aesthetic opening of the face further. It has been shown from different angles how European cultural faces are, even well into post-Christian times, in a sense all heirs to the Christograms; Deleuze and Guattari are not alone in their case-historical equation of Christ's face and the European face (minus the exaggeration). Taking their cues most obviously from Johann Caspar Lavater's *Physiognomische Fragmente zur Beförderung der Menschenkenntnis und Menschenliebe* [Physiognomic Fragments to Further the Knowledge and Love of Human Beings], published in four installments between 1775 and 1778, recent theologians, especially Protestant ones, have postulated a wealth of cunning analogies or echoes between God's incarnation and the transition of once tribal, unbaptized European faces to a Christ-like shape.[20] Recent theological physiognomy points out that precisely the faces of post-Christian times owe their specific visibility to protraction through the central Christian icons. Even Lavater's physiognomy, however, does not function only as an introduction to seeing God in everyone; it also provides a Christian recognition service that aims to read virtue and vice in the faces of inscrutable neighbors and strangers with occult pasts. All physiognomies of the Modern Age show an implicit policing aspect and a strategic approach to a knowledge of human nature; this already applies to the notorious animal-human analogies of Giovanni Battista della Porta from 1586, which, for all their unmistakable infamy, must be credited with exposing the problem

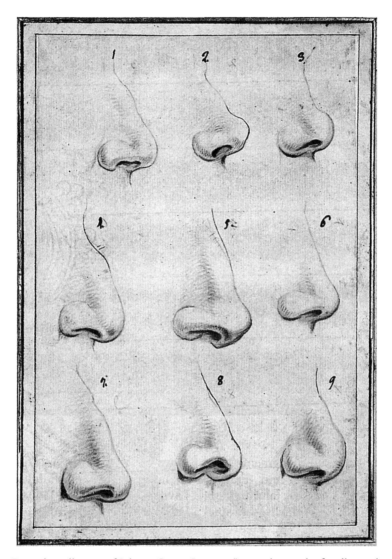

From the collection of Johann Caspar Lavater: "1. prudent and refinedly good, 2: prudent and crude, 3: noticeably weak, 4: the bridge somewhat more astute than the button and nostril, 5: complete without the side of the nose, 6: weakly good, 7: aside from the upper part, prudent, 8: somewhat unnatural at the bottom, but not entirely stupid, 9: weakly stupid"

of protraction as such in a garishly embarrassing and comical fashion. This is hardly less true of Lavater's moralistic descriptions of the virtuous and depraved temperaments, and what he alleges are their reliably identifiable facial features. Undoubtedly, Lavater was speaking above all to the noble, world-fearing soul of the early bourgeois period, which sought guidance amid the confused theater of relationships that had developed in the burgeoning market society. Referring to requests for a physiognomic key that promised to decipher the faces of strangers as characterological texts, Lavater's Christian-philanthrophic science of the face eagerly made itself useful to a wider audience:

> If one imagines being inside the spheres of a statesman, pastor, preacher, steward, doctor, merchant, friend, house father or spouse, one will quickly see what manifold, important use each one of these can make of physiognomic knowledge in their respective sphere.[21]

Naturally Lavater's notion of the sphere has nothing to do with the facio-genetic dynamics of intimate joy sharing; it simply points to the experience that bourgeois professional forms of existence create their own circles of interaction with respectively typical experiential radii. The reference to spheres here hints, as is generally the case in the language of Goethe's time, at the increasingly accented pluralism of life forms and segments of reality in modernizing society.

As far as the East Asian world in the time of advanced civilizations is concerned, one can scarcely overestimate the central-iconic formative power of Buddha depictions. Just as, in

Buddhist Protraction I: statue of the Buddhist ruler Jayavarman VII, Kompong Svay (?), turn of 13th century, National Museum of Cambodia, Phnom Penh

the Christian cultural area, crucifixes and transfigurative icons imprinted themselves on the faces and visions of Europeans through drawn-out modeling processes, the Indian, Indochinese, Chinese and Japanese world received a far-reaching facioplastic and protractive stimulus from the images of the Awakened One. In a physiognomic modeling process at least sixty generations long, the figure of Buddha, depicted in contemplation, cast its spell on the faces of monks and meditators of all social classes; his Nirvanic icon impressed upon on an entire cultural area the message of the dignity of sitting in meditation with eyes closed. It constitutes the most sublime shape of the ontological paradox of world-open worldlessness.[22] For over two thousand years, the image of the meditating Buddha has also presented the secular classes in Asian societies with a central icon of detachedness. It furthered the protraction of faces bearing an inclination towards the volition of non-volition. Although it is consistently portrayed as a still face, it holds an intimate promise of resonance for all who view it because, in its lively, animated calm, it shows the face of shared pain and shared joy. Its concentration conveys a heightened form of joy, as it exudes a concern for fellow beings beyond all mimic conventions and reflexes. It smiles beyond the gesture of smiling; in this, it presents the antithesis of the current American facial convention, which, as Europeans can meanwhile see—via film images—with the naked eye, has led to the pro-traction of a "fitness emptiness." Unlike the face of Christ, which aims either for final suffering or the representation of transcen-dence, Buddha's face shows the pure potential of an absolutely immanent touchability by whatever comes before it. By floating in a state of readiness to resonate, this face is itself the realization of the Gospel: it announces nothing, rather showing what is

Buddhist Protraction II: beaming Lokeshvara, Khmer statue, Preak-Khan, turn of 13th century, National Museum of Cambodia, Phnom Penh

already there. As an expressive manifestation of euphoric emptiness, the countenance of the Awakened One in contemplation is the opposite of the character heads of Western Caesars, modeled by violence and marked by determination.

It is not only the faces of spiritually "significant people" that have affected facial protraction in the millennia of turbulent history. Alongside the divine images and depictions of god-manlike mediators and teachers, likenesses of rulers have, since classical-imperial times, also played a part in the opening up of faces into the expansive. If the idea of a kingdom of God became visible in a human face, and if the concept of Nirvana had created its shaped visual manifestation in the countenance of Buddha, then the rulers' likenesses of the ancient world lent a physiognomic profile to the power of empire. In European antiquity, it was above all the images of Alexander and Augustus that—occasionally taking cues from the anthropomorphic Greek statues of gods—brought out a faciality in the principle of the world power. One could speak of a Caesaromorphism among the depicted faces in ancient worlds of power; for the spheric expansion of the archaic intimate space into the imperial universe inevitably inscribes itself in the faciality of the eminent representatives of power. Hence the faces of rulers can be presented like programs.

In the year 38 BC, in the middle of his power struggle with Mark Anthony, Octavian, the future Caesar Augustus, minted a coin on which the intimate *face-à-face* of two men was let out as the open secret of current imperial politics. On the Octavian denarius, left of the center, one can see in profile the wreathed head of Caesar, designated the divine Julius; facing him on the right is the head of his great-nephew and adoptive son C.

Coin of Octavian, 38 BC

Octavius, who was already unwavering in his wish to be addressed as *Caesar Divi Filius*: the son of God. It is easy to understand what this assignment of positions means in a culture that reads and writes from left to right: an intra-familial transferal of power from an older to a younger god. Octavian's coin and name politics was part of his strategy during the civil war— which was also waged using all available theological means—in which he forced his rival Mark Anthony to his knees after a thirteen-year struggle for sole dictatorship. The coin with the double portrait testifies to the core dogma of Augustan political theology: Octavian stands facing his father as "son by the grace of God."[23] The father places the imperial mission on his son through adoption; the son, for his part, chooses his own father as his idiosyncratic god. The Julian family theology effortlessly leads into the Augustian imperial theology. The most powerful religious-political fiction of the Old World is proclaimed on this little denarius: the doctrine of God's monarchy through Caesar's successors. The small coin contains the first Western gospel, the good news after Augustus. Two men look into each other's faces at very close range; the imperial mandate flows from the father to the son. The son cannot be a son without the empire that devolves upon him; and the father is not a father without the deification which the son returns to him. The future of the empire as a whole has contracted into an interfacial scene. From the start, contemporaries had noticed the young Octavian's resemblance to his father like a significant sign, and Octavian never had reservations about capitalizing on this similarity; at every point in his career, he seemed to be aware that, like his adoptive father, he bore the empire in his face as a power of command and a form of world. Octavian's battles at sea and on land were military prayers to the Caesar father: thy kingdom come. Like Pauline Christianity, the Caesarian empire is also a product of the romantic power to posit the father through the son—and the god through the apostle. In this, Augustus and Paul belong together as theologians and rival strategists; their methodic parallelism is the occidental secret.[24] In fact, the Octavian denarius was already the first model for a successful doctrine of the Trinity. For just as the power of the father is transferred to the son, the son's fury of succession places the father on the throne of thrones as the source of empire. The unity invoked by Jesus in the phrase "my Father and I" scarcely differs from that between the first Caesar and his successor. The third element that unifies the two father and their respective sons is the space-forming potency of their deep devotion to one other; the spirit circulating between them is that of empires. What the empire or the church are supposed to become was originally a *face-à-face*. Certainly the Jesuan kingdom initially consisted entirely in an intimacy with the Father that was emphatically not of this world; its third element is a love that claims to be higher than all striving for trivial success. The Roman father and his son, on the other hand, are unified by the holy spirit of imperial success. The first world market forms where this spirit rules: a monetary empire with omnipresent imperial money. Money is the third person in the Roman trinity—that is why anyone who sees the son of Augustus on the coin simultaneously sees the father. Father and son are united by the spirit of what is *valid*; the circular form of the coin draws the joined two together into the ideal form. As long as this coin was in circulation, one could indeed obtain everything with it; it is the pragmatic communion wafer of *Roma aeterna*. Once Octavian had defeated Mark Anthony, Romans could act officially in the name of Caesar, Augustus and the Holy Empire.

In advanced civilizations, one inevitably gains the impression that the entire history of their central facial icons is one of male faces. Christomorphy, Buddhomorphy and Caesaromorphy are the three most prominent manifestations of this male dominance in ancient and medieval faciality. The mere reference to the Marian images of medieval Europe, however, is sufficient to

Rex imago Dei; Deus imago regis: Roman rulers and their accompanying gods in double profile. Top: Postumus and Hercules; middle: Probus and Sol invictus; bottom: Constantine and Sol invictus

disprove the male monopoly in the field of represented faces. Marian iconography in Catholicism, for its part, simply meant the continuation of an immeasurably broad tradition of mother-religious cultic images by Christian means. Where the universe of the great mothers presents itself in pictures, the paradoxical nature of the older protraction at once becomes evident: the focus of humanization, the female, motherly face itself, remains invisible the longest. Although it is the source of the invitation to hominization as well as humanization, the old religions and their cultic images look past the woman's face—and indeed the human face in general. They protract and elevate the non-facial parts of female human beings: the buttocks, breasts and vulva, the attributes of female sexual power. The fact that beyond these biological details, the path of spiritualization, intimization and enlivenment has long since been trodden in the faces of women, especially mothers, is not evident in the oldest pictorial culture; a picture is not always worth a thousand words. The protraction itself does not appear in any portrait, the face-opening power of maternal faces remains undepicted. No trace of facial matriarchy, or indeed of the silent evolutionary work of the facializing process in general, finds its way into the oldest products of human visual power. Overall, people would have to wait until the age of the major religions and first philosophies for the absence of individualized faces in visual works to end: only then had humans reached the point from which seeing would be seen and thinking would be thought; and now they also found themselves faced with faces. Like early theory, which specifically emphasized thought and specifically examined the act of viewing, the discovery of the face through its depiction belongs to the reflexive dawning of the worldviews of ancient cultures.

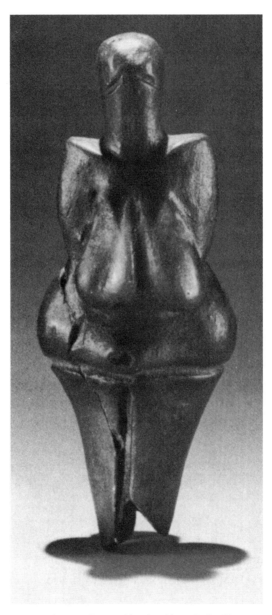

Ice Age deity with wing-like shoulders, Dolni Veston-
ice, c. 27000–26000 BC

Precisely this discovery, however, entirely ignores the maternal faces. Where the human face is protracted and established by representational means, it is always—in keeping with the way of the world—more likely to be the cultic image of male rulers, masters or gods. The female face, the evoking, invigorating, welcoming, rests like an archetypal preconscious on the foundation of all processes that depict history. By its nature, the earliest face of Our Dear Lady is more concealed than that of God, whom the Jewish ban on images aimed to prevent from being degraded through representations (because he was to be imagined as living, and so far there had only been portrait monuments of the dead). The first beloved face, the initial face, which was the first—and, as often, the only—good news, did not need to be sealed with a ban on depiction. Like a painted-over archetype, it has survived since time immemorial under the protection of non-recognition; more invisible than what is veiled, and more inaccessible than what is taboo. While it was once an aspect of theological maturity to prohibit man-made images of the One God, it will be an act of increasing anthropological reflection to understand why that animating first face naturally withdraws from all images.

The interfacial space—the sensitive sphere of bipolar facial proximity—also has its own peculiar history of catastrophe. It begins long before that estrangement through betrayal of which Giotto's kiss of Judas told us. Interfaciality is not simply the zone of a socio-natural history of friendliness; from very early times, the history of encountering strangers was also an eye training center of terror. Hence the solidarity between significant aspects of the archaic and modern periods. The oldest cultures did not

Large red and white terracotta vessel with engraved symbols from Vidra, Romania, 5th millennium BC

yet have the media to appropriate what was radically foreign, and modern ones no longer have any. Hence both depend on the mask as the means to encounter the inhuman or extra-human with a corresponding non-face or substitute face. In both archaic and modern times, depiction turns what was once a face into a shield to ward off what disfigures and negates faces. The mask is the facial shield that is raised in the war of sights.

Where modern art does still depict faces, it keeps a figurative record of a constant interfacial catastrophe. In analogy to archaic facial decoration, it shows faces that are no longer modeled within correspondences between intimate spheres, unacknowledged faces drawn by the world powers of emptying and disfigurement—including, not least, deformation through success, the permanent grinning of the victors, faces that no longer look upon human partners but rather monitors, cameras, markets and evaluation committees. The classical modern portrait, however, can no longer do justice to faces formed through interaction with monstrous and mechanical sights. It is therefore understandable to conclude that in much art of modernity, protraction itself has come to a halt—or started to emphasize the inhuman and extra-human aspects of the human face. Detraction and abstraction have won out over protraction as facioplastic morphological forces. Face-distorting and face-emptying powers have changed the portrait into the *détrait* and the *abstrait*, with a corresponding twofold tendency in facial art: firstly, the impulse to express states beyond expression, and secondly, the rebuilding of the face into a post-human prosthesis. It is no coincidence that the most distinctive new place in the innovated medial world is the interface, which no longer refers to the space of encounter between faces, but rather the contact point between the face and the non-face, or between two non-faces.

While Francis Bacon's screaming pope still shows a face in explosion, Andy Warhol's self-portraits attain the state of selfless-ness through self-sale. Both works still have a place on the edge of expressive art; for not only the laceration, but also the freezing of the face are subject to the principle of expression. Newer approaches to a facial aesthetic in visual art have clearly separated off from this. Cindy Sherman's montage *Untitled #314c* dissolves the face into a creased landscape of evil, self-willed pieces of tissue, with a mouth whose labia display an obscene opening up. Here there is nothing left of what Benjamin called the sex appeal of the anorganic; the flesh has become a synthetic copy of itself. There are surely few works in contemporary art that testify with such violence to the changing of the portrait into the *détrait*. Ironically undermined features tending towards the *détrait* are also disclosed in the series of quasi-self-portraits by the Cologne painter Irene Andessner, who eludes the viewer's facial expecta-tions by showing neither a face nor a mask. What she presents forms a sequence of pre-faces or preliminary stages of faces with a stern character—raw materials of the face, ingredients of beauty awaiting re-elevation, as it were, to the rank of the full female visage. We see an investigative energy staring through frozen eyes, permeating this female face like a changeable medium. The face in seven variations is illuminated by an unchanging, calm cruelty; coming from a distant place, it cannot quite become the face's own. It maintains the balance between a terrible, almost disfiguring truth and a will to survive that almost manages to produce a beautiful mask. Suspended between *portait*, *abstrait* and *détrait*, Irene Andessner's series of faces

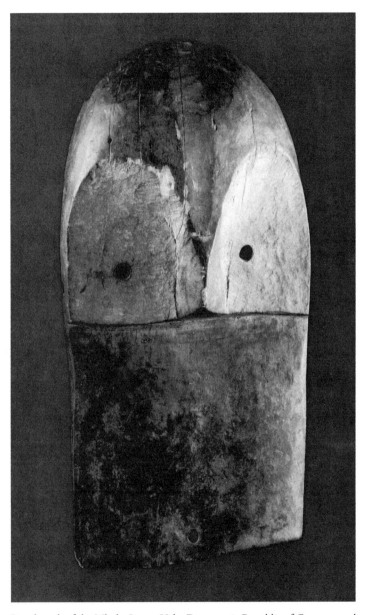

Board mask of the Mbole, Lower Uele, Democratic Republic of Congo, wood

illustrates a postmodern alternative to modern facial disfigurement; painted with a humor without laughter and a despair
without tears, it expresses the still-human face's waiting for its
withdrawn, adequate other. This is a waiting that simultaneously
postulates and doubts anthropomorphism; at the same time,
almost involuntarily, the series betrays an incredulous hesitation
about requesting the gratifying attention of the other. Just as
one could view postmodern ornamentation as a pastime while
waiting for unattainable beauty, Irene Andessner's painted preparation for beauty could be read as a sign of waiting for the
moment of the true face.

Looking at the entire early history of human faciality, one can say
that humans have faces not for themselves, but for the others.
The Greek word for the human face, *prosopon*, expresses this fact
most clearly: it refers to the sight one presents to the other's
gaze.[25] Initially, a face is only accessible to the view of the other;
as a human face, however, it also has the ability to respond to
being seen with a gaze of its own—and this gaze, naturally, does
not initially see itself, but only the face opposite. So the face
certainly contains the reciprocal intertwining of gaze and
counter-gaze, but nothing suggesting a self-reflexive turn.
Leaving aside the precarious reflections in the smooth water that
have always been possible, the self-encounter of human faces in
mirror images is a very late addition to primary interfacial reality.
For the people of the twentieth century, however, living in apart-
ments covered in mirrors, it would be asking the unimaginable if
one expected them to realize the meaning of a central fact: that
until recently, the quasi-totality of the human race consisted of
individuals who never, or only in highly exceptional situations,

Francis Bacon, *Study after Velázquez's Portrait of Pope Innocent X*, oil on canvas, 1953

Andy Warhol, *Six Self-Portraits*, silkscreen print, 1966

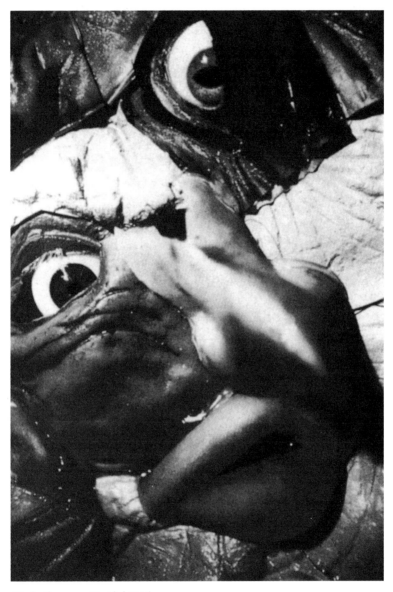

Cindy Sherman, *Untitled #314c*

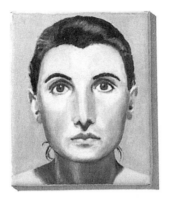

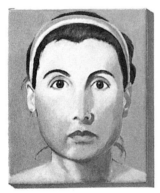

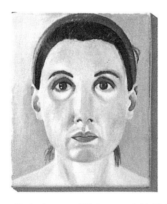

Irene C. Andessner, *Edition von 1 bis 7. Sieben Selbstportraits*, oil on canvas, 1992

saw their own faces. The first mirrors are typically equipment from the start of the Axial Age; until the Modern Age, they remained objects in the possession of a privileged few and cloaked in secrecy. They also soon belonged to the physical and metaphorical assets of those who invoked the rare commodity of self-knowledge. The renowned bronze elf mirror found in Hochheim has been dated to the fourth century BC; if geography had not proved otherwise, one could call it a pre-Socratic instrument. Glass mirrors of the type common today have only existed since c. 1500—and initially only in Venice. Supplying large parts of populations with mirrors only really began in the nineteenth century, and the process would not have been complete in the First World until the middle of the twentieth. Only in a mirror-saturated culture could people have believed that for each individual, looking into one's own mirror image realized a primal form of self-relation. And only in a population defined—across all classes—as mirror-owners could Freud and his successors have popularized their pseudo-proofs for so-called Narcissism and the supposedly visually transmitted primary auto-eroticism of humans. Even Lacan's tragically presumptuous theorem about the mirror stage's formative significance for the ego function cannot overcome its dependence on the cosmetic or ego-technical household inventory of the nineteenth century—much to the detriment of those who were taken in by this psychological mirage.[26] We should precisely *not* read the myth of Narcissus as evidence of a natural relationship between humans and their *own* faces in the mirror, but as an indication of the disturbingly unaccustomed nature of burgeoning facial reflection. It is not by chance that Ovid's version of the tale—assuming it even has a pre-Ovidian source—dates from the time in which it was possible

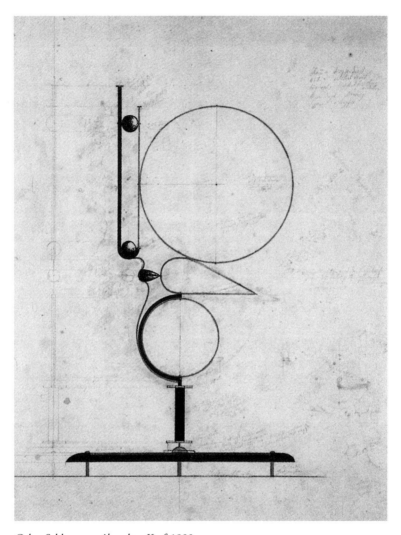

Oskar Schlemmer, *Abstrakter Kopf*, 1923

for the eye and the face—or, in more modern terms, the subject face and the object face—to be connected in a new, fateful way. If Narcissus wanted to embrace the face in the watery mirror, it was definitely also because it had not yet become his own; his stupid fall into the image presupposed that until then, every visible face had to be that of another. The Narcissan mishap constitutes an accident in the early stages of self-reflection. Before the ancient dawn of reflection, it was unimaginable that a visible face, particularly an enchanting one, could be one's own. Alcibiades seems to be the first historically identifiable figure in the European tradition whose characteristics point to an aesthetic awareness of his own face: Socrates refers to this by deliberately avoiding the subject of his pupil's vanity, talking his way around Alcibiades' beautiful face in order to address his soul directly. As far as the female side of facial dawning is concerned, Euripides lets Clytemnestra look smugly in the mirror after Agamemnon's departure and adorn her plaited hair with jewels, as if to anticipate her adultery and later crime. Among the Greeks, in any case, mirrors were reserved exclusively for women. Normally, a Greek man could only find out about his appearance from the way others regarded him. And it was only Socrates who made the amusing suggestion that the beautiful youths who surrounded him should look at themselves in the mirror as often as possible, to spur on their ambition to prove worthy of their physical merits also in the domain of the soul. The visually concretized notion of an "own face" formed, as these intimations illustrate, in the course of a drawn-out, individualizing evolutionary process— via stages that can be distinguished with varying clarity as ancient-medieval, modern and postmodern contributions to facial subjectivism.

The initial experience of faciality rests on the basic circumstance that humans who regard humans are themselves regarded by humans, and return to themselves by way of the sight of the other. In this sense the face, as vision, is the face, as visage, of the other. At first, then, a face is always something that can only be viewed over there and up there.[27] In the initial bipolar interfacial game, the gazes are distributed among the partners in such a way that each, for the time being, learns enough about himself by looking into the face of the other who is looking at him. The other thus acts as a personal mirror; but he is also the opposite of a mirror, for he permits neither the peace nor the discretion of a reflection in glass or metal—but above all because he produces not an eidetic reproduction, but rather an affective echo. One can only speak of a glance into one's "own" mirror face when the individual has turned away from the other and towards its face, which now appears and must be appropriated, in the reflecting image.

A face in the mirror that can be accepted as one's own, without any catastrophe of misattribution, only appears when individuals can habitually withdraw from the interfacial field of alternating glances—which, from the Greek perspective, is by definition also a field of alternating speech—into a state in which they no longer require completion through the present other, but can complete themselves through themselves, so to speak. Facial ego identity, as the possibility of having a face of one's own, thus depends on that rebuilding of the subjective space which began with the Stoics' invention of the self-sufficient individual. Only in European and Asian antiquity did it become possible for people to establish a form of intimate eccentricity in relation to themselves that allowed them to be themselves in one

Titian, *Venus in the Mirror*

Kiki Kogelnik, *Scissor Head*, glazed ceramic, 1977

place, and at once their own observer in another. In nascent individualism the individuals, as living observers—as inner witnesses of their own lives, one could say—adopt the perspective of an outside view on themselves, and thus augment their interfacial spheric opening with a second pair of eyes that, strangely enough, is not even their own.

Thus begins the history of the human who wants, and is meant to have, the ability to *be alone*. The separate actors in the individualistic regime become isolated subjects under the dominion of the mirror, that is to say of the reflecting, self-completing function. They increasingly organize their lives under the appearance that they could now play both parts in the game of the bipolar relationship sphere alone, without a real other; this appearance becomes stronger throughout the European history of media and mentalities, culminating at the point where the individuals decide once and for all that they themselves are the substantial first part, and their relationships with others the accidental second part. A mirror in each room belonging to each individual is practical life's patent on this state. Admittedly, the game of the individual's self-completion before the mirror (and other ego-technical media, especially the book, whether being written or read) would lose its attraction if it were not usable for the sublime fiction of independence—that dream of self-rule which has influenced the model of the wise life since the beginnings of classical philosophy. Because he knows himself, the wise man who can be his own master must no longer tolerate being penetrated by the gaze of a ruler, or indeed having any other fix him with their gaze. He would possess a quality that Hegel triumphantly called *impenetrable*.

Arnold Schönberg, *Tränen*, oil on canvas

It is thus not far from "know thyself" to "complete thyself." Both of these, self-knowledge as well as self-completion, are operations in a sphere of illusory bipolarity that, like an ellipse, only formally possesses two focal points. In truth, the face before the mirror has entered into a pseudo-interfacial relation to another that is not an other. It can relish the illusion of being in a closed field of vision, as it has expelled the other and the others from its inner space and replaced them with technical means of self-completion—the media in their modern function. Thus the world is divided into an inside and an outside that differ in the same way as the ego and the non-ego. Only where such expulsions have become the rule, and the conscious harboring and letting through of the other the exception, can a structurally modern society ensue, populated by individuals of which the majority live in the dominant real fiction: the phantasm of an intimate sphere with a single inhabitant, namely that particular individual. This real illusion underpins all individualistic circumstances; it secures the solitary confinement of every individual within an interconnected bubble. "You are self-contagious, do not forget. Do not let your 'you' gain the upper hand" (Henri Michaux).

CHAPTER 3

Humans in the Magic Circle

On the Intellectual History of the Fascination with Closeness

> In her magic circle bound,
> I must live as she deems sound.
> The change, alas! How great it is!
> — Johann Wolfgang von Goethe, "New Life, New Love"

Anyone seeking alternatives to an existence in stoical self-sufficiency or individual self-arrest in front of the mirror would do well to recall an epoch in which all reflection on the *condition humana* was pervaded by the evidence that between humans, whether in familiar proximity or on the open market, a restless play of affective infections was in progress. Long before the axioms of individualistic abstraction established themselves, the psychologist-philosophers of the early Modern Age had made it clear that the interpersonal space was overcrowded with symbiotic, erotic and mimetic-competitive energies that fundamentally deny the illusion of subject autonomy. The central law of intersubjectivity as experienced in premodern attitudes is the enchantment of humans through humans. If one wanted to adopt the traditional view, one could go so far as to say that humans are always obsessed by their own kind—leaving aside their extra-human occupiers for now. Among humans, fascination is the rule and disenchantment the exception. As desiring and imitating beings, humans constantly experience that they not only hold a lonely potential for desiring the other within themselves, but also that they manage, in an opaque and non-trivial manner, to infect the objects of their desire with their own longing for them; at the same time, individuals imitate the other's longing for a third element as if under some infectious compulsion. In the language of tradition this figures as the law of sympathy, which states that love cannot but awaken love. Hatred likewise generates its congenial response, and rivalry infects those after the same object with the vibrant greed of the competitor. Where philosophy of the early Modern Age mentions such effects of resonance and infection, it spontaneously draws on the vocabulary of *magological* traditions. As early as antiquity, it was reflection on affective causalities of the magical type that initiated the clarification of the interpersonal or inter-demonic concert which, from Plato's time on, was interpreted as a work of eros. Continuing along Plato's path, philosophers of the late fifteenth century launched a new erotological discourse whose echo extends into the depth-psychological activities of the early nineteenth century and the pop-psychoanalytical half-thoughts of the present.

When Socrates and Plato began to shine the light of discussion onto the dynamics of the human attraction to humans, they made it clear that the subject's desire for the beautiful other cannot only be its private and particular feeling, but must simultaneously be understood as a function of a public force

Man as microcosm—schema of influences. From *Livres des Portraits et Figures du Corps human*, 1572, ed. Jacques Kerver

field. Where desire flares up, an already existent, latent belonging of the subject to the desired becomes manifest; hence is no private property when it comes to longing for the other. For the psychologists of antiquity, that shared element which supplies the desirous and the desired from the same source reveals itself in the beautiful. Whatever humans desire from the other is— located on the right level—also a response to the attraction and accommodation of the other side. In this sense, being and attracting are the same thing. Hence intersubjective magic is based on the magic of completion, as described classically by Plato in the speech of Aristophanes from *The Symposium* with the myth of the human halves passionately striving towards one another. According to Plato, the binding forces between lovers come from a homesick longing for the round totality, whose traces point to the prehistory of the great couple. Like all mythical totalities, the round, autarchic primordial human is subject to the triple dramaturgical rhythm of primal completeness, separation catastrophe and restoration. Here this archaic romantic novel shares the formal law of mythical narrative, which is also that of dialectics. In this case, telling a story means wanting to heal the constitutive lovesickness. The maximum effect of attraction magic naturally lies between the second and third acts of the drama, when the bodies separated in the second act begin preparing for reunification. Where the severed halves find one another again we witness the abrupt formation of the interpersonal magic circle, which encloses the newly inseparable two like an invisible isolation tank. According to Plato's wise words, the radical-symbiotic couple would perish in there if its members did not have a means, in the form of relaxed genitality, of temporarily leaving each other alone and wriggling out of the totalitarian relationship. In Plato's account, genital sexuality was a later gift from the compassionate gods, who could not bear to see how the reunited half-humans, overwhelmed by a blind panic of embrace, forgot all their self-preservation and perished. From the perspective of the Platonic myth of the severed primordial human halves, sexuality appears as a valve added after the fact to contain excessive symbiotic pressure; a secondary eroticism whose task is to divert the totalitarian suction of primary eroticism. The second eros, the drive-controlled and relaxable form, is freed from the burden of the first, insatiable eros, which will only tolerate one thing—radiant fulfillment. Through sexual union, the lovers

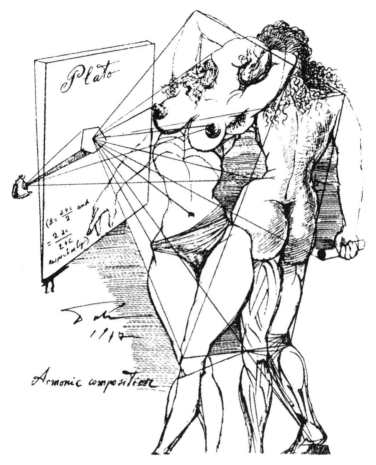

Salvador Dalí, *Harmonic Composition*, drawing, 1947

effect an intrinsically valuable distraction from the thing they truly desire from each other. What this true object of desire might be is a matter on which the erotology of the nineteenth and twentieth centuries and the love theories of the meta-physical tradition would scarcely agree. According to the refined theorems of recent psychoanalysis, all primary eroticism is based on a homesick yearning for the world-impoverished completeness of the fetus and the sheltered newborn—in the language of Béla Grunberger, the longing for the narcissistic monad's mode of being and prenatal "autonomy."[1] According to Marsilio Ficino's commentary on Plato's *Symposium*, however, the first eros is nothing but the longing to regain the bliss of possessing God (*beatitudio quae in possessione ipsius [Dei] consistit*). Because the first eros is founded on memory and homecoming— unlike the second, whose nature consists in curiosity and reaching out—Ficino, following Plato, must assume a lost primal presence of the soul in God. Without the ineradicable experience of his transcendent honeymoon with the absolute, the lover could not carry within himself any guiding idea of the state at which his desire is directed. Thus Platonism and psychoanalysis, for all the differences between their views of the amorous drama's substantial point of departure, do agree in the definition of its form: both teach that the primary, pre-concrete and super-concrete eros has its source in an obscured, never entirely forgettable and still ever-igniting biune past.

The first depth psychology of the Modern Age, as stated above in an anticipatory remark, emerged during the second half of the fifteenth century as a result of impulses from Florentine Neoplatonism. The criterion for depth-psychological thought can be considered fulfilled if mental and emotional processes are divided into an experienced front side and an unexperienced reverse—in such a way that the subjects learn to understand themselves in new ways through this distinction. Such models describe experiences through processes that, though they affect these experiences, are not represented as such in them;

nonetheless, the act of experiencing is itself reconfigured through insight into its psychological workings—partly by diverting interest, partly through cathartic reactions. It is precisely this mode of thought, which characterizes numerous modern psychological concepts from hypnosis to reframing, that we see forging ahead in Marsilio Ficino's theory of animal love. This, not his largely sterile superelevations of Platonic eros, which he terms Socratic, is where the originality of his contribution to a modern erotology lies. In his praise for the Socratic form of love, the author scarcely manages to break away from the conventions of idealism and its projections into the field of medieval love for God; in his reproach of vulgar love, however, Ficino—the son of the Medicis' personal physician—becomes one of the first phenomenologists of intersubjective enchantments. With the eye of a psychotherapist *avant la lettre*, he elevates the fascination of humans with their kind to a subject in its own right. Ficino remarks that humans normally do well what they do often—except in amorous matters, for "we all love constantly in some way, but almost all of us love only badly (*tutti quasi amiamo male*); and the more we love, the worse we love (*e quanto più amiamo, tano peggio amiamo*)." It would not be an exaggeration to call the seventh speech from *De amore* one of the founding documents of modern depth psychology. Already here, as in its later versions, pathology becomes the window to the soul through which the philosopher gazes in order to observe the inner workings of the machine.

Ficino's psychopathology describes the *amor vulgaris* between individuals of the same or different sex as a result of subtle inflections through the eye. According to well-known Platonic doctrine, seeing does not simply mean being affected by impressions of illuminated objects, but rather actively directing visual rays at them. The eye is itself sun-like to the extent that it illuminates objects with a light *sui generis*. The visual rays shoot forth like the projectiles of a cognitive artillery, and the existing, espied world is the bull's eye. At the same time, Ficino speaks of the world-espying ray as a transporter for ethereal essences sent out by the viewer. If one ventures the experiment of taking these concepts seriously, one can easily appreciate how Ficino reaches his understanding of ocular infections. When the gazes of humans meet, the space between their eyes is compacted into a highly charged radiation field and becomes the scene of a micro-drama of energies; interpenetrations must develop between gaze and counter-gaze, and it is the stronger gaze that injects its content— especially life spirits in the form of the finest *vapores*—into the other's eye. Thus the intersubjective space appears as a battlefield of life spirits that affect others through the eyes, but also through other forms of bodily radiation. Ficino remarks on this:

> Aristotle writes that women, when the menstrual blood flows down, often soil a mirror with bloody drops by their own gaze. This happens, I think, from this: that the spirit, which is a vapor of the blood, seems to be a kind of blood so thin that it escapes the sight of the eyes, but becoming thicker on the surface of a mirror, it is clearly observed. […]. Therefore, what wonder is it if the eye, wide open and fixed upon someone, shoots the darts of its own rays into the eyes of the bystander, and along with those darts, which are the vehicles of the spirits, aims that sanguine vapor which we call spirit? Hence the poisoned dart pierces through the eyes, and since it is shot from the heart of the shooter, it seeks again the heart

of the man being shot, as its proper home. [...] Hence follows a double bewitchment (*duplex fascinatio*). The sight of a stinking old man or of a woman suffering her period bewitches a boy, and the sight of a youth bewitches an older person, but since the humor of an older person is cold and very slow, it hardly reaches the back of the heart in the boy, and being awkward in making the transit, it moves the young heart very little, unless the heart, because of extreme youth, is very tender. But that bewitchment is very heavy by which a young man transfixes the heart of an older man.[2]

Despite its bizarre physiological concepts, which have long ceased to find any defenders, this discourse unmistakably belongs to the field of modern depth-psychological theories in structural terms, for it describes and conveys the experience of love as the effect of a non-experienceable psychophysiological process. At the same time, a latent idea of the unconscious is already present in Ficino's model: it belongs to the nature of neo-academically understood animal love that it is an effect of fascinogenic processes which can only be experienced by the subjects in their results, but not in their actual physiological mechanisms. By disclosing the psychomechanical reverse of experienced erotic passions, Ficino's discourse on vulgar love encourages the subjects concerned—in the style of modern psychodynamic enlighten-ment—to use the insight into the mechanically functioning components of their psychological apparatus to draw practical conclusions about how to cure themselves of pathological compulsions. From now on, someone experiencing vulgar or natural love would be in the picture about the mechanical reason for his exuberant desire for union with the other. Now he knows

that he is suffering the mental side effects of an ocularly transmitted infection with foreign blood; consequently, he is armed
with the enlightening knowledge to step back from his passion
and reflect upon it. It is the blood of the other, absorbed unnoticed and animated by foreign life spirits, that moves the lovers
to send their semen into their partner, or to burn to take up
the other's ejaculate in themselves. Once one realizes that the
frenzied desire for touching and unification is simply an effect of
unconscious transfusions, one has already taken the first step
towards disenchantment and cure. This step remains impossible,
admittedly, as long as the unfortunate succumbs to the compulsion to view his misery as something that will end in pleasure
after all; only once a critical level of suffering has prepared him
for conversion can he seek philosophical guidance in learning a
form of love that promises greater happiness. Where de-fascination
succeeds, he will be freed from the compulsion to act on the wish
for union. Where it does not, the subject risks repeating the fate
of Artemisia, whose dreary excess is mentioned by Ficino as a
cautionary example:

> That lovers desire to take the whole beloved into themselves
> Artemisia, the wife of King Mausolus of Caria, also showed, who
> is said to have loved her husband beyond the belief of human
> affection and to have ground up his body, when he died, into a
> powder, and to have drunk it (*ebibisse*), dissolved in water.[3]

As shown by the example of husband-drinking—which also
meant the continuation of incestuous excesses by other means, as
tradition has it that Mausolus and Artemisia were siblings—the
peculiarity of Ficino's theory of vulgar love lies in the fact that it

by no means explains the lovers' longing for union with an independent drive towards the genital object, but presents it as a doomed displacement of the symbiotic primary eros to the stage of sexual relations; coming five hundred years before Freud, Lacan and Kohut, this discovery is itself awaiting rediscovery. Admittedly, genital love as such would still have to wait a long time for its psychological justification; for centuries, the sexualized dual stood in the shadow of the magic dyad. Dual eroticism only managed to establish itself in its own right once the restoration of Jewish ethics had overcome the predominance of Greek philosophy in the contemporary balance of theories. It is not out of the question that this might one day be perceived retrospectively as the main event in the process of twentieth-century intellectual history. The ethics of psychoanalysis is, as one knows, rooted in the Jewish understanding of the law—it does not encourage merging, but constantly makes the case for constructive separations; its focus is not intimate fusion, but rather the discretion of the subject in relation to the other. The law itself is primarily there to bring out the distance between God and man, extending to all details of everyday life. Admittedly, the limits of the philosophically renewed Jewish dual ethics become apparent in its tendency to underestimate the infant's claim to intimacy: Freud's weakness, the unwillingness to think the mother, remains that of Emmanuel Lévinas, whose theory of the strong relationship between humans and their neighbors is excessively biased towards the father-son relationship.[4]

From Ficino's neo-Greek perspective, it is at least clear that sexualized enchantment can only lead to disappointment and exhaustion. His analysis of intersubjective fascination presents sensual love as a case of incorrectly addressed homesickness for the bipolarly integrated, microspheric primal state. Consequently, he views a conversion to the Socratic mode of love as the only promising method for curing oneself of vulgar love; only one who loves like the philosophers can place the correct address on the love letter of existence. When all merely human objects of love are potentially tormenting and disappointing, the divine super-object guarantees that one can shine the light of undisappointable kindness at the chosen adorant. Here Ficino remains tied to a medieval starting position: he still displays the theologian's disgust at the expectation that one could rely on mere humans to satisfy the highest needs of the soul. He repeats as a philosopher the monastic oath to allow completion by none other than God. The first erotology of the Modern Age could already have had the line from Kafka as its motto: "I came into this world with a beautiful wound; that is all I was furnished with." But at least, when a philosophical approach to desire fit for the Modern Age emerged in Florence in the late autumn of the Middle Ages, its concern was for this beautiful wound not to be closed up with any hastily-prepared dressings.

More than a century after Ficino, Giordano Bruno embedded the early modern magic of intersubjectivity in a general theory of discrete mutual bonds between objects. In his magical writings—which have only recently been translated into German[5]—especially the treatise "A General Account of Bonding" (*De vinculis in genere*), Bruno developed, in a sort of cosmo-erotological tone, a theory of strong interdependencies or correspondences between energy poles. Here the bond—*vinculum*—is the key concept; it forms the basis for an ontology of discrete multiple attractions. According to this ontology, the meaning of being for all things is no more or less than a play of constantly moving, manifold affiliations with corresponding elements.

> The bond thus consists in a certain correspondence not only between the members amongst themselves, but also in a certain corresponding disposition of the captor and the captive, if I may put it like this. [...] The bond does not capture the soul unless it can tie and bind; it does not bind it unless it reaches it; and it does not reach it unless it can be captured by something. In general the bond reaches the soul through knowledge, ties it through the affect, attracts it through pleasure [...]. (pp. 170f.)
>
> The bond is not the same in every binder, not in everyone who is bound. (p. 172)
>
> The binding occurs most strongly when the bond transports something of the binder, or when the binder controls something else through something of his own. Thus the fingernails and hair of the living are sufficient to gain control of the entire body [...]. (p. 174)
>
> We use a different bond each time to kiss children, our father, our sister, our wife, our female friend, a whore or a friend. (p. 176)
>
> Nothing is bound unless it has been prepared in a very suitable fashion [...]. (p. 172)
>
> The bond does not act in the same way from everything or on everything, nor always, but rather in the corresponding disposition on that which is correspondingly disposed. (p. 174)
>
> The bound flows to the binder through all the senses to such a degree that, when a complete binding has occurred, he

will wish to cross over to it or enter it, assuming it is the bond
of desire. (p. 200)

It is not possible to bind someone for oneself unless the
binding element is itself committed to them [...]. A woman
[...] will not actually be bound by a male friend unless he is
also actually bound to her. (p. 211)

In Bruno's thought, we find impulses from the older Florentine
magic of intersubjectivity elaborated into a general ontology of
attraction; this ontology integrates the psychology of interdependency into a comprehensive system of natural magic. For the
thinkers of the early Modern Age, magic was a cipher for the art
of conceiving of things and living beings as enclosed and pervaded by specific interdependencies. At all levels of being, the
relationships between things—in magological terms, their
binding power and bindability—take priority over their being-
in-itself. Hence for Bruno the dullest people, the idiotically
closed-up, are the least bindable, whereas the most brilliant individuals resonate in a world-fulfilled concert of bondings,
elevating themselves to operators or achievers of multiple creative
effects. The early Modern Age used magical terminology to
communicate about the human being who will make it his
business to perform acts hitherto believed impossible. What the
sixteenth century, the great time of empowerment and increase
in Europe, called the magus was the encyclopedically sensitive,
polyvalently cosmopolitan human who learned how to cooperate
attentively and artfully with the discrete interdependencies
between the things populating a highly communicative universe. The magus, as the shared prototype of the philosopher,
the artist, the doctor, the engineer and the computer scientist, is

no less than the operator-coupler in the world of correspondences, influences and attractions. He is the agent and meta-psychologist of the world's soul, whose universal expansion causes "everything to approach everything else" (p. 149). Bruno, the Dominican friar who broke out of his order, discarded the hood of monastic reverence for the eternally unchanging One along with the order's compulsions; in escaping the pull of the mystical light, he emancipated himself to become the thinker of a divine matter that was manifold and developed in changing partnerships, as well as its traces in the consciousness. As a Columbus of the Atlantic of relationships, he also discovered a new coast for the heroic homesickness of the soul that, like the legendary American one, presents a worldly hereafter in the world freed of boundaries.[6]

Alongside Bruno's body of magological writings, it is above all the work of William Shakespeare in which the ideas of influence and correspondence from the philosophy of the early Modern Age culminate. As René Girard has shown in his study on Shakespeare's dramatic plots, the plays of the master from Stratford-upon-Avon form a collection of investigations into the inflammability of humans through the "fire of envy."[7] His worlds of interrelations mirror social ensembles in which individuals incessantly infect one another with their desire for power and lust. Shakespeare's protagonists operate like psychological batteries charged by connection to the high tensions of rivalry—the only thing they can call their own is the infectability by images that direct their desire, and their excitability by the imitation of violence, under whose influence they keep up with their intense competitors in chaotic escalations. Throughout the darkening psychocosm of Shakespeare's late works we find an increasingly cruel analysis of that mimetic plague which turns those it infects into media for rapt envy and escalating imitative compulsions. In this sense, those literary sociologists who see a reflex of the emerging bourgeois-imperialistic society of competition in Shakespeare's dramatic universe may not be entirely wrong.

A fascination analysis of the first European depth psychology reveals two things about the nature of bipolar intimacy: as vulgar love, the attraction to the other constitutes the effect of a present infection through foreign life spirits; as sublime love, the yearning for the other is the effective trace left by the memory of coexistence with God. The present thus appears as the time of possession,[8] and the past as that of ecstasy. If the organ of the vulgar drive for union is the attraction and bonding system comprising the eyes, blood and heart, followed by its genital supplement, the organ of the longing for union with the sublime subject-object is the memory. Thus, under Plato's renewed stimulus in the center of the reopened question of the nature of intimacy, the deeper question of the possibility of memory appears. Neoplatonic analysis provides the tools to understand intimacy no longer simply as spatial proximity—neither between hearts nor between faces or genitally connected bodies; intimacy as memory introduces temporal depth into the play of attractable bodies by staging present closeness as the repetition of a past closeness. This sets in motion a thought based on concepts of transference: the agent of repetition is the archetypally powerful afterglow of an older state in the current one. Intimacy is time regained—in Platonic terms, time in God, and in psychoanalytical terms, the prehistoric biunity of the mother-child space. Following the path staked out by Plato's theory of memory, the depth psychology of the Modern Age revealed the essential historicity of everything concerning the soul. It shows how, in certain passions referred to by Renaissance thinkers as heroic, one finds the magnetism of a prenatal antiquity shining into the psychological present.

The second major formation of European depth psychology—the complex of animal magnetism, artificial somnambulism and hypnotism—which expanded into a multi-faceted therapeutic-literary universe primarily in Germany and France between 1780 and 1850,[9] is connected by numerous lines of tradition to the doctrines of early modern psycho-cosmo-erotology. This applies above all to the magnetosophical concepts that were passed on in almost unbroken continuity—albeit with increasing opposition—from the magi of the Renaissance, namely Paracelsus, Gilbert and van Helmont, via Jakob Böhme and Athanasius Kircher (*Magnes sive de arte magnetica*, Rome, 1641), to Newton and finally Franz Anton Mesmer (1734–1815), the true initiator of Romantic-magnetopathic medicine. In the case of Mesmer and his French school, however, the Platonic-anamnestic aspect retreated to the background in favor of a theory of presentist interdependencies between physical emanations of planetary and animal kinds. Nonetheless, Mesmer's impulse would enable Romantic psychology's understanding of magical-interpersonal intimacy to break through to a completely new understanding of the psyche as a memory of primal subjective relationships. Like Freud later on, Mesmer already used scientism as a productive pretext for innovative arrangements in the dramatic-intersubjective intimate space. Mesmer's patho-philosophical approach, which had been fixed in most aspects since his Vienna medico-physical dissertation *On the Influence of the Planets on the Body* from 1766, was based on cosmological notions of an interstellar attraction and a universal fluid that, through proliferation, reaches all bodies, mineral and animal alike, in the manner of magnetic radiation. It is not out of the question that Mesmer elaborated his doctrine from impulses in the work of the English doctor and natural philosopher Richard Mead (1673–1754), Newton's physician. For Mesmer, a psychology divorced from cosmology and general physics did not yet exist. His understanding of the intimate scarcely includes any references to the psychology of the individual; for him, humans are simply animal magnets that, like all other bodies, are moved about in a fluidal concert of inflows and outflows. If one transfers these nature-philosophical maxims to the erotic-personal sphere, one arrives directly at those psychochemical or magnetic elective affinities which Goethe integrated into the experimental strategy of his daring novel. Mesmer's significance for the spectacular and suspiciously viewed innovations of Romantic psychotherapy is due most of all to the fact that his easily imitable magnetopathic method triggered a wave of follow-up attempts in which new strategies for close encounters between healer and patient, artist and audience, and finally leader and mass could be acted out. Just as the alternative movements of the twentieth century were also influenced by wild psychoanalysis, the Romantic period from 1780 until the mid-nineteenth century was an age of wild magnetism—and only the fact that the seriously practiced magnetopathic approach in the healing arts did not manage to distinguish itself sufficiently in the public view from its wild forms, not least its overgrowth through spiritism, led to its science-historical catastrophe.

Mesmer's treatments brought impulses for new reflections on unusual intimate constellations to the doctors' practices, and to those parts of the public involved in discussion and experimentation. His idea that all bodies encounter one another as carriers of magnetic forces in an ether of animal gravity gave countless individuals of his time opportunity to expose themselves to ambiguous experiments with non-bourgeois experiences of attraction and closeness. These led to the far-reaching discovery of what was termed magnetic rapport, which, in today's terminology, could most feasibly be described as a transference relationship between the analyst and the analysand using archaic steps of regression. In 1784, Mesmer, who viewed himself to the end as a physicist-doctor rather than a psychologist, set out the principles of his curative method in a series of fundamental theorems at a Parisian secret society he had founded, speaking to a group of selected students including such contemporary and later celebrities as the brothers Puységur, General Lafayette, the lawyer Bergasse, George Washington and the banker Kornmann. A pirated edition from 1785, reprinted several times, made the central features of Mesmer's lectures—against the author's protests—known to a wider public. A comparison between these *Aphorismes de M. Mesmer, dictés à l'assemblée de ses Elèves* [Aphorisms of Mesmer, Dictated to the Gathering of His Students] and the later, authorized overview of his work by the Berlin doctor Karl Christian Wolfart, *Mesmerismus oder System der Wechselwirkungen* [Mesmerism, or, System of Interdependencies] (Berlin: In der Nikolaischen Buchhandlung, 1814), shows that the Parisian transcripts are mostly reliable. This early collection of 344 theorems on animal magnetism includes the following:

§79. There is a fixed law of nature that a reciprocal influence on all bodies exists, and this consequently affects all their constituent parts and properties.

§80. This reciprocal influence and the relationships between all coexistent bodies constitute what one calls magnetism.

§141. The condition of sleep in humans consists in the quantity of movement lost during waking being restored through the properties of the general currents surrounding them.

§160. Humans are constantly situated within general and particular currents, and are permeated by these.

§161. Currents exit and enter the most protruding parts or extremities [...].

§184. It is verifiable, and supported by strong *a priori* reasons, that we are also gifted with an inner sense that is connected to the whole universe [...].

§238. If two beings are affecting each other, their respective positions are not insignificant. Two beings have the greatest influence on each other if they are placed in such a way that their similar parts are precisely opposed. Consequently, two people must be face to face in order to have the strongest possible effect on each other. In this position they can be viewed as if they only constituted a *single* whole. From this it follows that one must touch the right side with the left arm and vice versa in order to maintain the harmony of the whole [...].

§309. There is only one sickness and only one cure; health consists in the complete harmony of all our organs and their functions. Sickness is merely deviation from this

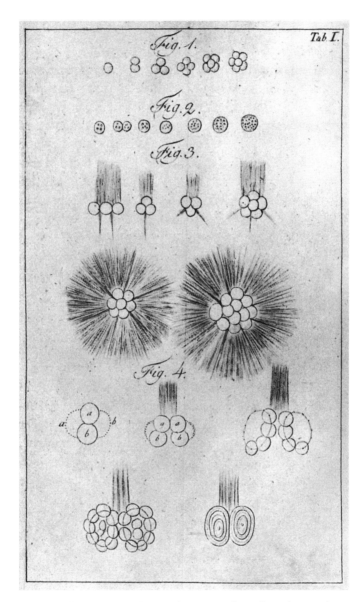

Drawings by Mesmer explaining the system of interdependencies, from
Karl Christian Wolfart's book of the same name

harmony. The cure therefore consists in restoring the harmony that has been disturbed.

§333. No sickness can be cured without crisis; the crisis is the striving of nature to disperse the obstacles inhibiting the circulation by an increase in movement, tone and tension.

§334. If nature alone is not sufficient to produce crises, one supports it through magnetism […].[10]

Because of their elemental and suggestive character, Mesmer's doctrines could easily be appropriated, verified and modified in a variety of applications by enthusiasts as well as skeptical and curious experimenters. F. A. Murhard's 700-page opus *Versuch einer historisch-chronologischen Bibliographie des Magnetismus* [Attempt at a Historical-Chronological Bibliography of Magnetism] (Kassel: Griesbach, 1797) gives a rough idea of the epidemic effect of Mesmer's impulses. Barely twenty-five years after Mesmer's emergence in Vienna during the 1770s, his ideas had developed into a turbulent and complex subculture. In the age of Romantic medicine, this subculture expanded into a major literary and clinical power. There are few cases in intellectual history where such an overwhelming proliferation of an idea was followed by such comprehensive secondary amnesia. This latter is not only due, however, to the aforementioned scientific discrediting of therapeutic magnetism through its theatrical and dubious imitators; one must also assume that the drive coming from Mesmer's ideas to experiment with interpersonal dissolutions of boundaries was destined to be thwarted by the general psychohistorical tendency in the later nineteenth and twentieth centuries to lend greater definition to bourgeois society's system of ego delimitations. With the progress of

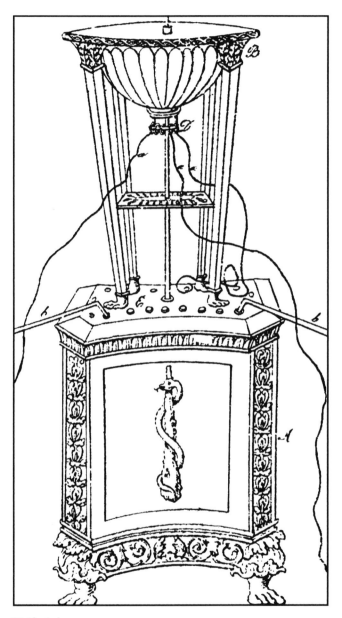

Wolfart's *baquet*

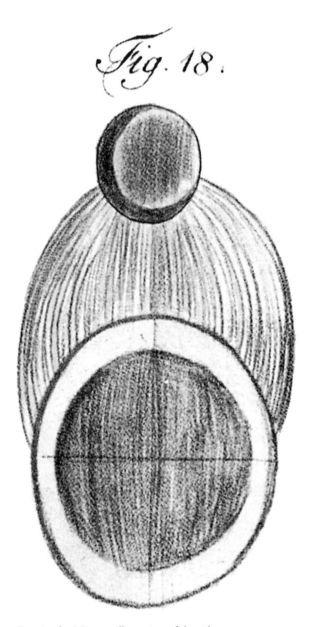

Drawing by Mesmer: illustration of the tides

goods trading society and individualistic abstraction, as well as the tendency towards the establishment of a more pronounced asymmetry of power between doctors and laypersons, the first great boom in ego-transcending magnetopathic methods petered out. It was only around 1900, primarily through the synergetic effect of Nietzsche's writings and the life-reforming ideas of the commune, that a second wave of interpersonal concepts for the dissolution of boundaries came about—bringing forth, among others, the psychoanalytical schools of Vienna and Zurich, which had to pay considerable tribute to the stricter norms affecting bourgeois and scientist rules of distance from the start. From a psychohistorical perspective, animal magnetism seems like a preliminary school for the Dionysian subversion of forms of bourgeois subjectivity as postulated by artists of the twentieth century; the path of the bourgeois subject from a magnet to a divine animal was shorter than established cultural history chose to acknowledge. The third wave—the counterculture movement of the 1960s, which was able to follow on from both its Romantic and vitalistic forerunners—is currently being thwarted by the heightened individualism characterizing the current thrust of telematic abstraction, as well as the aestheticistic neo-isolationism of postmodern lifestyle propaganda.

Around 1800, the magnetopathic arrangements of closeness gave rise to a wealth of far-reaching psychological discoveries within a very short time. Especially §238 quoted above, which clarifies the magnetopathic *face-à-face* as a form of bio-energetic communion, gives an inkling of the explosive procedures of closeness with which Romantic doctors and healers had begun to experiment. While Mesmer had believed

Ebenezer Sibly, *Mesmerismus: Der Operator löst eine hypnotische Trance aus* [Mesmerism: the operator triggers a hypnotic trance], copperplate, 1794

that he was simply effecting a fluidal equivalent of the tides in the individual human body, many of his students and emulators trained as authentic psychologists—though here the term "psychology" does not refer to the modern academic discipline but rather a general study of relationships, experiences and transformations. Armand-Marie Jacques de Chastenet, Marquis de Puységur (1751–1825), who established a large practice of his own on his country estate in Buzancy near Soisson after studying with Mesmer in Paris, increasingly concentrated on an aspect of magnetopathic treatment neglected by Mesmer, namely the phenomenon known as "critical sleep"—a hypnotoid depth regression of the patient tied to the presence of the magnetizer that often led to states of mental lucidity with heightened sensory perception and self-diagnostic insight. Puységur liked to conduct his treatments under magnetized trees to which the patients were connected with ropes—these are the magic trees of the folk medicine tradition, whose significance for intellectual history has only recently been reaffirmed. For Puységur, what he termed "artificial somnambulism" was the royal road to magnetopathic healing; he employed lucid trances to implant his will to heal the patient in the latter like an unconscious imperative. At the same time, he allowed his patients an autonomous participation unknown in any other form of medical relationship by drawing decisive information about the causes of their complaints, and hence about suitable remedies, from their own introspections and self-prescriptions while in magnetic trance. Puységur initiated the reinterpretation of the magnetic procedure as a transference of will from the magnetizer to the magnetized—a notion that impressed the thinkers of German idealism in particular.

From this emphasis on the will as the true agent of magnetic therapies, Immanuel Kant concluded that even self-healing through the will—the "sheer resolution"[11]—must be possible;

Goya, *Blind Man's Buff*, 1797

he thus became, almost a hundred years before Emile Coué (1857–1926), the discoverer of autosuggestion. Schelling's natural philosophy offers a comprehensive rationalization of animal magnetism; he himself tested magnetopathic procedures on people in his immediate circle—albeit with little success—and had connections throughout his life to a milieu of magnetizers and sympathizers of mesmerism. Among the most prominent of these were his younger brother, the state physician-in-chief Karl Eberhard von Schelling (1783–1854),[12] and the philosopher of religion Karl August Eschenmayer

The elm tree in Buzancy under which Puységur conducted magnetopathic treatments

(1786–1862).[13] Franz Xaver von Baader, Schelling's inspirer and colleague from his Munich days, referred extensively to phenomena of sleep-talking and magnetic lucidity in his writings on philosophical anthropology;[14] in his reflections on religious eroticism he further developed motifs from early modern enchantment analysis: "Love alone [...] does not separate [...] possessing from being possessed or allowing one-self to be possessed."[15] Fichte, in his late works, likewise turned to the study of magnetopathic theories and attended curative treatments of the Berlin Mesmerian Wolfart, who had one of the first German teaching positions for animal magnetism; by establishing such posts at universities, the Prussian minister Hardenberg, himself an adherent of Mesmer's ideas, and Wilhelm von Humboldt contributed—not least under the influence of the royal physician Johann Ferdinand Koreff—to the academic recognition of magnetism. After Berlin (Wolfart) and Bonn (Nasse, Ennemoser), the medical departments of the universities in Halle (Kruckenberg), Giessen (Wilbrand) and Jena (Kieser) also set up professorships for animal magnetism. Hegel integrated a considerable amount of mesmerist literature into his lectures on anthropology, which can still—especially in their copious verbal supplements—be read as some of the most complex discussions of the phenomena, principles and successes of magnetopathic psychology.[16] It is precisely the "oral Hegel" that testifies to the unbreakable bond between German Idealism and the first depth psychology.

Schopenhauer's high opinion of the new discipline came from the possibility of claiming Puységur's interpretation of the magnetopathic agent for his own metaphysics of the will, as precisely that will:

> Further, because the will manifests itself in Animal Magnetism downright as the thing in itself, we see the *principium individuationis* (Space and Time), which belongs to mere phenomenon, at once annulled: its limits which separate individuals from one another, are destroyed; Space no longer separates magnetizer and somnambulist; community of thoughts and the motions of the will appears [...].[17]

Key to the symbols used, from Bergasse, *La théorie du monde et des êtres organisés, suivant les principes de M.(esmer); gravée d'A.OE* [The Theory of the World and Organized Beings, Following the Principles of Mesmer; engraved by A.OE]

Furthermore, the effects of mesmerism were by no means restricted to its German school, even if that is where it managed to receive the highest academic and literary honors, primarily through its philosophical reception and amalgamation with idealistic philosophy. The motifs of Mesmer and Puységur are also ubiquitous in the French literature of the post-Napoleonic era; they inspire not only the Romantic Catholicism of the European Restoration, but also some of the early socialist systems, namely those of Saint-Simon and Fourier, in which Mesmer-like theories of attraction and gravitation, as well as the beginnings of a moral mechanics in the style of Pierre-Hyazinth Azaïs' compensation theory, play a decisive part. It is unnecessary to explain at greater length how all these motifs come together in the most significant narrative project of the nineteenth century: Balzac's *Comédie humaine* is simultaneously a world theater of moral and mental gravitational forces.[18]

With Puységur's deviation, the step from physics to psychodynamics, and from the energization to the intimization of the doctor-patient relationship, was complete. From that point on, the field of bipolar-interpersonal intimacy research was open; the way was paved for a reinterpretation of the psyche as a staged memory of the oldest relationships and a reproducer of past existential situations. Now the soul could be conceived of as a field of interpersonal resonances—even if numerous psychologists to this day have not realized the full possibilities offered by the magnetopathic experiment and its scenological rationalization. Mesmer himself, incidentally, opposed this transformation of his depth physics, probably mainly because the ahistorical nature of his theory of currents had no space for an introduction of time into the body. His physicalistic axiom that all solid bodies swim in currents of subtle matter remained entirely connected to presentist processes, excluding the notion of memories that affect events in the body and in relationships.

The fruitful moment in the theoretical penetration of magneto-pathic empiricism, which had grown immeasurably within a short time—and whose curative successes were to be viewed critically, but scarcely contested—came with the encounter between animal magnetism and early Romantic natural philoso-phy. To our knowledge, there is no record of any personal exchange between Mesmer and Schelling. But the numerous shared students led, as early as the 1900s, to those hybrids of the two streams of thought that produced the originary form of modern genetic psychology—the Jena, Weimar and Berlin schools of proto-psychoanalysis, so to speak. Where Mesmer's quasi-pantheistic fluidal physics and Schelling's ideas on the tem-poralization of nature came into contact, the critical spark was ignited that would develop into an evolutionary theory of matters of the soul and a classics of the life of intimate relationships.

The new alliance of the magnetopathic experiment in close-ness and evolutionary natural philosophy reached its early climax in Friedrich Hufeland's essay *Ueber Sympathie* [On Sym-pathy], published in Weimar in 1811. Hufeland (1774–1839) was court physician to the Duke of Saxe-Weimar and the younger brother of the well-known doctor and author Christoph Wilhelm Hufeland, whose book *Makrobiotik oder die Kunst, das menschliche Leben zu verlängern* [Macrobiotics, or, The Art of Prolonging Human Life] (Jena, 1796) initiated modern dietary science. Impressed by Schelling's theory of nature as the rise of matter to self-awareness, he converted to a worldview that subsumed the whole of nature under the concept of the organism. Here one still finds elements of older fluidistic concepts, which proved effortlessly combinable with the newer organism-based thought. Using the modernized notion of sympathy, Hufeland articulates the idea of lower and earlier evolutionary forms of the organic—especially the vegetative or herbaceous "sphere"—generally characterized by a capacity for passivity in relation to external influences. Animals already set themselves apart from the plant world by mobilizing independent activity and greater individuation. For Hufeland, the evolutionary sequence from minerals to plants, lower animals, higher animals and humans constitutes a rise of the organic from a mostly passive to a mostly active state—manifested in its highest form in human geniuses, who have achieved the unity of free moral self-determination and inventive-technical co-productiveness with nature. With the organism's increased individualization and active selfhood, the passive-sympathetic aspect of being falls to a negligible level—that is why man, as the most self-active being in the sequence of natural creatures, is simultaneously the most independent and the most open to the call of freedom. Nonetheless, even man, as the evolutionary product with the highest spontaneity index, is still susceptible to being affected by sympathetic influences from other living beings, especially in a state of vegetative introversion, during sleep and in states of fading self-awareness—but most of all in the case of a pathological disorganization of selfhood forces. In such a condition, the independent will of the sense of freedom and activity, normally largely immune to influences, is loosened and opens up the individual to the subtle effects of magnetic currents; Mesmer's term for these forces was "floodabilities"

Grandville, *Metamorphosis of a Dream,* from *Another World,* 1844

[*Flutbarkeiten*]. According to Friedrich Hufeland, the most important manifestation of the "ability of humans to enter a sympathetic relationship"[19] lies in the phenomena brought to light through magnetopathic practices.

For nowhere does the relationship we call sympathy, or the dependence of an individual life on a foreign sphere of life, reveal itself more clearly than in animal magnetism, whereby the magnetized subject, sacrificing its own individuality as far as possible without forfeiting its existence, and entering the magnetizer's sphere of life, is subjected to the dominance of the latter to such a degree that it seems to belong to it as one of its parts, to form one and the same organism with it. (*Ueber Sympathie*, pp. 107f.)

It is immediately clear in Hufeland's discourse how an object of fascination, namely sympathy, appears in conjunction with a scandal: the sacrifice of autonomy. It is characteristic of Romantic organism philosophies that they happily take this provocation on board to achieve their higher goal: the mediatization of humans within comprehensive totalities of life. In Hufeland's case, this undertaking involves a combination of medical motives and aspects of the holistic optimism found in Weimar and Berlin. The totality which the unstable subject is invited to enter appears on the one hand as the curative magnetopathic pact between doctor and patient, which aims to be fully infused with affirmations of trust, and on the other hand as the serene macrocosmic orb by which the individual, as the God-man in training, can know that he is enclosed without having to accept any reduction of his sense of autonomy. For a valuably precarious moment, philosophical-medical thought attained a complete balance of autonomy and devotion. Despite such edifying recommendations, critical contemporaries took exception to the excessive devotion demanded by magnetism; that already applied to Mesmer's Vienna phase, which was plagued by suspicions and jealousies—but all the more to the magnetopathic

Anonymous, *Crisis Room in Mesmer's Parisian Practice*, copperplate, c. 1780

movement at the height of its therapeutic and voguish success. The later nineteenth century, which has rightly been described as the age of strategic battles over rationality and of critique in the form of unmasking, advanced the co-evolution of expectations of abuse and the practice of distrust so far that Romantic curative optimism, with its devout joy in the therapeutic accessibility of the psyche through co-souls, inevitably fell behind the neo-bourgeois skepticism that sees exploitation, cheating and deception behind every corner—even among close partners. The first magnetizers fought this acute resistance from their contemporaries not only with their euphorias of discovery, but also through their unwavering faith in the integrity of their own therapeutic motives. Most of them would scarcely have understood the later criticisms of their paternalism and the magical-authoritative climate in which the doctor-patient encounters took place. For them it was evident in practice that even strongly asymmetrical psychological relationships, such as that between magnetizers and somnambulists, can remain embedded in an intact sphere of shared goodwill and moral equality. In addition, they could all see the decisive attribute of the new therapy quite clearly: never before in the history of healing had the patient been granted such a degree of dignity as a subject; the magnetopathic movement spawned a literary genre of case histories, which devoted a level of clinical and public attention to the patients unknown since the medieval biographies of mystics. A library of medical reports celebrated the healing unconscious as the hidden god of the dawning scientific century. Justinus Kerner's biography of Friederike Hauffe, the "clairvoyant of Prevorst," Clemens Brentano's notes on Anna Katharina Emmerich and Friedrich Schlegel's diaries of the magnetic treatment of the Viennese Countess Lésniowska between 1820 and 1826 are typical monuments of this new hagiography of the sick. This leads directly, albeit with a considerably cooler tone, into the case studies of Freud and his school, and lives on in the auto-pathographic literature of the twentieth century. Freud in particular was consummately skilled at turning every medical history into a novella, every neurosis into an anthropological monument. Romantic medicine loosened the tongue of sickness and made the patient himself the poet of its disorganization. As far as the magnetopathic approach is concerned, the precondition for this was indeed that the patients, as the magnetizing doctor's unconscious assistants, would become their own co-therapists. Just as the metaphysical age ultimately acknowledged only God as the one healer, the Romantic age clung to the principle *natura sanat*—which then meant that nature, in the magnetopathically affected patient, would cure itself as the whole-making unconscious.

Among the numerous authors who wanted to make the agent of these mysterious two-person healings known, the aforementioned name of Friedrich Hufeland, with his attempt at a natural history of sympathy, stands out especially. It was he who first stated in public what the psychogenetic key to the hazardous relationship of closeness in the magnetic cure was:

> There is only one relationship in organic nature in which sympathy expresses itself through the highest degree of dependency of the one individual on the other in a similar way to animal magnetism, namely that which we observe in the inseparable connection between the unborn child and its mother. The two relationships are essentially quite identical; their difference lies merely in the external form, and this is determined by the sphere of the organism that initially and originally enters this relationship. In animal magnetism we see an immediate dependency of the real animal functions—sensory activity, in part the voluntary muscle movements, and at times even higher intellectual activity, hence what we earlier termed the animal sphere—on the magnetizer, while the fetus in its vegetative sphere is perfectly dependent on the mother. The organismic activity of the latter directly affects that of the fetus; it is connected to the same central organ [i.e. the higher nervous system] that dominates the mother's sphere; if the mother's heart stops beating, its circulation is also inhibited, and thus the real source and center of the child's reproductive activity lies not in itself but rather outside itself, in the organism of the mother. (*Ueber Sympathie*, pp. 108f.)

This passage reads like a direct application of Schelling's thesis that the task of science is anamnesis. Scarcely anywhere else, however, has such a serious attempt been made to—once again in Schelling's words—raise the consciousness to consciousness through consciousness. Hufeland's model of fetal inhabitation of the mother offers—for the meantime—the most intimate and historically profound interpretation conceivable of the spheric union between subjects. For beyond the spatial incorporation of nascent life in the maternal body, Hufeland also conceives of the child's mental constitution as a relationship of direct sympathetic dependency on the central nervous functions, that is, the mother's animal-personal regulative centers. This essentially posits that the mother magnetizes the child within herself and animates it with her own, more highly organized life. A similar claim would be made by Hegel about the prehistory of the feeling soul in his anthropology lectures; using the leitmotif "The mother is the genius of the child," he explains that in the archaic mother-child relationship, there is only one available subjectivity for two individuals; the child participates in the self-hood of the maternal existence until it has matured into its own, substantialized being-for-itself.[20] For Hufeland, the fetus is like a plant in the womb of an animal that subsequently grows into an animal itself—an animal that will in turn open itself up to the world of the spirit. According to Schelling's natural philosophy, higher organisms preserve, as if in a somatic memory store, the integral recollection of their earliest modes of being. This sheds a first light on the otherwise entirely opaque circumstance that, between adult human beings, relationships are possible that can only be comprehended as reproductions of early "vegetative" ones. Not only is every human organism a result and memory store of ascending natural-historical processes from the stone to the sensitive, self-aware life form; each one also holds a memory that preserves its own history of becoming since its days in the mother's womb, and to which, under extraordinary circumstances—such as those created by magnetopathic treatment—they can return in an informative way. This possibility of return was the decisive condition of the new healing art; the patients of magnetism "remembered" a state of their selves, as it were, in which they were animated and coordinated from the center of the mother in the mode of ecstatic vegetability.

> Like the fetus, the sick of the variety described do not form a fully closed totality. Their animal sphere easily opens up to the predominant influence of a foreign organism, and only if they enter a foreign sphere of life can the energy missing from their inner life be replaced by forces from without; they take part in the more perfect life of the organism to which they are parasitically connected, delighting in an unaccustomed feeling of health and strength. Hence the life of these sick, like that of the unborn child, is like the dependent life of plants. For, like the child in the mother's body, the plant is rooted in the soil, receiving the positive principle of its life partly from without in the form of light, as those sick receive it through the stimulating influence of the magnetizer. (*Ueber Sympathie*, pp. 109f.)

Hufeland does not come close to drawing the seemingly obvious psychotherapeutic conclusions from his bold equation of magnetic rapport and the dyadic mother-child union during pregnancy. Above all, he avoids any inferences about an earlier fetal life based on the magnetic lucidity of the patients and their heightened sensory performance—especially their altered auditory perceptions, the oft-cited displacement of facial perception to the navel area and other peculiarities of the exceptional magnetic-hypnotic state. The author holds the key to a general theory of psychic transference phenomena in his hands, yet does not quite know which gate it is meant to open. Hufeland's speculative equation of fetus and plant inevitably blocked the seemingly inevitable progression of his reflections to an exploration of prenatal consciousness and a theory of genetic transfer. Connections of this kind were only developed systematically one hundred and fifty years later by the practitioners of a renewed prenatal psychology—Gustav Hans Graber, Alfred Tomatis, Athanassios Kafkalides, Ludwig Janus and others. Nonetheless, it remains Hufeland's supreme achievement to have connected the phenomenon of magnetic rapport to the history of the embodied relationship memory—not for the first time, but with irrevocable incisiveness. Hypnosis or magnetopathic trance is then a reproduction of the fetal position, which often appears in conjunction with a number of non-regressive mental acts. At the same time, Hufeland uses the analogy between birth and recovery to produce the first plausible interpretation of the end of the treatment and the expiration of the special relationship between the magnetizer and the magnetized.

> But just as the organization of the fetus, through the strength and nourishment the mother shares with it, gradually attains the necessary degree of development and completion to lead an independent life, and just as it separates from the mother once this goal has been achieved and the shared life of both is divided into two—in the same way, through the effect of animal magnetism, the afflicted subject is gradually led back to

a higher level of organismic completion, its animal activity revived, and, by having the higher functions of its subjective sphere put into regular effect, it regains its independence and now no longer requires the immediate influence of a foreign life. Thus every recovery achieved through animal magnetism has the same periods as the life of the unborn child until its separation from the mother. (p. 110)

Repeated application causes a gradual disappearance of the symptoms that came from the susceptibility of these patients, and with them the accompanying illnesses. The organism of the afflicted now begins once more to form a closed, clearly delimited sphere; their passive state comes to an end and they regain the independence granted them by nature, as well as the ability to assert themselves as something positive in the face of the outside world. (p. 137)

Now a state of indifference between the two subjects sets in, and, just as the fetus separates from the mother once it has the strength to lead an independent life, and the ripened seed from the plant, the cured patient now parts ways with the magnetizer, and his sympathetic connection with him, which he now no longer needs nor is able to maintain, ends. (p. 138)

Hufeland's interpretation of illness as a disorganization of organismic independence led directly to the discovery of the principle of regression. The vegetative bodily past and archaic symbiosis return in certain episodes of illness and their magneto-pathic treatment. Where illness appears, one also observes the organisms' own tendency to abandon the burden of their indi-viduating tension along with their independence and sink back into a diffuse overall relationship with an enclosing and completing other. For the patient who is willing to regress, the magnetizer acts as a form of "uterine cushion." In keeping with this, Hufeland's reflections lead into remarks that can be read as anticipations of Freud's metapsychological doctrines about the death instinct; on the other hand, those axioms prove that psychoanalysis as a whole belongs to Schelling's model of a temporalized nature. In Hufeland's diction, death appears as the fulfillment of a transpersonal sympathy between the individual life and the pan-organism:

> This possibility of return to organic unity and independence distinguishes that partial disorganization and the accompanying increase of human dependence on external nature from the complete loss of the inner principle of unity and the absolute, unbreakable unification with general nature that we call death; and if the striving for unification with the whole that is native to every individual, and expresses itself in the phenomena of sympathy as long as it asserts its existence, cannot be fully satisfied, death can be viewed as the true attainment of this goal. But also in the state of partial disorganization described above, the human organism enters a closer connection with nature in general and, sinking to a lower level of life, approaches the anorganism. (pp. 138f.)

It is notable here that for one brief, dangerous moment, Hufeland seems to have approached the limits of his natural theology.[21] While he places great value everywhere else on addressing the totality of nature as an encompassing organism and emphasizing the principle of life as the unifying motif of the universe, he lets a word slip out in this passage—"anorganism"—that could be read as the admission of a hidden fear: that nature as a whole is perhaps not a "womb," some preserving total life form, or the obscure foundation of an enfolding animality, but simply an anorganic aggregate whose totality remains pre-vital, and in that sense dead. It is, logically enough, the primal pain in the Romantic idea of nature that nature as a whole contains life, but cannot—or only in the form of a postulate—be integrated into the living realm as a whole. Within a narrow space, two opposing concepts of death come into contact in Hufeland's discourse. The first conceives of death in Romantic-holistic terms as a unification with the pan-organism, while the second understands it in naturalistic-nihilistic terms as a regression to the anorganic. The word "anorganism" points to the rupture in the world's life-warm shell; it reveals the Enlightenment's imposition—to conceive of the difference between inside and outside, between the organic world-womb and the anorganic death cosmos. Freud's doctrine of the death instinct merely represents a cooler, more resigned version of this notion of difference. It makes a concession to the Gnostic idea that it is not death that infiltrates life, but rather life that appears amid the general inanimation like a foreign intruder. In this, Enlightenment and dark Gnosis are allies; they both assert truths distant from humanity against the self-warming illusion of vitality. Nietzsche drew the philosophical conclusions from this quandary: "Let us beware of saying that death is opposed to life. The living is only a form of what is dead, and a very rare form."[22]

In the theologically-inclined musings of his late period, Johann Gottlieb Fichte perceived animal magnetism as a chance to defend the absolutism of the vital against the deadly imposition of thinking an autonomous outside. At the same time, he considered it a possible way to overcome the nature-philosophical deficiency that he increasingly saw in his own doctrine and arrive at a "physicization of idealism."[23] In September 1813—a few months before his death (on January 28, 1814)—Fichte visited the practice, already famous by then, of Professor Karl Christian Wolfart in Berlin, at 36 Französische Strasse, to sit in on a magnetic treatment.[24] Here he became acquainted with the most mysterious electrotechnical device of its time: Mesmer's invention, the *baquet*.[25] Following this visit, Fichte began a diary in which he wrote down his observations about Wolfart's practice, as well as excerpts from his extensive reading of mesmerist and Puységurist literature, during the following weeks.

> The essence of the conversation with Wolfart is this: magnetizing provides vitality, and thus healing, even without somnambulism. This latter, he says, is only one of the crises. While I admit that, I do wish to remind him that *clairvoyance*, the representation of complete consciousness, is the most complete and deeply harrowing crisis. Of course, it is an utter annihilation of selfhood for this very reason. Wolfart thinks it too great an attack; one should not aim for it, but rather leave it to nature to choose its most suitable crisis here too… But it is clear now, he said, that nature will only permit an annihilation of selfhood in so far as the latter is sick; one must therefore always offer it the whole. (*Tagebuch*, p. 299)

What Hufeland had described as the patient's complete dependency within the magnetic fusion is dramatized in Fichte's terminology, with phrases reminiscent of language games from the mystical tradition, into the annihilation of selfhood. The pathos of this formulation gives a sense of how the new medicine was to be connected to the old project of philosophy as the path to redemption. From Ionia to Jena, "great thought" had played with the motif of reaching salvation from death and externality through a living knowledge of essence. Thus also in Berlin during the autumn of 1813, only a few weeks before the Battle of Leipzig, in which Fichte had applied in vain to participate as a patriotic army chaplain; the Prussian ministry was presumably unwilling to give its most celebrated professor a chance to verify his non-belief in death in actual practice. Furthermore, Fichte's interest in magnetism came from his long-standing reflections on the nature of the obstacles to his manifold attempts to convey his own experiences of philosophical evidence to his audience in a tenable fashion. He was looking for an academically legitimate and publicistically effective linguistic equivalent of clairvoyance, that state in which magnetized patients seemed to achieve complete self-transparency. As a philosopher-priest, it was his ambition to lead his readers and listeners to the point where it would become evident to them that their free ego was medially incorporated in God's self-manifestation—in analogy to his own self-descriptions. In conversation with Wolfart, Fichte explicated to himself the feeling that his own teaching had always staged a form of logical-rhetorical magnetism. In fact, Fichte was no stranger to the idea that he might succeed in taking away his listener's cumbersome freedom in such a way that they benefited from it like an initiation into God's freedom.

Objects of examination: 1) the medium through which the first will of the magnetizer may here affect the stranger's personality. 2) The analogy with the sharing of evidence and convictions. (I shall keep to the latter, as it is of greater interest.) Why does attention beget attention, sorrow beget sorrow, etc.? Where does sympathy come from in the first place? The phenomenon that my listeners understand my words when they sit before me, but no longer once out of the auditorium, is of the same kind. [...] (The phenomenon of great attentiveness that I evoke in my lectures has its limits. Whence and how? E.g. at the start, when they come out of curiosity and still become embarrassed or unwilling, it fails. Who are then the receptive ones? Those who are unknowing, unbiased and new.) All wanting is universal, and takes freedom from the whole world. Hence if I can make the freedom of the other a part of my own, it is clear that it has been taken from the other. (*Tagebuch*, pp. 300f.)

In Fichte's reflections too, the magnetopathic element of scandal immediately steps into the center: the devotion of the passive part to the foreign will. Like the first magnetizers, however, Fichte relied on the assumption that his teacher's will was not the expression of egotistical feelings, but simply reproduced pure and loyal emotions for what was presently evident.

What, then, does the teacher do? [...] designs images, combinations, and waits to be struck by self-evidence. [...] he is guided by a law and force entirely unknown to him, and to which he is connected as the listener to the teacher. (*Tagebuch*, p. 301)

Admittedly, the teacher in Fichte's model, unlike the student, must already have an ego that has been posited and elevated to self-activity: he needs to have made himself freely as his own product. At this level, completed self-production can be reinterpreted as life from God that has been reached for or reached through.

> The student, by contrast, is directly aware of the teacher. His immediate observation goes further and outwards. And how is it with the correct devotion to the teacher? Answer: it is observation of the same, as the principle of the images [...]. The evidence then arises of its own accord. It is vital to have the absolutely individual, to have attentiveness; but this is pure devotion, a pure elimination of one's own activity. Therefore here, as in the physical aspect of magnetism, an effect of the individual on the outside and the central point of individuality are given; and all this is a model for devotion and self-elimination before God. (*Tagebuch*, p. 302)

With Fichte, then, *learning* means subjecting oneself to a magnetic thought treatment in the auditorium while in a state of attentive ecstasy, just like Puységur's somnambulists; exchanging vulgar self-awareness for a lucid state of illumination in which the ego conceives of itself as an organ of God. *Teaching* by Fichte's method, however, would mean letting oneself go in God's service through free rhetorical-logical construction. The speaker, an eloquent outpost of the absolute in the world of phenomena, uses words as the "element of intellectual communication"; for the free-moving speaker, the most complex becomes the most simple again: "The word provokes certain images in the state of devotion; the rest follows of its own accord." (Ibid.)

Thus Fichte's speeches unfold, like an autogenic training in enthusiasm, through what needs to be said: they tell of the virtual presence of the divine kingdom of reason; a continuation of Christianity by other, in Fichte's view, surely more perfect means.

Our idea-historical excursion into the two great formations of depth-psychological discourses and practices before the twentieth century, the intersubjective magic of the early Modern Age and the world of animal magnetism, has brought to light three clearly demarcated models of dyadic interpersonal union: magical rapture in erotic reciprocal enchantment; the hypnotoid reproduction of the mother-fetus relationship in magnetopathic treatment; the ecstasy of selfless attentiveness in Fichte's rhetorical self-proofs of God. Each of these configurations—lover-beloved, magnetizer-magnetized, teacher-listener—can be described like the realization of a temporarily closed bipolar bubble in which a single shared subjectivity is spread resonantly between two partners. The transition from the unenchanted to the enchanted, from the individuated to the merged, and from the absent-minded to the unconditionally listening state is achieved through different techniques respectively, however, and conveyed through diverse media; in each case it depends on the ability of the passive side to give itself up completely on its relationship with the active pole. Just as love magic is conditioned by the object's readiness to yield to the influence, mesmeric treatment likewise presupposes a patient's unbounded willingness to subordinate themselves to the doctor's fluid, while Fichte's psychagogic speeches, always suspended between appeal and proof, fully engage the compliance of the intelligent ear for their developments. It goes without saying that each of these procedures can only achieve success if it can lay down its own terms. So where erotic magic, magnetism and philosophical hypno-rhetoric are practiced, it is they themselves that produce the magic circle in which alone they can find their optimal state. Where the circle's formation fails, the effects become unstable—Fichte's reference to those listeners who are merely curious, and otherwise inattentive and unwilling, hints at a sound reason to be concerned about the desired effects. A much more far-reaching disturbance of Mesmer's circles and effects was caused by the academic commission set up by Louis XVI in 1784 to examine the scientific truth of Mesmer's theories and cures. The commission's negative report profoundly shook Mesmer's authority, and ultimately led him to close his Paris practice.[26] As far as the erotomagical theories of the early Modern Age are concerned, they were faced from the start with an opponent—the Catholic Church—that could place magic circles which had escaped their control under the capital sentence of sorcery. For them, any psychogenic effects of depth intimacy were potentially the result of demonic influences or diabolical pacts; the central religious administration aimed for a situation in which the church would only have to deal with disciplined individuals easily controllable through their dependency on Rome. Even as late as Schopenhauer, one finds mention of a circular sent by the Roman Inquisition to the bishops in 1856 in which they are called upon to join the battle against the practice of animal magnetism.[27] Four hundred years after Ficino's impulse towards the erotology of the Modern Age, it is still from the same intimacy-magical corner that the Holy Office sees dangerous tendencies approaching.

But the "magical" bi-personal bubbles are not only threatened by external disturbances; one occasionally finds motifs entering the inside of the circle that necessarily lead to ruptures from endogenous discrepancies. This became especially noticeable in the reception history of animal magnetism, which proceeded along two simultaneous paths from the outset: as a history of trust and a history of distrust. In its entire first wave, animal magnetism can be interpreted as a quarrel over the circle within which the magnetopathic cures would achieve their successes. Did it really have to be Newton's cosmic rays from the ether, as Mesmer claimed, that formed a healing energy circle between the magnetizer and the patient? Was it so indispensable to venture the presumptuous hypothesis of a "universal gravitation" that also pervades the human world? Would it not be sufficient for an explanation of all phenomena to assume that an auratic circle of bodily vapors and animal warmth develops between the healer and his subject?[28] Are the so-called crises genuine crises that must precede any successful cure, or does it not seem more justified to view them as pathological phenomena in their own right? Should somnambulism and clairvoyance not be understood as artificial illnesses only brought on by the treatment? And above all: can one fully rely on the moral integrity of the magnetizers themselves? And is there not a danger that magnetism, applied at the wrong time, does not cure the patient but instead leaves mental scars that can be worse than the initial complaints? These phantasms of suspicion, whose originators usually entered the magic circle for a short time themselves so as to flee better from it, were developed in a whole body of literature, the most prominent examples being Edgar Allan Poe's short story "The Facts in the Case of M. Valdemar" (1839) and

Jean-Jacques Paulet: *Satire on Animal Magnetism*, frontispiece from *Anti-Magnetism*, copperplate, 1784

Alfred Kubin, illustration for E. A. Poe's *The Facts in the Case of M. Valdemar*

E. T. A. Hoffmann's "The Magnetizer" (1813). Poe's macabre tale documents the encroachment of magnetism on the occult field—a tendency that had been evident in the Empire revival of magnetism, but most of all its Russian and American reception. The narrator tells of a macabre experiment, namely magnetizing a dying man *in articulo mortis*: its success was keeping the moribund soul in a physically dead body for seven months. The bound soul continued to speak to the living from its spirit hell, before finally withdrawing completely at the attempt to awaken the subject, leaving behind a corpse that dissolved in less than a minute into a liquid mass of disgusting putrescence. For Poe, unlike the majority of German natural theologians, the night side of nature is no longer an allied darkness that brings safety and salvation; his experiment means to show that the supposed world of the womb can invert itself into a kingdom of hell. E. T. A. Hoffmann, by contrast, reveals a moral night side in nature's night side: for who could prevent a shift within the magnetic space from the exercise of medical power to a lust for dictatorial political power? For Hoffmann the hero of his tale, the magnetizer Alban, symbolizes, like a Napoleon of occult forces, an unfettered will to power that cannot possibly content itself simply with curing headaches and other minor human ailments. The magnetopathic power no longer wants to be a mere means, and makes itself the purpose of its existence. It is in this spirit that Hoffmann lets his magnetizer present the philosophical program for the nihilistic-vitalistic age heralded by Napoleon:

> All existence is struggle and is born of struggle. The more powerful are granted victory in an ever-mounting climax, and it grows in strength with every subdued vassal [...]. The striving for that dominion is the striving for the divine, and the stronger the feeling of power becomes, the more blissful it is.[29]

Accordingly, Hoffmann's magnetizer will not let his victims go once they are under his spell, and sooner kill them than accept their freedom. This hints at the birth of modern psycho-sects from the spirit of intimacy exploitation. They develop as therapeutic-gurucratic parodies of the relationship between feudal lords and vassals. The aesthetic counterpart revealed itself in the twentieth century in Stefan George's auratic totalitarianism, where the word "circle" was made to represent as a sociological and spiritual emblem. Here too, we find feudalism shifted to a different milieu along with its entire metaphysics, psychology and spatial idea. In his defense of the circle, Friedrich Gundolf announced the following about the master:

> The circle is his aura, and none of the members have or need the pitiful ambition consciously to be a "personality" at all costs, for their purpose is to be air and element [...]. The same principle that makes the ruler the center of a living sphere, the drive towards unity [...] that same drive connects rulers and servants in the spiritual realm [...].[30]

Phantasms of this kind prove that the formal motif of the magic circle cannot be restricted to the intimate therapeutic encounter; it is capable of extending itself from the closeness-psychological biune figure to the group- and mass-psychological spell formula. Occasionally it expands from the fluidal union between the healer and the patient to a whirlwind of suction in the revolutionary collective of intoxication, where fortune-seekers dragged along and enchanted employees assist in the staging of their catastrophe to the point of self-annihilation. We will show later on, in the second book, especially in the description of the transition of the bipersonal bubble form to the political orb form, how projection onto the large scale takes place and which emotional errors of format and category appear when uterine relationships and their crises are reenacted in sociodramas.

Thought Transmission

To speak means to play with the body of the other.
— Alfred Tomatis

That my thoughts are invisible for others; that my head is a safe, full of notions and dreams that rest locked within me; that my reflections form a book which no one can read from the outside; that my ideas and knowledge belong exclusively to me, transparent for myself and impenetrable for others—to such an extent that even torture may not induce me to tell others what I know against my will: one cannot overestimate the significance which this syndrome of notions about the concealed nature of thoughts in the thinking subject has taken on in the recent history of private semblance. This perhaps makes it seem an even more provocative imposition to consider that precisely these notions have played a part in creating that semblance in the first place. In our cultural area they are only a little more than two and a half thousand years old—for a macro-historian, merely the young fluff on sturdy layers of older psychological realities. If they were not the dominant ideas today, they would hardly be of significance for the gravity of human history. For during the majority of the evolutionary process, almost everything individual humans thought and felt was so transparent that for the others around them, those experiences were like their own. The notion of private ideas had no grounding in emotional experience or the social concept of space: no cells had been made for individuals yet, either in the imagination or the physical architectures of societies. In small groups, under the law of reciprocity, the actions of one are the actions of the other; hence the thoughts of the one are generally also the thoughts of the other. This even applies to archaic "shame cultures," where individuals would like to make their inner selves invisible because they suffer from the excessive exposure of their affects to the empathy of the others. From a paleo-psychological perspective, hidden thoughts are perfectly absurd. The notion of a private interior in which the subject can close the door behind it, reflect upon and express itself was unknown before the early individualistic turn in antiquity; its propagandists were the men known as sages or philosophers—forerunners of the modern intellectual and post-modern singles. It was they who first gave the motif that true thought was only possible as independent thought, as thinking differently from the stupid masses, its revolutionary virulence. The meanwhile widespread model of the retreat within one's own mind is derived from those impulses: thoughts are free, no one can guess them[31]—initially, that only means that the thinkers of *new* thoughts become inscrutable for the guardians of conventional thoughts. In the world of new thoughts, the axiom that the thoughts of one are also those of the other in fact loses its validity: I cannot possibly detect in others a thought I have not had myself. In differentiated societies, other people frequently have different thoughts in their heads. In such societies, it is the psychotherapist's task to ensure that individuals do not drift off too far into the pathogenic otherness and ownness of their thoughts and feelings. The fact that thoughts were more like public matters in the old sociosphere was due first of all to a media-physiological factor: human brains, like genitalia, are fundamentally paired, probably even gregarious systems. While the statement "My belly belongs to me" can have a definable meaning in polemical contexts—namely that it should be the mother who has the last word in questions of abortion—the declaration "My brain belongs to me" would be both morally unacceptable and objectively inappropriate. It could neither truthfully mean that I am the author and owner of my thoughts nor that I am completely exempt from sharing them with others; and the claim that I can think whatever I want is also immanently untenable. A cerebral individualism would miss the fact that a brain only awakens to a certain level of performance through interaction with a second, and beyond that with a larger brain ensemble—no one would dare speak of optimal performance. Brains are media for what other brains do and have done. Intelligence only receives the key stimuli for its own activity from other intelligence. Like language and emotion, intelligence is not a subject, but a milieu or resonance circle. Preliterate intelligence, unlike literate intelligence, which is capable of abstraction, is oriented towards a dense climate of participation because, being entirely embedded in close-range communications, it requires the experience of a presentist brain and nerve communism for its development. In the age of reading, this would change into the quasi-telepathic republic of scholars, which does not have its zeitgeists for nothing; thanks to writing, the spirits of the distant past can return in current manifestations of attentiveness. It is also writing that enables individuals to withdraw from society in order to complete themselves with authorial voices: whoever can read can also be alone. Only with the advent of literacy did anachoresis become possible; the book and the desert belong together. Even in the loneliest retreat, however, it is impossible to have last instance thoughts of one's own. It is precisely through the withdrawal into the socially empty space that the idea of God as the first mind reader became dominant; by retreating to the desert, I necessarily draw God's attention to myself. And it was onto the God of the hermits that residues of the intimate participatory function in early groups were transferred: He guaranteed that the ascetic in the desert would never be without his great companion, who encloses him, observes him, eavesdrops on him and sees through him.

It was only writing that broke open the magic circles of orality and emancipated the readers from the totalitarianism of the current, locally spoken word; writing and reading, especially in their Greek, democratic, autodidactic modes of application, offered practice in non-emotion. In truth, the oral age was synonymous with the magical-manipulative prehistory of the soul, as the presentist obsession with the voices and suggestions of clan members was the norm then. Of course, an obsession with the normal, average and present is not conspicuous as such: in families, villages and neighborhoods it is considered the simple, direct, natural mode of communication. This keeps quiet the fact that in the oral world, all people are magicians who cast a varyingly powerful spell of normalization on one another (which can usually only be broken through a counter-spell, such as travels or conversations with strangers).

After the Neolithic revolution, the primary presence-magical potential was overlaid with the web of absence magics, then later also that of writing magics; it was only with these that what we today call the true magical functions were fulfilled, namely magic from the distance and communication with the dead. These spells bring to the fore those deceased god-kings and gods who have afflicted and perverted human intelligence since then; they have kept world history in motion as a series of wars between telepathic and influence-psychotic possession groups, better known under the name "cultures." The presence-magical conviviality of the oldest cultures depended on the neurolinguistic and neurosensitive domain: dense parallel programmings of the brain ensembles enabled the members of groups to function in great interpersonal proximity and intimate conductivity. That humans are capable of such densely mutually intervening participations is part of their oldest clan-historical makeup. Though this receded into the background in the medial Modern Age, that is to say the age of writing, it was never entirely eliminated. It seems plausible to suppose that the innumerable accounts of "thought transmissions" during magnetopathic treatments are based on a reactivation of preliterate and pre-verbal proximity functions. This also includes episodes of pain transmission from the patient to the healer—Fichte cites a French source describing such a case in his journal on animal magnetism.[32] That patients often seem to "read" the thoughts of their therapists, and the therapists somehow photograph the former's inner material, so to speak, in their "own" feelings and associations before bringing it back into the conversation with the patient—this has been one of the basic observations in the new practice of closeness since the founding days of modern psychology. Like William James and Pierre Janet, Sigmund Freud was impressed by the obstinate reality of "tele"pathic effects; he had no doubts that paleo-psychological functions are reactivated in them. But Freud hesitated to make any loud proclamations, and with good reason: he knew that it would have been ruinous for the psychoanalytical movement if he had led it into a cultural battle between occult-archaic and modern-enlightened models of communication. He was aware that psychoanalysis only had a chance as a specifically modern cultivation of closeness relationships in an alliance with enlightenment. It was in the nature of the matter that the analytical contours, as earlier in mesmerism, had to display those preverbal participatory effects that had been deformed into bizarre secrets under the semblance of individualism. But we can now better understand why they immediately returned as normal phenomena upon the first possible restoration of pre-individualistic situations of closeness.[33] In this respect too, the continuum between mesmerism and psychoanalysis is unmistakable. But as long as "thought transmission" has the reputation of an extra-normal phenomenon (while affective and scenic transmission would constitute psychological normality), it must be perceived as a fascinating curiosity, and as such drawn into the dynamics of the desire for enchantment and the pathos of disenchantment. Where these forces push their way to the foreground, there is no prospect that the critique of participatory reason, which describes the play of inter-intelligence on its own terms, might consolidate itself.[34]

CHAPTER 4

The Retreat Within the Mother

Groundwork for a Negative Gynecology

> Perhaps truth is a woman who has grounds for not showing her
> grounds? Perhaps her name is—to speak Greek—Baubo?
> — Friedrich Nietzsche, *The Gay Science*

Just as, in the time of Caesars and popes, all roads led to Rome,
where heaven and earth are supposedly closer together than elsewhere, all fundamental reflections during the discourse of origin
were drawn towards the vulva—the magical gate where the
uterine darkness of the inner world borders the public, illuminated and sayable domain. The reason for this vulva magic is the
elementary idea that the mother gate, which by its nature serves
as an exit, and only as such, must also be employed as an
entrance—less in a sexual-erotic, and hence partial act, than in
a religious, existentially encompassing sense. In fact, tendencies
towards a two-way traffic before the female opening, and
through it, can be identified from Paleolithic cave cults onwards.
Whether the archeological discoveries made so far genuinely
testify to formal Paleolithic magics of rebirth—that is, proto-
religious cults—may still be uncertain.[1] It is undeniable,

however, that there was a precise historical heyday for increased religious interest in the vulva. The massive crowd before the passage to the female interior can be culture-historically dated: it was only after the notorious Neolithic revolution that the fascination with the womb could develop into a world power. Only then, in the great Neolithic change, did those circumstances emerge that brought territorialism upon humanity; only then did the earthbound identities begin to blossom; only then were humans compelled to identify themselves by their place, their adhesion to territory, and finally their property. The Neolithic revolution lured the previously nomadic human groups into the trap of sedentarism, in which they attempted to prove themselves by simultaneously experimenting with rootedness and escape; thus begins the agro-metaphysical conversation with useful plants, pets, household spirits and the gods of the fields and meadows. It was only the early agricultural fixation on the soil that forced the epochal equation of the mother world and cultivated, fertile space. The age of work as mother-management begins with the settling of the earth, the "pig earth" (John Berger), which from now on must chronically bring forth additional produce, additional births, and a surplus of power. This age sees the internalized bond of mortals to a sacred-accursed and contaminated territory with huts, sewers and headquarters: where for generations, the fields need to be cultivated year after year, where stores make projects possible and dead ancestors measure out their grounds of return, two things form: a new spatial type, home, and a new thought type, land law—*nomos*.[2] The Neolithic equation of mother and cultivated earth led to the ten-thousand-year conservative revolution, which forms the substrate of the early settled cultures, archaic states and regional advanced civilizations. It was scarcely half a century ago that the European faction of humanity initiated a counter-revolution of mobility which restored the utero-fugal forces to predominance over the almost immemorial womb fixation of agro-metaphysical times.

The dual possession by the soil and genealogical compulsion drove the settled peoples into the arms of the possessing Great Mothers. As the soil binds the living and the dead to itself equally, some start to believe that the mothers want to keep their loved ones forever with them, and in a sense also within them. Now the hearth and the landscape, the womb and the field, become synonymous. In what resembled a first experience of fate's power, the settled populations in the early villages and towns are confronted by the necessity to identify themselves through terms of lineage. Before the state became fate, fate actually meant relation to territorialized dead. Just as fate means the inaccessible force of retribution, relation means the regulated connection of the elder to the younger, and of the elder to their soil-rooted ancestors. In early settlements, where being [*Sein*] consistently meant being related and existence [*Dasein*] meant being descended from, people had to learn to say which womb they came from and in what relation they stood to their mothers and soils. It is through this, the greatest transformation of thought forms in the old world, that the Paleolithic religiosity of birth and life began to move towards the Neolithic, already para-metaphysically shimmering religiosity of power and death.[3] With the shift to the genealogical compulsion of reason and allocation, the female womb, together with its portal and its hallway, is subjected to an incalculable alteration of meaning: from now on, it is no longer simply the

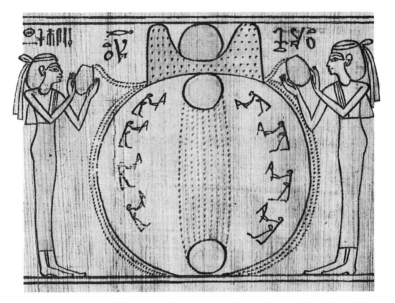

Funerary papyrus of the priest Khonsu-Mes; the northern and southern Nut
ensure the regeneration of the earth's shell by pouring the water of life on it.

starting point for all paths in the world, but also becomes a
term for the great homeward journeys that must be undertaken
for the sake of the now urgent search for ancestors, the interro-
gation of the dead and rebirth—in short, for the sake of
self-identification. For the restless living, the womb becomes a
place of truth; it imposes itself upon their thoughts and wishes
as the most intimate Yonder with which mortals have any business; what awaits them there will never be any less than insight
into their true selves. The womb idea exudes the evidence that
truth has a secret seat which can be reached through initiations
and ritual modes of approach. Hence by the end of the age of
uterine compulsion, when the first enlightenment was surfacing
in the etiological philosophies of the Greeks, people would

Scenes from the embalming process show the correspondence between bathing the corpse in caustic soda and pouring over the water of life.

descend to the mothers in order to find among them, and within them, something they would later refer to without the slightest blush as "knowledge." The self of this knowledge is concerned to plant itself in the most powerful interior; all trees of wisdom point down into the woman's interior. Mortals, those who are born, have their beginning and their end in caves of origin. One day people will even call for the entire horizon to become cave-immanent, and the phenomenal world will then have to become interpretable as an interior landscape. Not without reason did cultures of that proto-metaphysical epoch—primarily Babylonians and Egyptians—imagine the visible world as being enclosed by great rings of water: where the mother motivates

The gabled façade of the Lomas Rishi Cave in India, 3rd century BC, vulva-shaped cave entrance

thought, everything is inside. As long as motherhood and gestation define the form of thought as such, there is no longer meant to be any outside; for those who know, the only concern is to learn in what sense these mysteries of all-immanence apply. Whoever wishes to discover who they truly are under such conditions must, at least once in their life, travel to the source that is the only place from which grown life can understand itself. Once the female birth organ is no longer simply the exit, real and imaginary, but has also become an entrance through which the search for identity must pass, it charges itself up with ambivalent fascinations. The bleeding gate to life, whose gaping fascinates, outrages and repels,[4] now becomes a doorway to the lower and upper worlds. The uterus expands into the beyond, to which the vulva becomes the horrifying and inviting portal. It is now what Heidegger calls the inevitable. In the oldest world, being reasonable meant, first and foremost, acknowledging one thing: whoever passes through the gate inwards must part with his previous life— whether in a symbolic death, as ritualized for initiations, or through the real thing. Both deaths seem surmountable in the faith that dying, if the standard procedure is followed, very much aids a return to the mother interior. All truth-seekers in metaphysical times are therefore returnees to the womb. They strive for what seems *prima facie* unattainable: they wish to tie the end of the search to the beginning of life and reverse birth through radical struggles against themselves. Who is the hero with a thousand faces if not the seeker who journeys out into the wide world in order to return home to his ownmost cave? The tales of heroic truth-seekers celebrate the womb-immanence of all being. Wisdom is the realization that even the open world is encompassed by the cave of all caves. Because knowledge always leads home, and thus revokes birth or reveals its meaning in the first place, the heroic returnees must fight the dragon at the entrance to the maternal portal one more time; now it is a matter of repeating the struggle of birth in the opposite direction. If this fight is won, the insight into life before life, prenatal death, enables the striving for illumination to come into itself—and this illumination naturally causes total darkening. Increasingly, ordinary dying also takes on associations of return. Thus one not only finds an epidemic spread of re-fetalizing burial rites after the Neolithic shift; one could speak of a fetalization of worldviews as a whole. The equation of the grave and the womb—the mysterious and evident spatial premise of all early metaphysical systems, which know only immanence—begins its long reign over the imaginary realm of the post-Neolithic human world; it would cast its spell on the thought and life of early cultures for no less than two hundred generations.

It was only the ancient metaphysical systems of light and heaven that ended the womb's monopoly of the discourse of origin, by granting a share of the origin function to the male as the "transcendent." From then on, the great homecoming also takes on aspects of yearning for the divine paternal home; for millennia, Christianity developed the attraction of the idea of the paternal womb. It is only from the start of the recent European Modern Age that one can speak of humans breaking in significant numbers from the forms of life and thought that carried further—directly or indirectly—the suckling magic of the ontologies of maternal immanence. Only a few generations ago did philosophical stances emerge that no longer required their adepts to renounce their selves and, in a certain sense, die in order to enter the inner circle of truth; as late as 1810, the Nuremberg headmaster Hegel still deemed it fitting to tell middle school students that, like initiates of ancient mystery cults, their senses would have to reel before they could progress to real thought. Up until Romanticism, death was always viewed by the metaphysically resolute as a fair price for the privilege of returning to the place of truth as an isolated being. The price of transfiguration, on the other hand, was already negotiable early on. Death was not the only currency in which the fee for access to the concealed mystery of being could be paid; the Empedoclean leap into the crater was not the only form of admittance sacrifice. Often genital sacrifices also made in exchange for being close to the great maternal interior—the castrated priests of the Greek fertility goddess Cybele enjoyed the privilege of uniting with the goddess inside the earth's interior in *hieros gamos*. The institution of eunuch priesthood was as well known in the cult of the Roman and Phrygian *magna mater* as in that of the Anatolian Artemis and the Syrian goddess of Hierapolis, and also in the Indian cults of the Great Mother, in which tens of thousands of young men in every generation are still persuaded or forced to perform genital sacrifices to this day. Furthermore, there is much to suggest that the majority of Western philosophies were typological relatives of the holy eunuchs, for only those who understand the principle of all-immanence in its strict form could see fulfillment in absorption by the One. The secret of the highest metaphysics—what was it based on if not logical incest?[5]

The early para-metaphysicians grappled insistently, bloodily and ascetically with the original imbalance: being born and yet wanting to progress "into truth"[6]—something that is doomed to fail under human conditions, unless one could find a way of revoking birth and invalidating separation. How other than through self-dissolution can the born regain the position of the unborn? Post-Neolithic humanity devised a thousand and three methods to court the impossible. Whatever it achieved or gambled away in the process was always based on the same

Votive to a mother deity, presumably from a shrine in Veii, Southern Italy, terracotta

paradoxical intertwining of forwards and backwards. The one unmistakable truth is that the return to the mother constitutes the open secret about the secrets of the old world.[7] Death must therefore become the royal road of knowledge—provided one manages to discover a way of dying that can be experienced as regress rather than annihilation. No admittance to substance without re-fetalization. Where the great mothers still have the monopoly on thought, the civil war between philosophical reason and common sense, the fundamental cognitive event in advanced civilization, has not yet begun in earnest. For millennia, the wise and the profane gazed with the same fascinated eyes into the wombs of the encompassing mothers. In the ancient uteromorphic funerary urns of the Greeks, the *pithoi*, which later became significant as wine vessels in the Dionysia, the para-metaphysical equation of maternal womb and burial ground is palpable; they preserve the dead in a fetal squat. The custom of burial in uteromorphic vessels predates Greek culture, and there are numerous indications of its existence among Bronze Age Aegean cults. It appears to have originated from Asia Minor; analogous practices in South America suggest its growth from related constellations of elemental ideas. In Egypt, the noble dead had the image of the sky goddess Nut, the re-bearer, painted on the floors or lids of their sarcophagi. It is above all in the varied forms of earth burial, however, that the central idea of the reintegration of mortals into the womb of the Great Mother is especially prominent. Even Indian cremations do not lack a connection to the inescapable womb-grave equation, in that they stage transformations in which the exit from one form prepares the entrance into another—a change that cannot take place anywhere except in the inner space

The Egyptian sky goddess Nut

beyond all forms, namely that of the world mother. It is not only the post-Neolithic burial habits that came under the sign of the Great Mother, however. In most settled peoples of that time, inventions of worldviews were dominated entirely by utero-mythological motifs—their main symbols are earth and house, field and digging stick, birth and seed, harvest and underworld, sea and boat, cave and egg.[8]

There is no doubt: on our phenomenological expedition through the formal sequence of bipolar closeness and intimacy spheres, we have now passed the threshold to the narrower center of gravitation and gravidity. From here on, intimacy means proximity to the barrier which seals off the inside of the mother from the public world. If a confrontation occurs between the eye and the womb's entrance—recall Hindu sculptures at cave

entrances in the shape of the yoni-vulva—the examination of the field of intimacy enters its critical phase. This is where it transpires whether subject and object separate in the sense of the classical knowledge relation, or whether the subject enters the object to such an extent that the latter gives up its object character, indeed its presence and capacity for oppositeness as such. On the second of these paths, a bizarre epistemological affair develops between the vulva and its observer that will put an end to all externality and concreteness. In its own precarious way, the vulva belongs to those ungiven objects—Thomas Macho calls them "nobjects"—that we shall discuss directly here, and indirectly in all subsequent chapters. At the "sight" of them, the observer can be sucked in or de-positioned—up to a point where there is no longer anything concretely present

Sarcophagus of Tutankhamun

before him. He only sees the woman's thing as long as he stays before it as a frontal observer. If he chose this as his final position, he would not be a seeker in the sense of a para-metaphysical striving to contemplate the basis of things, but an observer, a voyeur, a neutralist, a scientist—for example a gynecologist, who studies the female genital system unimpressed by all effective metaphors of homecoming. At most, he could provide—as Hans Peter Duerr demonstrates in his book *Intimität* [Intimacy]—a baroque ethno-history of vulva-related ideas, practices and affects in different cultures.[9] With this relatively young cognitive attitude, it is possible to treat the vulva, as an anatomical or ethnographic object, descriptively and operatively without motivational derivatives of the post-Neolithic pushing and pulling behavior at the cave entrance coming into play. What sets positive gynecology—essentially a product of Aristotelian thoughts and its continuation in the neo-European life sciences—apart from older traditional wisdom is that it can stand fast before the once so magical female and maternal portal in an objectifying, and thus emancipating, certainty of distance. Where the investigative eye penetrates deeper, it simply produces additional surface views of levels situated further inside: uteroscopy is simply the continuation of vulvoscopy by technical means. One could call the organ image gained through this view a vulvogram. Where this is made proficiently using the imaging procedures available, the observer is not given any reason whatsoever to doubt his impartial eyesight. The visibility of the vulva as a facing object ensures that the observer is not absorbed by it. Seeing here means having the calm freedom to attain, in accordance with the axioms of the Greek epistemes and at the necessary distance from things, a dispository knowledge of them. It is quite different with the old para-metaphysical reverence before the gate to the inner world of the mother. Whoever believes in ritual acts of approach that they are standing before this entrance of all entrances, or envisages it in symbolic imagination, is immediately affected by a suction that is meant to make the beholder's senses reel. Where the real Baubo—Nietzsche's crown witness to a theory of truth made discreet once more—comes into view, seeing itself has little future. The seeker's eye here wants to, and must, be broken by its object. The pupils dilate before the sucking portal. As he comes closer, the beholder will feel as if a powerless warning legend had just glided past him: the last object before the great attainment of knowledge! And in reality, as soon as the entrants had passed through the grotto grate, they would encounter the

Udder-shaped bronze cauldron (*li*) from the early Shang Dynasty, c. 16th to 15th century BC, used for the preparation of sacrificial dishes

tropical night; and the fall of this exquisite night would mark the end of everything based on clearing, distance and concreteness. From now on, asking about the intimate has its price for the analytical intelligence too.

In the following, we shall weave the fiction that we are able to split our adventurous intelligence in such a way that one half of

IVSTI · IOVIS ARBITRATV ·

Fata homerica. Etching from J.-J. Boissard, *Emblematum liber* 1588. Even if it is the patriarch Zeus distributing the lots of fate, the lottery jars still constitute a form of hyperuterus. Whatever the nature of life, its form remains indebted to womb immanence.

it takes up position at the entry ramp to the mystical cave—still viewing it from the outside, that is—while the other half is initiated to enter the homogeneous totality of darkness. The two halves should remain in contact during the excursion—the one inside by reporting its states in the objectless sphere to the outside, and the one waiting *ante portas* by sending suggestions for the verbalization of the indescribable into the cave. This split arrangement takes into account that the focus of our investigation does not lie in the aim to produce mystical experience here and now, but rather in the project of advancing a theory of dyadic intimacy to the point where speaking theory has normally turned into silent theory. The all-too-familiar phenomenon of mystical muteness is due here to the fact that because of the observer's coalescence with the most intimate sphere, the bipolar structure of cognition and relation fades in his perception. Once the point of being-inside has been reached, all language games of observing and facing must indeed come to an end. A critical theory of being-in-the-cave only becomes possible through the introduction of a third element—in our case that means the doubling of the cave explorer, with one going bravely ahead and the other cautiously staying behind. This leads to a division of labor between yearning and skepticism, fusion and reserve. This arrangement involves conceding to the mystical tradition that the one inside will, indeed, inevitably repeat the insurmountable cave truth: that here, the One is everything. Someone who were truly all the way inside could only affirm the basic monistic doctrines of the last millennia, which the mystically interested from all areas so like to say are the same in all cultures. The observing partial intelligence at the cave entrance, on the other hand, here in the role of the participating third party, insists that whatever things the experimental mystic experiences in the cave can only be aspects of the dyad. If the pioneer claims to have found unimpaired unity within, one can tell him outright about the biune nature of his situation. In this manner, the union-mystical semblance to which the coalesced witness is exposed in the cave can be simultaneously respected and dethroned: interest in the progress of the dual theory is satisfied without having to deny the insights of mystical monism. Then the acute appearance of unity without a second element as a form of consciousness can even be understood as the most revealing figure of the bipolar-spheric coalescence taking place *in actu*. The reality of the relationship between the mother and the unborn includes, in a certain sense, the inexistence of this relationship as such for the

Lasciate ogni pensiero o voi qu'intrate: mouth of hell in the "Holy Forest" of Bomarzo, 1550–1580

child. As long as it is living inside the mother, it in fact floats in a sort of non-duality; in the perception, its containedness in the "mother" is confirmed by the termination of that connection as an acute proof of the given fusion. Whoever experiences the scene is either primarily or secondarily an *infans*, that is to say a fetus or a mystic, significantly speechless in both positions and with no connection to a facing opposite. The relation itself only exists in moments when it has to be denied or de-thematized. Part of the reality of this singular relationship is that where it exists, it precisely does *not* exist for the one contained: for the fetus there is no counterpart to which it might be interpersonally or inter-objectively related; there is nothing else to confirm its real being-in. The same applies by analogy to the mystic; in proximity to the actually present nobject, the subject

Pen and ink drawing of the mouth of hell, 1599

too is disarmed and dissolved. Taking up Thomas Macho's observations on the logic of basic psychoanalytical principles, we will examine this logical oddity—that one class of closeness relationships with the other is only real if these are denied or erased as relationships—more closely in the following.

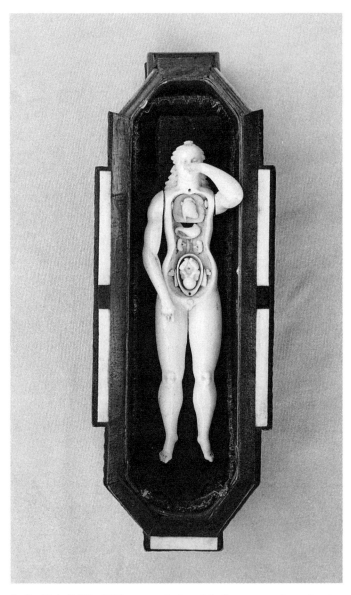

Stefan Zick (1639–1715), anatomical model of pregnancy, ivory figurine in wooden box

Excursus 2

Nobjects and Un-Relationships

On the Revision of Psychoanalytical Stage Theory

It is one of the publicized secrets of early Viennese psycho-analysis that it stopped halfway in its penetration of the intersubjective world of closeness, both in its therapeutic arrangement and its conceptual instruments. People were able to say—and rightly, for the most part—that it developed in theory and practice a system to fend off the unwelcome experiences of closeness that it inevitably brought about through its arrangement. Freud's obstinate scientism has often been the object of justified critique in recent decades—partly from a science-theoretical perspective, by proving that Viennese analysis described its own theoretical status incorrectly and sought to force a scenic-hermeneutical, language-theoretical and experience-scientific discipline into the mold of the natural sciences; and partly in psychodynamic terms, by attempting to show with what maneuvers and from what compulsive motives—mostly of matriphobic origin—the founder of Viennese psychoanalysis evaded the more disturbing deep layers in the field of intimate relationships he had newly described. All these points of criticism managed to remain immanent to the elastic approach of the Freudian model, however, and to be integrated sometimes more, sometimes less willingly by a psychoanalytical movement that was prepared to learn.

A substantially more radical critique, however, developed on a front whose development neither the immanent nor the external critics of psychoanalysis had reckoned with. It emerged from the combination of recent prenatal research and the conceptual rearrangements of the newer media philosophies. Against this background, the cultural philosopher and media anthropologist Thomas Macho has conclusively revealed a fundamental construction error in psychoanalytical terminology with reference to archaic and prenatal mother-child relationships.[10] It can indeed be shown that psychoanalytical notions of early communications are consistently formulated according to the model of object relationships—especially in the concepts of what is termed "developmental stage theory," in which one organ is bound as a subject precursor to an element from the outside world as the object pole: in the oral phase the mouth and the breast; in the anal phase the anus and its product, feces; in the genital phase the penis and the mother, as an object of love *sans phrase*. It is well known that Freud placed the fateful necessity of this third phase above everything else, because he was convinced that genuine individuation takes place as a development of sexual subjectivity in the resolution of the triangular Oedipal conflict. This, according to orthodox doctrine, marks the attainment of psychological object maturity, which is prefigured from the first time the child reaches for the mother's breast as a culturally binding and organically plausible goal of development. Macho, by contrast, has shown that the entire psychoanalytical terminology for early relationships is fundamentally deformed by the object prejudice—and beyond this, that the fixation on thinking in object relationships is responsible for the almost grotesque misunderstanding of fetal and infantile modes of reality in early psychoanalytical orthodoxy. It would then be a futile, not to say pathogenic undertaking to attempt a description of the early mother-child reality in terms of object relationships, as there are not yet any traces of subject- or object-like aspects in the actual situation. Only an elaborated theory of psychosomatic mediality could, one day, be capable of representing the intimate webs of the earliest dyads in a correspondingly finely woven language of reciprocal solubility and suspension in a bipolar ether of relationships. This would presuppose a replacement on all levels of psychological organization of the previous, eccentric and occasionally even dangerously disinformative descriptions of object relationships by medial analyses. Only through medial formulations can the mode of being in the child's earliest presentist encounters be adequately expressed in language. What is more, one must assume at least three pre-oral stages and forms of condition before the supposedly primary oral phase, each of which, in its own particular way and according to the nature of its elements, can itself already be viewed as a regime of radical mediality.

1. First of all one must conceive a phase of fetal cohabitation in which the incipient child experiences the sensory presence of liquids, soft bodies and cave boundaries: most importantly placental blood, then the amniotic fluid, the placenta, the umbilical cord, the amniotic sac and a vague prefiguring of the experience of spatial boundaries through the

resistance of the abdominal wall and elastic walling-in. A fore-taste of what will later be called reality presents itself in the form of an intermediate fluidal realm that lies embedded in a dark, spheric spatial factor softly cushioned within firmer boundaries. If there were already early "objects" in this field, their state could only ever be that of object shadows or things of emergence—contents of a first Yonder from which a first Here conceives itself, both combined in a vaguely contoured encompassing space with an increasing tendency towards tightness. Possible candidates for such object shadows are primarily the umbilical cord—which may be sensed by touch early on—and the placenta, which, like a nurturing primal companion to the fetus, has an early diffuse presence as the harbinger of a first counterpart. (The two following chapters deal with the "relationship" between the fetus/subject and the placenta/companion.) Objects that, like those we have named, are not objects because they have no subject-like counterpart, are referred to by Macho as "nobjects": they are spherically surrounding mini-conditions envisaged by a non-facing self, namely the fetal pre-subject, in the mode of non-confrontational presence as original creatures of closeness in the literal sense. Their being-close-to-here (which is precisely not yet a demonstrable being-there) communicates itself to the child most of all with its first gift, the placental blood. Among the nobjects of the earliest world of "experience," placental blood has the incontestable status of the earliest. Consequently one must assume, as the most original of the pre-oral regimes, a suspended stage whose essential content lies in the constant placenta-mediated exchange of blood between mother and child. The blood, which is not only the blood of the one, but automatically also creates the first medial "bond" between the dyadic partners interlocked in bipolar intimacy. Through the blood, the biunity is constituted as a trinitary unity from the start; the third element turns two into one. It is not for nothing that many cultures describe the closest form of connection between relatives as a blood relation; in the everyday sense this refers to the imaginary blood of family trees, but at a deeper level also implies a real blood communion: with its characterization as a network of "relatives," the archaic circulatory community is elevated to a symbolic representation. For the ancient Egyptians, it was the mother's blood that nourished the fetus by flowing down from her heart. In medieval Europe, and even into the eighteenth century, it was widely believed that unborn children survived by drinking the mother's menstrual blood.[11] In reality, the fetal *modus vivendi* can be described as a fluidal communion in the medium of blood. It lives on in all postnatally transformed fluid cultures—from drinks to baths, ablutions and aspersions. The new media-theoretical version of the intimacy motif makes it clear why blood is indeed a very special juice: it is the first material between two individuals who will one day—when they become modern people—speak on the telephone. From the start, the history of the self is first of all a history of self-conveyance. Its protagonists are beings who come from respectively unique circulatory communities and drinks communions—and who keep reviving that uniqueness in ever different translations. It is these fluidal communards that Rilke addresses in his appeal to lovers from the second *Duino Elegy*: "When you raise lips to the lips of the other, drinking each other / ...strange, how those drinkers depart from it all." It would scarcely do justice to the medium of blood, however, if one sought to interpret it as the carrier of a prenatal "dialogue" between mother and fetus; obstinate fixations on verbal communication have seduced many analysts into using the misleading term "dialogue" to describe medial exchange in the archaic dyad, and even the great psychologist René A. Spitz showed a lack of the necessary acumen in tolerating a media-theoretical absurdity in the title of his well-known book *Vom Dialog* [On Dialogue].[12]

2. The second aspect of the pre-oral media field concerns the psychoacoustic initiation of the fetus into the uterine sound world. It is logical that acoustic events can only be given in the nobject mode—for sonorous presences have no tangible substrate that could be encountered in the attitude of standing opposite something. From the physiology of listening as a state of being set in sympathetic vibration, it is evident that acoustic experiences are media processes which cannot possibly be represented in languages of object relationships. This applies, incidentally, to the position of open air listening as much as to the fetal position, which is why music is the continuum art *par excellence*; listening to music always means being-in-music,[13] and in this sense Thomas Mann was right to call music a demonic realm—when listening, one is genuinely possessed by sound at that moment. (As far as the formation of intimacy through fetal acoustics is concerned—especially as discussed in the extensive research of Alfred A. Tomatis—we will examine this in Chapter 7 below. It is not least the medial character of the amniotic fluid, which transforms sound waves into vibrations of auditory and full bodily relevance, that becomes apparent in the light of this research; but the transmission of sound through bone seems even more significant.) Macho, for

his part, places less emphasis on the fetal bonding through the mother's voice than on the immediate postnatal self-experience of the newborn in the use of its own voice, which secures the connection to the mother outside the bodily enclosure as a vocal-magical medium. As a form of acoustic umbilical cord, it offers a replacement for the lost actual umbilical connection; Macho emphasizes that this coming together through listening in the extra-uterine dyad remains the nucleus of all communal formations, and that connection to others through acoustic umbilical cords is the central principle of psychosocial synthesis.[14] At the same time, a pre-oral, medial ego core develops in the child when it hears its own voice; the incipient subject's lifelong history of mediations with itself and its vocal extensions begins in crying, crowing, babbling and word-making; this is where the archaic production pole of music and the art of language is located. That is why Macho speaks of a vocal-auditory phase in the pre-oral space.[15] Because voices are not objects, however, it is impossible to have a "relationship" with them in the usual sense of the word. Voices produce acoustic coverings of spheric-presentist expansion, and the only mode of participation in vocal presences can be described as being-in within the current sonosphere;[16] the vocal umbilical cord, like the physical one, is also nobjectal in its structure. When the mother and her child exchange vocal messages in a direct play of affection, their interdependency is the perfect self-realization of an intimate-acoustic bipolar sphere.

3. The third pre-oral phase that needs to be newly conceived is referred to by Macho as the "respiratory" phase. In truth, the newborn child's first partner in the outside world— before any contact with the surface of the mother's skin—is

the air it breathes, which now replaces the lost amniotic fluid as the successive element. The air is also a medial factor, and as such it can never be defined in object terms. For the child, extra-maternal being-in-the-world first and last of all means being-in-the-air and participating without struggles—following an episode of initiatory breathing difficulty—in the wealth of this medium. The air, as experienced in the child's first encounter with it, possesses unmistakable nobject properties, as it affords the incipient subject a first chance at self-activity in respiratory autonomy, but without ever appearing as a thing with which to have a relationship. It is no coincidence that until recently, no psychoanalyst—except for the belated fluidist Wilhelm Reich—had anything quoteworthy to say about the complex of air, breath and self,[17] probably because even the simplest breath analysis would have revealed how fundamentally inappropriate it is to speak in terms of object relationships.[18] Precisely the most elementary medial process, taken on its own terms, would have made psychoanalytical pretensions and conceptual habits come to nothing. Macho concludes his deliberations with the observation that even in its theoretical language, psychoanalysis has remained a prisoner to old Western grammar, even where it has long discovered reasons in its encounter arrangements to sublate ostensible subject-object relationships into medial processes. Only through a revision of its basic principles could psychoanalysis—which, in its theoretical and therapeutic potential, is still the most interesting interpersonal practice of closeness in the modern world—present itself in a suitable language of closeness. Then it could state openly that every animation is a media event, and that all psychological disturbances are distortions of participation—

media sicknesses, one could say. The fixation on objects is itself the logical matrix of neurosis. It need hardly be pointed out which civilization suffers from this like no other.

What, after all this, is negative gynecology? It is first of all a method to ensure that the woman and her organs do not enter any form of objectivity. A gynecology is negative or philosophical if it maintains a renunciation of two things: the obvious possibility of looking at the vulva from the outside and conceiving it as an object (gynecological and pornographic vulvograms); and the temptation, never entirely absent, to pass through the vulva again as an initiation, as the gate to the inner world. Once these two attitudes and modes of perception are disabled, the nobject character of the female non-opening can be made apparent with ease. It is the non-thing experienced by every naturally born individual in a single sequence of events; it is the narrow primal something that only "exists" once in an unrepeatable, dramatically extended scene. What the observing intelligence before the cave views as the soft female organ is experienced by the half that has entered, if it wishes to be reborn, as a giver of the most monstrous severity. In the nobject view, this organ which, understood as an object, seems familiar, straightforward, congenial and yielding, is a tunnel of decision in which the fetus is motivated to brace itself and become the ultimate breakthrough, a "here I come" projectile. Conceived as a medium, the birth canal or vulva convey the present experience that there is an impenetrable wall which must at once also be an opening; this opening is a function of banging one's head against a wall. For the new arrival, the hopelessness of standing before the wall turns directly into the compulsion to break through it. As a nobject, the vulva is the mother of granite. It is evidently impossible to penetrate this wall at the moment of struggle; by passing through it nonetheless somehow, however, *in extremis*, the initiate who exits experiences himself as the harder stone, the stone that breaks stone. For most of the born, being born means defeating a wall.

The arrangement suggested above, where the cave explorer is split into two halves, and one dissolves experimentally in the dark interior while the other captures the diurnal worldview outside, seems eminently suitable for gleaning nobject research results first hand; it feigns something that psychoanalysis cannot presuppose, namely the existence of a fetus that is capable of description. The inside part would then be a sentient probe in a state of uterine immersion; it would only have to avoid being silently fulfilled in the experience and instead, supported by the part keeping guard outside, remain capable of intellectual satisfaction as a phenomenologist of its own being-in-the-cave—in Heideggerian terms, its not-yet-thrownness.

Chinese traditions from the heyday of Taoism provide an eminent example of the paradoxical position of being-outside-and-inside-at once. The legend about the birth of the master Lao Tzu, almost unknown in the West, perfectly illustrates the phantasm of a pregnancy incorporating both a maturing time

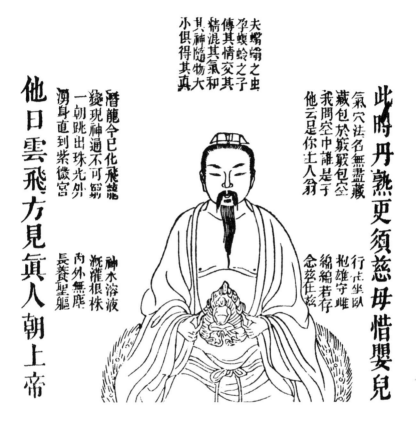

"The Genesis of the Newborn": meditation image from Taoist alchemy. The union of *k'an* and *li* produces an embryo that represents the immortal soul created by Taoists.

within the cave and studies outside of it. In the ancient Chinese worldview, the implantation of the child in the womb was already considered the actual birth. The intrauterine period was thus included in the reckoning of human age; newborns were termed one-year-olds. The ten lunar cycles of the intrauterine night form the equivalent of a solar year. In addition, the inner life constitutes a proportional equivalent of outer existence: because the mother's gestation period provides a model for the actual lifetime, its duration determines the length of existence in the outside world. Ten moons correspond to the life span of an ordinary human; divine heroes remain in the womb for twelve months, the great wise men for eighteen. Lao Tzu's life in the inner world, which is given as eighty-one years, indicates a longevity equal to that of heaven and earth: it is the full cycle of earthly time as a gestation period.[19] In Taoist doctrine—as often expressed by Chuang Tzu—the inner always takes precedence over the outer. The central principle of the divine sphere in Taoism is the True One, which inhabits the inner realm as an immortal embryo. Theogonic tales describe in manifold variations the former life of Lao Tzu in his mother Li, who has been known since the 4th century as "Mother Plum Tree, Jade Maiden of the Obscure Mystery."[20] In his sympathetic study on the mystical and social physics of Taoism, the Sinologist Kristofer Schipper reproduces a version of Lao Tzu's birth myth he wrote down in Taipei in August 1979 after the oral account of a 74-year-old Taoist master:

> There was once an old woman who belonged to the clan of the Pure Ones. The Old Lord did not have a name. One might say that originally he was an incarnation. He was born in (the womb of) a chaste woman. She had no husband, but had become pregnant after absorbing a drop of "sweet dew."[21] Her belly grew bigger, that is to say, during the day she was pregnant; but she was not pregnant at night, for then the Old Lord would leave her body to go study the Tao, and so he was not there.

This Old Lord was not just anyone! Having taken the form of an embryo in his mother's belly, he wished to delay his birth to the day when there would be neither birth nor death in the world. Thus he waited for more than eighty years, unable to appear.

The God of the Underworld and the God of Heaven spoke to each other, saying: "This here is the incarnation of the Constellation of Destiny. How can we not let him be born? Let us choose a day when we allow neither birth nor death so that he may be born on that day."

It was the fifteenth day of the second moon. On that day the Old Lord was born. He came into the world through his mother's armpit [author's note: cf. the birth of Gautama Buddha through his mother's hip]. At that very moment, oh! his hair and beard were all white. Since he knew how to walk, he set off right away.

His mother said to him: "You! My old child! Why are you leaving without letting me have a look at you? Why are you going off as soon as you're born? I won't even know how to recognize you later!" so he turned around abruptly, his beard and hair flying… Seeing him, his mother took a fright. She fainted and died on the spot.

He continued to walk straight ahead, without stopping until he reached a plum orchard. There he leaned against a tree and said to himself: "I know neither my name nor my family. I am leaning against this plum tree [*li*]. Why not take *Li* as my family name? And what should be my personal name? My mother called me 'old child'! So, my name will be 'Lao Tzu.'"

"Old Lord" is a title of respect. In fact, his name is "Old Child."[22]

History of a scandal and initiatic tale: Schipper's characterization of the myth points both to its intimately didactic function and its paradoxically self-entwined metaphysical logic. It would require an extensive study to probe its full implications: Lao Tzu's fatherlessness; the mystical self-fertilization of his mother; his heterologous birth through the (left) armpit; the numerological implications of the number 81; the refusal of birth and the call for a birthless and deathless world; the date chosen by the gods; the immediate separation of the old child from the mother; her death from fright upon seeing her monstrous offspring; the genealogical zero point situation and his self-naming; the connection to fruit tree culture[23]—all this would, among other things, demand detailed narrative-theoretical, culture-historical, cosmological and religion-philosophical explications. We shall limit ourselves to two aspects of this unusual story: the motif of the learned embryo and the relationships between being-in-the-mother and experience in the world. In both cases, one finds a natural link to our methodic trick of connecting uterine immanence and external observation despite the strict impossibility of their simultaneity. What else would the fetal student of the Tao, who exits his mother at night and lives in her belly during the day, be but a precise embodiment of the notion that it is possible to overcome the difference between being inside and being outside in a unity of a higher order? If one looks more closely, the reference to Lao Tzu's nocturnal study trips outside his mother transpires as a union-mystical thought figure: it makes it clear that the divine sage cannot have reached the maternal interior through external conception; what appears to be the mother's body is in fact its inhabitant's own creation. The difference between inside and outside is itself located within

Lao Tzu's interior: the child contains the mother and the child—it is not for nothing that Lao Tzu is known as the Old Child who constitutes the fetus and the cosmos in one. Even if the text does not explicitly state that the sage is his own mother, the tale's immanent logic unmistakably leads towards this thesis. Someone who spends eighty-one years in the womb must himself be the lord of the inner world; the external mother can only appear as a shell and supplement, which is why his separation from her is so easily achieved. In other variations on the myth, Lao Tzu actually projects his mother Li outwards from within himself in order to enter his own uterine form. If, after eighty-one years of gestation, everything external—even death—has been taken up into the internal, and no event from the non-interior can surprise the perfect sage anymore, the mother must not remain any real external factor. The mythical act takes place in the form of a paradoxical loop; what the mother has to give to the fetus is in fact what the fetus gives itself through the mother—the eternal capacity for being-inside in deathless, self-circling being. The sage is born so that he will not simply enter the world as a born mortal; he enters a mother's womb precisely to avoid entering a short-lived human life cycle. Other variations on the myth not mentioned here have a similarly paradoxical form; in these, the short phase of encounter between mother and child is described as a time in which Lao Tzu is initiated by his mother into the very secret of longevity that is already demonstrated by his overextended stay in the womb. The same paradox reappears in the circumstance that Lao Tzu is born on a day when birth and death do not exist—his birth is not a birth into the outside world, and his emergence remains a movement within outsideless immanence. Thus the Taoist sage ultimately views himself as a gestating woman who is pregnant with himself; the finite maternal gives birth to the infinite maternal that spawned it. The maternal has the power to keep the very difference between outside and inside on the inside. Self-referential paradoxes of this kind belong to the inventory of logical forms in all metaphysical systems where the infinite is supposed to be made manifest in finite media. The finite Son of God who wandered around the Sea of Galilee also became known as his own infinite father via the paradox of the Trinity. This paradox appears slightly more extreme in the New Testament Apocrypha, in which Jesus was supposedly an angel among angels before his incarnation; as the angel Gabriel he brought his own mother the annunciation of his birth.[24] When the legendary Saint Christopher carries the baby Jesus across the water while the infant holds the entire globe in the palm of his hand, an equally paradoxical question is raised: where is Saint Christopher to place his feet while carrying the boy, when the river he is wading through is undoubtedly part of the world held by the child riding on his shoulders?

Taoism arrives—assuming these sparse intimations have such far-reaching consequences—if not at a negative, then at least a polarity-philosophical gynecology. The abstractions in its conception of the world have not yet been taken to the point of making the dyad invisible. In its most sublime concepts of unity, the bipolar mediation and reciprocal animation of child and mother are present as leitmotifs. From its ontology of uterine immanence it derives that ethic of feminization for which it has recently also become known in the West. "Know the male but cling to the female; become the valley of the world" (*Tao Te*

Ching, Chapter 28). As far as the inner realm is concerned, its approach is admittedly more evocative than investigative. The learned embryo that slips out of the cave at night to study the Tao explores not so much its own small, dark cave, but rather the great round object that is the illuminated world cave. If we desire more concrete psychophysiological insights into the form of being in the narrow, unlit cave, we must look around for the findings that other researchers, both outside and inside the cave, have brought to light.

One of the outstanding pioneers of modern psychognostic cave research is the psychosis therapist and psychoanalyst Ronald D. Laing (1927–1989). He gained his reputation as an avant-gardist of psychological theorizing through the radical derestriction of the psychogenetic model and an opening towards ultra-deep sources of mental disturbance; in his famous knot models he described interpersonal closeness as spindles or whirls of intertwined expectations and expectations of expectations—the absurd theater of intimacy. As a therapist, he impressed his contemporaries with his self-endangering determination to accompany the mentally ill into even the most extreme states. Laing was disposed to cave research chiefly because he did not enter the inward path merely in search of happiness; for him, the cave was not only a place where thought ends in gratification, but equally a source from which the oldest pain and the earliest injuries could flow into the present of a disturbed life. (From which follows the epistemological maxim that analysis goes further than illumination.)

Laing sought to balance out the existential hindrance that the researcher naturally has no access to the cave of the past any longer through the method of free regressive association.

He analyzed the cave indirectly by reading the current mental traces of being-formerly-inside-it as indications of the original situation, and then elaborating them into theoretical notions; his method follows the model of the scenic-autobiographical exploration technique in psychoanalysis. In the notorious fifth chapter of *The Facts of Life* from 1976, which deals with life before birth, the author developed a three-stage schema that places disproportionate emphasis on inner stages, with no consideration of outer duration. According to Laing's concept, two out of three acts in our life "cycle" fall into the category of prenatal "existence." Our quotations will show that the civil war between philosophy and common sense which had affected the intellectual balance of occidental civilization since the founding of Plato's Academy, if not earlier, returned after its apparent subsidence as a civil war between depth psychology and vulgar ontology. Idea-historically speaking, Laing's speculations are obviously close to the counterculture movement and orientalism of the 1960s.

Stages in My Life

A	conception to implantation
B	implantation to birth
C	my postnatal life
M0	mother before conception
M1	mother from conception to implantation
M1.1	mother from implantation to completion of birth
M2	postnatal mother

One of our great tasks seems to be coming to the realization that $M0 = M1 = M2$

Do we have a genetic mental map of our whole life cycle with its different phases—mental patterns which reflect biological forms and transforms?

It seems to me credible, at least, that all our experience in our life cycle from cello one is absorbed and stored from the beginning, perhaps especially in the beginning. How that may happen, I do not know.

How can one cell generate the billions of cells I now am?

We are impossible, but for the fact that we are.

When I look at embryological stages in my life cycle I experience what feel to me like sympathetic reverberations, vibrations in me now with how I now feel I felt then.

Photographs, illustrations, films of early embryological stages films of early embryological stages of our life cycle often move people very much.

If you were to die now, and be reconceived tonight which woman would you choose to spend the first nine months of your next lifetime inside of? That many people feel similar, and often strong, *sympathetic vibrations* (resonances, reverberations) when they unguardedly allow themselves to imagine how they might have felt from conception to and through birth and early infancy is a *fact*.[25]

Laing's meditation on the form of the life cycle resembles the ancient Chinese view in significant aspects—in particular, his insistence that this cycle does not only begin at birth, but rather at conception, expressly restores to the cave year its dignity as the defining introit of every biographical form. The implantation of the fertilized egg cell in the uterus would then have to be taken seriously as the primal event in a life's history, even if no one can be sure whether it has an experienceable side and a projective repetition thereof in later experiences. One can read this as if, through his inclusion of the earliest stage, Laing had sought to escape the conspiracy against the unborn in which almost all those social authorities of modernity—including women—that wish to make abortions a matter of course directly or indirectly participate. One can perceive figures of a less Taoist than Platonizing cast in Laing's view that an overarching memory of all states and changes is built up from the first cell. Hence the strong feelings that can arise from involuntary contact with embryonic motifs in humans, according to Laing, have the character of reminiscences; they are a mode of self-experience in archaic material. The starting point of Laing's attack on both the vulgar and normal psychoanalytical worldviews is his radically monadological imposition of understanding the life cycle as the *Bildungsroman* of the ovum. This ovum, Laing argues, is not sheltered within an inner world *a priori*, but must first attain its protected interior position through a hazardous transition.

Implantation

Implantation may have been as horrific and as wonderful as birth; Reverberating through our lives, and being resonated by experiences of being sucked in, drawn in, pulled in, dragged down; of being rescued, revived, succoured, welcomed; of trying to get in, but being kept out; perishing through fatigue, exhaustion; frantic, helpless, impotent, etc. [...] To put my proposition succinctly: birth is implantation in reverse and the reception one receives from the postnatal world generates a sympathetic resonance in us of our first adoption by our prenatal world. (pp. 45f.)

Contrary to the impression these lines may give, Laing is not only interested in a historical monadology—the epic tale of the destinies of the ovum as a unity; beyond that, the history of the egg is the history of its embedding in a pre-objective space as such.

The world is my womb, and my mother's womb was my first world.
    the *womb* is the first of the series

                  of contexts
                  containers
                  whatever one is *in*
                  a room
                  a space
                  a time
                  a relationship
                  a mood

            whatever is
                around
                whoever[26]

is felt as
around me
one's atmosphere
one's *circum*stances
one's surroundings
the world.[27] (pp. 45f.)

Starting from these associative notes about being-contained in surroundings, Laing sketches a delirious diagram that connects the myth of the hero's birth—based on Otto Rank's famous study—to the egg as the cellular hero. Here the author stops asserting facts in well-formed sentences; instead, he covers the page before him with word lists, individual words and blocks whose placing on the page hints at connections in their content. They can best be read from left to right as parallels.

BLASTULA

… a dome of many-colored glass that stains the white radiance of eternity

a geodesic dome	a space capsule
a sphere	flying saucer
a balloon	sun-god
the moon	football

the zygote and blastula in the zona pellucida

zona pellucida	a box	first clothing
	a casket	
	an ark	
	a swan	

uterine tube	the water	the ocean	a river

journey along uterine tube time in ocean,
                          or drifting down river,
to implantation in womb till picked up
                          by animals or shepherds, etc.

thus conception	in myths birth
uterine journey	exposure to sea or river in

	a box or casket
implantation	adoption by animals
uterine endometrium	or reception by lowly people

I am not considering whether these analogues are "right," if that is a sensible issue, but merely that they are actual. All of them I have heard or read, as well as made myself, before or after having heard or read them.

May there be a placental-umbilical-uterine stage of development preceding the breast-oral stage? (p. 59)

We have quoted so extensively so that we can at least use Laing's example to illustrate fluctuations between regular argumentation and dreamy association. His cave probings do not only work with the known methods of psychoanalytical affect recollections; if one assesses Laing's procedure in his theoretical-autobiographical experiment as the creative projection of an archaic spatial understanding, one might conclude that the associative lists on the loosely written pages are themselves related to their amorphous object in a quasi-representational fashion. They make it clear that there are no well-formed sentences in the place from which the author is attempting to speak; intrauterine daydreams know no orderly lines of text— at this point, everything that will later belong to the syntactic realm is only distantly sensed. Fetal being-in-space is indeed reproduced more accurately in the fragmentary, sentenceless floating of key terms in a bubble than by discourses. Because Laing dreams his way eccentrically into the fetal position in the act of writing, his thought develops a creatively vague solubility; his text aims for a suspension in a space with neither verbs nor a thesis—a dreamtime of reason in which the possible reabsorbs the real. Words glide across the pages like daydreams, part of an amorphous text that precedes all other texts. It would thus seem that the biographical-speculative daydream itself takes on a fetality-mimetic quality. Nothing is genuinely stated in it, no system is built, and no sentence is sent off into the real domain; contemplation remains entirely in that possibility-shaped guise which fully formed discourses discard in order to say something; it is where deconstructions seek to return. No more is given of the things that could be said than a semantic plasma— the dream of a true context that, appearing as a thesis, would definitely be a mistaken one.

If it were permissible to draw conclusions from Laing's cave-daydream experiment about the nature of its object, a first finding would be this: the cave is a container to which the inhabitant can only gain access as an intruder. First of all, it is necessary to move into the uterine home in a daring act of approach. Whether implantation processes, be they smooth or problematic, can leave traces within the experiential is, of course, impossible to determine; the question could not even be posed without a certain inclination towards ovular Platonism. After implantation, however, intrauterinity means freedom from drama and decision-making. From that point until the final period of narrowness, the sojourn in the uterine interior has a floating character throughout; the fetus is submerged in dream-like indecision, but gradually dreams its way forward. It does not yet know any "superstitious belief in the existent"; as a floating being, it keeps itself at the zero point of sentences—in the neutral core of the slumbering concatenations, as if pre-syntactically sovereign. If the fetus already had a conception of the world, its relationship to it would be that of Romantic irony; the mute sovereign would make every figure melt down to its foundation; if it already had a conception of logic, it would be a monovalent one that distinguished neither between true and false nor between real and unreal, as in certain Indian mythologies where the world appears as the dream of a god: for the god, nothing really happens in the phenomenal hurricane of events, desires and sorrows.[28] The fetal sensibility is one of "medial indifference";[29] it occupies a medial position in which an incipient extension begins to become apparent. For the fetus of the optimal floating months, there is truth in Friedlaender's aphorism: "Indifference is the immaculate conception of the whole world."[30] In kinetic terms, the fetal sensibility means a suspension that is in the process of gathering coercive weight; though entirely locked in its maternal retreat, it is affected by a pretendentious swelling. Despite some aspects of Nirvana, the arrows of tendency springing up in it point towards the world—or, carefully put, towards something. Through this incubation-towards-the-world—and through a first shadowy defining of polarity in a medial exchange with inner nobjects— the fetus, though it perhaps fulfills certain attributes of the divine, eludes the extreme idealizations of mystical theologies— such as the uncompromisingly negative image of Nirguna-Brahman painted by the Indian logician Shankara: a God without qualities who sits enthroned above mountains of negations. In its bland, slightly tonicized sub-euphoric dark gray, everyday fetal life contradicts the para-theological phantasms of some psychoanalysts, who saw fit to effuse about a fetal "I-am-who-I-am" and intrauterine feelings of omnipotence, immortality and purity.[31] Compared to such flights of fancy, Kazimir Malevich's

Black Circle offers a realistic snapshot of fetal reality. Whatever truth there might be in the equation of the womb and Nirvana, one certainly cannot claim that the incipient individual experiences a state of complete emptiness at any point. The fetus with which the mother is pregnant is itself pregnant with its own tendency to fill out its space and affirm itself within it. The child's movements, with their cheerfully enigmatic "cat in the bag" impressions, testify to this intra-uterine expansionism. And recent findings in the field of psychoacoustic fetal research dismiss any such illusions about an initial emptiness of experience once and for all: the floating being in the amniotic waters inhabits an acoustic event space in which its sense of hearing is subjected to constant stimulation.[32]

No author of the twentieth century has found such evocative formulations for the tendentious nature of fetal swelling as the expressionist Schellingian Marxist Ernst Bloch. In the generative center of his reflection we find a changing figure of pregnancy-mimetic character. Bloch sees tensions of tendency arising from the darkness of the lived moment in every conscious life, and these move towards clearing, world formation and liberation by turning to the concrete. His famous initiatory formulas are like mottos of a fetality that has been made to speak:

OUT OF ITSELF
I am. But I do not have myself. Thus we are only becoming.

The am of *I am* is within. And everything within is wrapped in its own darkness. It must emerge to see itself; to see what it is, and what lies about it.[33]

TOO CLOSE TO IT

So I am at myself. But the *am* precisely does not have itself; we only live it aimlessly. Everything here can only be sensed, quietly boiling and quietly roaring. I can certainly sense it, but this too hardly stands out. Almost everything in this sentient muffledness of mere living still restrains itself...

ROTATION IN VIEW

We do not, at any rate, see what we experience. Whatever is to be seen must be turned before our eyes...

(*Experimentum Mundi, Frage, Kategorien des Herausbringens, Praxis*)[34]

If one reads these darkness-to-light formulas as peri-natal figures of the urge to be born, there is an error of number: from a psychological perspective, coming-into-the-world precisely does not mean the movement from I to We, but rather the splitting of the archaic biune We into the ego and its second element, simultaneously crystallizing out the third. This splitting is possible because the medially conditioned nature of the biunity means that it always has three parts; in undistorted developments, the dyadic triad is always simply reshuffled, concretized, expanded and modernized:

1 fetus—2 (placental blood/mother's blood)—3 mother;
1 newborn—2 (own voice/mother's voice/mother's milk)
    —3 mother;
1 child—2 (language/father/mother's partner)—3 mother.

Because the middle element gains complexity, the child gradually develops into a competent exponent of its cultural system. The trinitary structure of the primary dyad is given from the start, however. What we call "mother and child" in the abbreviated terms of subject-object language are, in their mode of being, only ever poles of a dynamic in-between.

Therefore, as follows from these reflections, there can be nothing in the earliest life of the psyche that one could rightly describe as "primary narcissism." Rather, there is a relationship of strict mutual exclusivity between the primary and the narcissistic. The confused narcissism concepts of psychoanalysis are above all an expression of its fundamentally skewed conceptual disposition, and of the way it was misled by the object and imago concepts. The true issues of the primary fetal and peri-natal world— blood, amniotic fluid, voice, sonic bubble and breath—are media of a pre-visual universe in which mirror concepts and their libidinous connotations are entirely out of place. The child's earliest "auto"eroticisms are *eo ipso* based on games of resonance, not mirrorings of the self. Hence the mature subject status lies not in the supposed turn towards the object, but rather in the ability to master inner and outer acts at higher medial levels; for the adult subject, that includes libidinous genital resonance with sexual partners—which presupposes a well-tempered departure from the oldest media and their sublation in the later ones. This is what a media-theoretically reformulated theory of sexuality would have to show.

In our exploration of the space of bipolar intimacy, these references to the fetal retreat within the mother have brought us into contact with the outside of the inner ring. Of all the things we have said here we shall, in the following, hold onto the fact that through the basic rule of a negative gynecology one must reject the temptation to extricate oneself from the affair with outside views of the mother-child relationship; where the concern is insight into intimate connections, outside observation is already the fundamental mistake. The intimate Atlantis cannot be moved to rise from the sea again for the purpose of its exploration; and it is even less feasible to go on direct diving missions as a researcher. Because the lost continent lies sunken in time, not space, the only means of reconstruction are archeological—especially the reading of traces in ancient emotional finds. The current Atlanteans, the new fetuses, refuse to give us information; yet we should no longer draw the wrong conclusions from their silence. By observing incipient life with delicate empiricism, one can attempt to sketch outlines of its being-in-the-cave.

Excursus 3

The Egg Principle

Internalization and Encasement

> Omne vivum ex ovo.
> Omne ovum ex ovario.
> — Eduard von Hartmann, *The Philosophy of the Unconscious*[35]

On the title copperplate of William Harvey's animal encyclopedia *De generatione animalium* from 1651 we see the hand of
Jupiter, father of the gods, holding an egg in two halves.
Numerous creatures have hatched from it, including a child, a
dolphin, a spider and a grasshopper, and it bears a legend: *ex
ovo omnia*. In the hour of modern biology's birth, the philosophy of origin was allowed—as if for the last time—to be the
force behind the publication of the very thing that forced its
demise. The ovum of the biologists is no longer the egg of the
mythologists of origin; nonetheless, the incipient modern life
sciences also fall back on the old cosmogonic motif of the genesis
of all life, indeed the world as a whole, from an original egg.
Through its magical symmetry and its quintessential form, the
egg had served as the primal symbol for the cosmization of
chaos since Neolithic conceptions of the world. It could be

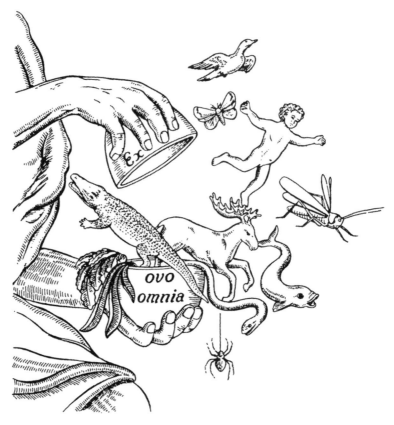

Detail from the frontispiece of Willam Harvey, *De generatione animalium*, 1651

used to show, with the self-evidence of elemental ideas, that natal creations always constitute a bipartite action: firstly the production of the egg through a maternal power, and secondly the self-liberation of the living being from its initial capsules or shells. Thus the egg is a symbol that teaches us, of its own accord, to think of the sheltering form and its bursting as a unity. The origin would not be itself if what emerged from it did not free itself from it. It would be rendered powerless as the origin, however, if it were unable to bind its products to itself again; where being is interpreted through emergence, the original bond ultimately negates freedom. Because of the parametaphysical need for form, the broken vessels cannot have the last word on the true shape of the whole, and so what is inevitably lost in each individual case is restored on the larger scale as the unlosable overall shell encompassing the world and life; the celestial domes of ancient times were set up as cosmic guarantees that isolated human existence would remain encompassed by indestructible containers beyond its exit from capsules and caves. That is why, in the classical age, existence never means suspendedness in nothingness,[36] only the move from the narrowest shell to more distant proximity.

The transition from the mythology of origin to the biology of the egg in the work of William Harvey is not without a certain objective irony; just this once, it is science that goes further and speaks more effusively in the definition of an object than myth. Harvey's investigations reinforce the egg principle to an overwhelming extent, expanding and universalizing it. In this singular matter, demystifying the myth means generalizing the object of examination in an unprecedented fashion. Although Harvey had no sufficiently powerful microscope at his disposal, he developed individual observations into the hypothesis, later triumphantly confirmed, that the embryos of all living beings come from egg cells, most of which—unlike the more noticeable eggs of birds and reptiles—are inconspicuous, even invisible to the human eye. More than a generation after Harvey, the Dutch amateur biologist and microscope builder Anton van Leeuwenhoek (1632–1723) showed that numerous small creatures do not result from

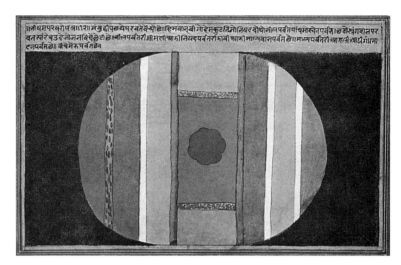

The Primal Separation Within the World Egg, Rajastan/India, 18th century, gouache on paper

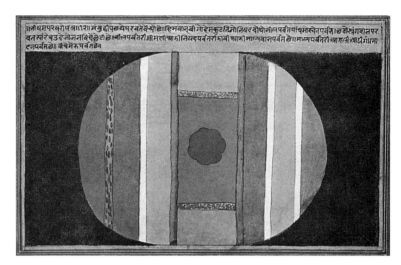

spontaneous generation in different creative milieus, as had long been thought, but rather from tiny eggs placed in the sand, wheat or mud by their mothers. Thus myth was outdone by science; in the ontogenesis of sexually reproducing life forms, the egg phenomenon was assigned a quasi-universality of which even the mythologists of origin had never dared to dream. It is only with the egg principle that the ontogenetic motif of living things emerging into the open from a place inside gained its maximum biological validity. The egg is the only cell able to survive outside of the organism that produces it; it thus acts as the model for the idea of the microcosmic monad. The relationship between the egg and the non-egg prefigures all theorems of the organism in its environment. One could almost say that later monadologies and system theories are merely exegeses of the egg phenomenon. From the perspective of the egg as a gamete, every environment becomes a specific being-around-for-what-emerges-from-the-egg.

Understood as in its biological universality, the egg instructs biological thought to give the endogenesis of the living priority over all external relationships; as a consequence, being outside can now only ever be a continuation of being inside in a different milieu. Thus the earliest form of what would later be called the "autopoiesis" of systems established itself from a reproduction-biological perspective. For the Modern Age, being-from-the-egg became the emergency situation of endogenesis. For living things, existence now means—more bindingly than in all mythology—coming-from-within. The containers functioning as eggs, whether membranes, gelatinous capsules or shells, represent the boundary principle; they seal off the inner from the outer. At the same time, they allow highly selective communications between the egg and its environment—such as exchange of moisture and ventilation. As materialized entities for differentiating between inside and outside, shells and membranes thus act as media amid border traffic. In accordance with the specific needs of the inner world, they only permit an extremely reduced amount of external information and substances through: primarily gas, warmth and liquid.

As far as human embryogenesis is concerned, it is subject—as among the related warm-blooded, live-bearing mammals—to the evolutionarily late and highly jeopardous condition that the egg is no longer deposited in external media or containers, as with the vast majority of species, but rather implanted in the mother organism itself. This internalization of the egg assumes such revolutionary organ creations as utero-genesis and placentogenesis—in organ-historical terms, transformations of the yolk system into womb-immanent nest and nourishment systems. It is in these that the evolutionary sources of hominid-typical interiority lie; only through them are births necessitated as tribe-historically new event types in the ontogenetic process. Because of inward ovulation, the exit from the womb ascends to the position of the proto-drama of animal emergence. It supplies the primal type of an ontic change of location that is of ontological relevance: through birth, that which is close and innermost is abandoned to an inescapable tearing-open by the distant. What in ontological terms is openness to the world is ontically co-conditioned by the compulsion to be born. The luxuriant development towards the interiorization of the egg—along with the chronic, endogenous ovulation cycles—creates the background for the hazardous gain of the outside through the new organism.

In warm-blooded live-bearing mammals, birth constitutes a triple shell rupture: firstly, the bursting of the amniotic sac, which must ensure the separateness of the fetus in the maternal milieu as an elastic equivalent of the eggshell; secondly, the exit from the uterus through the uterine orifice—the organic exodus made possible by the contractions; and thirdly, the passage through the birth canal into the extra-maternal, *completely other* milieu, which transpires as the true outside world compared to the intrauterinity and amniotic immanence. From a topological perspective, however, this process of triple de-shelling does not necessarily plunge the infant into a shelless mode of being because, under normal conditions, the lasting proximity of the mother compensates, as the spheric fourth shell, for the loss of the material first three. This muted change of milieu from an inner to an outer uterine space takes place among all higher

Detail from Hieronymus Bosch, *The Garden of Earthly Delights*

life forms that produce highly immature and nest-dependent offspring. Hence all these life forms are essentially psychopathizable: their maturation to participation in adult games of behavior can be distorted through injury of the extra-uterine fourth shell. Among all creatures, *homo sapiens* enjoys—along with his pets—the precarious privilege of finding it the easiest to become psychotic, in so far as one understands psychosis as the trace of the failed change of shells. It is the result of that miscarriage which each of us, as the suffering-attuned subject of a mis-move into the crutchless and shelless realm, represents. Using this notion of psychosis as the reverberation of an earlier spheric catastrophe, it becomes clear why psychosis has to be the latent primal theme of modernity. Because the process of modernity implies an initiation of humanity into the absolute outside, a theory of substantial modernization can only lead to credible and existentially handleable formulations as a transcript of the

Fortunius Licetus, *Head of Medusa, Found in an Egg*, frontispiece of *De Monstris*, 1665

ontological process psychosis. As the age of the systematic shifting of boundaries, collective husk pathologies and epidemic shell disturbances, the current epoch calls for a historical anthropology of processive madness.

Excursus 4

"In Dasein There Lies an Essential Tendency towards Closeness."[37]

Heidegger's Doctrine of Existential Place

Only a few Heidegger exegetes seem to have realized that the sensational programmatic title of *Sein und Zeit* also contains an embryonically revolutionary treatise on being and space. Under the spell of Heidegger's existential analytics of time, it has mostly been overlooked that this is rooted in a corresponding analytics of space, just as the two in turn rest on an existential analytics of movement. That is why one can read an entire library about Heidegger's doctrine of temporalization [*Zeitigung*] and historicity—ontochronology—and a few studies on his principles of movedness [*Bewegtheit*] and ontokinetics, but nothing—aside from unquotable pietistic paraphrases—on his work towards a theory of the original admission of space,[38] or ontotopology.

Heidegger's analytics of existential spatiality arrives at a positive tracing of the spatiality of Dasein as *approach* and *orientation* in two destructive steps. And indeed, the spatial concepts of vulgar physics and metaphysics must be done away with before one can address the existential analytics of being-in.

What is meant by "*Being-in*"? Our proximal reaction is to round out this expression to "Being-in 'in the world,'" and we are inclined to understand this Being-in as "Being in something" ["Sein in..."]. This latter term designates the kind of Being which an entity has when it is "in" another one, as the water is "in" the glass, or the garment is "in" the cupboard. [...] Both water and glass, garment and cupboard, are "in" space and "at" a location, and both in the same way. This relationship of Being can be expanded: for instance, the bench is in the lecture-toom, the lecture-room is in the university, the university is in the city, and so on, until we can say that the bench is "in world-space." All entities whose Being "in" one another can thus be described have the same kind of Being—that of Being-present-at-hand—as Things occurring "within" the world. [...]

Being-in, on the other hand, is a state of Dasein's Being; it is an *existentiale*. So one cannot think of it as the Being-present-at-hand of some corporeal Thing (such as a human body) "in" an entity which is present-at-hand. [...] "In" is derived from "*innan*"—"to reside," "*habitare*," "to dwell" [*sich aufhalten*]. "*An*" signifies "I am accustomed," "I am familiar with," "I look after something." It has the signification of "*colo*" in the senses of "*habito*" and "*diligo*." [...] "Being" [*Sein*] as the infinitive of "*ich bin*" (that is to say, when it is understood as an *existentiale*), signifies "to reside alongside...," "to be familiar with..."[39]

In his reference to the Old High German verb *innan*, "to inhabit," Heidegger already discloses the crux of the existential analysis of spatiality early on in his investigation; what he calls being-in-the-world is nothing other than the world "inside" in a verbal-transitive sense: living in it and benefiting from it already have been explored in prior acts of attunement and reaching out. Because existence is always a completed act of habitation—the result of a primal leap into inhabitation—spatiality is an essential part of it. Speaking about inhabitation in the world does not mean simply attributing domesticity within the gigantic to those who exist: for it is precisely the possibility of being-at-home-in-the-world that is questionable, and to presuppose it as a given would be a relapse into the very physics of containers that is here meant to be overcome. This, incidentally, is the primal error of reasoning that is found in all holistic worldviews and doctrines of uterine immanence and hardens into pious half-thought. Nor is the house of being a casing in which those who exist come and go, however.[40] Its structure is more like that of a ball of care [*Sorge*] in which existence has spread out in an original being-outside-itself. Heidegger's radical phenomenological attentiveness removes the foundation of the multi-millennial rule of container physics and metaphysics: man is neither a living being in the world around him nor a rational being in the firmament, nor a perceiving being inside of God. Consistently with this, the talk of the environment that has been on the rise for the last twenty years is also an object of phenomenological critique: biology does not think, any more than any other standard science. "Nowadays there is much talk about 'man's having an environment'; but this says nothing ontologically as long as this 'having' is left indefinite." (*Being and Time*, p. 84) But what is meant by the "aroundness of the environment"?

> From what we have been saying, it follows that Being-in is not a "property" which Dasein sometimes has and sometimes does not have, and *without* which it could *be* just as well as it could

Schulbank im Weltraum [School Desk in Outer Space], photo montage, conceived by Andreas Leo Findeisen and realized by David Rych

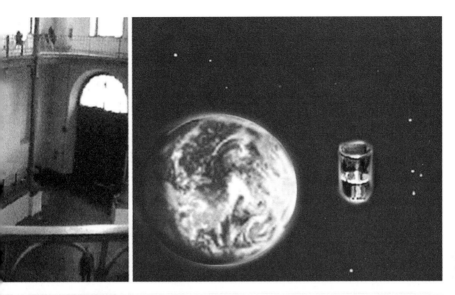

with it. It is not the case that man "is" and then has, by way of an extra, a relationship-of-Being towards the "world"—a world with which he provides himself occasionally. Dasein is never "proximally" an entity which is, so to speak, free from Being-in, but which sometimes has the inclination to take up a "relationship" towards the world. Taking up relationships towards the world is possible only *because* Dasein, as Being-in-the-world, is as it is. This state of Being does not arise just because some other entity is present-at-hand outside of Dasein and meets up with it. Such an entity can "meet up with" Dasein only in so far as it can, of its own accord, show itself within a *world*.[41]

The existential blindness to space in conventional thought manifests itself in the old worldviews in the fact that they integrate humans more or less automatically into an encompassing nature as cosmos.[42] In modern thought, Descartes' division of substances into the thinking and the extended offers the most pronounced example of the reluctance to consider the place of "meeting" still questionable in itself. Because everything Descartes has to say about spatiality remains connected to the body-and-thing complex as the only possessors of extension, the question of where thought and extension converge is one that cannot come up for him. The thinking thing remains a worldless authority that, strangely enough, is seemingly able to submit to the whim of sometimes entering into a relationship with extended things and sometimes not. The *res cogitans* bears some of the traits of a ghostly hunter, bracing himself up to go on forays into the realm of the recognizably extended before withdrawing once more to his worldless fortress in the extensionless domain. Contrary to this, Heidegger insists on the original being-in of Dasein in the sense of being-in-the-world. Knowledge too is merely a derivative mode of staying in the spaciousness of the world disclosed through circumspective concern:

> When Dasein directs itself towards something and grasps it, it does not somehow first get out of an inner sphere in which it has been proximally encapsulated, but its primary kind of Being is such that it is always "outside" alongside entities which it encounters and which belong to a world already discovered. Nor is any inner sphere abandoned when Dasein dwells alongside the entity to be known, and determines its character; but even in this "Being-outside" alongside the object, Dasein is still "inside," we understand this in the correct sense; that is to say, it is itself "inside" as a Being-in-the-world which knows. And furthermore, the perceiving of what is known is not a process of returning with one's booty to the "cabinet" of consciousness after one has gone out and grasped it; even in perceiving, retaining, the Dasein which knows *remains outside*, and it does so as *Dasein*.[43]

In his positive statements about the spatiality of Dasein, Heidegger emphasizes two characters in particular: de-severance and directionality.

> "De-severing" amounts to making the farness vanish—that is, making the remoteness of something disappear, bringing it close. Dasein is essentially de-severant […]. De-severance discovers remoteness. […] Proximally and for the most part, de-severing is a circumspective bringing-close—bringing something close by, in the sense of procuring it, putting it in

readiness, having it to hand. [...] In Dasein there lies an essential tendency towards closeness. (pp. 139f.)

Dasein, in accordance with its spatiality, is proximally never here but yonder; from this "yonder" it comes back to its "here"[...]. (p. 142)

As de-severant Being-in, Dasein has likewise the character of directionality. Every bringing-close [*Näherung*] has already taken in advance a direction towards a region out of which what is de-severed brings itself close [*sich nähert*]. [...] Circumspective concern is de-severing which gives directionality. (p. 143)

When we let entities within-the-world be encountered in the way which is constitutive for Being-in-the-world. This "giving space," which we also call "making room" for them, consists in freeing the ready-to-hand for its spatiality. [...] In concerning itself circumspectively with the world, Dasein can move things around or out of the way or "make room" for them only because making room—understood as an existentiale—belongs to its Being-in-the-world [...] the "subject" (Dasein), if well understood ontologically, is spatial. (p. 146)

Whoever expected these mighty rhetorical overtures to be followed by the piece itself would be sorely disappointed. The existential analysis of "where" abruptly switches to an analysis of "who," without the slightest mention of the fact that the author has only pulled out the beginning of a thread that is still mostly wound up. Had it been unraveled further, it would inevitably have opened up the multi-significant universes of existential spaciousness addressed here under the catchword "spheres." Inhabitation in spheres cannot be explicated in detail, however, as long as existence [*Dasein*] is understood primarily in terms of a supposedly natural inclination towards loneliness.[44] The analytics of the existential "where" demands for all suggestions and moods of essential loneliness to be parenthesized, in order that we can verify the deep structures of accompanied and augmented existence. In the face of this task, the early Heidegger remained an *existentiale* in the problematic sense of the word. His hasty turn to the "who" question leaves behind a lonely, weak, hysterical-heroic existential subject that thinks it is the first to die, and remains pitifully uncertain of the more hidden aspects of its embeddedness in intimacies and solidarities. A quixotic "who" in a confused "where" may have nasty surprises in store for itself if it attempts to anchor itself in the next best collective. When Heidegger, carried away by imperial enthusiasm, sought to rise to greatness in the nationalist revolution, it became apparent that without a radical clarification of its position within the political space, existential authenticity leads to blindness. From 1934 on, Heidegger knew—albeit only implicitly—that his fervor for the National Socialist awakening had been a being-sucked-in: time had become space. Whoever falls prey to this suction lives in a different sphere while seemingly still here; on a distant stage, in an uncomprehended Yonder. Heidegger's late work discreetly draws the conclusions from this lapse. The cheated *völkisch* revolutionary has few expectations left of the history unfolding around him; he has retired from the work of the forces. In future he will seek salvation in even more intimate exercises in closeness. He doggedly sticks to his anarchic province and offers guided tours of the House of being, language—the perfect magical concierge, equipped with heavy keys, always ready to offer profound hints. In emotional moments he invokes the sacred Parmenidean orb of being as if he had returned to the Eleatic, weary of historicity as an unholy specter. Heidegger's late work keeps acting out the figures of resignation offered by a revolutionary deepening of thought, without ever returning to the point from which he might once more have taken up the question of the original admission [*Einräumung*] of the world.

The present project, *Spheres*, can also be understood as an attempt to recover—in one substantial aspect, at least—the project wedged sub-thematically into Heidegger's early work, namely *Being and Space*, from its state of entombment. We believe that as much of Heidegger's interest in rootedness as can be salvaged comes into its own here through a theory of pairs, of geniuses,[45] of augmented existence. Finding a rooting in the existing duality: this much autochthony must be retained, even if philosophy attentively continues to practice its indispensable emancipation from the empirical commune. For thought, it is now a matter of working anew through the tension between autochthony (*ab ovo* and in terms of the community) and release (in terms of death or the infinite).

CHAPTER 5

The Primal Companion

Requiem for a Discarded Organ

> Che farò senza Euridice?
> Dove andrò senza il mio ben?[1]
> — C. W. Gluck, *Orfeo ed Euridice*

> We cannot let our angels go; we do not see that they only go
> out that archangels may come in.
> — Ralph Waldo Emerson, *Compensation*

The black of the eye has to expand for the sight to be maintained in the dark. If the dark grows as deep as in the exquisite night, it would be helpful if the eye could become as large as the eye itself. Perhaps such a spheric eye would be ready for what lies before us: the journey through a black monochrome. If the subject in the dark had become wholly a pupil, the pupil wholly a tactile organ, and the tactile organ wholly a sounding body, the homogeneous massif of that orb of blackness could unfold into landscapes already sensed. Suddenly a world before the world would begin to transpire; a vague, ethereal universe would take shape, as delicate as breath and pre-discrete. The salty night

Odilon Redon, *Divine Omniscience*, lithograph, in *Dans le rêve*, 1879

would remain safe in its unspeakable density, and its circle would still be sealed with no possible exit; and yet an organic something would begin to stand out, like a sculpture of black mercury against a black background. Within the undifferentiated, sketches of areas would diverge, and in the intimate closeness a first Yonder would polarize itself, enabling an incipient Here to return to itself.

What could one do to attune oneself to the silent expeditions in the monochrome night? At what other scenes—or unseens— would the eye be schooled for the journey into the black land? Would it be helpful to assume the lotus position, close one's eyes and temporarily renounce all things visible and imagined? But how many have boarded the boat of meditation only to drift out into the immaterial, where research ends in lack of curiosity. Should one experiment with drugs, and travel through alternative universes as an inquisitive psychonaut? In most cases, however, such interior journeys only replace everyday images with eccentric ones, which flicker through the cave like endogenous action films; such apparitions dilute the dark space as such all the more, and the art of reading figures in the black monochrome does not get any further. If one casts a glance at the reports from LSD sessions written by patients of the drug therapist Stanislav Grof about their supposed amniotic regressions, one has the impression that these people experience what they have read, and reproduce eloquent images of the *hortus conclusus* as a uterine fantasy; they pass off educational tours of the gynecological atlas as their own experiences; images of paradise from Sunday school mingle with archaic spatial memories; in garishly visual imaginings, they see heavenly fields and choirs of light surrounding the divine throne, sights to which no womb-dweller has ever been privy. This suggests that at best, even the psychognostic wonder drug LSD only produces synthetic conglomerates of experience in which early scenic elements are mingled with later verbal and visual ones to such a degree that one can scarcely speak of a return to some authentic primary state. So what is to be done when even truth drugs yield disinformation? Would it be better to accompany miners on their journey into the shaft and follow their trail into the drifts, without light or site plans, to pause somewhere in the depths and gauge how the mountain spreads its density out in all directions around the breathing life point? Such an exercise would only be a sporting self-test, however, and would end with the examinee being left at the mercy of his own heartbeat in the silent stone space, having to restrain the incipient panic of his excited thoughts; so this undertaking also fails to lead back to the scene before all scenes. It would not advance the exploration of the only nocturnal cave that concerns us. Descents into foreign tunnels do not lead you back into the incomparable black monochrome background from which your life began to emerge as a vibrating figure long ago. Seeing in the only darkness that concerns you cannot be practiced on a different darkness; there is no alternative to confronting your own black monochrome. Whoever tackles this will soon understand that life is deeper than one's autobiography; writing never penetrates far enough into one's own blackness. We cannot write down what we begin as.

The first "where" still lacks the slightest outlines of structure or content. Even if I knew that this is my cave, all it would initially mean is that I am lying here as a deep gray Hegelian cow in my own night, indistinguishable from anything or anyone else. My

Kazimir Malevich, *The Black Circle*

being is still an uncreased heaviness. As a black basalt ball I rest within myself, brooding in my milieu as if it were a night made of stone. And yet, as self-sufficient as I might be, some inkling of difference must already have dawned inside the dark massif in which I live and weave. If I were merely a basalt black, how could it be that a vague sense of being-in is taking root within me? What is the meaning of this feeling, this floating bulge? If my black were seamlessly joined to the mountain's eternally dead interior of the same black, why would I feel a hasty beating

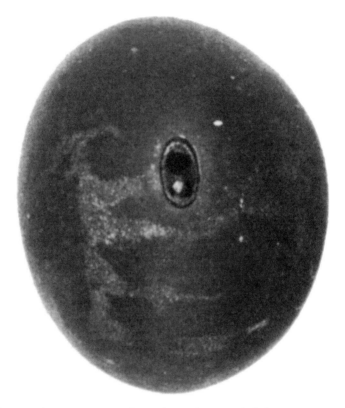

Salagrama (memento stone for Indian pilgrims): drilled stone containing ammonite, length 90 mm. The drilled hole represents the beginning of creation through an opening outwards.

stirring within me, and above it the slower distant drum? If I were indistinguishably merged with the black substance, how could I already be something that senses a space and makes first stretching movements within it? Can there be a substance that is simultaneously sensation? Are there mountains that are pregnant with non-rocks? Has anyone ever heard of a basalt that will develop as animation and self-awareness? Strange thoughts, vapors from dark vaults—they seem to be the sort of problems on which the dead pharaohs ruminate in their crypts for millennia without making any progress. Mummy meditations, glimmers in the mineral, brooding without a subject. Can one conceive of an incident that would make such questions become those of a living human?

For the time being, however, we will have to look around for assistance—though not from gynecologists; they run through the female interior with organ names and street shoes like tourists from afar through oriental establishments, blinded by their booked interests. No: the observer at the entrance whose support we should now seek can, at this stage, be any-one except a user of anatomical terms. He should be more like an aging psychoanalyst, or a hermit whom people with con-cerns that evade words seek out—perhaps a person who devotes himself to what we referred to above as magnetopathic procedures of closeness; a person, at any rate, who knows how to be present without intervening in the other's existence except in ways that are themselves given through his discreet, attentive presence. To progress in our inner observation we must now, as stated above, introduce an additional view from the outside that is connected to these goings-on not through interference, merely through witness. Let us therefore make an appointment with the helper in front of the cave, and let us give him the task of advancing the hesitant elucidation of the spheric night.

In his study on what he calls "monadic" communion, the psychoanalyst Béla Grunberger has published an example of an encounter in the core area of the bipersonal intimate space that is as questionable as it is thought-provoking:

A young man went into analysis because of various difficulties with relationships, a number of somatic symptoms and sexual disturbances, etc. After the therapist had told him the basic principles, he lay down on the couch and said nothing for the rest of the session. He came to the next one, and for a few months acted in exactly the same way. Then, in one particular session, he finally broke his silence and said: "We're not there yet, but it's getting better." After that he fell silent again, and after another few months in which he said not a single word, he stood up at the end of one meeting, declared that he was feeling well today, believed he was cured, thanked his therapist and left.[2]

This bizarre case history—almost a legend in its tone and content—would never have come to light if various circumstances had not coincided to lead to its publication. Firstly, its narrator is an author of such authority in his circles that he could take the liberty of digressing into problematic areas without any immediate danger to himself; thus the therapeutic idyll of his account could pass unassailed under the mantle of his integrity. Secondly, it seems that these events took place in the practice of a colleague; so, if the analyst's part in the silent duo dictated by the patient had been a professional error—which, without contextual knowledge, cannot be ruled out—it would be that of his colleague rather than his own. Thirdly, the author believes he is presenting an innovatively precise theory of early mother-child communion for which this peculiar case history can be declared a piece of evidence. It is in fact Grunberger's ambition to develop a theorem of "*pure* narcissism" that is meant to lead to a concept of psychoanalysis "beyond drive theory." According to

Grunberger, the characteristics of *pure* narcissism include the subject's freedom from drive tensions and its striving for a splendidly omnipotent, disturbance-hostile and blissful homeostasis. This *pure* tendency can *ipso facto* only unfold under the protection of a form that provides the subject with a sufficiently sealed-off mental incubator—and the scene described offers, in the author's opinion, both a daring and a perfect example of this. Grunberger calls this protective ideal form the *monad*—undoubtedly in conscious modification of Leibniz' term, and consciously ignoring the fact that the content of this monad corresponds to what other psychoanalysts call the dyad. The objective reason for choosing the former term over the latter is that the monad is a form with a unifying container function; the one acts as the shaping capsule that harbors the two. The monad would thus be a bipolar matrix or a single psychospheric form entirely in keeping with the concept of the primary microsphere expounded here. For Grunberger, monads—as formal units—can be assigned variable content; hence they appear both in the original mother-child combination and in reassociations and substitutions reached at different points in life. The monadic motif asserts itself whenever individuals enjoy their imaginary perfection in an intimate psycho-spatial community with the ideal other. Primary union can equally be represented in Romeo-Juliet relationships or in Philemon-Baucis symbioses; it appears as the playing community of child and animal or child and doll—indeed, the monadic pact can even be made with virtual animals and heroes from computer games; in its most mature form, it may present itself as a relationship of admiration between an adult and a charismatic personality; and finally, it can be enacted as a therapeutic contract between the analyst and the client. This great scenic variability confirms that the monad is indeed a formal concept that, like an algebraic formula, can be applied at will within certain boundaries. As Grunberger notes, "the monad consists of content and containers,"[3] and hence a stable form of biunity and a large repertoire of filling-in material offered by concrete bipolar models of closeness—in so far as these are capable of supporting the phantasm of the unchallenged authority of self-enjoyment in the shared interior.

What, one wonders, actually went on during that young man's months of wordless sessions with the silent analyst? Can this joint waiting in stillness, which seems ultimately to have led to some form of cure, really be interpreted as a monadic creation of form in Grunberger's sense? Does the scene, in effect, involve nothing other than the patient's dive into the healing dual, which lays down no premises except the unreserved permission to stay in a space impregnated by the proximity of the benevolent intimate witness? It is reasonable to ask where the young man finds the willful confidence to dominate the situation through his persistent non-speaking, when psychoanalysis, especially in France, has the reputation of being a verbal therapy—not to say an exercise in verboseness or a school for budding novelists. What kind of complicity did the patient draw his analyst into when he succeeded in imposing his silence upon him in a game of two halves, each lasting several months? However one chooses to answer these questions, one thing seems obvious: based on the description of the scene, there is no evidence of a pre-Oedipally symbiotic mother-child relationship between the young man and the analyst. If the client came to the analyst like a problem infant to its substitute mother, such an encounter would contain the seed for dramatic developments that would have to be reenacted in the analytical relationship as a tense back-and-forth. Someone who remains in silence with his analyst for months, then goes home claiming to be cured, could be many things—but not a subject that has realized and acted out its subsequent demands of a failing mother with the analyst. Rather, the latter is here deprived of the role to which his title refers. He is stripped of his interpretative authority and power to differentiate, and remolded into a being that is supposed to provide the conditions for a curative self-integration merely through his silent co-existence. But in what role can the analyst—who would be more accurately termed an integrator or monitor here—provide such effects? What old stage forms the setting for this silent meeting between a man on the couch and another in an armchair? It only becomes clear how much of a riddle this question is when one calls to mind that in the repertoire of early forms of mother-child closeness, there is not one scene that could remotely have acted as a model for this duel-like fusion of two silent partners over a period of months. Whatever might take place between mother and child, the two do not form a sound-less meditation group at any point in their interaction process. So what game are the figures in Grunberger's case history playing? What does each represent for the other—and what blind site is the location of their meeting? Where is the Yonder from which the two mutes return to their Here?

Our suspicion seems well-founded: we could be dealing here with a scenic equivalent of the fetal night. In the analyst's studio we find ourselves, just this once, in the middle of the therapeutic monochrome: the monadic field, it seems, conjures up the black primal scene in which the speechless subject is pre-linguistically contained and nurtured by an encompassing milieu. Though this scene does not feature anything that could be called an event, it contains—provided that the young man's final claim was based on something substantial—an integrative togetherness with concrete life-practical effects. Naturally we cannot be sure whether the shared nothingness does contain some traces of words that elude the outside observer; what is certain, however, is that the homogeneous dark and signless space has divided itself into an archaic bipolarity. A first amorphous other has appeared, with neither eyes nor voice. Let us suppose that the young man is our cave explorer: then who is the other, waiting in his analyst's armchair and facing his client's silent presence with his own hour after hour? Whose revenant is this precarious other? To what lost existence does he lend his present body? What role does he play by remaining so humbly and patiently in his seat close to the patient, refraining from all expression of his own? What mission from what past might it be which demands that the analyst put aside his own life, his temperament and his knowledge to such a degree that no more of him remains in the space than a sponge, absorbing the patient's silence and nourishing it with its counter-silence?

The analyst, then, does not represent the mother in the usual sense, although he forms one part of the therapeutic monad, that is to say the metaphorical-uterine immune form. Should one instead assume that he is the uterus itself, the egoless organ or milieu in which the individuation of an organism takes place? Is he the velvet wall on whose surface the egg once settled after its first journey? Does he keep himself available, like the maternal mucous membrane in which the egg has implanted itself as a grateful parasite, just as certain mushrooms accumulate on the trunks of old trees with the aim of multiplying peacefully? Such an assumption may seem suggestive for a moment, but it quickly loses its plausibility as soon as one transfers it to the given therapeutic scene: over many months, two men persistently meet in a closed room to wage a fightless fight in the inaudible. Each of them spreads out his dome of silence around him, searchingly holding out his own stillness to that of the other. This pre-dialogic, almost dueling aspect of the silence-to-silence, ear-to-ear events is quite different from a mere nesting on a living wall, and more than simply the irresponsible license to swim in a bubble that demands nothing and permits every freedom. One already finds a pre-confrontational dual structure developing in this silence *à deux*; the silence of the one is not identical to the silence of the other. The two domes of silence bang together, creating a silent chord with elements of an earlier Here-Yonder structure.

So whom—or what—does the analyst represent in this scene? He stands, it would seem, for an archaic, unpopular organ whose task is to make itself available to the fetal pre-subject as a partner in the dark. In physiological terms, this organ of the first other and the original togetherness is absolutely real: anyone who wanted to enter the womb by endoscopic means would be able to see it with his own eyes and touch it with his own hands; he could photograph it and make anatomical maps of it; or he could write dissertations about the vascular system and the villous structures of the curious tissue, precisely describing its function in the exchange of blood between mother and fetus. But as we are committed here to applying the methods of negative gynecology, it is pointless for now to label that organ which, in the original inner togetherness, is *yonder*, with its anatomical name. If this name were uttered too soon, the investigation would degenerate into uninformative externality and once again con-fuse anatomical imagining with first psychology. How quickly such things can happen can be seen in the barely established, yet in this respect rapidly dated field of perinatal psychology. Here too, the men in street shoes are on the move in the pre-objective realm, bringing false daylight into the night with reifying termi-nologies. To avoid straying onto the misguided path of object relationship theory, we shall give the organ with which the pre-subject floats in communication in its cave a pre-objective name: we shall call it the *With*. If it were possible to cross out the term "fetus" too, and replace it with a similarly de-reifying name, this retreat to anonymity would be equally preferable in its case; unfortunately, the prenatal pre-subject is associated too strongly with its medical name, and any butcher in professor's clothing can speak of fetuses like public objects. If we were to give this being a new name, it would be called the *Also*, as the fetal subject only comes about through returning from the With yonder to the Here, the "also here." As far as the With is concerned, its quality of presence is neither that of a person nor that of a subject, but rather a living and life-giving *It* that remains yonder-close-by. Facing the With thus means returning from the Yonder, which marks a first location, to the Here, where the Also grows. Hence the With acts as an intimate usher for the Also-self. It is the first close factor to share the original space with the Also by nurturing and justifying it. The With therefore exists only in the singular—what the With of another would be can *eo ipso* not be the same as mine. Thus the With could, with good reason, also be termed the *With-me*—for it accompanies me, and me alone, like a nourishing shadow and anonymous sibling. This shadow cannot follow me—not least because I would not know how to get moving myself—but by being there and appearing to me, it constantly shows me my place in the space before all spaces; by being consistently faithful and nurturingly close *Yonder*, it gives me a first sense of my lasting Here. What will one day be my speaking ego is an elaboration of that delicate place to which I learned to return as long as the With was close to it. In a sense, the shadower goes ahead of the shadowed; in so far as it exists, I also exist. The With is the first thing that gives and lets things be. If I have what it takes to turn from an Also into an ego, it is not least because the With has let me sense the place in which I have begun to find a rooting as an augmentable creature that feels across and is open in a polar fashion. Like an imperceptible, drawn-out lightning bolt illuminating the nightscape, the With introduces an inexhaustible difference into the homogeneous monochrome by imprinting ways to approach the back-and-forth into the reawakening Here-Yonder sphere. From it, energies flow to me that form me. Nonetheless, it remains unassuming in itself, never demanding its own presence. We are accompanied so naturally by the With that scarcely any pre-idea of its indispensability can form in either the personal or the general consciousness. As the humblest, quietest something that will ever have come close to us, the With immediately retreats as soon as we seek to fix it with our gaze. It is like a dark little brother placed by our side so that the fetal night would not be too lonely; a little sister who, at first glance, is merely there to sleep in the same room with us. One could think its only mission is to share its peace with yours. Like an intrauterine butler, it stays close and on the fringe, discreet and nourishing, privy to our two-party secret, which no one except you and it will ever know about. The With does have properties of a physical organ, but for you—because you are yourself still a creature without organs—it is not a real bodily thing; and if it were, it would only be one that was formed purely to accompany you, an organic angel and secret agent in the service of the Dear Lady whom you inhabit because she invited you to come. The With is an intrauterine probation officer for you alone, you, the untroubled problem child of the alchemical night. Just as Kafka's supplicant before the gate of the law that was kept open only for him waits until his end, the most intimate and general organ of relationships, the With, is only connected to you, and it disappears from the world the moment you appear as the main person; then you cease to be an Also, because your external appearance is immediately accompanied by a proper name that prepares you for becoming an individual. The With, on the other hand, is not baptized, and disappears from the eyes of the living—including yours. Although the With was your private reagent that shared your distilling flask with you, your catalyst and mediator, it remains condemned to be merely your lost surplus. You are the *Opus One*; the With will perish. You will forever be spared from thinking about it—and without thinking of what was lost, there is no cause for reflection or thanks. Because your With consumes itself in its existence as an organ-for-you, and disappears as soon as it has served its purpose, there is a certain aptness in the fact that you do not know it, and do not even know how one would go about asking after it. If you met it in daylight—who could promise that you would not turn away in disgust? Would you be able to recognize a bloody sponge, a flat, reddish brown gelatinous mass as your soul sibling from the time before time? One can be absolutely certain: if gynecologists or midwives were to call it by its anatomical name in front of you, it would remain the most

Figurine pendant, ceramic Neolithic period, 5th millennium BC

distant It for you, and would consider it out of the question that you had been ever entertained a relationship with it. That is why it remains important to the end that we understand the With as essentially nameless and devoid of appearance; we would bounce back, probably fighting to hold back our disgust, if this spongy something appeared to us in its visible form—this most wretched phantom in the opera of the entrails. We would be reminded of Sartre's analysis of the slimy [*le visqueux*]; upon touching this, we would experience not an immersion in clear water, but rather a stickiness that we would consider an obscene attack on our free-dom.[4] We would have to suspect ourselves of being monstrosities if we sensed the imposition of developing a feeling of kinship with the visually perceived With-lump. Viewed by real eyes, the external With would infiltrate us "like a liquid seen in a night-mare, where all its properties are animated by a sort of life and turn back against me."[5] Motives of denial cannot entirely erase the historical truth and the genetic reality, however: in its impor-tant period, the With was our private nymph fountain and our sworn genius; it was more of a sibling to you than any external sister or external brother could ever be. What it means to us is probably demonstrated better by certain archetypal dreams and symbolic-pictorial projections than by any anatomical represen-tation, and even someone who rolls up gratefully under their quilt in bed before going to sleep has already learned more about the With than external glances upon it ever could. In fact, beds and their utensils—especially pillows, duvets, feather beds and quilts—show a connection both clear and discreet to the initial organ-for-you. In friendly inconspicuousness, these everyday objects continue the function of the With as the original augmenter and creator of intimate spaces for adult subjects too.

French four-poster beds of the 18th and 19th centuries

As soon as we prepare for the night, we almost always slide into a state in which we cannot help disposing ourselves towards a self-augmentation in the dark in which an appropriate With-successor will play its part. Even those who do not believe in angels or doppelgangers can rehearse the secrets of pre-personal friendship with their closest sleep helpers, and whoever has no friend can at least have a blanket. The theory of With-projections will not least permit a psychohistorical deduction of bed cultures.

As long as the With appears and circulates in the cultural space in the form of such free anonymous elements, sublimated and symbolically concealed re-encounters with it are neither impossible nor uncommon. The young man who practiced the art of silence with his analyst over many months also seems to be among those who knew how to summon their lost With to a rendezvous outside of the bed. If this suspicion were correct, the answer to the question of what role the analyst had to play in Grunberger's legend would be this: he embodied the lost and regained With of his client. During months of mute rehearsal in feeling-With,[6] the "analysand" would have become sufficiently sure of the With's presence to know one day that he would henceforth be able to keep the augmenting element with him "alone," that is, outside of the therapeutic monadic form. In his case, then, being cured would have meant nothing other than the reassured reconnection with the inner prospect of the inner companion's shadow presence, which would not be lost again so easily. To avoid distorting the With through externalizing de-projections and reducing it to the anatomical-material level—which usually has a more blinding effect than the usual never-thinking-about-it—one must seek pictorial projections in which the With-nobject can be brought to light at an appropriate level of sublimation. The elevation of the With to the non-anatomical sublime would be complete once its pictorial representation were able to do justice to the originally space-forming polarization energy of the With-Also-sphere. One can find numerous documents of this in the symbol history of early and advanced civilizations, not least in the field of integration symbolisms, in particular the wide morphological cycle of trees of life (cf. Excursus 5) and mandala figures. The most current symbolization of psychological primary duality, however, occurs in the mythologies of doppelgangers, twins and soul siblings that we shall examine in their own right in the following.[7] To mark the extremes of this With-symbolism, let us first comment on two eminent models of fetal space creation: the first gives us theological, the second artistic access to the With as a phenomenon.

In an account by Hildegard of Bingen from the first part of her record of mystical visions written in 1147, *Scivias*, we find an unprecedentedly sublime intrauterine-theological communion. Hildegard famously wrote about her audio-visionary experiences in a verbal paraphrase first, then adding commentary in additional interpretations of the images; last of all, her visions were translated into pictorial forms by a manuscript illustrator. The legend of the fourth vision from the first cycle of *Scivias* reads as follows: ✗

> You see a most great and serene splendor, flaming, as it were, with many eyes, with four corners pointing towards the four parts of the world. [...] this shows the mystery of the Celestial Majesty, which, as you see, is presented to you in this image of great loftiness and profundity. In it appears another splendor like the dawn, containing in itself a brightness of purple lightning. [...] You see also on the earth people carrying milk in earthen vessels and making cheese from it [...] One part is thick, and from it strong cheeses are made. [...] And one part is thin, and from it weak cheses are curdled; [...] one part is mixed with corruption, and from it bitter cheeses are formed. [...] And you see the image of a woman who has a perfect human form in her womb. [...] And behold! By the secret design of the Supernatural Creator that form moves with vital motion [...]. So that a fiery globe which has no human lineaments possesses the heart of that form [...] And it also touches the person's brain; [...] and it spreads itself through all the person's members. [...] But then this human form, in this way vivified, comes forth from the woman's womb, and changes its color according to the movement the globe makes in that

Hildegard of Bingen, *Scivias, The Creation of the Soul, illustration from the Rupertsberg Codex*

form. […] Many whirlwinds assail one of these globes in a body and bow it down to the ground. […] But that globe, gaining back its strength and bravely raising itself up, resists them boldly.[8]

The corresponding illustration from the Rupertsberg Codex translates essential aspects of the vision into the language of external visuality. The picture's longitudinal axis is cut in two by a trunk or rope rising with curious, or perhaps alarming concreteness from the belly of the fetus inside the mother, lying on the oval ground, to the floating eye rhombus covered with eyes in the upper section. If there was ever a depiction of the With protected from anatomical de-sublimation, here is a concrete example. It seems that the animating *vis-à-vis* of the child in the womb is being directly elevated to the magical crossing in the heavens;[9] through its eccentric umbilical cord, the fetus is vividly connected to the sphere of the divine spirit, which manifests itself as an accumulation of pure intelligences and world-founding eyes in the upper world. That this crossing, filled with eyes, indeed symbolizes an emanation very close to God is shown by the first *Scivias* vision, in which Hildegard perceived, directly beside the overwhelmingly radiant shape of the Most High, "an image full of eyes on all sides, in which, because of those eyes, I could discern no human form."[10] Hildegard's vision of the creation of humans and their souls thus conceives the With not as an intrauterine phenomenon, but rather as a heavenly body of subjectivity connected to the fetus from a distance through a hyper-umbilical cord or angel cable. At a particular moment, a spherical individual soul descends from the With on high to the child through this cord—just as if one of the eyes at the top were separating from its heavenly ensemble and entering the heart of the fetus through its navel. Thus the pychognostic character of the fourth *Scivias* vision becomes evident: it offers a complete view of human ontogenesis. While the eccentric umbilical cord makes the intimate long-distance connection of the fetus to its animating With in the space close to God, the people in the oval bringing their cheese in vessels represent the creation of mankind. To understand the cheeses as symbols of the human body, we should recall the very old notion, made ubiquitous in Christianity by the Book of Job, that the human body in the mother's womb comes about no differently from cheese in fermented milk: through thickening and curdling. Just as a solid body concresces from liquid material in the production of cheese, the human form grows inside the womb through the clotting of blood.[11] This enabled Job to ask God in his accusations:

> Did you not pour me out like milk and curdle me like cheese? [...]
>
> Why then did you bring me out of the womb? I wish I had died before any eye saw me. (Job 10:10 & 18)

But, just as not all milk curdlings produce good results, not all instances of concrescence in the womb produce solid human bodies: Hildegard knew through her own chronic sickliness how precarious a matter human bodily creations can be; she herself was a typical product of "weak cheese"—though one should acknowledge that this undoubtedly has its own value, and need not be considered a bad result *a priori*; the lean is also a legitimate result of procedures in the workshop of creation—indeed, esoteric psychologists claim, the first manufacturer often has special plans for it, in so far as the lean ones are the better media. The only thing humans must avoid like damnation is becoming bitter. In Hildegard's model, pregnancy repeats the creation of Adam: physically as the formation of a solid from a liquid through concrescence, and psycho-pneumatically as the inspiration of the soul through the descent of a spirit orb from the angelic space into the fetal body. According to the traditional view, the latter takes place around the middle of pregnancy—that is, at a point equated in earlier doctrines of female wisdom with the beginning of palpable movement in the womb. It is the orb, having descended from close to God and been absorbed by the child's body, that forms the center of human destiny, even after birth; its calling is to prove itself amid worldly opposition.

Alongside Hildegard's theological vision of With-structure, any psychological or endoscopic conception of the intrauterine partner will seem prosaic and trivial. Even if contemporary analysts will not be able to follow on directly from the details of Hildegard's religious mindscape, they will find in her account a document showing how high older vision discourses elevated the mysterious togetherness of the fetus with an animating other. The umbilical cord is more than a vein between the child and the bloody sponge in its proximity—it forms the physical monument to the real connection of incipient life to an inflowing augmentative force. People may parenthesize these concepts today because of their effusive religiosity. In their musical pitch and form, however, they protect modern researchers in this field too from the physiological idiocy of presumed expertise in womanhood, along with its gynecological vanguard and its pop-psychological rearguard. They indicate the necessary level for any discussion of intrauterine bipolarity if the risk of an inappropriate de-sublimation is to be eliminated.

Equally valid formulations from our own time would be expected most in the field of fantastic visual art, where psychological depth symbolisms were developed into visual figurations. One eminent recent example of this can be found in some mysterious images of trees by the surrealist painter René Magritte, especially a work from 1964 with the title *La reconnaissance infinie* (Infinite Recognition). Magritte's painting, a small-format gouache, shows two small gentlemen wearing hats and long dark coats, viewed from behind, in the middle of a tall, heart-shaped tree with dense, sponge-like, fine-veined leaves; they seem like twins, and are standing in the upper third of the foliage—the heart area of the tree, as it were. Their presence in the tree gives the impression of being completely natural, even though the two figures seem both small and a little lost within it. The picture could be read as a cryptic treatise on belonging together: what these two very similar figures, standing amid the leaves like miniature Chaplins, have to do with each other remains as unclear as the reason for their association with the tree—and yet these two unexplained circumstances seem interwoven; the one unknown comments on the other. The title of the painting does not tell us whether this infinite recognition—which could also mean infinite gratitude—takes place between the two men, or rather refers to their position inside the tree. In both cases, this recognitive thanking or thinking refers to the tree itself: in the one case as the discovery of similarity between the two figures, in which case they would be standing in a tree of knowledge, and in the other case as a testimony to the affiliation of both with the tree as such, which would then have to be understood as a tree of life. Thus Magritte's symbolic image discourse, though entirely based on the intrinsic artistic value of

René Magritte, *La reconnaissance infinie*

the forms used, enters a dialogue with old Judeo-Christian mythological traditions. If one concedes that the motif of the tree of life is an original With-symbol, Magritte's enigmatic picture forms a direct introduction to the field of archaic bipolarity: the place in the tree is in fact that from which both infinite recognition and unlimited gratitude originate. At the same time, the tree symbol discreetly and sublimely maintains the antonym of the With, ensuring its presence in visual perception without betraying it to anatomical triviality.

This applies even more to the famous series of paintings entitled *La voix du sang* (The Voice of Blood), in which Magritte meditated on the motif of the wonder tree between 1948 and the early 1960s. In one picture dominated by deep sea blue and greenish black hues, whose format of 90 x 110 cm reinforces its suggestive presence, the mythical motifs of the tree of life and the tree of knowledge are combined into one. The picture itself seems to dictate a perception in three stages of viewing: first of all, in the center, the trunk with the two flaps catches the eye. The compartments stand open like windows in an Advent calendar, displaying naïve symbols of happiness—the closed white ball and the illuminated house with its promising interior. It does not seem out of the question that a third window, almost concealed by the leaves, might open above the ball in this festive tree. The first glance has scarcely moved away from the figural attractions in the middle before it is drawn upwards, in a second act, to the archetypal branches of the giant tree, which fills out the entire upper half of the picture with its dark, irrefutable authority. The foliage, in its detailed, spongy-spheric structure and with the blue background shining through it, forms an organic antithesis of the geometric-artificial figures in the trunk's interior. Although the picture seems devoid of people, it actually discusses a humanly significant contrast: that between the organic form represented by the branches and leaves and the intellectually idealized and constructed figures of the house and

René Magritte, *La voix du sang*

René Magritte, *La voix du sang*, detail

ball. But how does the voice of blood become audible? It sounds as the call of the tree of life itself: it is this voice that mediates between the geometric fetuses in the tree trunk and the nourishing foliar sphere. The tree, which bears the ball and the house in its "womb," is obviously not concerned with fruits of its own species and genus. As the tree of life and knowledge in one, it does not produce its own and organically similar offshoots, but rather its opposite: the anorganic intellectual forms that are significant for thinking subjects because they testify to their own constructiveness. Hence Magritte's tree stands for a With that, as vegetative nature, supports intellectual inhabitants. The tree of life is pregnant with houses, balls and human subjectivity. That is why the intrauterine poles are clearly contrasted inside the Advent tree: in the trunk the Also, the geometric image fetuses, and in the organic foliage the With, the life-giving creature of closeness. As for the third view of the picture, it is only permitted once our observation has resigned in the face of the impenetrably open secrets of the tree of life. At some point one looks past the tree's intimate sphere into the distance, which surprisingly transpires as a genuinely liberated zone: a deep river landscape opens up, with mountain ranges on the left and an open plain on the right. It is a landscape without the burden of symbols or the gravity of riddles. In order to reach it, one would have to break out of the sonic circle in the foreground, in which the voice of blood rules over everything. Would it be entirely mistaken, then, to suppose that the artist himself is hiding in this blue distant space, from where, a little willfully and without faith in his own symbols, he presents the figures in the foreground to his viewers like false riddles?

What conclusions can we draw from these symbolic representations of the With about its structure and mode of being? These images certainly assign the intimate spatial partner a powerful status in the real domain. Whether one imagines it as a crossing close to God, full of eyes and soul orbs, or as an Advent tree of life and knowledge, both projections feature the With as an autonomously augmentative authority that would give the ego cause for warm and grateful remembrance. Nonetheless, it remains a justified question whether the With can genuinely only become visible in such sublime projections and indirect manifestations. Does the "other organ" really depend on being remembered purely in sublime paraphrases? Can one only speak of it like the invisible monarch of a neighbor state, whose goodwill we depend upon for our own fortune even though we could never welcome him on an official visit? Is there no way to receive the intimate other than as a guest, without underestimating him or losing sight of him through improper superelevations? If it was an indispensable partner in our cave life, what prevents us from checking whether the other is appearing at the same time when we leave the cave? If the With has shared that most personal cave with you—not as a ghost and imaginary nightshade, but as a real, indispensable, bodily second party—it is inevitable that it will leave the cave together with you once it is time for you to make that move.

In the case of that move, the above arrangement with the twofold observer inside and before the cave seems a useful one: the outside witness would have to be capable of saying without further ado whether my With had come out into the open along with me, the first class arrival. In that case, we would not have to worry that we had fallen prey to the misguided prose of a gynecological view from above; it would then not be a matter of inappropriately dragging inner truths outside and de-sublimating them through crude classifications. The outside observer would have no more to tell than the things which must come to light of their own accord in the increasingly drastic and sublime natal drama at the cave exit. So what would the outside observer put on record about what came with you? Would he tell you outright that you had come alone? Or would he confirm that there were two? It is precisely at this moment of choice, however, that the observer we are hoping for will usually disappoint us. Only now can we judge the full extent of our quandary: of all the people we know, did any of them ever have a chance to consult their midwife or family doctor? And how perfectly normal it seems that among millions of people, not one interrogates their own mother about such things. We ask no questions from the start, as if the impossibility of receiving answers were a proven fact. While it is certain that an outside observer would have witnessed the newborn and its With first hand if they had seen the light of day successively, it is also difficult to verify after the event, as the witnesses can virtually never be consulted. If the With had emerged at the same time as I did, I would no longer be able to assure myself of its existence—unless I found ways to break through the wall of silence built around me and my augmenter as soon as my life began. If the With ever existed, I am clearly the one who is meant to be fundamentally separated from it.

A wall of silence—indeed: the more clear or contoured the intrauterine monochrome becomes, the more stubbornly it resists description. Even if I allow myself to be consumed more and more by the assumption that back then, in the exquisite cave, there were always two of us, all the traces left by my life history point me exclusively to myself. So was I deceived from the start? Was my With secretly removed and exchanged, like a Kaspar Hauser among the organs? Could it still be alive, held captive at some other location, underground, neglected and lonely, like the unfortunate Kaspar, the phantom of Karlsruhe, the child of Europe in his Franconian dungeon? And if it were dead, and I an orphan, why did it not receive a proper burial, even if it were only in a cemetery for organs related to us? Who decided that we should be beings who neither seek nor visit our lost With—not on our birthdays and not on All Souls' Day? What is the sense of this With-lessness to which every person is condemned today, as if by general arrangement? What could be done to circumvent this perfect alliance of silence, which managed to turn the With into the absolute anti-topic?

There is, at least, one detail from the whispering of midwives that enters the general public's knowledge: one can only consider a birth successfully completed when the afterbirth has also left the womb without residue. This is where the conspiracy of silence against the With has its weak point: in truth, obstetricians know that there are always two units which reach the outside in successful births. The child, which naturally receives the lion's share of the attention, never emerges from the cave alone—it is followed by an inevitable organic supplement known in old France as *arrière-faix* or *délivrance*: the afterbirth, the after-burden, deliverance. Only birth and afterbirth together meet the requirements of a complete delivery. Since around 1700, the medical term "placenta" has become the standard word for the afterbirth in German and the other European national languages. The word is a learned derivation from the Latin word for flat cake or flat bread, *placenta*, which itself comes from the synonymous Greek *plakous*, whose accusative form is *plakounta*; this, in turn, is related to *Palatschinke*, the Austro-Hungarian word for pancake. The term's metaphorical roots clearly lie in the imaginative field of the old baker's craft; its place in life was in the field kitchen of the Roman legions. In fact, Aristotle had already compared the relationship between the womb and the child with that between the oven and the bread dough. For him, the child's stay within the mother meant a creation through concretion or a solidification of the soft. According to earlier traditions of midwifery, however, the dough baking in the maternal oven was not so much the child itself as that mysterious placental cake on which the child evidently fed *in utero* until it was ready to see the light of the world and drink its milk.[12] Thus the pregnant womb was always imagined by mothers and midwives in earlier times as a twofold workshop: a placenta bakery and an intimate child kitchen. While the child itself is prepared in the uterine cauldron, the mother's second work, the flat cake, ensures the appropriate nutrition during the longest night. It therefore comes as the second delivery at birth, and is even referred to in recent gynecology as *secundinae mulieris*. Where notions of a magical uterine kitchen predominated, it goes without saying that the placenta, as the mother's *opus secundum*, an essential co-phenomenon of every birth was received with great esteem, even numinous awe. Every newborn child was given something unspoken on its way in the form of the afterbirth that seemed—especially for the female community in the district of birth—to be fatefully connected to the child's life. Often the afterbirth was viewed as its double, which is why the placenta could not possibly be treated with indifference. It had to be guarded like an omen and brought to safety like a symbolic sibling of the newborn. Above all, it had to be ensured that no animals or strangers gained control of it. Often the child's father buried it in the cellar or under the staircase so that the household would profit from its fertile power, and sometimes barns or stables were also used as burial sites.[13] In some cases the placenta was buried in the garden or the field, where it was meant to decay as undisturbed as possible. It was a widespread custom to bury it under young fruit trees; one factor in this may have been the morphological connection between the placental tissue and the root systems of trees, as a sort of analogy magic. The habit of burying the umbilical cord under rose trees also stems from analogy-magical ideas.[14] In Germany, pear trees were chosen for the placentas of boys, and apple trees for those of girls. If fruit trees were planted on top of buried placentas, however, these were supposed to be sympathetically connected to the children for the duration of their lives; it was thought that the child and its tree would prosper together, fall ill together and die together. In other traditions the placenta was hung up to dry in hidden corners of the house, for example fireplaces—a custom that supposedly still persists erratically in Northern Portugal. In many parts of Europe, dried and ground placenta was considered an impeccable remedy for numerous ailments; it is already mentioned in the *Corpus Hippokraticum*, and was praised from the days of the medical school of Salerno to the seventeenth century by doctors and pharmacists, most of all as a cure for liver spots, birthmarks and acute growths, as well as epilepsy and strokes. As far as gynecological disorders and fertility problems are concerned, these seemed to demand unequivocally the use of placenta powders. The placenta was also ascribed exceptional significance for the reanimation of lifeless newborns; people thought that the

睿	= 예	Ye	} Proper name
宗	= 종	Yong	
大	= 대	Dae	} Great King
王	= 왕	Wang	
胎	= 태	Tae	Placenta
室	= 실	Shih	Chamber

Grave of the placenta of a prince, the later eighth king of the Korean Yi Dynasty (1468–1469). It is located in front of the national museum of Jeonju, the capital of North Jeolla Province. The inscriptions on the tortoise stele (tortoise = symbol of longevity) are explained beside the picture.

afterbirth, which was applied as a warm compress, would have a restorative effect—one last time—on the unfortunate creatures that had emerged from the struggle of birth in a state of apparent death. The travelers of the sixteenth century did not neglect to express their wonder or shock that among some peoples, for example indigenous tribes of Brazil, it was customary to eat the placenta directly following birth—as can also be observed among the majority of mammals. Among the Yakuts, the placenta meal is a ritual that the child's father is obliged to perform for his friends and relatives. In Europe too, it was a widespread belief until the eighteenth century that it was advantageous for nursing mothers to eat at least a small piece of fresh placenta. A cookbook belonging to Hildegard of Bingen contains recipes for beef olives stuffed with placenta. As late as 1768, a midwifery handbook passionately discussed the question of whether Adam ate the placenta following the birth of his offspring.[15] In Pharaonic Egypt, the afterbirth was assigned great cultic importance—especially in the case of royal births. The Pharaoh's placenta was considered the incarnation of his outer soul; it was described as his "secret helper" and occasionally appeared in pictures. Impressive details of elaborate placenta-cultic institutions have survived in ancient Egyptian sources.[16] The Pharaoh's placenta was not infrequently mummified after birth and preserved as a talisman for his entire life; this "bundle of life" had protective and supportive effects—it was considered the king's mystic ally. The placenta mummy was looked after and guarded by temple priests with great reverence. The ancient Egyptian custom of carrying the pharaoh's placenta ahead of the ruler in processions was upheld from the fourth millennium BC to the Ptolemaic age; later flag cults were derived from it.[17] During the fourth, fifth and sixth dynasties there was a special office whose representatives acted as "openers of the royal placenta." It was presumably their task to open the Pharaoh's "bundle of life" symbolically after his death so that the outer soul would be freed for the journey to the underworld; at the same time, this farewell ritual made way for the successor to the throne. The placenta mummy was then either interred in special alabaster urns or placed in the king's tomb together with his embalmed body as a cap or pillow. An x-ray of a royal mummy in the British Museum shows a placenta bound to the back of the corpse's head with bandages. In some parts of North Africa, the custom of wearing leather pouches containing placental or umbilical amulets throughout one's life is apparently still upheld today. In the Old Testament too, one finds traces of the notion that the placenta, as a little bag of life, held a second soul or *alter ego* of humans:

Pharaonic Procession with placental standards

> Even though someone is pursuing you to take your life, the
> life of my master will be bound securely in the bundle of the
> living by the Lord your God.[18] But the lives of your enemies he
> will hurl away as from the pocket of a sling. (1 Samuel 25:29)

In Korean tradition it was usual to give up the placenta to the sea,
or to burn it together with rice and millet husks and scatter the
ashes on paths for good luck. Numerous cultures have the custom of hanging up placentas in trees; occasionally the afterbirth
is dressed in a cotton shirt, girded with a rope, given headgear
like a human being and fixed to the branches of trees. The four
main methods of placenta care—burial, hanging up, burning
and immersion in water—correspond to the elements, to which,
as forces of creation, that which is theirs is returned. Among
northern peoples, placental ash was considered a powerful magical

cure. If the placenta is thrown into a pit latrine, on the other hand, a folk superstition—most widespread in old France—has it that the woman will suffer cancer and a miserable death after her menopause.

Whatever the nature of the ritual and cultic procedures of placenta care may have been: in almost all older cultures, the intimate correspondence between birth and afterbirth was beyond doubt. Dealing with the child's placental double in an inattentive fashion would universally have been considered a curse-worthy neglect of the most necessary duty. It seems as if the beginnings of a disenchantment of the entire perinatal field, and thus also a de-sanctification of placenta awareness, only appeared with the advent of Hellenistic medicine; but even these tendencies—as the example of Hildegard's vision shows—were not sufficient to trigger a general de-sublimation of the fetus-placenta alliance in post-Hellenistic European birthing practices.

It was only in the second half of the eighteenth century, starting from the courtly and upper class sphere and its doctors, that a radical devaluation of the placenta took place. From that point on, obstetric literature standardized an attitude of disgust and embarrassment among childbearers and witnesses alike to that macabre object which comes out of the mother "afterwards." In an epoch-making example of disgust training, middle-class women—but also poets and fathers from the enlightened parts of society—unlearned how to keep a space open for the afterbirth in the cultural imaginary realm. For the intimate With, an era of unconditional exclusion began. Now the placenta became the organ that does not exist; in the light, what had been the authority of a first There-is becomes something that is itself absolutely without existence. The innermost second element becomes the

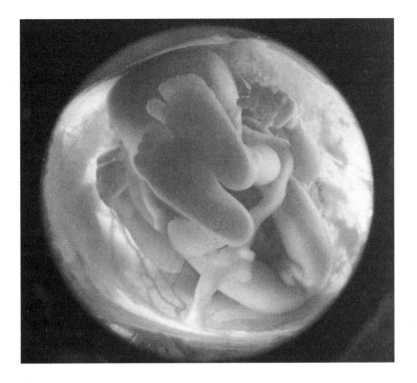

unconditionally vanished, the repulsive reject *par excellence*. It was, in fact, only from that time onwards that those conducting births, whether in hospital or at home, became accustomed to treating the placenta as a waste product. Now it was increasingly discarded as carrion and "disposed of" as garbage—which means destroyed. In the twentieth century, the cosmetic and pharmaceutical industries developed an interest in placental tissue because it came into consideration as a raw material for remedies and regenerative facial masks; this interest also informs the more or less blind consensus that clinics are the correct place for births; for where if not in clinics can one set up such collection points? If the placentas are not used for pharmaceutical purposes, it can happen that they are granulated together with stillborn fetuses and employed as combustive agents in garbage incinerators—that is the current state of technology in the German capital after the reunification.

Admittedly, it would be an exaggeration to say that the placenta has been thrown in the garbage in modern times. In the new world of unaccompanied single persons, the organ that prepares us to count onwards from two and travel here from yonder will, officially, never really have existed. The subject is isolated retroactively, and now portrayed even in its prenatal being as a first without a second. There are some indications that modern individualism could only enter its intense phase in the second half of the eighteenth century, when the general clinical and cultural excommunication of the placenta began. The medical establishment took it upon itself to ensure, like a gynecological inquisition, that the correct belief in unaccompanied birth was firmly anchored in all discourses and emotional dispositions. Bourgeois-individualist positivism established—against weak resistance from exponents of soul-partnership Romanticism— the radical, imaginary solitary confinement of individuals in the womb, the cot and their own skin throughout society. Robbed of the second element, all single humans immediately became mothers, and directly after that a totalitarian nation that reaches through its schools and armies for the isolated children. The founding of civil society began an age of false alternatives, in which the only choice individuals had was ostensibly that between reveling solitarily in the bosom of nature and embarking on potentially fatal power adventures with their peoples. It is no coincidence that one finds the master thinker of regression into absorptive nature or into the pathos-laden national state, Jean-Jacques Rousseau, as a charming and grotesque figure at the portal to the structurally modern, individualistic-holistic world. Rousseau was the inventor of the friendless human, who could only conceive of the augmentative other as either a direct maternal nature or a direct national totality.[19] With him began the age of the last men, who are not ashamed to appear as products of their milieus and isolated examples of social-psychological laws. That is why, since Rousseau, social psychology has been the scientific form of contempt for humanity.

Where, on the other hand, as in antiquity and popular traditions, a space was left open for the soul's double in the cultural imaginary, people could—up to the threshold of modernity—assure themselves that they were not directly connected either to their mothers, "society" or their "own" people; rather, they remained primarily connected throughout their lives to an innermost second, the true ally and genius of their particular existence. Its highest formulation shines out from the Christian commandment to obey God more than humans. That means: no human is simply a "case," because each one is a secret—the secret of an augmented loneliness. In ancient times, the placental double could also take refuge effortlessly among the ancestors and household spirits. The archaic, intimate means in itself affords the subject distance from the two primary forces of obsession that become manifest in the Modern Age: obtrusive mothers and totalitarian collectives. But where, as in the most recent part of the Modern Age, the With-space is annulled and withdrawn from the start through the elimination of the placenta, the individual increasingly falls prey to the manic collectives and total mothers—and, in their absence, to depression. From that point on, the individual—especially the male one—is driven ever deeper into the fatal choice between an autistically defiant descent into loneliness and devourment by obsession communities, whether in pairs or larger groups. On the way into apparent willfulness, one arrives at something else: the human without a protective spirit, the individual without an amulet, the self without a space. If individuals do not succeed in augmenting and stabilizing themselves in successfully practiced loneliness techniques[20]—artistic exercises and written soliloquies, for example—they are predestined to be absorbed by totalitarian collectives. For the individual whose double disappeared in the garbage always has good reason to prove to himself that he was right to survive without his With, rather than keeping his intimate other company in the garbage.

Indeed: since people stopped burying the intimate With in the house or under trees and roses, all individuals are latent traitors who have a guilt without a concept to deny; with their resolutely independent lives, they deny that they are constantly repeating the betrayal of their most intimate companion in their remorselessly autonomous being. Sometimes they think they are discovering a depth of their own when they feel lonely; in doing so, however, they overlook the fact that even their loneliness is only half their own, the smaller half of a loneliness whose larger half the thrown-away With took upon itself. The lonely modern subject is not the result of its self-choice, but rather a fission product from the informal separation of birth and afterbirth. Its positively willful being is tainted by a fault to which it will never admit: that it rests on the elimination of the most intimate pre-object. Its own singular value was purchased with the descent of the second element into the garbage. Because the ally disappeared in the refuse, the subject is an ego without a double: an independent, unrepeatable meteor. In relation to its navel, the released individual finds, instead of the With-space, not the addressable other but distracting business and nothingness. If the subject were to practice what one contemptuously terms "navel contemplation" in the West, it would only find its own unrelated knot. It would never comprehend that for its entire life, the severed cord in the imaginary and psycho-sonorous realms inevitably points across into a With-space. In terms of its psychodynamic source, the individualism of the Modern Age is a placental nihilism.

In modern urban delivery rituals, both in clinics and homes, the imaginary and practical equation of placenta and nothingness has largely established itself; the only exceptions to the general trend were small islands of tradition where traces of older generation psychology and doctrines of female wisdom survived almost unnoticed. In more recent times, a resistance to clinical positivism and its cultural superstructure developed from these islands, not least in the form of neo-archaic obstetric practices. In these, the severing of the umbilical cord in particular regained a certain ritual meaning and symbolic accentuation. Where such aspects are absent, it is usually the umbilical cord's opposite pole, the placenta, that is perceived as a waste product from which a separation cannot have any significance for the subject. One can even suppose that for the majority of modern mothers, it is not even clear in physiological terms what is actually severed when umbilical cords are cut off—there is, in general, merely a vague notion of the fact that the child lies on one side and the mother on the other.[21] In truth, the fetus and its placenta, ascending together from the underworld, are a couple like Orpheus and Eurydice; and, although Eurydice is destined to be lost through the *vis maior*, the modes of her separation are not insignificant. Obstetricians and midwives must know that when they perform the cut that is constitutive for the subject, they must, as it were, adopt an explanatory and clarifying attitude towards the child as mature givers of separation. They must understand themselves as cultural officiants who convey this cut as an original symbolic gift, indeed as an initiation into the symbolic world as such.

In terms of its dramatic content, what one generally calls "cutting the cord" is the introduction of the child into the sphere of ego-forming clarity. To cut means to state individuality with the knife. The one who performs the cut is the first separation-giver in the subject's history; through the gift of separation, he provides the child with the stimulus for existence in the external media. The obstetrician can only act as a separation-giver, however, if he himself, in mature circumspection, has both poles of the designated separatee in view. If Orpheus is to be delivered in the correct, adult fashion, then Eurydice too must be bid farewell in a sensitive and adult manner. Being able to act towards the child as an adult essentially means nothing other than being able to give the right separation at the right time. Modern individuals who have themselves already grown up in the regime of placental nihilism, however, have lost their competence to perform adult gestures. Where they should give the first separation with positive clarity, they normally seek infantile-nihilistic refuge in gestures of shameful disposal and hurried aid to disappearance. They act as garbage disposal men for Eurydice. Hastily, informally and cluelessly, they exterminate the afterbirth and destroy in Orpheus the beginnings of the melody that would be born from his free asking after the other part. Hence the muse's primal scene is covered up among the badly delivered subjects of modernity; the freedom to lament the lost other is smothered by dullness and unceremoniousness. With this, culture

Votive to a mother deity, presumably from a shrine in Veii, Southern Italy, terracotta

squanders its first scene in the individual. How will the child ever learn that angels only go so that archangels may come in?

Of course, the umbilical cord is still tied off everywhere in modern times, in all imaginable ways; to this day, the navel on the subject's body constitutes the hieroglyph of its drama of individualization. But the navel has lost its idea, its melody, its question. The modern navel is a knot of resignation, and its owners have no use for it. They do not understand that it is the trace of Eurydice, the monument to her withdrawal and demise. Originally, it is the source of everything that will be spoken or intoned with decent resolve. Using the symbolically living body, it testifies to the possibility of leaving behind blood communions in order to cross over to the world of breath, drinks and words—a sphere, then, that will one day, in the most favorable case, develop into table fellowships and reconciled societies. In modernity, even poets scarcely know that mature language is the music of separation: to speak means to sing through one's navel. In recent time, only Rilke seems to have touched the deep language pole:

> Be dead in Eurydice, always—climb, with more song,
> climb with more praise, back up into pure relation.
> (*Sonnets to Orpheus*, Second Part, no. 13)[22]

Our requiem for the lost organ thus ends with an additional demand for clarity. Thinking the With first of all means deciphering the hieroglyph of separation from it, namely the navel. If the attempt to renew psychology by philosophical means proves successful, its first project should be a hermeneutics of the navel— or, to put it somewhat Greekly and metaphysically: an omphalodicy. Just as theodicy was the justification of God in the face of the world's failures, omphalodicy is the justification of language, which constantly wants to go across to the other, in the face of the severed umbilical cord and its trace on one's own body.✗

Among the few authors who have commented on the navel as an existential engram, the French psychoanalyst Françoise Dolto deserves special attention for her theory of navel castration (*castration ombilicale*). Dolto has pointed out that the acquisition of a navel means far more than simply a banal surgical episode which takes place during an unexperienced early phase of human life. In speaking of umbilical castration, she underscores the hypothesis that cutting the cord constitutes a first culture-founding gesture acted out on the infant body. Dolto speaks of the child's body like a passport that should contain the description "navel-castrated" in the section "particular features." Her choice of words becomes more understandable if one takes into account that in the French psychoanalytical tradition, the term "castration" is used to refer to personality-forming separations, denials and prohibitions. It stems unmistakably from the theory of the Oedipus Complex, in which the child—in the orthodox analytical view—must learn to become free from its own generation for later genital partners through a thoroughly internalized renunciation of the forbidden intra-familial love object, namely the mother or father. Symbolic genital castration—that is, the ban on incest—separates the future genital subject from its immediate longing for the obvious first love partner. Only a thoroughly internalized castration can teach the genital subjects, their desire now curtailed, as it were, to steer clear of the ultimate forbidden erotic goal; their libido is thus extraverted and directed extra-familially; it is freed from the comfortable, yet unbearably burdensome obsession with the nearest, most logical first love object. Thus the abstention from the absolutely forbidden would be the start of the subject's later erotic availability; it creates the conditions in which the subjects, in more mature days, can choose a non-mother or non-father as an erotic partner. But even if one acknowledges a certain plausibility to this clearly overly simple and optimistic model—why should the severing of the umbilical cord already have a castrative meaning? Like other psychoanalysts of the French school, Dolto uses the term "castration"—sometimes, it must be said, with a hint of helplessness—as a technical synonym for progressive weanings, precisely in the pre- and extra-genital field; she occasionally places it in quotation marks, undoubtedly aware that it may have an alienating or even repellent effect on impartial listeners and readers. But as the author, for all her self-assurance, seems bound more to the school than the public communication community, she repeats the castration formula like a pledge of allegiance to analytical scholastics, even though one could easily invent other, less provocative terms for the matter in question, namely the symbol-creating emancipation of the child from its obsolete first partners in desire.

It is not our aim here to poke fun at the outmoded terminological frocks of an improperly school-based and subservient psychoanalysis. In truth, this language convention is based on a very serious, secularistically and scientifically concealed religious motif: like the Jewish practice of circumcision, castration reminds us that humans, if they are to be autonomous, capable of culture and obedient to rules, cannot be owned solely by the impulses of their momentary libido; they should break away from the limited and impatient enjoyment of primitive goods in order to ascend to an unrestricted and patient joy over objects of more mature sympathy. This corresponds precisely to one of the Jewish religion's constitutive ideas: freedom under the law. Only through a series of successful separations, sublimations or indeed "castrations"—at the respective developmental stages of orality, anality and genitality—can the child that lives forwards unmutilated master the free use of the world. The properly separated, desiring, fertile subject can—correctly understood—rule over the earth. Even in its terminological peculiarities, classical psychoanalysis still advocates a pathos-dominated concept of adult, properly disenchanted life. Complete adulthood, it believes, comes about through a curriculum of world-disclosing renunciations. In renunciation, wisdom and freedom coincide; abnegation makes the subject fit for culture and community and anchors it in living language games among adults who are capable of cooperation. With its doctrine of liberating abstinence, psychoanalysis in the French style thus produced a suggestive reformulation of Jewish spirituality and its Christian offshoots— a formulation that is the more suited to missionary attempts the less the protagonists realize what line of succession they are thinking and acting in.

According to Dolto's conviction, these separating "castrations" are not merely symbolic actions, but themselves symbol-creating or "symboligenic" acts; they set the *infantes* on the way to language. Symbol formations serve the de-fascination of the subject and its opening-up to the wider world; they emancipate it from the obsessive directness of relation to the first milieu and its libidinous content. If, consequently, we are already to consider the cutting of the umbilical cord a form of castration, it is because for the child, this coincides with the imposition of forgoing the comfortably immediate blood communion with the mother and accepting the more hazardous and variable circumstances of oral nourishment and external embraces. Drinking, whether from a breast or a substitute thereof, is a communion that replaces a communion. In this—and only this—sense, it constitutes a step towards the symbolic. Anyone drinking from an external source is at least free from the longing for an exchange of blood—unless they drink, as some alcoholics do, to the point of self-liquefaction and the dissolution of the world's contours. Milk and equivalent drinks replace the oldest sanguine communion. Because it is in the nature of the symbolic to replace earlier elements with later ones and material media with subtler ones, the child's progression out of uterine immediacy can be viewed as a castration in the precise technical sense—all the more so because Françoise Dolto leaves no doubt that the infant itself must be ascribed some "understanding" of the necessity of these progressive transitions. This becomes more plausible if one considers that the open-air newborn not only exchanges blood communion for breathing, but also masters a post-uterine use of the voice; this gives it the power to make itself insistently heard by its mother in case of need. The voice secures the dispensability of the blood community because it "signifies" the summonability of milk. Being outside means being able to call; I call, therefore I am; from this moment on, existence means existing within the success space of one's own voice. Thus symbol genesis, like ego formation, begins with voice "formation"; Thomas Macho and others have rightly assigned properties of a vocal umbilical cord to the voice that leads to the mother's ears.[23] The physical umbilical bond must indeed have a successor to ensure that unbound life too will remain under the sign of attachment.[24] The development of symbolic abilities thus presupposes a continuum principle; this articulates the demand for the earlier not simply to be lost in the substitution process, but rather functionally preserved and replaced by its expanded form at the next stage. Successful symbol formation in the mental process occurs through conservative-progressive compromises.

If, however, no acceptable new balances of desire are offered to replace the lost older ones, the subject comes up against an insurmountable obstacle and is shattered by its lack of desire. Now the good world becomes unattainable. No progression can occur with the frustrated infant, and its life, which had ventured this far, is now trapped; it is too late to turn back, and there are no longer adequate transitional aids in sight for it to go forwards. Thus a rigid continuum is inscribed upon its organism; a white point grows in the symbolic field, the pain remains imprisoned in non-linguistic bodily processes, and the pressure to live is incapable of transforming itself into an expressive libido. From this perspective, Dolto's view that the missed or poorly communicated umbilical separation can become an early catastrophe of symbol formation is well-founded. For then the subject will not experience the productive game of resonance with its mother that would convince it of the advantage of being born. Hence the phrase "umbilical castration" refers not only to the act that brings about the liberating division of mother and child with the knife or the scissors; it stands for the entire effort of converting the child to the belief that it is advantageous for it to be born.[25] On this level, "castrating" successfully would mean establishing a store of good experiences of resonance in the outside world with lifelong effects. The ability to believe in promises rests on this pre-linguistic hoard of primary impressions that confirm the attainability of the world; what is usually termed "faith" is simply another word for a pre-linguistically established trust in language. This grows exclusively in the hothouse of successful communions; whoever lives in it constantly witnesses the advantage of speaking and of listening to the spoken. Perhaps language only managed to become such a species-wide anthropogonic factor because it articulates the siren force that ties us to life? What could be a more powerful advertisement for human life than passing on the advantage of being able to speak to the speechless who are on the way to language? Where the speakers do not succeed in convincing the not-yet-speakers, the abandoned subject develops leanings towards going on a primal strike against the disappointing outside and its deaf, tiresome and superfluous signs; the ungreeted, unseduced and unenlivened are—rightly, one is inclined to say—agnostic towards language and cynical about the idea of communion. They do not move into the house of being in the first place. For them, language remains the epitome of counterfeit money; communication is nothing but the forgers' attempt to bring their own duds into circulation along with all the others. ✓

Excursus 5

The Black Plantation

A Note on Trees of Life and Enlivenment Machines

> And the leaves on the tree
> are for the healing of the nations.
> — Revelation 22:2

As individuals, human beings are constituted by a separating cut that does not usually remove them from the mother, but certainly forever from their anonymous twin. It is to be expected, then, that the individual, as a de-coupled, de-siblinged and uprooted residual subject, will experience the formation of a psychological and symbolic navel alongside the physical one— or, more precisely, an umbilical field on which memory traces from the formative phase of placental supplementation remain inscribed. The incipient subject can, it seems, only develop with integrity if it is able to connect to the reserve of an intimately-partnered parallel life from which it receives nourishing, supportive and prophetic signs that assure it prosperity in attachment and freedom. Plutarch's ingenious idea of reciting the life stories of great Greeks and Romans in biographical pairings therefore holds,[26] beyond its historiographic wit, a

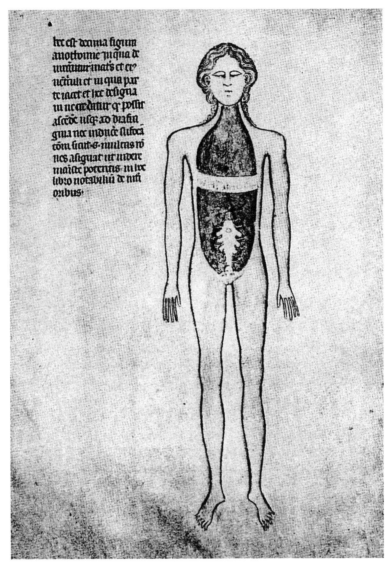

The seven-chambered uterus of medieval gynecology as an occult hybrid tree.
From Guido da Vigevano, *Anatomia designata per figuras*, Paris, 1345

religion-philosophical and depth-psychological potential that can be revealed as soon as one applies the principle of *bíoi parálleloi* not to two analogous human lives, but rather to the manifest life of an individual and the occult or virtual life of its original companion. Among countless variations in popular notions, one finds the idea that there must be spiritual double or magical, vegetative parallel life, in particular the trees of life mentioned above with reference to works by René Magritte. As a rule, the planting of such trees takes place directly after the birth of a child, usually with fruit trees, and not infrequently in the place where the child's umbilical cord or placenta was buried, normally in the immediate vicinity of the house of birth. Martin Luther's famous saying about the apple tree that would have to be planted even if one knew that the world would end tomorrow can only be understood through this idea of alliance: a human is undoubtedly more closely tied to its tree of life than the two of them are to the rest of the world.

The mythology of the tree of life offers the most convincing and widespread way out of a dilemma that is constitutive for all cultures: that the placental double must neither appear nor not appear either to individuals or groups. Its special status of being between necessary concealment and necessary acknowledgement lends it the dark radiance of a proto-religious (mis)creation. If it were too readily visible, it would—viewed as a mere organ-thing—invoke the risk of a nihilistic crisis, as it initially remains an unreasonable expectation that humans should imagine the conditions of their existential integrity in terms of this superfluous and rejected lump of tissue, and yet its complete absence would abandon each of them to a state of individualistic loneliness. One could classify cultures by how

Tree of life from the altar of abbey in Stams, Tyrol

they solve the problem of the simultaneously forbidden and imperative placentophany, whether through hypostases of vitality in allied plants, the representation of the vital principle in specific animals, especially soul birds,[27] or the allocation of protective spirits and invisible spiritual doppelgangers—which can, moreover, be expanded into integrative community spirits, city gods and group geniuses. The placentophanic alliance with the nourishing other can also be lifted into a livable symbolic form through a connection to an eminent amulet or a figure of spiritual guidance such as a guru or great teacher. What we call religions are essentially symbolic systems whose purpose is to transform the intimate ally of individuals into inner supervisors.

The case of modernity, admittedly, demonstrates the possibility of cultural climates in which the placentophanic dilemma can no longer be articulated as such (although its latent power becomes greater than ever), because individuals are imagined either as creatures of freedom that do not require significant augmentation, or as bundles of pre-personal partial energies for which the connection to an integrative second element no longer comes into view. In addition, modern self-supplementary life forms have achieved the breakthrough to technical media, and thus opened up a genuine post-human horizon. Andy Warhol provided the classic expression of this:

> So in the late 50s I started an affair with my television which has continued to the present [...]. But I didn't get married until 1964 when I got my first tape recorder. My wife [...]. When I say "we" I mean my tape recorder and me. A lot of people don't understand that.[28]

The goddess Isis, seen here in the form of a tree, nurses the Pharaoh; from the tomb of Thutmose III, Thebes, Valley of the Kings, 18th dynasty, 15th century BC

Pre-nihilistic cultures—one could also describe them as societies that did not possess any *technical* media of self-augmentation—were condemned to finding, at all costs, a mythical answer to the following question: into what grounding alliances should the souls of individuals and peoples be integrated? No religious or metaphysical psychology has ever reached its goal without being able to offer a conceptual framework for the imperative of placental doubling. As far as this task is concerned, the Babylonian and later the Essene mythologems of the tree of life are among the most impressive symbolic arrangements, as one finds the transcendent parallel life appearing in doubled projections. On a figural frieze from the ninth century BC in the palace of Ashurnasirpal II in Kalhu, one can make out a series of cherub-like bird-men or winged warrior geniuses, each of which seemingly has the task of looking after a tree of life. Evidently the total field of the double soul is here given visual form, with the alliance between the spiritual-anthropic and vegetative souls becoming particularly evident.[29] It seems, however, that the link between angel doctrines and the tree of life model was perhaps closer than any other in the cult of the Essenes, which the angelologist Malcolm Godwin summarizes as follows:

> Central to their belief was the Tree of Life which had seven branches reaching to the heavens and seven roots deep in the earth. These were related to the seven mornings and seven nights of the week and correspond to the seven Archangels of the Christian hierarchy. In a complex cosmology, which is both macrocosmic and microcosmic, man is situated within the middle of the tree suspended between heaven and earth.[30]

Assyrian tree of life, alabaster relief from Nimrud, 9th century BC

Here the tree of life is not only elevated to the integrative symbol of the sect; the spiritualistic counter-society, even more than the imperialistic first society, clearly needs to consolidate itself through a powerful psycho-cosmological symbol of integration—in this case an image of the *arbor vitae*, which acts as a world interior and communicating cave in one. Undoubtedly, a sociology of community-forming deliria could find its strongest corroborations in doctrines of this type.

When Saint Boniface felled the Donar Oak near Geismar on his missionary offensive in 724 AD, or when the agents of Charlemagne, under the influence of Lullus, Archbishop of Mainz, destroyed the Irminsul at the Eresburg fortress, the

Saxon sacred pillar thought to represent a world tree, these gestures were more than simply expressions of the usual Christian polemic against pagan symbols. Rather, this war against the trees consisted of frontal attacks on the placentophanic integrative figures of the alien society, that is, strikes against the imaginary and participatory resources from which the rival group had drawn the ability to create its symbolic and spheric coherence. Anyone seeking to introduce different structures of obedience must first replace the group's previous tape recorders. This is also evinced by the fact that the Christians tended to replace the toppled heathen tree symbols with their own *arbor vitae*: the cross, as the speaking wood on which death had been defeated. The history of fighting salvation associations, which emerge as religious peoples and ideologically virulent states, is always also a war between trees of life. It would be mistaken to view this simply as a trait of archaic and premodern societies, for it is precisely mass-medial modernity that produced the means to make giant populations froth up in synchronized polemical deliria and violence-steeped phantasms of regeneration. Did not one of the founding fathers of American democracy, Thomas Jefferson, formally decree that the tree of freedom demands to be watered with the blood of patriots in each new generation? The call for everyone to water the communal tree assumed an efficiently structured educational, postal, military and media system; the nationalization of the masses under revolutionary trees of freedom or patriotic lindens is a large-scale psychopolitical project that has been keeping European populations on tenterhooks since the founding of nation states. Anyone wishing to escape from the shadow of the totalitarian tree could only have done so by seeking refuge in opposing

The ash tree Yggdrasil as the world tree, from *Northern Antiquities*

media: the only protection against the total people's community comes from impenetrable symbioses between individuals and subversive literature; in recent times, submergence in the idiocy of one's own tape recorders has also proved an effective exile. The totalitarian effect of recording media can only be undone by media of self-insulation.

Shortly before the trees of life from immemorial agrarian folklore transformed into the trees of freedom in the French Revolution, the suggestions of the Viennese doctor Mesmer and the Marquis de Puységur led to the metamorphosis of the tree of life into the emblem of that first modern psychotherapy movement discussed above with reference to intersubjective practices of closeness.[31] In his study *The Discovery of the Unconscious*, Henri F. Ellenberger captured the primal scene of this new method under the "magic tree":

> The public square of the small village of Buzancy, surrounded by thatched cottages and trees, was not far from the majestic castle of the Puységurs. In the center of that square stood a large, beautiful old elm tree, at the foot of which a spring poured forth its limpid waters. The peasants would sit on the surrounding stone benches. Ropes were hung in the tree's main branches and around its trunk, and the patients wound ends of the rope around the ailing parts of their bodies. The operation started with the patients' forming a chain, holding one another by the thumbs. They began to feel the fluid circulate among them to varying degrees. After a while, the master ordered the chain to be broken and the patients to rub their hands. He then chose a few of them and, touching them with his iron rod, put them into "perfect crisis." [...] To

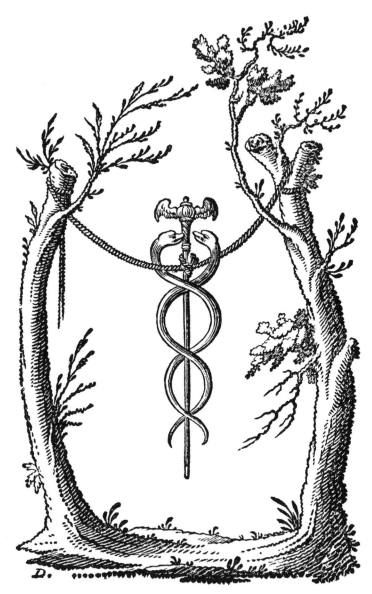

Magnetized trees, cover illustration of *Bockmanns Archiv*, 1787

"disenchant" them (that is, to wake them from their magnetic sleep), Puységur ordered them to kiss the tree, whereupon they awoke, remembering nothing of what had happened.[32]

For all its primitive and bucolic aspects, the scene nonetheless constitutes the decisive moment in Puységur's psychological secession from Mesmer's doctrinaire nature-philosophical physicalism. For, by leading to the discovery and systematic application of what would later be known as "hypnosis," this bizarre arrangement under the tree of life with its umbilical connections constituted the breakthrough to the scenic principle in psychotherapeutic treatment, and hence to that historization of the soul's space whose philosophical principles were brought to fruition by Schelling and Hufeland, and whose biographical-physiological substrate was developed fully in Freudian psychoanalysis. In addition, it is more than likely that Puységur's idea of connecting his patients to the magnetized elm with ropes came from the model of the magnetic baquet whose cables Mesmer had connected to his clients in his Paris practice. It seems logical to view the elm and the baquet as two means of staging the same contact-magical motif, namely therapeutic deep regression; this would mean that the tree of life in Buzancy constituted a herbaceous magnetization machine and the baquet, conversely, a mechanized tree of life. In both arrangements, the ropes and cables imply a metaphorical umbilical cord intended to place the individual in a melting relationship with its re-proximated companion. Both constructs represent the difficulty for modern psychology of reminding us of the lost, unknown and embarrassing double as the condition of possibility of psychological augmentedness.

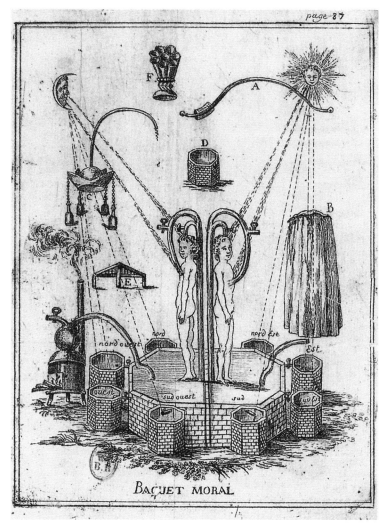

Franz Anton Mesmer, *Correspondance de M. Mesmer sur les nouvelles découvertes du baquet octagonal, de l'homme-baquet et du baquet moral, pouvant servir de suite aux aphorismes* [Correspondence of Mr. Mesmer on the New Discoveries of the Octagonal Baquet, the Man-Baquet and the Moral Baquet, Which Can Serve to Follow the Aphorisms], Paris, 1785

Baquet belonging to Franz Anton Mesmer, 1784

For, while the progressive factions of civil society set about constructing a humanity devoid of original sin in which every person has the freedom to be potentially perfect in themselves, the more radical modern psychologists attempt a reformulation of the *conditio humana* in which original sin returns as primal separation. You do not need to have "done anything wrong" yet to share in the universal human ability to despair. No one articulated this more clearly than Franz Kafka, who noted down the following during the First World War:

82. Why do we complain about the Fall? It is not on its account that we were expelled from Paradise, but on account of the Tree of Life, lest we might eat of it.

83. We are sinful not only because we have eaten of the Tree of Knowledge, but also because we have not yet eaten of the Tree of Life. The condition in which we find ourselves is sinful, guilt or no guilt.[33]

If one reproduces the religious category of sin with the psychological concept of separation, it points to the heart of unanalyzability. A few lines later, Kafka responds to the insistence on that separation which seeks to elude the understanding of one's mere fellow humans with the motto: "Never again psychology!"[34]

CHAPTER 6

Soul Partitions

Angels—Twins—Doubles

Further, Damascene says that where the angel operates, there he is.

> — Thomas Aquinas, *Of the Angels in Relation to Place*[1]

The unconscious is housed. Our soul is an abode. [...] Now everything becomes clear, the house images move in both directions: they are in us as much as we are in them.

> — Gaston Bachelard, *The Poetics of Space*[2]

Now tell me in what society, or *beside* whom, you live, and I will tell you who you are; describe your double, your guardian angel, your parasite, and I will recognize your identity.

> — Michel Serres, *Atlas*[3]

All births are twin births; no one comes into the world unaccompanied or unattached. Every arrival who ascends to the light is followed by a Eurydice—anonymous, mute and not made to be beheld. What will remain, namely the individual that cannot be separated again, is already the product of a separating cut that

Apotheosis of Antonius Pius and Faustina. The emperor's genius, holding the imperial sphaira, carries the ruling couple up to heaven.

divides the previously inseparable parties into the child and the remainder. Eurydice perishes, yet only seemingly vanishes without trace, for aside from the navel—that fleshly monument to the former connection with her—she also leaves behind a spheric lacuna in the space around her child, her protégé and twin. The companion, which was originally *yonder* in the first closeness, discreetly departs by leaving open the place of its absence. After it is cleared out, the first Yonder leaves behind the outline of a first Away. For a moment, while the With is disposed of, the child is exposed to a hint of unaccompaniedness—yet this precarious moment normally remains a fleeting one that is "forgotten," as new presences immediately stake their claims in the extra-uterine position. For the abandoned, exposed child, it seems as if Eurydice has been lost in the commotion and will reappear shortly; and indeed, what she was does return in a sense—but as something else. Once as a new balance has been established, other authorities take Eurydice's place. The great shift, as dramatic as its forms and consequences are, seems entirely lawful and natural; everything is now completely different, and yet it all remains vaguely the same as before. Thus every newborn gains early experience of revolution; somehow the total other will, after all, be like the situation it overturns. This affects every-thing that comes afterwards, for the important passages and successful revolutions—are they not the ones that establish a continuum of continuum and non-continuum? The successful revolution is the transition to the total other that still manages to follow on from the good old days.

The beginning of being outside, like that of philosophy, is amazement. Eurydice's farewell gift to Orpheus is the space in which replacements are possible. Her Away creates a free sphere for new media. Eurydice gives Orpheus his strange freedom; thanks to her withdrawal, he can devote his eternal infidelity to his former companion. Replaceability is Eurydice's inextin-guishable trace; it enables her separated lover to be constantly involved with others, whose changing faces always appear in the same "place." The "mother" will be the first of these others who materialize in that certain place. Her bodily emanations and discharges, the pillow-like qualities of the womb—these are the first With substitutes; they introduce new levels of resonance into the Orphic bubble. Orpheus is now forever dead in Eury-dice, but Eurydice lives on in him in her replacements. Through his interaction with ever new Eurydice substitutes, Orpheus is constantly re-adjusted for more complex scenarios. If the psyche is a historical element, it is because its progressive recastings and enrichments of the primitive spheric dual lend it a disposition towards what one thoughtlessly terms "growing up."

The teachings about gods and spirits in European antiquity display uncoded traces of a relatively uncomplicated awareness of the dual. Around 238 AD, the rhetorician Censorinus presented an erudite celebratory speech on the forty-ninth birthday of his patron Caerilus entitled *de die natali*, a merry collection of the knowledge of his time relating to the day of birth. It includes a reflection on the question "What is a Genius?", a being that supposedly accompanies the life of every human, "and why do we venerate him especially on our birthdays?"

> 1. A Genius is a god under whose protection each person lives from the moment of his birth. Whether it is because he makes sure we get generated, or he is generated, in any case, it is clear he is called our "Gen-ius" from "gen-eration." 2. Many ancient authors have handed down that the Genius and the Lar, the household god, are the same thing [...]. It was believed that the Genius has the greatest, or rather absolute, power over us. 3. Many believed that two Geniuses should be worshipped, at least in married households. Euclides of Megara, the follower of Socrates, however, said that a double Genius has been appointed for each of us [...]. And so we offer special sacrifice to our Genius every year throughout our lives. [...] 5. Our Genius, on the other hand, has been appointed to be so constant a watcher over us that he never goes away from us for even a second, but is our companion from the moment we are taken from our mother's womb to the last day of our life.[4]

The document expresses clearly that for Romans, there was no such thing as a single birthday, as humans are never born alone. Every birthday is a double birthday; on that day one not only commemorates the supposedly joyful event, but—even more so—the indissoluble link between the individual and its guardian spirit, which exists *coram populo*[5] from that day on. Roman birthdays were thus celebrations of an alliance—they were honored like jubilees of foundations or contracts; on those days, individuals commemorate their partnership with the companion spirit, which accompanies them as an outer soul in an unbreakable spheric alliance. Hence the individual is connected less directly to its progenitors, even its mother, than to its genius (unless one wanted to identify the mother as the child's true genius, as Hegel did);[6] it is immediately related only to the intimate god who will lead a parallel life in the closest and most intimate position for the full length of the individual's existence. That is why it can—as its only epithet—be termed an *observator*; but the observer is simultaneously a conserver: a specialized god whose area of attention and protection only extends to the one individual life. Certainly a human can be an observer in relation to other humans and things, but in existential tandem with the genius, he is exclusively the observed—the partner and recipient of an attention directed purely at him. For Romans, then, the central principle of philosophy in the Modern Age—*cogito ergo sum*—would have remained completely incomprehensible, as they would only ever have been able to expect the passive formulation: "I am thought of, therefore I am."[7] (Only in much later periods, when the observer-genius was completely interiorized, would the still-dominant concept of the self-augmenting, self-contemplating, self-caring individual emerge,

Apotheosis of Antonius Pius and Faustina. The emperor's genius, holding the imperial *sphaira*, carries the ruling couple up to heaven.

which understands itself as an autonomous, self-transparent orb. It is in this orb, indeed, that all imagining must be accompanied by an "I think" and all actions by a parallel "I know what I am doing"; conscience-time, writing-time, time of the genius that has been transferred from the outside to the inside.)[8] Birthdays serve to seal the pact of companionship between individual and genius and anchor it in reciprocity. This does not at all mean, however, that the subject guarded by the genius could also observe the observer; if someone expressly focuses on their genius on their birthday, this occurs in the form of devoting a ritually structured commemoration to it out of reverence and a duty to show gratitude. The individual celebrates its alliance of animation with the genius by satisfying the divinity exclusively assigned to it with well-defined sacrifices. These include, above all, libations with unmixed wine. Under no circumstances should animal sacrifices be made, for it is forbidden for humans to take the life of any creature on the day when they came into the world. It seems especially significant that no one is allowed to sample the offering made to the genius before the maker of the offering, the birthday child. Not even a pontiff is permitted to mediate between the subject and its genius, for when it comes to the personal life spirit, each Roman individual is like a protestant *avant la lettre*, and must therefore become a priest for itself once a year. Nonetheless, this private day of celebration is also a social event, and it is not without reason that the relatives and *familiares* celebrate the birthday together with the jubilarian. Aside from all that, Censurinus leaves the precise conditions of the bond between child and genius open. Whether the genius itself brings about conception, or is co-conceived, or only joins the child after conception in order to take over responsibility for it—this can remain undecided for now. In the latter case, the genius would be a form of divine precursor to the father, for in the Roman view it is the fathers who give their progeny a status in life by taking them in their arms (*infantem suscipere*), and thus acknowledging them as their legitimate children.[9] It is no coincidence that the general Roman understanding of the *genius* was first of all the man's specific life force, while women received life from Juno. Censorinus does not provide any information about the formalities of Roman women's birthdays. The identity of geniuses and *Lares*, which the author considers certain, at least seems to grant the protective spirits a certain domestic jurisdiction and *stabilitas loci*; for, since time immemorial, the household spirits—the Lares—have been considered place-bound, space-filling presences that are usually ancestral spirits. They are the close-range divinities *par excellence*. If, however, the ancestors cling to their houses, it is because houses were almost always also graves in ancient times, with urns or coffins kept in precisely specified places: the ancestral shrine or the Lararium. What would later be considered haunting was initially merely an occupation of the domestic intimate space by spirits of the dead, something that had come to be considered entirely natural in many cultures in times of sedentarism. The liaison of house and spirit highlighted by the Lares remained in force everywhere throughout the entire process of civilization, up until very recent times; it lives on in modern ghost stories, which still confirm the connection between the casing and animation.

When the narrator in Henry James' splendid doppelganger novella *The Jolly Corner* seeks out his dastardly and unkempt alter ego, this takes place with psycho-topological necessity in the interior of a large, empty house that offers a providential setting for the drama of an uncanny self-augmentation. James lets the companion mutate into a *genius malignus*, a para-noogenous pursuer; but the external setting, the secret and weird house in the middle of the metropolis New York, still provides the exact spheric form in which the split subject can be left at the mercy of its stalking double.[10]

In truth, there can be no domesticity without the inhabiting subjects expanding and establishing themselves in their respectively particular ways. The building of houses initiated interior creations of direct psycho-spheric significance. From the start, the poetics of the domestic space corresponds to mental partitions between the poles of the intimate field of subjectivity. Initially, living in house-like containers always has a dual character: it means both the coexistence of humans with humans and the community of humans with their invisible companions. It has, in a sense, always been the household spirits that have given an inhabited building dignity and meaning. The interior is born from the connection between architecture and invisible inhabitants. In fact, it is not unlikely that the oldest Mesopotamian notions of guardian spirits related to buildings, especially temples and palaces, and were only later transferred to individuals and personal representatives. Assyrian palaces were first guarded by those famous winged bulls, the *kerub* colossuses whose imago supposedly entered Christian angel iconology after long journeys through Jewish and Hellenistic phases. These guardian spirits were not yet mobile divine couriers, but rather place-bound keepers of a monarcho-sphere in the stricter sense—that is, a royal interior that constitutes a special kind of "power-protected interiority." The space shared by the prince and those close to him must be architecturally secured before the routine long-distance communications emanating from the palace can be set up. As the house is, so is the kingdom: if the kingdom outside is not secured, the ruler cannot yet withdraw to his palace, the broadcasting center of calm power, but must himself act as the messenger of the power he is assigned, bringing this to mind at critical sites with the risk of physical violence. It is characteristic of the monarch that he views not only the palace, but his entire domain of rule as the extension of himself; if the kingdom were not present within its bearer as a spatial idea and a task of concern, it could not be maintained outside either. But as soon as an inner world with the dimensions of a kingdom including a palace interior has been consolidated, there is a need for volatile, fast-travelling intermediate beings that ensure the swift accessibility of all points in the large-scale interior. The time of established kingdoms would therefore become the golden age of winged and wingless messengers. They are the new media of heavenly and earthly communication for kings—their business is *angelia*, bringing the lord's message, be it good or bad. The political theologians of earlier advanced civilizations never hesitated, moreover, to place whole empires—like animated houses—under the protection of the spirits and gods of the kingdom, and the Christian kingdoms seldom made exceptions to this rule. At Charlemagne's request, Pope Urban VI made the Archangel Michael, who distinguishes himself in transcendent campaigns as the commander of the heavenly host, the patron of the Carolingian kingdom; the Catholic Church celebrates his day on September 29th. It cannot be said that Europe's military archangel failed to live up to his task; under his banner, the army of Otto I repulsed the Hungarian cavalry in 955 at Lechfeld.

Figure of warrior with club and "second ego," San Augustin Archeological Park, Colombia

One should recall this event if one wishes to call to mind (for the last time) the difference between a substance-based Europe, unified by its angel, and a function-based Europe that would seek its motif of unity in a common currency.

The Roman genius is a representative from the immeasurable collection of soul companions and guardian spirits of which the mythologies of peoples and major religions tell. From a religion-typological perspective, it belongs to the morphological circle of outer souls which, like the Egyptian Ka or the Mesopotamian guardian spirits Ilu, Ishtaru, Shedu and Lamassu, were assigned to the inner life forces of individuals as external supplements.[11] Even the Socratic *daimonion*, though it already tended to articulate itself as an internalized guardian spirit, like an early argument for the conscience, still belongs typologically to the external or supplementary souls as a threshold figure; Socrates speaks of this subtle guest, which intervenes in his monologue, as if it came from an external space of closeness. Properties of the outer soul are also found in the character-*daimon* which, according to the great myth of the hereafter in the tenth book of Plato's *Republic* (620 d–e), is assigned to every soul that has chosen a new earthly fate by Lachesis, one of the three Fates.

Like most figures of this type, the Roman genius appears as an unmodulated fixture; it accompanies its charge's affairs like a benevolent silent partner with no claims or demands for development; its constancy stems from the fact that it is a spirit with few qualities. With an unchanging form and as a mysterious union of the wonderful and the reliable, it ensures that the psychological space inhabited by the ancient subject discretely and continuously borders on a proximate transcendence. Hence the ancients could never imagine the individual life simply as a distinctive soul-point, a trapped spark or striking flame; existence very much has a spheric and medial structure, because the subject is always placed inside a demigod-like field of protection and attention. Each individual floats in ghostly surroundings, whether one imagines the guardian spirit as a person-like companion residing in an invisible vis-à-vis or conceives it in auratic-environmental fashion as a "divine milieu" that wanders with the subject. Whatever the case may be, the presence of the genius ensures that the individual not only incorporates its psychological principle within itself like an isolated point of force, but in fact wears its innermost other around itself like a force field—and is equally carried and enclosed by it. The field creates closeness from within itself, because it is peculiar to the genius that it never moves far from its charge. (This is where the Roman idea of the protective spirit deviates significantly from that of many archaic peoples, who believe that outer souls can withdraw and go astray in the distance; the practice known as shamanism is, among other things, a technique for tracing stray free souls and bringing them back to their hosts—the historical prototype of all treatments for depression.)[12] As far as the structure of the dual field in the psychohistorical discourses and symbolisms of antiquity, it is evident that it does not yet know any real modifications within the dual; it is rigid by nature, and scarcely tolerates any biographically conditioned developments. We are still a long way from a non-theological, dynamic concept of spheres. It is not without reason that Censorinus describes the guardian spirit as "placed alongside," *adpositus*, the individual; this apposition clearly involves no internal modulations, let alone recastings or upgrades in the registers of resonance. At most, the brief reference to the doctrine of Socrates' pupil Euclides concerning the two geniuses (*binos genios*) holds the seed for a dialectical view of the companion spirits; Euclides may have meant that there was a division of labor, perhaps even quarrelling, among geniuses, where one of these could perhaps be envisaged as a good demon, the other as an evil one.[13] But even with double accompaniment, the structure of the metaphysically imagined dual space remains unchangingly rigid. A dynamic and psychological view would only become possible through the modern concept of augmentative variables, which describes the separate, yet connected poles of the dual appearing at new levels through altered volume and richer contents. This provides the tools for an analysis of sphere-immanent recastings—and only from this analysis can one formulate a phenomenology of the fully matured spirit: a mature subjectivity would be one that had developed its geniuses from micro- to macrospheric functions without breaking the continuum. The new microspherology thus creates the conditions for the discussion of the dual space to emancipate itself from religious languages, without depriving these of their virtual truth content. Only in spherological terms can one repeat those elements of psyho-spheric knowledge preserved and protected by mythical-religious discourses from corruption through false concept formations.

That the allocation of roles between the individual and its companion spirit cannot be conceived of in a religious-metaphysical imaginative framework without logical complications is shown by numerous documents from the ancient world. For, as soon as the subtle guardians are no longer imagined as permanent, discreet presences in the individual's immediate surroundings, instead approaching them as episodically appearing delegates—which is the rule in the biblical world—a precarious epistemological relation develops between the subject and its companion. In most cases, the subject does not directly recognize the manifested angel as "its" angel, as *no* relation of familiarity exists between them. That is why the stereotypical form in which angels address humans in the Bible is "Be not afraid!" (*Et dic ne timeas*).[14] The fear of God is preceded by the fear of the angel and the cancellation of that fear by the messenger himself. When Saint Peter is freed from the dungeon of Herod Agrippa, the apostle does not even realize that he is experiencing a "real" angelic intervention, as opposed to a dream vision (Acts 12:7–10). By contrast, some Neoplatonically oriented angelologists have proposed that angels can, as pure spirits, not know individuals, as they have knowledge only of general concepts, not individual beings (*singularia*). Thus angels can have intentions about peoples, communities or the human race as a whole, but not detailed knowledge about individuals, let alone local relationships with them; this theory is supported by the mystical authority of Pseudo-Dionysius, whose text *Celestial Hierarchy* was, for a while, understood as meaning that angels only operated on a general, not an individual level. In his treatise on the nature of angels, Thomas Aquinas attempted to refute this excessively Platonizing view, which destroys the personal element of angel-to-human contact in the Bible, through the authority of the scriptures and with reference to the consensus among scholars and the people. To him, it was clear that God's omnipotence worked through these angelic second causes and had a direct influence and foreknowledge that also extended to individual details.[15]

Be not afraid, Matthias Grünewald, Isenheim Altarpiece, inside of outer wing

The mystery of accessibility: Carlo Crivelli, *Annunciation*, 1486, oil on wood

Seraphim on a mural in the Church of Sant Climent, Taüll, 13th century

To avoid the tensions inevitably resulting from the imbalance between incorporeal and corporeal spirits—one could call it the ontological difference between angels and humans—numerous pious authors of accounts describing individual angels chose a sly way out: they let the personalized angel appear in the form of a twin. One finds the model for this in the first of the legends about Saint Anthony in the *Apophtegmata Patrum Aegyptiorum*:

> When the holy Abba Anthony lived in the desert he was beset by *accidie*, and attacked by many sinful thoughts. He said to God, "Lord, I want to be saved but these thoughts do not leave me alone; what shall I do in my affliction? How can I be saved?" A short while afterwards, when he got up to go out, Anthony saw *a man like himself* [my emphasis, P. S.] sitting at his work, getting up from his work to pray, then sitting down and plaiting a rope, then getting up again to pray. It was an angel of the Lord sent to correct and reassure him. He heard the angel saying to him, "Do this and you will be saved." At these words, Anthony was filled with joy and courage. He did this, and he was saved.[16]

The edifying twin pantomime removes, from the start, the sting of one possible problem of knowledge that could impair the human-angel relationship. The man "like himself" is an immanent-transcendent apparition unambiguously intended for Anthony; a mirroring space between the desert father and his double comes about in which informative communication immediately occurs. The benevolent angel is the reply to human upset; the twin appears as a precisely dosed angelic simile for its human pendant. He heals him by acting as a model—a case of monastic homeopathy. In our context it is unimportant that we have the primal scene of *ora et labora* (pray and keep fit) before us; the decisive aspect is rather the turn towards an individual angelology, which here seems to take place both naïvely and emphatically. At the moment when the angel takes on the form of a twin, a kind of micro-species comprising two individuals is born. The twin pair of human and angel consists of two singularities that together form a species, something biune and general. In this particular case, the angel's side would already be something individual and general in itself, as it founds a species on the basis of the unique, namely the quality of Anthony-shapedness. It therefore possesses, wonderfully enough, an *a priori* knowledge of the individual.[17] The human side also draws ontological profit from this augmentation and encounter, for, despite being singular, as an individual, it is taken up into a sacred biune quantity in which it stabilizes itself metaphysically; it can tell from the angel that it is itself an idea of God. In cognition-theological terms, there is much to suggest that a divine intellect could only remember such biune human-angel quantities; isolated humans would be invisible to it, and would elude all co-knowledge through their singular autism.[18] Thus the individual angel is, as it were, the optical lens through which the divine intellect espies the individual. If the angel disappears, the intelligent individual is also extinguished; from that point it could only be registered, but no longer recognized. The angel-less subject could be described externally, as modern psychology does with "unanalyzable" ones, but it could certainly no longer be reached through communicative intentions.

The twin angel phantasms of late antiquity reach their climax in the accounts associated with Mani (216–276), the founder of the Gnostic, semi-Christian two-principle religion which became notorious as Manichaism—that is, the "Mani lives" movement—and whose name, thanks to successful Catholic campaign of denunciatory propaganda, is still used pejoratively in today's secular culture.

> Mani acquired the art of wise words at a very young age. And at the completion of his twelfth year, he was inspired from above by (a being) he called the King of the Gardens of Light [...]. And the angel that brought him (this) revelation was called al-Tawm, from the Nabatean word meaning "companion." [...] (So) when he turned twenty-four, al-Tawm brought him forth saying: "Now is the time for you to appear [...]."
>
> Mani claimed that he was the Paraclete, foretold by Jesus.[19]

Naturally the proximity between the name *al-Tawm* and the Aramaic *toma*, "twin," catches the eye. That Mani's "companion" or Syzygos indeed had qualities of a transfigured twin is unmistakably clear from the tales of Mani's vocation in the Cologne Mani Codex, as well as Middle Persian sources:

> [...] from the spring of the waters there appeared to me a human form which showed me by the hand the "rest" so that I might not sin and bring distress on him.
>
> In this way, from the age of four until the time when I reached my physical prime, I was (secretly) kept safe in the hands of the most holy angels and powers of holiness.[20]
>
> [...] At the time when my body had reached completion, that well-formed, impressive mirror image of my person came and appeared to me.[21]

[...] Now too he accompanies me, and he himself shelters and protects me. With his strength I fight against Az and Ahrmen, and teach mankind wisdom. And this work of the gods and the wisdom and knowledge of the gathering of the souls, which I received from the twin [...].[22]

The case of Mani is primarily informative because it shows how the intimate psychological supplementation through the twin can be combined with a missionary function of cosmic implications. That the twin—if we read correctly—first spoke to Mani from a mirror image in the water offers a variation on the myth of Narcissus, albeit with the difference that no fatal confusion of subject and image ensues, just as the appearance of the double seems devoid of the implications of death or doom that are so common in doppelganger mythology; rather, the individual encounters a heightened alter ego in which it recognizes its ego ideal and the teacher for its life program. Enlightenment variations on this myth from late antiquity, incidentally, granted Narcissus the company of a sister whom he loved above all else, and who looked and dressed exactly as he did; after her death, he sought relief from his disconsolate state in the sight of his own mirror image in the water.[23] In this version, the motif of the augmentative twin gains primacy over the fatal confusion of doubling; it is, admittedly, the twin sister who now has to pay the price for the pathological equation of double-appearance and death. As far as Mani's twin is concerned, who belongs to the group of bright augmenters, he no longer has the modest features of the Roman genius. Certainly the double of the religion-founding Mani is also connected to his existence in a genius-like, intimate microspheric alliance; at the same time, however, the twin has charged himself up with the expansive elan of Middle Eastern missionary religiosity, and is steeped in the cosmic pretensions of Judeo-Christian and Hellenistic universal theology. Mani is thus not only subtly supplemented by his twin, but also spurred on by him to undertake ventures of world-spanning scope. Typologically speaking, Mani's twin liaison has parallels to Mohammed's alliance with the Archangel Gabriel, who would later dictate the Koran. We are clearly in the heartland of monotheistic mediumism: here, being a subject *eo ipso* means carrying a prophetic load. In this sense, one can say that prophetology is the basic science of the subject in expansive monotheism of the post-Jewish type.[24] The case of Mani—like that of Jesus—shows a state of the world in which micro- and macrospheric structures can be effectively nested within each other. From this historical turning point on, intimate religion already has the authority to speak the language of universal religion. We reach the age of individuals who, endangered by estrangement, can only find salvation on paths of internalization, defying the way of the world and avoiding imperial coercions. Before there could be any robust, cosmologically relevant battle of principles between good and evil in Manichaism, however, the subtle idea of an integral dual form first had to be found in the account of Mani's own development. Only in this way could the intimate religiosity of the twin-spirit faith be connected to universalist and expansionist programs. Religion responds to the political breakthrough to the idea of worldwide empire by postulating casings for the divine spirit in the form of a worldwide church. We will discuss how this took place in the case of Christianity later on.[25] It is no coincidence that Mani—who died after being kept in chains for twenty-six days in 276—left behind a church extending from Rome to China. The thermal center of this para-Christian empire of preaching was the young Mani's silent encounter with the image of his twin in the water. How such expansions from microspheric dyads—Mani and his twin, Jesus and his Abba—to worldwide churches became structurally and psychohistorically possible will be examined in the second volume.

The genius, the twin, the guardian angel and the outer soul form a group of elemental and enduring concepts for the second pole in the psycho-spheric dual. All these figures result from recastings of the first There, which left a vacant space for supportive, close accompanying elements. But while the original fetal There and With is essentially anonymous and unconscious, the later companions must be presented under public names and observable concepts—whether in analogy to natural persons, as with the twin, or taking notions of invisible force subjects or spirits, which can be found in the imaginary realms of all cultures, as a model. One could call the aforementioned soul companion concepts, where they appear as successors to and substitutes for an archaic anonym, figurations of the placental double; in truth, these elements would not be able to develop their soul-space-securing qualities if they did not already find, set up in the intrauterine bubble, a primitive Yonder-Here structure that they could enter as Yonder-figures and allies on a higher level. One can see that the subtle partitions in the soul space are, in psychological terms, archaic companion figures under suspicion of immaturity. Where such figures occupy a lasting place, they threaten to hinder their replacement by their rightful evolutionary successors, most of all the imaginary parents that are meant to establish an inner double model of fruitful life in a healthy tension between genders.

Therefore, according to analytical orthodoxy, the images of angels and twins must also perish so that their place can finally, through further recastings, be taken by the models of sexual maturity—and, beyond these, by the cultural models. The individual is not meant to remain the inseparable companion of its primitive, intimate alter ego forever, but rather to develop into the pole of a mentally and physically fruitful couple. In his play *Nathan the Wise*, Lessing skillfully shows how the image of the saving angel must perish in the soul of a girl for that of the real man to emerge in its place. The homoerotic couple in the middle of a very earthly household would—according to the psychoanalytical Vulgate—be the minimum goal in every history of mental maturation. Logically speaking, maturation means nothing other than the increasing readiness to count to three, four and five; it would be the final stage of a recasting process rich in phases as well as transitional subjects and objects.

As far as the placental doubles are concerned, their appearance already testifies to the formation of a mental space with pronounced attributes of a microcosm. The ego and its alter ego, the individual and its genius, the child and its angel: they all form microcosmic bubbles in which the dense worldlessness of the intrauterine position, with its blueprint for the Yonder-Here structure, has already cleared a little and been modified into the moderated worldlessness of the early ego-alter ego dual; it is this dual that foreshadows later, more complex realities.

Five structural elements are constitutive of the small world: the first two, trivially enough, comprise the holders of the Here and Yonder poles—that is, the self and the With-self, which, as shown above, are always connected from the start in original augmentation, and which are further enriched and differentiated through separations and reconnections. The third is provided by the container form in which the Here-Yonder field is embedded. The fourth characteristic is the free mutual accessibility of the two poles, and it is typical of the twin, the angel and their counterparts that they have no problems in accessing their other—the companions are always in the room already. The angel, like the genius, does not seek; it finds. For it, the creature of closeness that is always *there* from the start, the other pole is disclosed *a priori* through resonance; for the subject, however, in so far as it turns towards the companion, a degree of sheltered being-outside-itself is the norm. Inside the bubble, ecstasy, being with the other, is the usual state: because the bubble is the absolute place, I am always in place when I am in it—and in it at the other pole. In the following chapter, we will show that this is first and foremost a psychoacoustic relationship which comes about through the ecstasy of anticipatory listening.

The fifth structural element of the small world are the membrane functions that are native to the companion from the outset. As an original augmenter, the companion ensures both the formation and opening of the space and its care and closure. In this sense, the subject's "chance and misfortune" depend entirely on the quality of the mental membrane that simultaneously provides and denies access to the world. The twin is a manner of sluice through which the metabolic exchange between subject and world takes place. The degree of its opening determines whether there is dehydration or flooding. If the companion's membrane is not sufficiently porous to let through increasing amounts of world, it can become a prison for the subject; it closes it off from the "outside world"—or rather, the extra-symbiotic spheres. If, on the other hand, the companion is lost prematurely, or remains indifferent or absent for a long time, the subject will suffer an openness shock, tumbling "out" into the harmful ecstasy of a fear of destruction; it becomes acquainted with an exospheric outside in which it cannot bear itself. Both extremes—twin autism and pathological fear of the outside as a space of destruction—are typical consequences of a failure of the companion's membrane function. They show what consequences an excessive or a deficient protection of one's space in early psychological processes can have. The case of the British twin sisters June and Jennifer Gibbons, who closed themselves off from the outside world for years through their persistent silence in order to live in radical-symbiotic fashion in their "own world," received great attention, including coverage in the tabloid press.[26] They testify to the risk that the intimate companion—if it appears in too real, obsessive and impermeable a form—may seal the bubble off to the outside so strongly that a hermetic inner life will start to blossom in forms of two-party autism. Such cases have the merit, at least, of demonstrating to profane viewers—that is, anti-depth psychologists—the reality of internal psycho-spheric relationships in palpable forms. On the other hand, numerous cases of autism in early childhood, dealt with in the landmark studies by the psychologists René A. Spitz and Bruno Bettelheim, can be read as traces of invasions by a malign infinity of the early intimate space. The empty fortresses of autism are first and foremost defense systems that protect the subject from spatial panic and death by abandonment. They show the opposite extreme of the destruction of the soul space; for while the over-accompanied soul threatens to remain trapped in hermetic communions, the under-accompanied one withdraws into an uncommunicative, frozen state as a

Jennifer and June exchange their secret sign, from Marjorie Wallace, *The Silent Twins*

security measure, rendering itself unreachable to all overtures from the outside world. The fate of the autistic children shows that the fear of death comes from the same side on which the integral companion should have shown itself—which is why the treatment of autism can only make progress as the establishment of a second trust and new circles of resonance, bypassing the scar of destruction. Where the discreet companions perform their membrane duties well, however, the subject grows up in the oscillating area of that protected openness which provides the human optimum—that is, in well-tempered ecstasy.

The outer soul—a membrane: this concept can help to understand why it is only through this medium, this sluice, this exchanger, that a world can be constructed at all in the subjective field, that is, in the symbiotic sphere and the spaces that follow it. As a two-sided form, the membrane firstly ensures that the world can only reach into the subject, so to speak, via the "twin"—which temporarily presents itself primarily as the mother—and secondly, that the self is always already outside with its double. Together, the subject and its augmenter initially form a worldless—or own-worldly—intimacy cell; because the subject is informed by its double, and initially *only* by it, about the volume of "world" in the given culture, however, the incipient subject's access to the outside depends entirely on the membrane qualities of the inner other. By flying towards the cherished other, it develops in the direction of that other's wider world. The openness of the world is the gift of the double as membrane.

Only if the subject has constituted itself in a structure of protective-permeable twinship from the start—and the prefiguration of this dual begins, as shown above, in the prenatal space—can the enrichment of the subjective field through additional poles develop into a fitness for community: the adequate mother is not the direct second, but rather the third in the alliance of twins, in which the ego is the manifest and the primal companion the latent part. Mother and child always form a trio that includes the child's invisible partner. If the field is built up further, the figure of the father adds a fourth pole, while the siblings (as the close strangers) and unrelated persons (as strange strangers) form the fifth. Adult subjectivity, then, is communicative mobility within a five-poled field. It is the ability to enter differentiated resonances with the genius, the mother, the father, with siblings or friends and with strangers. Translated into musical terms, the elementary development progresses from the duet to the quintet. At every stage, it is the companion that formats its subject and makes it available; a discrete genius evokes a discrete individual in an adequately defined world.

In traditional cultures, children must become at least as mentally spacious as their parents in order to move into the world house of their tribe. In advanced cultures, this factor is joined by professional spirits of provocation and soul expanders—which, in the case of the ancient Greeks, led to the discovery of school and the transformation of demons into teachers. (The teacher historically appears on the scene as a second father; he oversees the sensitive transition from the quartet stage, which is still limited to the family, to the quintet—that is, to the minimum form of society. Since the advent of teachers, fathers have found themselves observing dissimilar sons.)

The history of formal pedagogy shows that in all higher cultures, mothers are deprived of their psychocratic monopoly on the children when the threshold between rearing and educating is reached. When Hegel says in his lectures on psychology that "the mother is the genius of the child," he is describing—albeit inadequately—the starting point of parenting on the level of the sentient soul and the sensing, yet still aconceptual subjectivity. Certainly the individual, after its placental and fetal-acoustic conditioning, must first of all be infused with the mother's soul and, as Hegel puts it, made to "tremble"; once it has completed its education, however, the spirit of the individual—according to the idealistic schema—is supposed to be infused purely with the self-assured concept, which no longer trembles.[27]

The mode in which the companion's presence is experienced at the start is initially mostly a non-visual one, as the subject's ancient history lies entirely in the pre-visual and pre-imaginary realms. As far as the (in)existence in the uterine night is concerned,

Joseph Beuys, *Die Hüterin des Schlafs* [The Guardian of Sleep]

this goes without saying; for the newborns too, however, it is—leaving aside the elementally significant fascinogenic eye contact with the mother—the non-visual media of physical contact and relationships that are clearly predominant. In the child's earliest perception, even a genuine twin brother would for a long time be not so much a sight as a sensed presence, a sound center, something touched, a pulse, an aura, a source of pressure actions—and only lastly something visible too. This applies all the more to the early concepts of the present and absent other that develop in the child in its interactions with the face and body of the mother in place of the archaic With. The presence of the genius and the experience of closeness are thus firstly and lastly a matter of feeling; visual evidence can only join the field's foundation of self-sensation as a secondary augmentation. Even the child's supposed early self-"image" is, in reality, not so much a matter of pictorial imagination or an *imago*[28] as something in the sensed self-field. To the great detriment of theory and practice, classical psychoanalysis already sought to make the early ego fundamentally dependent on visual self-images, thus going against all probability; for the *infans* certainly gains immeasurable experience of itself and its integrity or disintegration through the sensual exchange with its mother, but it assimilates relatively little auto-eidetic information of any significance. Even the reflection in the mirror that it may see and recognize is inevitably interpreted in the inner light of its prior self-sensation. The decisive information about the nature of the self is always already present as a vague holistic complex of sentiments in the sensed field, and it is only as a visual supplement to the lived prejudice of its self-sensation that the mirror image of the ego can come into its own as a phenomenon in the visually disclosed space.[29]

For the ordinary, more or less umbilically separated individual, one of the banal givens in its existence as a single being among other single beings is that the place opposite its navel—which was occupied in the fetal space by the connection to the With—must now remain forever vacant, though not empty. That is why humans perceive a stark difference between the physical awareness of their back and front sides: the front is the face side, the genital side and, above all, also the navel side. This front not only includes the most important orifices and sensors; it is also where the scar of separation is inscribed upon the body. The navel is located on the human's front like a monument to the unthinkable; it reminds people of the thing that no one remembers. It is the pure sign of that which lies on the other side of the consciously knowable— which is why, if one thinks about it, those who are unwilling to speak about the navel should also keep quiet about the unconscious. It signifies the knowledge of an event that concerns me more than any other, even though I am not eligible as the current subject of this knowledge. For his entire life, the navel owner looks past the memorial at the center of his body, like someone who walks past an equestrian monument every day without ever wondering whom it represents. This disinterest in one's own prehistory has cultural method, for Europeans have always been raised under a ban on navel contemplation: they are supposed to feel shame for even thinking it possible to refer to themselves at this point. Attached to the discreet recess in the middle of our body is the commandment to refer always and without exception to other things: the navel is the symbol of our obligation to extraversion. It fundamentally points forwards into the panorama of things and subjects that exist for us and with us. The world is meant to become everything that is the case opposite the navel.

In a short story entitled "Scenes from the Life of a Double Monster," Vladimir Nabokov describes the case of a pair of Siamese twins born near Karaz, by the Black Sea, who were bound together by a "fleshy cartilaginous band" at their navels—"*omphalopagus diaphragmo-xipbodidymus*, as Pancoast has dubbed a similar case."[30] The fascination of such grown-together twins seems primarily to be the fact that they show the normally vacant place opposite the navel as an occupied one. Thus the curiosity aroused by these monsters—in the sense of showpieces and cautionary creatures—is not simply one variety of the aspecific interest in all things abnormal, curious, anecdotal or surprising. At fairs and circuses the visitors, who come in throngs from far away to see the double monster, sense a connection to the secrets of their own individuation. The hunger for this Siamese obscenity conceals the inarticulable question of the double, which invisibly accompanies all individuals without its connection to the navel ever becoming explicit. In the case of the Siamese twins, the intimate companion has simultaneously adopted all three of the forms that the With-successor, also known as the placental augmenter, can have: it is double, genius and pursuer in one. As the double, the twin embodies two as the prime number of the soul space; as the genius, it testifies to the ego-forming happiness of positive augmentation; and as the pursuer, it incarnates the basic risk inherent in animation, namely that your innermost point of access might belong to your denier. (In this sense, hereditary political enemies are also Siamese twins on the level of psychohistorical accretions—and their separation is most likely to occur in the surgical war that is followed by making peace. In the words of Theodor Däubler, quoted by Carl Schmitt: "The enemy is our own question as a figure.")

Nabokov's Russian twins, Lloyd and Floyd—though these are their later names as an American variety act—are inseparable figures in which the archaic shadow has materialized into a physically present brother. In them, the unthinkable has become flesh and dwells among us, and the world is happy to recognize it—no means as an aspect of its own truth, however, but as an external sensation and a part of nature's comedy. Wherever the twins have to endure being gawked at, a macabre and cursed zone comes about in which the sacred shines out from the curious. Because the mystical bond is viewed as a cruel whim of nature, something that normally remains hidden between saints and their God can be observed like a zoological fact. For the exhibited conjoined children, what makes their situation particularly torturous is that people demand for them to play and communicate with each other as if they were normal, separate brothers:

> Our folks bullied us into gratifying such desires and could not understand what was so distressful about them. We could have pleaded shyness; but the truth was that we never really *spoke* to each other, even when we were alone, for the brief broken grunts of infrequent expostulation that we sometimes exchanged [...] could hardly pass for a dialogue. The communication of simple essential sensations we performed wordlessly: shed leaves riding the stream of our shared blood. The thoughts also managed to slip through and travel between us. Richer ones each kept to himself, but even then there occurred odd phenomena.[31]

It has been suggested by doctors that we sometimes pooled our minds when we dreamed. One gray-blue morning he picked up a twig and drew a ship with three masts in the dust. I had just seen myself drawing that ship in the dust of a dream I had dreamed the preceding night.[32]

The refinement of Nabokov's story lies in the narrative decision to develop it from the perspective of one of the twins, so that the reader follows this existence as a double monster from within, like a normal individuality. The twins themselves—as portrayed by Nabokov—scarcely comprehended their unusual nature in the first years of their life. Floyd, the narrator, thought of himself as an average human being with a constantly present partner by his side, and only came to appreciate his extraordinariness much later:

> Each was eminently normal, but together they formed a monster. Indeed, it is strange to think that the presence of a mere band of tissue, a flap of flesh not much longer than a lamb's liver, should be able to transform joy, pride, tenderness, adoration, gratitude to God into horror and despair.[33]

This is how Floyd explains the death of his mother, who perished out of sorrow over the monster's birth. For Floyd, the primal scene of his realization took place at the age of seven or eight, when they encountered a child the same age peering at them from under a fig tree:

> I remember appreciating in full the essential difference between the newcomer and me. He cast a short blue shadow on the ground, and so did I; but in addition to that sketchy, and flat, and unstable companion which he and I both owed to the sun and which vanished in dull weather I possessed yet

another shadow, a palpable reflection of my corporal self, that I always had by me, at my left side, whereas my visitor had somehow managed to lose his, or had unhooked it and left it at home. Linked Lloyd and Floyd were complete and normal; he was neither.[34]

Nabokov poses the question of the criterion for a normal soul from the perspective of the Siamese twin who assumes that being joined to the second is the primal state. Equipped with this new vision, he sees through the halved nature of the others: one has to be a monster of completeness not to realize that the normal individuals are those who can detach their companion. From Floyd's perspective, the strange boy is a monster of isolation— and it will take a while for him to understand that the monstrous quality lies with him, not with the separated who have left their augmenters at home or wherever else. The Siamese twins embody the neglected "umbilical castration," the missed letting-go of the other. In their umbilical field, unlike those of ordinary individuals, no invisible companions and dreamy intentions of desire for them were able to establish themselves. For these twins, the double remains carnally, all too carnally present. That is why Siamese twins can be exhibited at fairs: they stand before the fascinated crowd as individuals who have caught their angel in a trap—their companion is condemned to appearing, their genius must endure a descent into the body. Faced with this monstrous exception, even the dullest gazer senses the law of human incarnation: where there was a physical bond, there will now be a symbolic one. Whoever sees the twins breathes a sigh of relief and is glad that God, should He exist, has stayed in the background in their own case. In no temple could this truth be more

Circus theology: Chang and Eng—or: The trapped augmenter

explicitly proclaimed than it is on the variety stage: no mirrors, no glass, no optical illusions—only pure, obscene nature. Here the real twin has pushed himself into the umbilical field, asserting his presence against liberating recastings. Without any palliative veil, the observer has the sacred bondage of the chosen in view. For the conjoined, the way out into psychological banality, which is open to all normal individuals, is blocked; they are condemned to constant accompaniment, just as the mystic is chronically defenseless against the God who floods him or dries him out as He pleases. Life under possession by a genius that does not keep its distance is monstrous. The grown-on second—

does he not represent what should never have become visible, not now, not here, and not in so recalcitrantly corporeal a shape? It is placentophany as a brother staggering along at one's side. At least the macabre comedy of the sight acts as a sheltering incognito for the monster, "making us look, I suppose, like a pair of drunken dwarfs supporting each other."[35]

In the third and fourth parts of his novel *The Man Without Qualities*, Robert Musil adopts the motif of the Siamese twins as a metaphor for fusionary eros. The Siamese bond appears here in a completely dematerialized and internalized form, admittedly, acting as a symbolic pointer in an epic exploration of the condition of possibility of intimacy between partners who seduce each other into an excessive openness to one another. The fact that the poles of Musil's fusion experiment, Agathe and Ulrich, are biological siblings is only a literary, not a psychological necessity. Musil does not neglect to locate the starting points of the merging process as far apart as he can: the two siblings— who are also of different ages, not being actual twins—had lived separately and had lost sight of each other, emotionally as well as literally, for many years. It was only the death of their father that provided the occasion for a renewed encounter, which would mark the beginning of a boldly constructed magnetopathic-incestuous liaison. The sibling bond between Ulrich and Agathe is necessary for Musil's narrative economy for two reasons: firstly, to provide the simplest and most plausible explanation for the simultaneously erotic and symbiotic *a priori* attraction between the two, and secondly, to examine the question of the boundaries of eros using an exceptional and illegitimate case of sibling love. In the process, the search for a

Leonardo da Vinci, *Leda and the Swan* (detail). Her four children have hatched from the two eggs.

thousand-year kingdom for two emerges as a violation of the basic law of all societal formation. It is not without reason that the cycle of chapters on the siblings in Musil's magnum opus was meant to bear the title "The Criminals" [*Die Verbrecher*]. Agathe and Ulrich have to be siblings so that the equivalence between incest and mystical communion becomes apparent. For, just as the genealogical order of society as a system of distances and differences could not remain in force if there were sexual relations between mothers and sons, fathers and daughters or brothers and sisters, so too reality could not establish itself as an overarching symbolic institution if that mystical temptation which seeks to liquidate the institutionalized distance between subject and object were to gain the upper hand. Indiscretion—or refusal of distinction—is the ontological crime to which all generally binding constructions of reality, all ethical worldviews, object. Even if individuals always long to merge into the undifferentiated on some level, culture is based on the categorical imperative of discretion: thou shalt distinguish! And thou shalt view the first distinctions as absolutely valid laws, even if it seems to you that the law, like the emperor in the fairy tale, is naked—or willful and indifferent, which amounts to the same. All constituted conceptions of the world are rejections of undifferentiatedness. At the same time, an anarchic de-differentiating tendency can be expected among countless individuals. Indifference towards everything accounts for more than half of mysticism. The devil-may-care attitude that takes the end of the world into consideration as a permanently current solution to all problems of reality is not only a specialty of the Austrian social character. Ontological anarchism is a temptation that is found, at least in traces, in all advanced civilizations and all milieus of achievement. Musil's essayist art imagines itself as an experiment to investigate the difference between an existence that remains trapped and sheltered within valid distinctions, and one in which constitutional differences are abandoned to dissolution. This can only lead to a permanent conflict between the normal condition and the "other condition." Musil's great theme is the rivalry between the realistic and mystical modes of existence. In the novel's universe, as we know, Ulrich, the man without qualities, figures as the living intersection between the discrete and indiscrete forms of being. His supposed lack of qualities marks the life-practically impossible position on the boundary between pure observation and absolute participation. His idea of sibling love takes into consideration the utopian coincidence of *epoché* and fusion:

> (Ulrich): "The moment you're ready to go all out into the middle of something, you find yourself washed back to the periphery. Today this is the experience in all experiences!" […] (Agathe): "So your experience tells you that one can never really act with conviction and will never be able to. By conviction," she explained, "I don't mean whatever knowledge or moral training have been drilled into us, but simply feeling entirely at home with oneself and with everything, feeling replete now where there's emptiness, something one starts out from and returns to—" […]
>
> "You mean just what we were talking about," Ulrich answered gently. "And you're also the only person I can talk to about these things. […] I'd have to say, rather, that being at the inner core of things, in a state of unmarred 'inwardness'— using the word not in any sentimental sense but with the

meaning we just gave it—is apparently not a demand that can be satisfied by rational thinking." He had leaned forward and was touching her arm and gazing steadily into her eyes. "Human nature is probably averse to it," he said in a low voice. "All we really know is that we feel a painful need for it! Perhaps it's connected with the need for sibling love, an addition to ordinary love, moving in an imaginary direction toward a love unmixed with otherness and not-loving." [...]

"We'd have to be Siamese twins," Agathe managed to say.[36]

Excursus 6

Spheric Mourning

On Nobject Loss and the Difficulty of Saying What Is Missing

> Richer treasure earth has none
> Than I once possessed—
> Ah! so rich, that when 'twas gone
> Worthless was the rest.
> — J. W. von Goethe, "To the Moon"[37]

If psychologists were still allowed to speak in openly mythological forms—they have never stopped doing so in coded forms anyway—they could, in order to pinpoint the theoretical and therapeutic nuisance of the depressive or melancholic disposition, take refuge in the formulation that melancholia is the mental trace of a single twilight of the gods. The advantage of this wording would be that of explaining the melancholic-depressive disorder with an authentic bereavement in the subject's immediate vicinity, which would also deprive the supposed structural difference between mourning and melancholia, to which Sigmund Freud assigned considerable importance in his frequently interpreted essay of 1916, of much of its theoretical attraction. Then the melancholic would first of all be a mourner like everyone else, except that the loss he had suffered would go beyond the usual interpersonal separations. It would be the genius or intimate god that had been lost in the individual twilight of the gods, not simply a profane relative or lover; mourning a lost beloved person would only take on aspects of melancholia if this person had simultaneously been the genius of the abandoned individual. Both the loss of the genius and the loss of an intimate partner constitute psychologically real, and thus objective bereavements, and the task of a psychology that knows anything about spheric laws is certainly not to play off the reality of one against the unreality of the other, but rather to establish the psychodynamic causes for the subjective equivalence between the loss of a life partner and the loss of a genius. Psychology can only identify itself as the science of distributing subjectivity through its competence in describing inner circumstances according to their own laws. If—with all the necessary methodological and ideological reserves—it described melancholia as a chronic form of mourning for a lost genius, it would be defining the nature of the depressive-melancholic disorder as a form of individual-atheistic crisis: in a religious culture, the melancholic would be an individual who had extended the official doctrine of "God exists" with the private, subversive and rebellious addition "but He is unable to animate *me*." That is why, in the Old European metaphysical tradition, problem-laden images of the genius' withdrawal to zones remote from the world and from God could become suggestive; it is no coincidence that Dante and Milton, with their portraits of the gloomy Satan, practically developed official views of the original mental illness: having a different opinion from God. In an atheistic culture, on the other hand, the melancholic individual would be a subject that had augmented the officially licensed thesis "God is dead" with the private addendum "and my own ally is also dead"—though it would hardly matter at first whether these private thoughts affects the subject consciously or unconsciously. Depressive impoverishment is the exact depiction of the state of no longer having anything to say after the removal of the most important augmenter; that is why, in the ancient world, real melancholia was primarily the illness of the banished and the uprooted who had lost their families and ritual contexts through wars and pestilence. But regardless of whether an individual is forced to go without the cult of its gods or its divine partner, the depressive-melancholic subject embodies the certainty of the genius' no-longer-being. Falling prey to melancholia means nothing other than devoting oneself with undivided intensity of belief to the conscious or unconscious statement that I have been abandoned by my intimate patron, accomplice and motivator. Melancholia constitutes the pathology of exile in its pure form—the impoverishment of the inner world through the withdrawal of the life-giving field of closeness. In this sense, the melancholic person would be a heretic of the faith in his lucky star—an atheist in relation to his own genius, or the invisible double who should have convinced him of the unsurpassable advantage of being himself and no one else. The abandoned subject responds to the experience of a metaphysical deception with the deepest resentment: it was seduced into life by the great intimate other, only to be given up by it halfway. Faced with the melancholic sorrow over the lost animator, the therapy—remaining in the mythological mode—would consist of strengthening the isolated subject's potential for a renewed faith in the possibility of mental augmentation. This can essentially occur in three ways: the therapist can offer himself to the patient as a temporary substitute genius, as necessarily occurs in the demanding transference relationships of long analyses; he can make the mourner aware of a higher-ranking non-deceased god, as is customary in pastoral-theological counseling and sect communications.[38] The third variation would involve the subject allowing itself to be initiated into the use of non-religious, non-intimate self-augmentation techniques. Andy Warhol brought out the central features of this:

> The acquisition of my tape recorder really finished whatever emotional life I might have had, but I was glad to see it go. Nothing was ever a problem again, because a problem just meant a good tape, and when a problem transforms itself into a good tape it's not a problem anymore. An interesting problem was an interesting tale. Everybody knew that [...].[39]

Not really everybody. As long as the reformulation of mental problems as media problems is not generally accepted as an autotherapeutic rule, the two older, essentially individual-theological methods seem to be the only viable ones in the treatment of the melancholic disorder—with the inevitable consequence that human listeners have to be introduced instead of technological measuring devices. In a thoroughly psychologized civilization, however, priestly counsel also becomes increasingly obsolete, or it transforms itself into a religiously-cloaked psychotherapeutic service, with the result that this service is left as the only form of personal care for melancholia. The methodological problem with the genuinely psychological approach, however, is that its basic doctrines, especially the Freudian ones, operate under a total ban on speaking mythologically, which is why it rejects the possibility of defining the treatment of melancholia as the restoring of faith in the genius or a higher divine representative—or as the bestowal of spiritual meaning on empirical abandonment. It must therefore gloss the bereavement from which the melancholic patients are suffering in a non-mythological language, and is condemned to developing a psychological notion of healing without drawing on the concept of the regained faith in the genius—with the result that initially, and in reality until the end, it can no longer say what the melancholic's lost property is actually supposed to be. This inevitable encryption of a basic psychological circumstance that was previously very easily formulated, albeit not at all easy to analyze, was demonstrated by Freud with impressive circumspection in his well-known essay on mourning and melancholia:

> In one set of cases it is evident that melancholia too may be the reaction to the loss of a loved object. Where the exciting causes are different one can recognize that there is a loss of a more ideal kind. [...] In yet other cases one feels justified in maintaining the belief that a loss of this kind has occurred, but one cannot see clearly what it is that has been lost, and it is all the more reasonable to suppose that the patient cannot consciously perceive what he has lost either. This, indeed, might be so even if the patient is aware of the loss which has given rise to his melancholia, but only in the sense that he knows *whom* he has lost but not *what* he has lost in him. This would suggest that melancholia is in some way related to an object-loss which is withdrawn from consciousness [...].[40]

The excommunication of mythological and poetic formulations forces psychoanalytical discussion of the melancholic psyche into the interesting semantic maneuver of having to describe the severing of the relationship with the constitutive other with references to the patient's "object loss." This operation is informative because it is doomed to fail, yet never becomes futile: its relative success will be measured by its ability to locate the moment of failure ever later, so that before its termination it will bring to light a wealth of previously unseen and unspoken connections from the field of interwoven consubjectivities. Freud himself took the first step in this direction in his aforementioned essay, in which he presented far-reaching hypotheses on the intricate nature of the melancholic attachment to the lost object. What is decisive here is that the analyst arrives at the view that the melancholic, like every mourner, initially "withdraws" his "libido"—imagined as his private capital of sexually directed life energy—from the lost object into the ego; not to invest it in a new love object, however, but to tie itself in a far more radical way—though Freud's premises do not make it clear exactly how this is to happen—to the lost old object. Emotional bankruptcy and utmost impoverishment of the soul are the inevitable consequences of this. The formula is now: "identification of the ego with the abandoned object."[41] This nonsensical clinging to the ruinous libido investment is tentatively defined explained as follows:

> Thus the shadow of the object fell upon the ego, and the latter could henceforth be judged by a special agency, as though it were an object, the forsaken object. In this way an object loss was transformed into an ego loss [...].[42]

If one bears in mind that this refers to the silent tragedy we have summarized in the mythological-poetic notion of the loss of the genius, one is struck first of all by the objectifying tendency of these formulations. Nonetheless, one can hold the view that the danger of reification that appears with such discourses is amply balanced out by the gain in differentiation in the interpretation of the melancholic subject's self-relationship. This now appears in a light in which the couple relation with the intimate second element transpires as internally doubled: what the real other means to the subject is repeated in the subject with reference to itself. Thus the subject is simultaneously itself *and* the trace of all its experiences in dealing with the other. If the real other is really lost, its "shadow," as Freud mysteriously puts it, falls upon the ego. In technical psychoanalytical discourses, what exactly happens in this ego umbration is outlined with more or less fabulous, often very complicated interpretations whose only firm essence in all cases is the claim that the subject, to its own detriment, yearns to live on in an oversized, illusory, ambiguous and possibly also hate- and guilt-ridden, but certainly immature, proximity to the indispensable object. It seems that under these conditions, the essential other cannot be lost without the subject being deprived of fundamental aspects of its own life—unless it had already trained itself to lose the other in such a way that its disappearance would not be followed by ego loss. The nuisance of melancholia for the formation of psychoanalytical theories and its underlying individualistic and thing-ontological dogmatism is that, in melancholic loss, something undeniably vanishes that, according to the theoretical model, should not exist in the first place: an object that never really was one, as it is so intimately close to the subject that for the latter to be left behind alone in an intact state after the withdrawal of the former proves a psychological impossibility. Hence the melancholic does not lose the object as the rules would have it, namely in such a way that he is left *in fine* as the winner of the separation, existentially free for new libido investments and symbolically inspired to creative lament; rather, with the "object," he would lose the most significant part of his communicative and musical-erotic competence. This makes it clear, however, why the concept of object loss is out of place here. In a correctly understood conception of the object, this clear demarcation from a subject must already be implicit so that a real object loss, in the precise sense of the phrase, could under no circumstances cast doubt on the ego's enduring presence. In an objective duet, the first violin can procure a replacement for the second if the latter has disappeared owing to some incident. In the pre-objective or constitutive duets of life, however, the playing of the one is always that of the other too, and if the incipient subject were deprived of its counterpart the music would die, for the compositions are not differentiated to the point of objectivity and the instruments have not crystallized to the point of being independently playable. If torn out of the rehearsal context, the single player cannot simply continue his part acontextually somewhere else. A meaningful psychological theory of this relationship would therefore suggest that one should view the melancholic as an involuntary soloist, left without a piece, an instrument and the animating force of practice after his separation from the constitutive duet partner. The references to object loss show that in their first attempts to speak within the vague field of archaic dualities, psychologists were not able to understand their own words; for objects in the psychological sense can only exist once the pieces and instruments can be separated from the players without causing them to lose their performative potential. If it is productive to take into consideration something like the existence of psychological objects, then only if these are defined as relationship poles that can be replaced and transposed by the ego without acute self-impoverishment. Only something that can be occupied *and* let go is an object. What we call psychological objectivity is born from a crystallization of dialogic competence to form a repertoire that can also be played with other partners. The strong characteristic of the psychological object is its losability—or its replaceability and the replayability of the rehearsed piece with other partners, which amounts to the same in this case. Conversely, an object that has not (yet) crystallized as losable, abandonable, replaceable and translatable cannot constitute an object in the psychological sense.

We shall refer to this unabandonable intimate something, without whose presence and resonance the subject cannot be complete, using the term coined by Thomas Macho, as the nobject.[43] Nobjects are things, media or persons that fulfill the function of the living genius or intimate augmenter for subjects. These elements, which were often thought of as outer souls in the pre-psychological tradition, should, even in a psychologized culture, by no means be viewed in terms of the thing-form, as this would postulate or presuppose a separability from the subject—or rather the pre-subject—that precisely cannot be attained from a psychological perspective as long as the subject is still in its formative stages. It will only learn its transferability once it has achieved mastery of its own part in formative duets and constitutive trios (we need not speak of the quartets and quintets here). If the nobject augmenters are torn from the hearts of the individuals prematurely, however, whether by a higher power or the higher overpowering that operates ubiquitously in trivial misery, the depressive-melancholic disorder is the nobject-amputated individual's adequate response to the withering of its mental field. Hence the core of that consubjectivity which psychological theory would have to reconstruct appears neither in straightforward relationships between subjects and objects nor in affective transactions among subjects, but only in those subject-nobject unities which are ahead of all other material and communicative activities as resonating cells of the mental metabolism. One should, incidentally—as intimated above—cancel out the term "subject" or "ego" with a corresponding negative, as it too displays the mistaken postulate of separability from its augmenters and allies; so one should speak of a pre-subject or n(ego), a terminological tendency that can indeed be observed in the after-ripened psychoanalytical discourses of the last generation.

A portion of the thoughts the nobject concept provokes were already addressed by Jacques Lacan in his well-known lecture series *The Ethics of Psychoanalysis*, given from 1959 to 1960, in which, speaking of "the thing" (*la Chose*), he sought to articulate a pre-objective psychological object. Its primary aspect, he stated, was that it must always be considered lost, yet its absence is always in the subject's best interests. Lacan's brilliant reflections on *la Chose*—in whose concept we hear an overtone series reaching from Meister Eckart's concept of God to Kant's thing-in-itself—are riddled with irresolvable ambiguities that make it impossible to filter out precisely which aspects point towards an analysis of nobjectal communions and which aim for the edifying, psycho-analytically and psycho-hygienically renewed Pauline doctrine of

Marcel Duchamp and Eve Babitz pose for the photographer Julian Weasser in the Pasadena Art Museum, 1963 (detail)

the prohibition that enables desire. What remains unacceptable, however, is the invasiveness with which Lacan's affirmation of the ban on incest, whose discussion draws attention to his Catholicism, turns into an idiosyncratic tragic anthropology: here the "loss of the mother"—whatever that might mean—is declared a universal human fate on an archaic level. All humans appear as creatures with equally good reason to become melancholics, for let us face facts: we are all mother-amputees. All men are equal before the unattainability of the *Chose*. You think you have been robbed of more than others? Not at all: look around you, we are all but orphans of the *Chose*. As strong spirits, however, we would do well to accept that loneliness begins in the cradle! With this leveling of psychotic and neurotic conditions into universal human patienthood, psychoanalysis *à la parisienne* abandons its attention to mental suffering and the need for help, instead turning into a philosophical *schola* of a neo-ancient variety. Lacan's stoical-surrealistic ethics aims for the refutation of therapeutic hope: you have not been helped until you comprehend that no one can help you. If one draws the appropriate conclusions from this message, then the third way of treating melancholic disorders—the therapeutic one—also proves a dead end. My genius is dead, and the thing I took for my helper as his temporary replacement has turned out to be a talking dummy. Is this a reason to despair? At the exit of Lacan's practice, Warhol is waiting with his tape recorder. "When a problem transforms itself into a good tape it's not a problem anymore. [...] Everybody knew that." Word gets around. Where there was disconsolation, there will now be media performance.

On the Difference Between an Idiot
and an Angel

It is the shared achievement of Dostoyevsky and Nietzsche to have introduced the concept of the idiot into modern religious discourse. The significance of this term becomes clear as soon as one distinguishes it from that of the angel, as whose opposite and contrast agent it gains its value. What an angel is, and how it intervenes in profane life: the Old European religious tradition developed this question in a thousand variations according to its curiosity and hunger for images. It remained the task of the greatest psychological novelist of the nineteenth century and the author of *The Anti-Christ*, however, to understand that there is also an idiot figure which affects human life. For both writers the word "idiot" is Christologically charged, as both take a chance in probing—albeit from opposite perspectives—the typological secret of saviordom using the adjective "idiotic." This is a religion-psychologically explosive undertaking, for all known attempts to deduce the appearance of redemptive figures had inevitably drawn on the angel or messenger model, that is, the notion that an envoy would appear to mortals with a transcendent message and liberate them from physical need and moral deviance as a savior-hero. Hence the savior is initially merely a heightened form of messenger—it was only with Hellenized Christology that the categorial leap took place whereby the messenger now no longer *brought* the message, but rather *was* the message. In its heyday, the messenger or angel schema was clearly powerful enough to support the savior doctrine. To establish the savior as the messenger of all messengers, Christian theologians had to make him the son of substance and proclaim him the only fully adequate sign of being.[44] It testifies to the capacity of the angeletic[45] model that it was capable of taking this strain. Classical Christology shows the metaphysics of the envoy and the message at the height of its power. It belongs to a world situation and state of theory that was characterized by the dogma of the strong sender. Perhaps the discursive structure we were accustomed to calling "metaphysics" was actually no more than a reflex to subordinate thought to the notion of a being that, as the absolute sender, has the monopoly on all thrones, forces and powers, along with their associated signs and mediators. In this absolute being-a-sender, it was possible for the God of the Bible and the God of the philosophers to converge.

If one agrees here on the formula that the Modern Age is an information process that forces the crisis of sender metaphysics, one already has the means to understand why a time-sensitive theology after Gutenberg can no longer rely on an angeletic doctrine of the savior as an envoy. In the modern multiplication of sender forces and the messenger inflation on the free message market, a hyper-messenger of the "savior god" type, made manifest by his apostolic representatives, cannot assert his position of feudal primacy. In future, anyone who wishes to have a liberating effect on humans in a specific sense must be not so much an envoy with a transcendent message as a human being whose directly evident otherness fully replaces the bringer of news from beyond in a real presence. It is a sign of Dostoyevsky's religion-philosophical brilliance that he was the first to recognize the chance to shift the focus of Christology from angeletics to idiotics and thought it through to its limits.[46] Precisely because the modern world is so full with the noise made by the messengers of power parties and the artistic hullabaloo of geniuses drawing attention to their works and delusional systems, religious difference can no longer be highlighted convincingly in the messenger mode. The present God-man cannot reach the mortals as a messenger, but only as an idiot. The idiot is an angel without a message—an undistanced, intimate augmenter of all coincidentally encountered beings. His entrance is like the appearance of a phenomenon; not because he invokes a transcendent radiance in the earthly real, but because he embodies an unforeseeable naïveté and disarming benevolence in the midst of a society of role players and ego strategists. When he speaks, it is never with authority, only with the force of his openness. Though a prince by lineage, he is a human without signs of his status—he belongs unreservedly to the modern world; for while hierarchy is characteristic of the angel, the idiot is marked by an egalitarian streak. (Hierarchies of angels go without saying, but hierarchies of idiots would be baffling.) He moves among humans of high and low society like a big child who never learned to calculate its own advantage.

Starting from these modern religion-aesthetic findings—let us not forget that Dostoyevsky had conceived the figure of the idiot as an attempt to depict the "completely *beautiful* human being" and his inevitable failure amid human ugliness—Nietzsche drew the corresponding religion-psychological conclusions in his polemic *The Antichrist* of 1888. For him, the historical Jesus can already be summed up in Dostoyevskyan typology—in

Nietzsche's terminology, he is the incarnation of a *décadent avant la lettre.*

> It is a pity that there was no Dostoyevsky living near this most interesting decadent, I mean someone with an eye for the distinctive charm that this sort of mixture of sublimity, sickness and childishness has to offer.[47]

Consequently, all characterizations that seek to project the language of heroism and genius culture onto the historical Jesus—or the language of fanaticism and apostolic-apologetic arrogance—are unsuitable; all these simply express the anger of representatives and ambitions of succession. As far as the concrete type of the evangelistic savior is concerned, one should finally approach him with the only applicable medical category: "The rigorous language of physiology would use a different word here: the word 'idiot.'"[48]

The sublime, the childlike and the sick—in his turbulent polemic against Christianity, Nietzsche does not take the time to unravel the riddle of how these aspects could come together in a single qualifier, namely "idiotic," to the great disadvantage of divinity and general psychology. If one wished to piece Dostoyevsky's and Nietzsche's intuitions about the equation of idiotology and savior doctrine together patiently, it would produce a far-reaching revision of traditional notions of religious process.

In standard angeletic systems, the savior appears to humans as a metaphysical informant and moves them, adopting the attitude of sender-reinforced strength, with his penetrating message. In the idiotic system, on the other hand, the savior is a nobody without any higher client behind him. His statements are viewed by those around him as childlike trivialities, and his presence is perceived as non-binding and incidental. Dostoyevsky makes this trait in particular absolutely clear; of one figure in the novel, *Ganya*, he writes: "He behaved exactly as though he were alone in his room and made no attempt to keep up appearances before Myshkin, as though he looked upon him as absolutely of no consequence."[49] Nonetheless, the presence of Prince Myshkin is a trigger for all events that take place in his vicinity; he decisively catalyzes the characters and fates of those who encounter him. It is precisely as a non-messenger that he solves the problem of access to the inside of his opponents with a method that no one can see through. Neither siren nor angel, he unlocks the ears of his conversational partners and their centers of mental activity. Nor is it his childlike character in the ordinary sense that gives him his special access to others, unless one gave the word "childlike" a heterodox meaning: it could refer to the willingness to interact with others without asserting one's own self, instead keeping oneself available as the augmenter of the other. If such a possibility of childlikeness solidifies into a general attitude, the result is what Dostoyevsky articulated with the word "idiocy"—a word that was clearly only meant to sound pejorative in its most superficial usage. With the title "idiot," Dostoyevsky pinpoints, as a philosopher of religion and a critic of subjectivism, an ego position that he considers noble and—at least in relation to others—salvific, though it can in no sense be attributed to an angeletic potency. The idiotic subject is evidently the one that can act as if it were not so much itself as its own double, and potentially the intimate augmenter of every encountered other. There is a rough saying in various cantons of Switzerland, "it looks like they brought up the afterbirth instead of the child in your case," and one should perhaps take this as a psychological discovery. The idiot placentalizes himself by offering an inexplicable experience of closeness to everyone who crosses his path, like some intrauterine cushion—a sort of immemorial connection which creates an openness between people who have never met before that may otherwise only be found at the Last Judgment or in the wordless exchange between fetus and placenta. In the presence of the idiot, harmless good-naturedness becomes transforming intensity; his mission is seemingly to have no message, but rather to create a closeness in which contoured subjects can dissolve their boundaries and remold themselves. His morality is the inability to hit back. This is the aspect that had to interest Nietzsche about supposed Jesuan idiocy, as it embodies the ideal of a noble life free of all resentment—albeit not on the part of the active self, but rather the companion, the patron, the augmenter. This would mean a noble idiocy that expressed itself in a pre- and superhuman availability and willingness to serve. The idiotic savior would be the one who did not lead his life as the main character in his own story, but had rather exchanged places with his afterbirth in order to make space for its being-in-the-world as itself. Is this a pathological excess of loyalty? A case of prenatal Nibelung loyalty? A delirium of yolk and cushions in which the subject confuses itself with the archaic patron and spirit of closeness? Perhaps the idiot's wisdom lies in the fact that he descends to his intimate waste, the placental sister, in her forlornness? Would he rather continue her life for her than betray their common origins in a state of augmented floating-together? "Unless you become like children…?" Perhaps Jesus should rather have said: "Unless you become like this idiotically friendly thing…"?

CHAPTER 7

The Siren Stage

On the First Sonospheric Alliance

> I have really become hard only by thin layers;
> If anyone knew how marrowy I am at bottom.
> I am gong and cotton and snowy song,
> I say so and am sure of it.
>
> — Henri Michaux, "I am Gong"[1]

> Where do I call You to come to, since I am in You? Or where
> else are You that You can come to me? […] So speak that I may
> hear, Lord, my heart is listening; open it that it may hear Thee
> say to my soul *I am thy salvation*. Hearing that word, let me
> come in haste to lay hold upon thee.
>
> — Saint Augustine, *Confessions*, Book I, II & V[2]

In the beginning, the accompanied animals, humans, are surrounded by something that can never appear as a thing. They are
initially the invisibly augmented, the corresponding, the encompassed and, if there is disarray, those who have been abandoned
by their companions. That is why investigating humans philosophically means, first and foremost: examining paired

structures, both obvious and less visible ones, those that are lived with congenial partners and those that create alliances with problematic and unattainable others. Only the *ideologia perennis* that drifts in the mainstream of individualistic abstraction speaks of the unaccompanied single person. Psychology may cultivate its twin research, and social science will continue to chase its chimera, *homo sociologicus*; pair research and the theory of the dual space are constitutive for the philosophically reformulated science of mankind. Even what newer philosophers have termed "human existing" is thus no longer to be understood as the solitary individual standing out into the indeterminate openness, nor as the mortal's private suspendedness in nothingness; existing is a paired floating with the second element, whose closeness maintains the tension of the microsphere. My existence includes the presence of a pre-objective something floating around me; its purpose is to let me be and support me. Hence I am not, as current systemists and bio-ideologues claim I think, a living being in its environment; I am a floating being with whom geniuses form spaces. "If anyone knew how marrowy I am at bottom."

How can we understand the nature of this marrowy softness? How can the same voice speak of itself as cotton and snow song, yet also the gong that echoes with the unbearable? It seems that our journey through the nobjectal zones has still not touched on the innermost ring. For even if it can be made plausible that humans, both in archaic horde formation and in times of classical empires and modern project cultures, are spheric beings that only master life's hazards in the world's openness in the interplay with their augmenters, companions and pursuers, this still does not articulate the mystery of their receptiveness to the encouragement of their creatures of closeness. Let us admit it: the genius does not seek, it has found; the angel does not knock on the door, it is in the room; the daimonion does not ask to be announced, it already has the subject's ear! But how, in these intimate circumstances of partition, can the one have assured itself of the other's disclosedness beforehand? On what store do the prestabilized intimacies that enable an unhindered transmission of feelings between the inseparably connected parties draw? How can it be that for billions of messages, I am a rock on which their waves break without resonance, while certain voices and instructions unlock me and make me tremble as if I were the chosen instrument to render them audible, a medium and mouthpiece simply for their urge to sound? Is there not still a mystery of access to consider here? Does my accessibility to certain unrefusable messages not have its dark "reason" in an ability to reverberate that has not yet been adequately discussed? How is the standing-open that enables Socrates to hear his demon intervening in his monologues with admonitions possible virtually *a priori*? And what of that obliging receptiveness,[3] termed "immaculate," that allows the angel of annunciation—which usually enters from the left—to speak the impossible news in Mary's ear without her submission turning into refusal? On what wavelength is the speech broadcast that puts you in a state of unreserved resonance, and whose audition makes the ear open and swell up, as if it were suddenly involved in ardently singing a hymn whose sounds contain its earliest and most recent expectations?

If one inquires as to the most elemental and interior layers of mental accessibility, one must also desire to know how to re-disarm a hearing sense that has become hard, careful and narrow. From a psychoacoustic perspective, the shift to intimate listening is always connected to a change of attitude from a one-dimensional alarm- and distance-oriented listening to a polymorphously moved floating listening. This change reverses the general tendency to move from a magical, proto-musical listening to one revolving around alarm and concern—or, to put it in more enlightened terms: from uncritical participation to critical awareness. Perhaps history itself is a titanic battle for the human ear in which nearby voices struggle with distant ones for privileged access to emotional movedness [*Ergriffenheit*],[4] the voices of the mighty with those of the counter-mighty. Using gestures claiming the right to move, power has always presented itself as truth; in the refusal to be moved, however, one sees a laboriously acquired strategic cunning which knows that the gullible ear also takes in lies. Those who become wise distance themselves from Cretans, priests, politicians and representatives.

Through resistance, the subject posits itself as the power point of a non-movedness. By the psychohistorical standards of the last two-and-a-half millennia, only those who have subjected themselves to comprehensive de-fascination training can be considered adults. This training is meant to take the subject to the threshold from which it can have unmoved dealings with consent-demanding rhetorical and artistic demonstrations. That the ear too is taught to separate spirits and favors shows the tension that advanced civilizations have to maintain in their carriers in order to combine an increased openness to the world with a heightened non-seducibility. Critical subjectification is based on de-fascination as a restraining of movedness. Since written culture successfully asserted its law, being a subject has primarily meant this: being able, initially and usually, to resist the images, texts, speeches and musics one encounters, except for those which, for some reason, have already been granted the right to

Red-figured vase from Volci, 5th century BC. The Sirens fly around Odysseus as birdlike women.

force my agreement and attunement—we call them icons, holy books, writings of the fathers, hymns and classics. In these, we recognize the culture-bearing potentials to convince, which have passed the examination of critique often enough to be allowed to disarm even us, the present carriers of denial, to a certain extent. "Convincing" is merely a name for post-critical movedness—it indicates the return of the affirmative judgment at the heights of self-reflection. It is not only the official dogmas of shared, mature convincing that have the license to circumvent our barriers of distance, however; in effect, enchantments from sources that are questionable or frowned upon can suspend our basic right to listen without applauding, turning us into degenerate listeners. Should we simply shrug our shoulders and allow whatever people like? Perhaps it would be useful to remember that higher culture can only exist for as long as it manages to produce sufficient numbers of individuals who feel a need to defend the distinction between hypotheses and enchantments.

In the twelfth book of the *Odyssey*, Homer depicts the primal scene of the old musical overpowering and a new form of resistance against it. Odysseus, whom the gods want finally to complete his homeward voyage, receives the advice from the sorceress Circe, his lover for a year, to beware the deadly seduction of the Sirens' song while at sea. Odysseus now tells his comrades about this as they journey:

> The prophecies of Circe are not meant
> for one or two of us; they must be shared,
>   my friends: beforehand, know that we may meet death
> or may, escaping destiny, be spared.
> Above all, Circe urges us to flee
> the song of the beguiling Sirens and
>   their flowered meadow. I alone—she says—
> may hear their voices. Tie me then hard fast—
> use knots I can't undo. I'll stand erect,
> feet on the socket of the mast; and let
>   the rope ends coil around the shaft itself;
> and if I plead with you to set me free,
> add still more ropes and knots most carefully. (XII, 154–164)[5]

What is the source of Homer's conviction that the Sirens bring death to all men with their song? How does the bard even know about the existence of these bewitching creatures—there are initially only two, it seems[6]—and by what spells do they manage to tempt the unadvised? What charms do the deadly songbirds in women's guise employ to make all who hear them lose their minds? What do the Sirens know about their victims that enables them to get so close to them? How do the two voluptuous singers penetrate their listeners' ears so deeply that they gained this reputation: "Whoever, unaware, comes close and hears the Sirens' voice will nevermore draw near his wife, his home, his infants: he'll not share such joys again." And why in the world is it that "round about them lie heaped bones and shriveled skin of putrefying men"? (XII, 40–46) What fear, what experience and what imagination were able to create this association of song and destruction among the Greek myth-tellers? Even if most of these questions cannot be answered with certainty as far as Homer's views and their sources are concerned, the Siren episode in the *Odyssey* does make one thing clear: the early patriarchal Homeric world learned to fear a particular kind of aural magic. Not everything that reaches the ears of seamen can be perceived by them as a music that consoles them or transports them home. Now that the men who have traveled far and hear much have become more numerous, we must consider a state of the world in which even our ears must be prepared for deadly deceptions. The ear, which is by nature the organ of gullible devotion to all things associated with the mother tongue, the fatherland and the household muses, can be fooled by songs that sound more attractive than what is most native to them—and yet, it seems, are the music of a hostile principle. The Sirens' voices create an auditory suction that disarms battle-tested men and worldly-wise travelers at the wrong moment; it dupes them with an illusion of being at home and at ease that before Odysseus, who was better advised in such matters of sonic enchantment, none had been able to

"The Air Full of Notes"—mosaic from Dougga, 300 AD

resist. It is a foreign music in the world, and it is precisely the most diligent who should beware; for these sounds, as the mythologists tell us, lead their listeners not to themselves, into their own well-being, but rather into a death far from home. Death at the hands of the Sirens comes not in a horrific guise, but as an irresistibly flattering melody that reaches the innermost ear of each listener. It is as if a homesickness trap were set up on the high seas,

at the flowery Siren coast, a trap that men burn to enter as soon as they find themselves in the sonic circle of the two women's voices singing as one. Homer makes an effort to demarcate the power field of these strange musicians quite clearly: where the Sirens sing, the wind ceases to blow, and ships glide silently through the water, driven only by their oars; no sounds of nature, no roaring of the sea and no flapping sail compete with the magical voices for the ears of the victims. The sea turns into an otherworldly concert hall, the listeners row silently into the divine sound bell, and the winged singers pour the milk of their voices into the men's hedonistically opened ears—unless, like those of Odysseus' crew, these have been sealed with wax as a precaution.

What kind of music is it, what melody and rhythm, that gives the Sirens such power over the ears of mortal men? As soon as one attempts to get closer to the Siren concert, it becomes clear that the secret of their successful seductions does not lie with the singers themselves. Certainly the epithet "seductive" is associated with the Sirens as stereotypically as the attribute "almighty" with the monotheistic God, and being-seductive is ascribed to these lethal minstrels like a fixed trait. This would make falling prey to the Sirens the normal consequence of Siren perception, and the men's striving and pining to reach their clawed feet would be the most adequate analogue to the charms of those Greek soubrettes. Are they not, in essence, showing the seamen a little too much cleavage of their throats? In truth, the seductive element of the Sirens' music does not stem from a nature-like sensuality, as Adorno still mistakenly supposed. Rather, it seems to be the nature of these singers not to display any charms of their own: their concert is not the presentation of a lascivious program that has, so far, been popular among all who sail past—yet might already encounter its first critical or indifferent listener tomorrow. The secret reason for the irresistibility of the Sirens is that they, with a peculiar lack of scruples, never perform their own repertoire, only the music of those who pass by; the very idea of a melody of their own is foreign to them; even the sweetness of their voices is not a musical quality irremovably tied to their performance, and in tradition their voices are more often termed shrill than beautiful. The Sirens found eager victims in all listeners up until Odysseus—and especially in him—because they sing from the listener's own place. Their secret is to render precisely those songs in which the passing sailors' ears yearn to immerse themselves. Listening to Sirens thus means entering the core space of an intimately touching musical key and wishing to remain at the source of this indispensable sound from that point on. The fatal singers compose their songs in the ear of the listener; they sing through the larynx of the other. Their music is that which finds the simplest solution to the problem of the accessibility of otherwise closed ears. With nefarious accuracy, it performs the exact sonic gestures with which the listening subject will unlock itself and step forward. For Achilles, had he not fallen before Troy, the feathered singers would have recited verses to Achilles whose magnificence would have rendered him defenseless against his own song; for Agamemnon, if he had passed by, they would naturally have sung hymns to Agamemnon across the water, wickedly pleasing and irresistibly glorifying, and how could the endangered hero not have yielded to the song issuing from the hill as if from his own interior? The Siren's art is to place the subject's own self-arousal into its soul. The meaning of irresistibility in this case is transporting the subject to the center of the hymnic emotion that seems to well up in itself and transports it to a place among the stars. It is not surprising, then, that the Sirens have prepared carefully attuned hymns to the well-traveled Odysseus—an *odyssey* within the odyssey, a musical oasis to which the hero is invited for a rest, as if he had returned home after so many strenuous adventures. These compositions are adapted with such wonderful precision to his hearing, modulated by many dangers and ordeals, so that it is out of the question for the recipient of praise not to be moved. The Siren song sings of him, the approaching, who glides towards his song; he sings along with what he hears in spontaneous affirmation, as if this unique listening moment already contained the outcry of his own singing. Seduction is an awakening of the source of that melody which is absolutely mine to sing. Homer did not neglect to include in his tale of Odysseus those Siren verses that simply had to enchant the hero. These verses would undoubtedly have caused him to perish on the Sirens' meadows if he had not, tied to the mast, been rowed through the arousing music funnel by his wax-deafened comrades.

> Remarkable Odysseus, halt and hear
> the song we two sing out: Achaean chief,
> the gift our voices give is honey-sweet.
> No man has passed our isle in his black ship
> until he's heard the sweet song from our lips;
> and when he leaves, the listener has received
> delight and knowledge of so many things.
> We know the Argives' and the Trojans' griefs:
> their tribulations on the plain of Troy
> because the gods had willed it so. We know
> all things that come to pass on fruitful earth. (XII, 184–191)[7]

Siren music rests on the possibility of being one step ahead of the subject in the expression of its desire. Perhaps such an ability to be ahead is the anthropological reason for the interest of non-artists in artists, which reached its zenith in modern societies and passed it in postmodern ones. Thus the Sirens' song does not simply move the subject as if from without; it rather sounds as if the ownmost sentiment of the subject, which now rises up, were being uttered in perfection and for the first time.

In a so far inexplicable fashion, these singers solved the problem of access to the subject's center of artistic feeling; it remains uncanny that they succeed in this not only occasionally, with isolated individuals, but with many different victims, as if the ability to infiltrate the human ear that dreams of itself were not some coincidentally effective intuition, but rather a virtuosically mastered psycho-technique. For the Greeks of Homer's time and later, such abilities would have been unthinkable without demigod privileges. To them, the Sirens were like melodic seeresses—and indeed, mantic farsightedness and divine cognizance are required in order even to suspect that precisely this dark ship passing the Siren cliffs holds none other than the cunning returnee from Troy. If one has this knowledge, it no longer seems such an impossible leap to the infiltration of the hero's innermost ear; for what would a heroic seafarer, his homeward voyage delayed by fatal winds and female guile, want more to hear about than the ordeals of his compatriots before Troy, his current trials and his unknown destiny. With a sure sense of key, the Sirens immediately render the epic that tells of the hero Odysseus—yet they sing it not in the style of that people-forming muse which succeeded in making the name of Odysseus intelligible for the whole of Greece as the emblem of a new, post-heroic form of humanity; they sing of the world-famous Odysseus for Odysseus alone, as if he had lost his horizon and forgotten his project. They beguile him, as if to say: "Let the Aegean shrink to your most private body of water! After proving yourself among others as a hero and making people speak of your deeds among the deeds of others, there is an inland sea of notes waiting for you here in which you alone will be glorified! Abandon the noise of the world and immerse yourself in your own music, your first and last!" Let us not forget: even Odysseus resists this song not because he is able to mobilize the powers to reject it himself, but only because he has countered the overpowering pull of the music with the ropes that bind him to the ship's mast. Is it mere coincidence that the Greek name for these ropes scarcely differs from that of the singers pulling on them from the other side? Did Homer already know that bonds can only be broken by more bonds? Was it already clear to him that culture in general, and music in particular, is essentially nothing other than a division of labor in bewitching?

Even in the case of Odysseus, then, the Sirens' song is completely successful: it overcomes the listener as a higher power in musical form. Only through a cunning division of binding powers does the hero escape their suction. Nonetheless, there is no reason to claim that we have correctly understood the attraction of the Siren music. For it is still unclear whither the man who does not keep still when he hears the Sirens' voices, like every other citizen in the concert hall, but is rather seized by the overpowering urge to approach these singers physically, is actually striving to go. What is the nature of this desire to get closer? What primal scene of being-close might it be that the plunge towards the singers reenacts? From where does the principle of transference take effect in the case of this acoustic enchantment? Only at the second listen does the particularity of the Siren scene become clear: if such music is irresistibly sweet for this one and only sung-about and singing listener, it is because it feigns to the hero that his constitutive wish has been fulfilled. The singers hold the key to the listening subject's heavenly ascension, and their method of seduction gives the decisive clue to the intimate zone of the hearing sense, which is willingly open to certain insinuations. Here a successful seduction can be used to deduce the tendency of the wish itself—and more, namely that the Siren song as such is the medium in which the wish originally forms. The song, the wish and the subject have always belonged together. In truth, the subjectivity of heroic times can only form through listening to the epic and mythical glorification. In the nurseries of advanced civilizations, as in most pre-literate societies, the ego is formed in a promise of song: a future of notes is sent ahead of the ego's own existence. I am a sound image, a verse flash, a dithyrambic feeling, compressed into a form of address that already sings to me in my infancy who I can be. The hero and the heroine: they will be those whom they hear in advance—for life in the age of heroic subjects is always on the way to versification. Every subject, as long as it resists discouragement, moves towards its current musicalization. Only monotheistic priests revel in the self-referential misconception that man wants to be like God. If the priests are not in attendance, it transpires that humans desire not to be like God, but like a hit song. Being on the way to the rhapsodic moment gives one's existence the feeling for its forward and upward motion. An immemorial inclination towards frothing up in the cantilena precedes the ego; its frequency is its substance. That is why, to this day, tenors and prima donnas can arouse entire stadiums and make large houses tremble; they show even the most musically impoverished a simple route to the frothing of the self in vocal exhibitions. *Sursum—boom boom—* and none shall sleep.[8] Pop stars descend even further into the underworld of ego orgasms at discount prices by simulating their emergence with jaws locked around the microphone. But tenor

In anticipation: Werner Schroeter, *Willow Springs*, 1972

hysteria and pop action would not be so attractive if they did not still offer touching projections of old powers which lead to ego formation via the ears. They seduce the listener to the extent that they plausibly promise the subject's appearance in the song's core. The primitive-artistic journey to madness has psychological method. The listeners' expectant readiness to leap into the frothing of their ownmost sonic gesture testifies to the reality of an archaic, ego-forming siren stage in which the subject hooks itself into a sonorous phrase, a vocal sound, a sonic image, to hope from then on for the return of its musical moment. The aspects of truth that Lacan included in his aimless theorem of the mirror stage apply not to the visual, but rather the auditory and audio-vocal self-relationship of the subject. Through its advance hearing of the ego motif the individual forms a pact with its own future, from which it draws the joy of living towards fulfillment. Every unresigned subject lives in the orthopedic expectation of its most intimate hymn, which will simultaneously be its triumphal march and its obituary. This is what makes so many dream of musical appearances and bursting out in recitation: those who hear their hymns have triumphed. For the unsung the battle continues, even if Troy has long since fallen. For them, the truth that the subject comes closest to itself in the act of intonation still lies ahead. Whoever steps on stage to present their sounding gesture is not sight-reading, and above all, knows nothing of self-*images*; for in the oral world, the incipient subjects do not look in the mirror, but rather into the song—and that part of the song which promises me my emotion motif, my hymnic rhythm and my self-fanfare. Like most people today, the early humans did not want to look like something; they want to sound like something. It took the unleashing of the modern machinery of images, which has been forcing its clichés into the populace since the Baroque, to conceal this basic circumstance and bring the masses under the spell of visual individualism with its quick views, its mirrors and its fashion magazines. It is not without reason that the video clip is the symptomatic genre of contemporary culture, which works towards a visual gluing-up of the ears and a global synthesis through images. The old songs of great men and women, by contrast, are still at home in a regime of sonospheric common spirits; they erect sounding monuments, halls of fame or sonorous burial mounds from which the heroes rose to sound on in the ears of subsequent generations. From the stricken ear, the

Eternal Promise

subject is led to itself. In its early acoustic or rhapsodic memory, a few magical rhythms and sonic gestures accumulate and ring ahead of the individual like leitmotifs from a hymnic heaven—as yet unplayed and postponed, yet always on the point of finally being performed. This is how I sound—and this is how I will be once I am. I am the frothing up, the sound block, the liberated figure, I am the beautiful and bold passage, I am the leap to the highest note; the world echoes with my sound when I show myself as I have been promised to myself.

Does the pleading of Odysseus to be untied from the mast not reveal his willingness to cooperate with the acoustic illusion of his perfection? Struck intimately at his pole of arousal, he wants to reach the place from which his song is being sung: is the cosmos not created so that when I navigate around it I can, in a providential place, hear myself perfectly?—It is no coincidence that according to Greek traditions outside of the Odyssey, the Sirens normally performed a lament for the dead. Their power is borrowed from the underword and its lords, Hades and Phorcys; hence their voices are especially suitable for hymns of praise and songs for the dead. Their foreknowledge concerns human destinies and their unknown end. The ancient authors describe the Siren voices as simultaneously honey-sweet and shrill—which perhaps reminds us that the music of antiquity did not produce its oft-cited magical effects through those elements known to post-Romantic listeners as melodies and harmonies; instead, it forces itself upon the listener through a form of ecstatic relentlessness—magically over-articulated, penetratingly incisive and sustained to the point of exhaustion. Ancient recitative places the ears of those gathered in a state of emergency: a clarity that magnifies them, arouses them and makes them defenseless. The muse's speech is inscribed upon the hearing in capital letters, as it were; its singers advance towards the listeners like intoxicating verse-writing machines, and the rhapsodists draw their circle around the tonicized listeners as living drums. Without tolerating contradiction, the muse loudly and clearly stakes its claim to move, which the dialectally mumbling everyday subject is helpless to resist.

Such a sonic phenomenon tears trivial time apart. Whoever hears it must find a new balance between patience and arousal; whoever dissolves in it will not be returning soon; and whoever does finally return knows that from now on, life is a waiting for the return of the verses. There are certain indications that for modern ears, Homer's Siren music would be most similar to the wailing of female mourners, organized in waves, that is said to have survived in various cultural niches of the Eastern Mediterranean. (Did Nikos Kazantzakis not remind us of this in *Zorba the Greek*?) Nonetheless, the Sirens' listeners find their own superhumanly sweet spot in their bitter recitals, just as the Sirens hit the musical spot in their listeners whose arousal tells the subject that its hour has come. Tied to the mast, Odysseus throws his head back and begs for his release upon hearing the rattling hexameters from the coast. "Remarkable Odysseus, halt and hear…" —these words ring out across the water while his deaf comrades row on. So these are the heavenly sounds that seek out Odysseus in his ropes. The Sirens' recitation permeates the immobilized, intensely aroused listener like a eulogy from beyond. To hear them is to recognize that one's transformation into song is complete, and one's goal in life thus attained. Odysseus is no exception to this song-metaphysical rule. Whoever hears such songs of himself can assume that his own life is now a topic of conversation at the tables of the gods. This, then, is why the Siren rock becomes the cliff on which the prematurely honored perish. There is no path leading back to everyday, unsung existence from the song-grave in their own lifetime.

Odysseus is the first to escape his entry into song alive; he stands at the beginning of a story that saw godly heroes end as returning humans. Epic monsters would ultimately become wily virtuosos—and names in the culture supplement. That is why successful artists in more recent times had every reason to acknowledge the crafty seafarer as their ancestor. For just as the ancient hero took on an element of the swindler to survive his transformation into song, modern artists, as soon as they experience success, must creep out of the catalogues and art histories like confidence tricksters preparing their next coup in secret. Post-Homeric commentators also drew typological parallels between Odysseus and Oedipus, and claimed that the Sirens suffered a fate which clearly duplicates that of the Theban sphinx: supposedly they leapt to their death out of grief over Odysseus' escape. The logic of this relationship seems transparent: either Odysseus or the Sirens must die. The gentle wooliness of modernity, however, dreams of everyone surviving, both artists and reviewers (whose voices are still more often shrill than sweet). As far as the ancient Sirens are concerned, it remains peculiar that for an entire millennium—from Homer to his late Hellenistic commentators—barely a word was written about the material reason for the death of the men on the Sirens' island. It seems that all recipients darkly accept the connection between being honored in song and having to die as a given. Their only certainty is that the Sirens do not touch their victims in any way; direct violence is not the singers' business. Everything suggests that their victims died of what was known in medieval times as "wasting away": the prematurely celebrated men perish of hunger and thirst on the exterritorial island because it has nothing to offer except rhapsodic seduction.

The notion that beauty knows no better fate than to be buried in song anyway was still espoused—or rather espoused again—around 1800 by Friedrich Schiller, as the nationalthanatologist of the bourgeoisie, as if it were a self-evident higher truth:

> Even to be a lament on the lips of the beloved is glorious,
> For the lowly descend to Orcus unsung.
> ("The Gods of Greece," 1788)

In such verses, we see the new bourgeois public sphere preparing for the task of configuring mortality and the collective memory in a contemporary manner within a burgeoning mass culture. From 1800 on, cultural history became a song in which the eminent people wanted to find their place of idealization. The great narratives describing the procession of artistic powers through the different stylistic periods attract the highest ambitions, and the bourgeois museums open their doors to anything that supposedly deserves to survive in the national collection. For the others, communal cemetery administrations offer places of rest under modestly inscribed tombstones. Those with the merciful gift of faith can go on trusting that God, who has no storage problems, can remember people better than the mundane media can. In bourgeois times, one must always reckon with a degree of advance condemnation to oblivion among all those who do not stand out especially; only the world-historical individuals who gained Hegel's blessing through his concept and the art-historical individuals who were elevated to the honor of altars in the aesthetic religion escaped the general fate of disappearing more or less unsung. Were it not the case that many are still capable of positive involvement in the idealization of the great other, then Andy Warhol's dull witticism about fifteen-minute fame for all would indeed describe the final horizon of a civilization in which, more than any currency, fame is devalued through inflation.

The storyteller Jean Paul, that contemporary of Schiller experienced in contemplative fervor, showed deeper insight into such matters than the modern cynic when, in the novel *Titan*, he wrote of his hero: "He read the eulogies of every great man with as much delight as if they were meant for him."[9] With this observation he touches on the psychodynamic functional secret of bourgeois societies, which could never survive without that "as if they were meant for him." From antiquity on, layered societies are fame-distributing systems that synchronize their public choruses with the intimate song expectations of individuals. The space of fame arches over the peoples of history like a political concert hall; here the individual life, once its transformation into song is complete, is sung about by the masses. Odysseus tied to the mast—today that would be the winner of an art prize sitting through the eulogy with bowed head. Where it proves possible to combine the Siren effect with the pantheon effect, the sound wave of culture spreads discreetly and irresistibly among the subjects. Culture is the sum of all expected and spoken laudations.

Our analysis of the encounter between Odysseus and the Sirens has expanded to include references to a theory of moved communication in large societies. What touches the individual listener intimately and gives him the certainty of hearing his own song is that specifically siren-like music which recites in the open what arouses his own personal emotion. Homer's Sirens demonstrate the ability to access the other's audio-vocal center of feeling. But the art of making seafaring heroes melt is not the only siren capacity. The skeletons of the seduced on the singers' island only show one part of the effect of siren music—and, as we will see, not the most significant. In truth, siren components come into play whenever humans abandon themselves to moved listening. In listening to the outer voice, as shown above, the listener's most native, personal emotion wells up. So it is when sirens—that is, sounds that move and demand unconditional affirmation—become audible that things become serious for the subject's sense of self. Hearing sirens means hearing "oneself"; being called by them means moving towards them out of one's "ownmost" desire. It is, incidentally, one of the typical self-revelations of the twentieth century—and one of its characteristic cynicisms—that it referred to the wailing machines on factory roofs, and in wartime also the alarm systems that spread panic in cities being attacked from the air, as "sirens." This choice of name plays with the insight that sirens can trigger archaic feelings among those who hear them, but it distorts this with wicked irony by associating the siren with a forced alarm. The most open form of listening was thus betrayed to terror, as if the subject were only close to its truth when running to save itself. At the same time, this renaming of the siren voice inappropriately coarsens it, instrumentalizing it for the most brutal mass signals. Sirens of this kind are the bells of the industrial and World War age. They do not mark the sonosphere in which a joyful message could spread. Their sound carries the consensus that everything is hopeless and dangerous to all ears that can be reached.

When we speak here of a siren effect, on the other hand, this refers to the intimate accessibility of individuals by sonic messages that transmit a form of hypnosis via happiness, a feeling of attaining the fulfilled moment. That some listeners can be reached and awakened by certain sounds would be unimaginable if the sound itself were not met by a spontaneous urgent accommodation on the recipient's part. As our reflections on the effects of the Sirens' recitation about Odysseus have shown, the irresistibility of song rests not on a sweetness particular to music, but rather the alliance of the sound with the subject's most discreet listening expectations. The ear comes with its own selectivity, which waits persistently for the note that is unrecognizably its own; if that note does not sound, the intimate sonic expectation stays in the background and the individual continues its everyday business unmoved—literally—often without even the possibility of sensing an other condition.

Recent psychoacoustic research, especially that of the French otorhinolaryngologist and psycholinguist Alfred Tomatis and his school, has attempted a suggestive explanation of the unusual selectivity of the human ear that manifests itself in the siren effect. Not only do these investigations into the human auditory sense and its evolution show beyond doubt that unborn children can already hear extremely well because of the ear's early development—possibly from the embryonic state onwards, and certainly in the second half of pregnancy; in addition, there are impressive observations showing that this early listening ability does not result in the fetus being passively at the mercy of the mother's sonic inner life, or of the water-filtered voices and noises of the outside world. Rather, the fetal ear already develops the ability to find its bearings in its ever-present, invasive sonic environment actively through independent, lively listening and non-listening. As Tomatis untiringly emphasizes, the child's stay in the womb would be unbearable without the specific ability not to listen and to mute large areas of noise, as the mother's heartbeat and digestive sounds, heard in such close proximity, would be like the noise from a 24-hour building site or a lively barroom conversation. If the child did not learn to avert its ears at an early stage, it would be ravaged by permanent noise torture. Numerous prenatal and perinatal myths remind us of the risks of such primary cave noises and infernal rackets, for example the Egyptian books of the underworld, which describe crossing a desert of noise on the nocturnal voyage of the soul. So when human children come into the world without having been harrowed by intimate noise, it is because one of the first impulses of their "I can" sense is to refrain from listening. This contradicts the common myth of the fatefully unclosable ear. Not listening and listening are original modes of pre-subjective ability—in so far as ability is always connected to having an alternative. With the help of this earliest sensory competence, a primary distinction is introduced into the intrauterine night: it establishes the difference between those sounds which concern the listener, and are accommodated by him, and those which remain indifferent or repulsive to him and are blocked out. With this primal choice between turning towards and turning away, the first difference of communicative behavior comes into effect. The ear decides, within certain boundaries, how welcome or unwelcome the various acoustic stimuli are. This distinction precedes that between significant and insignificant ones. It is a typical error of contemporary semiotics to view the significant as something that is brought to light through selection from the insignificant—as if the subject made an arbitrary choice among an initial, indifferent assortment of noises of which it has an over-"view" in order to obtain privately meaningful data. In reality, the field of the insignificant only comes about when the ear turns away from the bothersome noise presences; these are hence "posited" as uninformative or indifferent, and consequently excluded from the waking perception. There is not first a field of indistinct noise and then a filtering of information from this; rather, the indistinct noise arises as a correlate of averting the ears from unwelcome sounds. At the same time, however, our hearing approaches in a special way those sounds it expects to grant particular enlivenment. In listening closely, the ears carry out the primal act of the self; all later instances of "I can," "I want" or "I come" by necessity follow on from this first manifestation of spontaneous liveliness. By listening closely, the incipient subject opens up and moves towards a particular mood in which it can perceive what is its own with wonderful clarity. Naturally such listening can only apply to what is welcome. For the subject-to-be, only those sounds which tell it that it is being welcomed are themselves welcome.

One must seemingly assume that once pregnant women notice their condition, they begin to speak for the intimate witness in their body—and, to an extent, directly to it. If a woman's acknowledgement of her pregnancy is accompanied by positive feelings, a fabric of delicate anticipations of togetherness with the new life develops in her behavior, and the mothers begin to act as if they were under discreet observation from now on. They pull themselves together a little more than usual for the witness inside them—they hear their own voices more clearly, they feel they are being held responsible for their moods and their successes in life, and they know that they themselves are not merely an indifferent marginal condition for the successful beginning of the new life. In particular, they feel—however discreetly and implicitly—that they must be happy for the child's sake. Act in such a way that your own mood could at all times be a reasonable standard for a shared life: that is the categorical imperative for the mother. The law of sharing the good and bad fortune of one's partner in the intimate sphere goes deeper than the moral law based on following the most generalized norms. The duty to be happy is thus more moral than any formal or material decree; it expresses the ethics of creation itself. In the best case, the pregnant women become exhilarated actresses, demonstrating existence to the eyeless witness inside them like a sounding pantomime of happiness; demonstration and seduction become one and the same. Even if the mothers have reasons to be unhappy, they now have a stronger to show greater happiness than they can feel. It is their good fortune to be reminded very seriously that they must be happy, and the only completely unsuitable mother would be one who refused to want what she *must* do. The child's state as the object of the mother's expectations is conveyed by audio-vocal means to the fetal ear, which, upon hearing the greeting sound, unlocks itself completely and takes up the sonorous invitation. By adopting a posture of listening, the happy and active ear devotes itself to the words of welcome. In this sense, devotion is the subject-forming act *par excellence*, for devoting oneself means rousing oneself into the necessary state of alertness to open up to the sound that concerns you.

This going-outside-oneself is the first gesture of the subject. Above all, proto-subjectivity means feeling an accommodating impulse and vibrating in the greeting. It can only be accommodating because it too has been accommodated. In straightening up to listen, the pre-subject is persuaded of the advantage of hearing. Up to this point, hearing means an active anticipation of friendly messages. It results in the birth of intentionality from the spirit of listening for sounds of greeting and enlivenment. Enjoyment as the first intention also begins in such listening. What phenomenological research describes as intentionality or the noetic striving towards concrete ideas, then, initially comes from the fetal ear's accommodation of sounds made by the adequately good maternal voice. From the subject's earliest beginnings, the ray of intentionality with which it "relates" itself to something given has an echo character. Only because it is intended by the mother's voice can it intend the enlivening voice itself. The audio-vocal pact creates two-way traffic in a ray; enlivening forces are answered with a raising of the self to liveliness.

The theory of the siren effect thus leads into an investigation of the first greeting. What initially seems no more than seduction by something aspecifically very pleasant—the sonic magic of sirens—transpires, in the study's final perspective, as the repetition of a constitutive greeting of the human being in its first atmosphere. The human being is the more or less well-greeted animal, and if its center of feeling is to be reactivated, one must repeat the greeting that originally marks its initiation into the world. The correct greeting or welcome is the deepest correspondence a subject can experience. Certainly the Sirens' song from Book 12 of the *Odyssey* can also be heard as a greeting hymn. The heroic song, after all, only means—without the listener knowing what has hit him—a welcome in the hereafter, for the fabulous Sirens, as the ancients knew, belong to the other side. Their song closes the file of a hero's life with the remark "sung and completed." But while the Homeric singers dribble irresistible invitations to completion into men's ears, the good mothers' voices invite the witnesses in their wombs to begin their own existences energetically. The peculiarity of the siren effect, then, is that it creates a form of evangelistic intimacy: it creates good news that can by its nature only be heard by one or two parties.[10]

If we take this audio-vocal act of intimacy as the criterion, then Christian evangelism also partakes in the siren effect in several ways: the angelic greeting obliges the mother of the extra-ordinary child to look forward to the coming event at the highest spiritual frequency. The mystical sermon commands the individual to become pregnant with the divine spark and bear the Son within itself. And in its vital functions, the Christian message generally has the intention of raising up dejected life: *evangelizo vobis gaudium magnum.*[11] What characterizes Christianity as a cultural power is that time and again, it has managed to find a balance between the individualizing and community-forming compo-nents in the effects of evangelistic communication—an equilibrium between the muse and the siren, one might say. While siren religiosity releases intimistic and mystical tendencies, in precarious cases also sect magic and suicidal madness, the muse's *religio* leads to communal integration and the coherence of the people's church, but at its dangerous extreme also mass psychoses and belligerent chosenness offensives.

If one gives credence to the findings of the latest psychoa-coustic research, the fetus receives a fateful acoustic baptism in the womb. This happens not so much through its factual immersion in the intrauterine Jordan as through diving into the exquisite sound that becomes audible when the mother's voice speaks to the arriving life at her greeting frequencies. Baptizing and greeting are identical; they place the indelible seal on the welcomed being. With this mark begins the little-examined history of the affective power of judgment: it is the ability to interpret overall circumstances in terms of their atmospheric shadings. Because it is able to listen, the fetal ear can selectively highlight the mother's affirming voice amid the constant intrauterine noise. In this gesture the incipient subject experiences a euphoriant stimulation; according to Tomatis, it is the overtones of the mother's soprano voice in particular that offer an irresistible stimulus of joy. To make these claims plausible, Tomatis interpreted the mother's entire body as a musical instrument—albeit one that does not serve to play a piece to the listener, but rather brings about the original tuning of the ear. The transmission of high and extremely high frequencies in the soft, sound-swallowing bodily milieu is enabled, according to Tomatis, by the unusual conductivity and resonant quality of the skeleton; the mother's pelvis in particular is supposedly capable of conveying the subtlest high frequency vibrations of the mother's voice to the child's ear like the back of a cello. This ear listens at the mother's pelvic floor and spine as a curious visitor listens at a door behind which he suspects delightful presents. What the little guest cannot yet know is that this listening is its own reward, and that seeking to reach the other side would be futile. The joy of anticipation already contains the wealth of the enjoyable.

Clearly, current psychoacoustic research has given traditional beliefs concerning the formative effects of pregnant women's experiences on their unborn children new relevance, as well as lending them physiological concreteness by pointing to the specific transmission channel, namely auditory contact. Long-term influence can only be exerted via the ear, admittedly, if the fetus already has the sufficient neurological equipment to record and retain acoustic engrams. Such neural "engravings" or imprintings would then—like acquired acoustic universals, so to speak—pre-structure everything yet to be heard; hence they act as effective Platonic ideas of the hearing. Through prenatal auditions, the ear was equipped with a wealth of heavenly acoustic prejudices which, in its later work in the noisy pandemonium of reality, facilitate orientation and especially selection. The wonderfully biased ear would thus be capable of recognizing its primal models at the greatest distance from the origin: so for listening too, memory is everything. And just as Plato, in his discourse on the effects of the beautiful face, speaks of torturous unrest and hot flushes, as well as the lover's inclination to make sacrifices to his beloved as if he were a god,[12] the new audio-psycho-phonologists recount the startling effects of altered maternal voices (simulated using the Electronic Ear) on their patients. With barely any exceptions, and largely independently of age, they experience sudden excursions into prenatal states and begin radical reflection on their original talent for existing in integrity, connectedness and welcomeness. With his Platonic acoustics, Alfred Tomatis constructed a memory apparatus that allows the soul to follow on from its states in the hyper-heavenly place—more reliably and effectively, at first sight, than any philosophical anamnesis. In acoustic deep regressions, it grants the ears of the hardened, the fixated and the unhappy an audience with the original voice.

This shows that humans emerge without exception from a vocal matriarchy: this is the psychological reason for the siren effect. But while Homer's Sirens produce sweet obituaries, the mother's siren voice is anticipatory: it prophesies a sounding fate for the child. In listening to it, the fetal hero embarks on his own odyssey.[13] The irreplaceable voice utters an immediately self-fulfilling prophecy: "you are welcome" or "you are not welcome." Thus the mother's vocal frequency becomes a Last Judgment shifted back to the beginning of life. Mothers indeed greet whom they please, and their will to greet is not assured under all circumstances; they seldom refuse to offer any welcome at all, however. In this sense, the Last Judgment at the beginning is more merciful than that at the end—also because it knows a second, therapeutic authority.

Showing great psychological and logical consistency, Saint Augustine assessed the fallen soul's chances of being called back to God at the final verdict as very slim; his eschatology describes a divine economy in which only the few are spared and return home, while most are lost—bound into the great lump of perdition (*massa perditionis*). That is where the dark majority remain imprisoned, having failed to make adequate use of their second chance, the gospel of the true religion. They are left with the prospect of remaining in a personal God-forsaken hell as their final, continuous state. Depth-psychological proto-acoustics develops a somewhat more conciliatory doctrine by reformulating the final judgment as an initial judgment passed on each individual life: the prejudice of the initial attunement. This judgment can now be revised with psycho-phonological methods. In the therapeutic revision process there is a good chance of an acoustic rebirth—provided one can induce the mothers of troubled individuals to record their voices with a belated message of love to the child, which is then acoustically transformed in order to match the intrauterine milieu. If accounts of the method's consequences are not deceptive, it can have extraordinary effects. They not infrequently cause almost magical regressions to lost beginnings of lives. For countless people, such acoustic immersions appear to have opened up a second route to a good life. In substance, these psycho-phonological manipulations constitute first steps towards a theotechnic process. They reconstruct the second stage of Adam's creation—his pneumatic animation—using the means of the most advanced audiophonic technology; they reenact the first love in the virtual space.

In this manner, psychoacoustics establishes itself as the technique of the first things. It defines the prototype of the radically transformative, immersive and regenerative psychotherapy that must replace the exhausted religion of salvation in our time. Audiophonic psychotechnics negates the specific difference between proto-musicality and proto-religiosity. Whoever advances into these regions can no longer—as Max Weber so pithily said of himself—be religiously unmusical. Here it is sufficient to hear the high sounds that welcome your life in order to become both religious and musical, and both in the freest and most flexible form. At the same time, audio-vocal technology dissolves the boundary between soul and machine. As in some forms of traditional music, intimate therapeutical emotion transpires as something that can, to a degree, be produced on demand. The innermost ring of closeness techniques belongs not to mesmerist treatment and hypnosis, but rather to psychoacoustic, neuromusical and neurolinguistic procedures.

In our attempts to reveal the cause of individuals' accessibility to the messages of their own kind, we have now touched on the region of the most subtle resonance games. What we call the soul in the language of immemorial traditions is, in its most sensitive core area, a system of resonance that is worked out in the audio-vocal communion of the prenatal mother-child sphere. Here, human bondage begins as acuteness or hardness of hearing.[14] The accessibility of humans to intimate appeals has its origin in the synchronicity of greeting and listening; this movement towards each other forms the most intimate soul bubble. When the mother-to-be speaks inwards, she steps on the primal scene for free communion with the intimate other. With a sufficiently good greeting, the fetal ear can filter an adequate amount of high enlivening frequencies from the maternal milieu: it stretches out towards these sounds, and in its ability to hear well, it experiences the pleasure of being in the ascendant through its ability to be at all. Now the original unity of alertness, self-stimulation, intentionality and anticipation is rehearsed almost automatically. In this quaternity, the first blossoms of subjectivity open up. And what the happy underwater tube does is not content to be asked twice; if it is to believe the beloved voice, the latter must repeat its message a hundred times—but the repetitions are as easy for the adequately good mother as it is for the adequately addressed fetal hearing to attune itself to the recurring vibration, listening out anew each time as if it were the first. It notices the intention and is exhilarated; here repetition is the crux of happiness. Long before the glittering in the mother's voice returns in her eye, it prepares the child for its reception in the world; only by listening to the most intimate greeting can it adjust to the unsurpassable advantage of being itself.

In its earliest exercises, then, intimacy is a transmission relationship. Its model is not taken from the symmetrical alliance between twins or like-minded parties, where each mirrors the other, but from the irresolvably asymmetrical communion between the maternal voice and the fetal ear. It is the unconditional emergency of encounter, but it does not involve the two approaching each other from their respective spaces or situations; rather, the mother is the situation of the child, and the child's situation is nested within the maternal one. Acoustic communion gives the primordial encounter its location in the real. There is nothing between this voice and this ear that could be considered a mirroring, and yet the two are inextricably related in spheric union. Genuinely distinct, they are genuinely united. The voice does not speak to itself, and the ear has not withdrawn to listening to its own sounds. Each is always already outside-and-with-itself: the greeting voice in its turn towards the intimate co-listener, and the fetal ear in listening for the euphoriant sound. This relationship has no trace of narcissism, no unwarranted self-enjoyment arising from deceptive blind spots in the individual's self-reference. What characterizes this unusual relationship is an almost boundless surrender of the one to the other, and an almost seamless interlocking of the two sources of feeling. It is as if the voice and the ear had dissolved in a shared sonorous plasma—the voice entirely geared towards beckoning, greeting and affectionate encasement, and the ear mobilized to go towards it and be revived by melting into its sound.

Upon reflection, these observations cannot really contain anything new, as they describe fundamental conditions that have always had to be known and cared for via some idea or other. The novelty in these matters can only ever lie in the electric, perhaps demonic explicitness of their presentation. If the unfolding of the theory is to be effective, one must hear the rustling of the wrapping paper in which something almost familiar and almost forgotten is handed to the owner once again like something new. This is the typical sound accompanying the gifts phenomenology has to offer, for giving phenomenologically means giving nothing new in an entirely new way. Obviously midwifes, mothers and grandmothers have always looked after this area of knowledge correct intuitions, and it is only through the victorious individualistic abstractions of the last centuries that the sphere of fetal communions has been pushed ever further away from the feelings and the cognizance of individuals. In Chapter 3 above, which deals with the social history of recent practices of closeness, in particular mesmerism and animal magnetism, we outlined a striking wave of recent intimacy techniques whose offshoots are still potent to this day, and there was an opportunity to show how the most prescient authors of this movement interpreted the peculiarity of magnetic rapport as a direct reproduction and reactivation of the fetal position. It was above all Friedrich Hufeland and Hegel who were most explicit in this. They not only conceived of the fetus as a plant growing up inside an animal, striving towards an animality and spirituality of its own; they also understood the incipient subject as a form of malleable psychoplasma in which intense ideas harbored by the mother are capable of leaving their imprint.

Nonetheless, the classic articulation of the modern theory of the mother's psychoplastic effects on the fetus is over a century older than psychomagnetism and its consideration in German Idealism; it was already made in Nicola Malebranche's *Recherche de la vérité* from 1674. In his uncommonly radical theory of imagination, the author develops a resolutely medial theory of motherhood characterized by the possibility of long-distance viewing and feeling. The Oratorian monk and psychologist Malebranche conceived of wombs as projectors through which good or bad images—almost like primal prejudices about the outside world—are cast onto the soft matrix of the child's soul.

Thus, children see what their mothers see [...]. For basically the body of the child is but a part of the mother's body, the blood and spirits are common to both [...].[15]

About seven or eight years ago, I saw at the *Incurables* a young man who was born mad, and whose body was broken in the same places in which those of criminals are broken. He had remained nearly twenty years in this state. Many persons saw him, and the late queen mother, upon visiting this hospital, was curious to see and even to touch the arms and legs of this young man where they were broken.

According to the principles just established, the cause of this disastrous accident was that his mother, having known that a criminal was to be broken, went to see the execution. All the blows given to this miserable creature forcefully struck the imagination of this mother and, by a sort of counterblow, the tender and delicate brain of her child. The fibers of this woman's brain were extremely shaken and perhaps broken in some places by the violent flow of the spirits produced at the sight of such a terrible occurrence, but they retained sufficient consistency to prevent their complete destruction. On the other hand, the child's brain fibers, being unable to resist the torrent of these spirits, were entirely dissipated, and the destruction was great enough to make him lose his mind forever. That is the reason why he came into the world deprived of sense. Here is why he was broken at the same parts of his body as the criminal his mother had seen put to death.

At the sight of this execution, so capable of frightening a woman, the violent flow of the mother's animal spirits passed very forcefully from her brain to all the parts of her body corresponding to those of the criminal, and the same thing happened in the child. But, because the mother's bones were capable of resisting the violence of these spirits, they were not wounded by them. [...] But this rapid flow of the spirits was capable of sweeping away the soft and tender parts of the child's bones. [...]

It has not been more than a year since a woman, having attended too carefully to the portrait of Saint Pius on the feast of his canonization, gave birth to a child who looked exactly like the representation of the saint. [...] his arms were crossed upon his chest, with his eyes turned toward the heavens [...]. He had a kind of inverted miter on his shoulders, with many round marks in the places where miters are covered with gems. [...] This is something that all Paris has been able to see as well as me, because the body was preserved for a considerable time in alcohol.[16]

These excerpts from Malebranche's deliberations make it clear how much reflections on prenatal phenomena were biased towards visual models already in the early Modern Age. The bizarre idea that *images* of horror from the mother's soul should be traced onto the child's body proves that the intimate communion between mother and child was thought of primarily graphically or eidetically. Nature as the creator is here imagined as a draftswoman who, via the mediation of active life spirits, can inscribe the outlines of pathological outside-world objects and scenes through the mothers and into the fetal plasma.

The idea that this visual imagination is accompanied by a constitutive sonic imagination which plays an even more important part, indeed the decisive one, in the incorporation of the child into the world was, to our knowledge, first developed seriously by

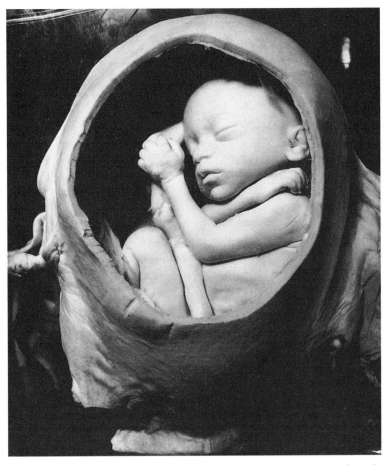

Anita Gratzer, *Pulcherrima*, from *Human Time Anatomy*. Now housed in the Federal Museum of Pathology and Anatomy, Vienna

psychologists and otologists of the twentieth century; and it is no coincidence that they usually did so in contradistinction to the dogmas of the Zurich and Vienna schools of psychoanalysis, whose imago-oriented view and its continuation in the theory of inner objects and the doctrine of archetypes paid tribute uncritically to the dominant visual prejudices of their milieu. Those who assert the primacy of the sonic imagination can refer to impressive evolutionary evidence that give the ear a key role in the development of higher forms of organization for life in general. Among songbirds one already finds traces of auditory formability *in ovo*: experiments have shown that the chick in the egg enjoys a species-specific music education through the mother's singing. Young birds incubated by mute mothers become vocally insecure or songless, while those brooded over by singing mothers of a different species show the tendency to adopt the melodies of that species. Anyone seeking to naturalize Plato and uncover evidence of prenatal information on the "soul" would find the most suggestive corroboration in such observations. The listening conditions among mammals support these conclusions even more. Here the bond between the fetal ear and the mother's voice develops further, to the point of unambiguous individualization: according to evolutionary biologists, newborn piglets or kids are immediately capable of recognizing their mother's voice with absolute certainty among thousands of similar ones—an achievement of early shaping that can only be explained by a form of prenatal "tuning." Among humans, the process of subtle symbiotic attunements in the audio-vocal resonant space is even more highly differentiated, encompassing emotional keys,[17] recitative-like accents, types of sonorous milieu and, above all, individual frequencies of welcome. As it attunes itself to the sounding space that will later bear the name "mother," the hearing of the human fetus develops the decisive rudiments of motoric-musical subjectivity. People come into the world through chamber music; only there can they learn that listening to the other voice is the precondition for having anything to play oneself. One can therefore

Wolfgang Rihm, *Im Innersten*, Third String Quartet. Text: "In this movement, there is not a single crescendo or decrescendo. The dynamics indicated always apply to the full note value or note group. There should be no transitions between dynamic levels, even when, for example, the harmonic context seems to demand it in keeping with traditional performance practice."

> kein einziges crescendo und decrescendo.
mik gilt immer für die ganzen Notenwerte
Es sollen keine übergänge zwischen den
u stattfinden, auch dort nicht wo es z.B.
ntext im Sinne traditionellen Spiels zu

say that the human being's time in the world is defined, more than with any other living creature, by the necessity of staying within a psychoacoustic—or, more generally speaking, in a semiospheric—continuum and developing there.

As we have stated and shown several times in the course of our reflections, humans are sphere-dwellers from the start, and in this specific sense they are creatures predisposed towards a division of the inner world. Now we are in a position to offer a closer characterization of the central fabric of this constitutive interiority, namely its contribution to producing an intimizing sound phenomenon. It is the constitutive listening community that encloses humans in the immaterial rings of mutual accessibility. The ear is the organ that connects the intimate and the public. Whatever might present itself as social life, it initially comes about only in the specific width of an acoustic bell over the group—a bell whose sonorous presences, especially in European cultures, are capable of textualization. Only in the social sonosphere can chamber music turn into choral politics; only here, in the stream of speech, is the mother-child space connected to the stages of adult myths and the arena of political quarrels over right and wrong. In a synergetic area of natural-historical and symbol-historical influences, human ears rose to become the leading agencies of ethnic associations. It is only through the arousing extreme development of the hearing that human existence within a sonospheric hothouse became possible. Even if natural languages had developed into phonetic systems without any claims to reference or meaning—if there were only choirs, no working groups—humans would be exactly the same in all fundamental respects as they are now (minus the workers' autisms). In the wall-less house of sounds, humans became the animals that come together by listening.[18] Whatever else they might be, they are sonospheric communards.

Excursus 8

Illiterate Truths

A Note on Oral Fundamentalism

There is a distinctive and not entirely powerless tradition in European intellectual history that truth is something that cannot be articulated through speech, let alone writing, but only through singing—and most of all through eating. This concept of truth is concerned not with the representation or imagining of a matter in a different medium, but rather the absorption or integration of one matter into a different matter. Clearly there is a collision here between two radically different models of truth-enabling adequation: while the generally noted and respected representational truth involves an alignment of intellect and thing or statement and fact, the comparatively unacknowledged absorption-based truth aims for an equivalence of content and container or devourer and devoured. Semioticians and theologians have worn us down often enough with the corresponding examples: the statement "It is raining now" is, as we have heard, true if and only if there is genuinely reason to believe that it is raining now. My listening to music, on the other hand, is only true listening if I myself become music-shaped in the presence of the piece, and my eating of the communion wafer only assists my salvation if I myself become

Christ-shaped by swallowing the offering. There is clearly something special about the mode of adequation in the last two examples. It is obvious that we are not simply dealing with different concepts of truth and equivalence, but that entirely incomparable dimensions of appropriateness and the ability to be precise also come into play here. While one can usually say sufficiently precisely with representational truths when the preconditions for their validity are fulfilled, one can never be quite sure of this in the case of absorption-based truths. The correspondences arising from absorptions are constitutively vague; this vagueness should not be viewed as a deficiency, however, but rather as defining the particular mode of being and chance of this truth field. Perhaps I can go unchallenged in stating that this sleeve, if and because it fits, is a true counterpart of this arm. I would surely encounter objections, however, if I specified where the listener is when he immerses himself in the event space of a present piece of music, or where Christ is when the wafer disappears down the throat of the communicant.

Absorbing something into oneself and letting oneself be absorbed in something: with these two gestures, humans secure for themselves what one could call their participatory competence. Through consumption they absorb food and drink, and by taking place in a round of consumers they make their absorption into a table fellowship visible. The non-insane, non-perverted human possesses the power of judgment not least because of the ability to discern where he participates as an absorber and where as an absorbed. If he has not lost all reason, that is to say his sense of correspondence, he will always know with sufficient accuracy when he is the vessel and when its content, when he uses something up and when he himself is used up. One could say that all oral truth is based on the differentiation of tables. In order to be adequately complete human beings, we must learn at which tables we are the eaters and at which we become the eaten. The tables at which we eat are called dining tables; those at which we are eaten are called altars. But are we, as human beings, directly altar-capable? Is it possible and permissible to describe humans in terms of their suitability to be put on the table? It is the axiom of all culture that communicating people come *to* the table rather than being put *on* it. The man put on the table legitimately would—speaking within the Christian horizon—would no longer be a man but the God-man, who wants to make himself present in us through oral communion and integrate us into his imaginary body; and the table set for this would precisely no longer be the profane dining table, but rather the altar—that is, the table of the Lord, where such food is permitted as we can eat in the awareness that it will eat us or spit us out later on. The other table belongs only to God, who gives and takes without restrictions. The edible God is the founder of the table fellowship as the true commune whose members have agreed on exophagia. Only by refraining from endophagous relationships can humans recognize one another as their own kind. In the true community, all are ultimately equal only before the law not to consider viewing one another as food. And if we do eat meat, it must at all costs be foreign meat—firstly that of permitted animals, which feed us as a profane group, and secondly that of the true God, who unites us as a holy group.

The field of absorption-based truths is of fundamental significance for the construction of human reason because it is precisely there that the essential distinction between true and false comes into effect. As in the field of representational truths, it is the case here too—and above all here—that the false ultimately brings death; that which enables and extends life, on the other hand, can be considered the true. Whoever takes poison will die, as will anyone who lands inside the wrong whale. That is why, even in a culture as extremely geared towards representational truth as our modern one, it is vital that the awareness of absorptive and participatory relationships and their respective degrees of truth and error does not fall into neglect. There is reason to note that the critique of absorption-based relationships is in a worse state than ever before; philosophy in particular, which was traditionally responsible for this, has, if one examines the last two centuries, descended into a cluelessness that is culture-historically unprecedented; had this space not been filled by psychological and myth-critical disciplines in the course of the twentieth century, the area of responsibility of a philosophical critique of participatory reason would be in even more desolate condition than it currently is. The formula "participatory reason" implies the thesis that there are appropriate and inappropriate participations whose difference is akin to that between true and false. Even the appropriate and inappropriate forms of participation should not be imagined only as voluntary memberships in public projects, however, but also as an inclusion in consumptive communions—under the premise that even among non-cannibals, there are necessary, discreet and welcome endophagous relationships.

The positive paradigms for this can naturally be found in the world of early mother-child relationships: if one could characterize normal pregnancy as the mother's devotion to her own consumption by the foreign body inside it, the breastfeeding period would be the active accommodation by the female body of its cannibalistic use by the infant. If one focuses on the child's perspective, it transpires that the incipient subject claims the unconditional right to settle as an absolute consumer in the milieu it finds—a milieu that has obviously existed since primeval times and seemingly knows no other purpose than to fulfill the needs of the intruder at all costs. The ontological irony of the maternal milieu is that no fetus, no infant, no young child—in short, no human being—can know in advance that the world only has the character of a magically available milieu shows how she is accessible as an inhabitable, cannibalizable, retrievable mother. And there is nothing to suggest that she might one day become inaccessible, as long as the sufficiently good, sufficiently edible mother takes the side of the cannibal's longing for her. She signals to the child that it is completely right to desire nourishment initially only from her and through her. Thus the original oral truth function, the elemental consistency of the child's consumptive participation in the mother, is reinforced by the consumed party. The mother-eater is always right, and is right to be right: its drive to absorb is based on an immemorial biological truth relationship, in the sense that its claim to nourishment through the mother generally encounters the accommodation of the mother's breasts; where there is an unmistakable appetite, there is also the unmistakable dose. One could speak here of an *a priori* synthesis in the somatic. In the maternal milieu, a child that is not overly frustrated acquires the proto-religious faith that an eternally valid pragmatic equation is in force between calling and drinking. This conviction forms the core of the child's belief that it can perform magic—a belief without which the opposite of magic, namely work, must ultimately remain pointless; for one can only work successfully as long as one still believes that effort calls for happiness, and that it will accordingly come once the work is done. Growing up consists in accepting that the magic-enabling equation of call and success has the tendency to fade, and ultimately disappear almost entirely. But how, if those who seek no longer find? If what is called no longer comes? The first magic gradually dissolves into struggle and work, until the point is reached where the subject—on the threshold of bitterness—admits that whoever does not work should not eat, and that whoever cannot refrain may not indulge. The word "work" sums up a state of the world in which it is no longer enough simply to call or use magical formulas in order to find satisfaction. Where work has entered the horizon, the experience that calling helps can only be defended by religious or aesthetic means. And the belief that the happiness one has called will come after an appropriate time is only sustained by the fact that the question of who should ultimately be considered the giver of our daily bread can be left open. Religion survives as a memory of the days when calling still helped.

As archaic as it may be, consumptive participation in the maternal milieu through one's own *infans* voice is not the earliest form of absorption magic. Before the subject could experience the necessity of calling in order to eat, it was granted an even deeper form of participation that, as a fetal, sanguine, endo-acoustic communion, offered the absolute maximum of absorbed life. That is where those who want neither to work nor to call strive to return in order to find that archaic homeostasis once more. Before the *infans*, the non-speaker, comes the *inclamans*, the non-caller. It is characteristic of modern mass culture that it has learned how to bypass the tables and altars of high culture and offer new, direct ways of fulfilling the desire for homeostatic communion. This is the psychodynamic purpose of pop music and all its derivatives: for its consumers, it stages the possibility of diving into a body of rhythmic noise in which critical ego functions become temporarily dispensable. Anyone who witnesses the behavioral gestures at discotheques and sound parades as an impartial observer must conclude that the current mass music audience strives for an enthusiastic self-sacrifice by plunging—voluntarily and at its own risk—into the sound crater. It clearly longs to be drawn inwards by the acoustic juggernaut and transformed inside its innards into a rhythmicized, oxygen-deprived, pre-subjective something. Pop music has overtaken religious communions—Christian ones—on the archaic wing by outdoing the chances of absorption found at altars with the offer to join psychoacoustic abdominal cavities and follow passing audio gods.[19] This was especially evident at the Berlin Love Parades of the 1990s and their replicas in European cities, which, in cultural-anthropological terms, are interesting as particularly explicit displays of "true" absorption relationships. According to their immanent concept, they could just as easily be called "Truth Parades," as their aim is to absorb large numbers of people, all of whom value the attributes of their individuality, into happy, symbiotic, reversible and thus "true" sonospheres. These communions with the audio gods or the rhythmic juggernauts are based on the same truth model as post-Freudian psychoanalysis—with the difference that the latter recommends that its clients develop a strict individual rhetoric of mourning for the lost primal object, while integristic music therapy in the streets relies on drug-assisted group euphorias that may advance flirtation with absorption into a spheric primal body in the short term, but yield little profit for the participants' medial competence in the sobering periods that follow. But the Love Parades, as well as countless other forms in which collective ecstasy is enacted, do reveal how modernity works on making the basic relationship among human ensembles, namely psychoacoustic integrism, producible in ever more direct, unabashed and religion-free ways.

In this sense, the couch and the ecstasy of the disco belong together like the concave and convex sides of a single truth lens. They have the same theotechnic connection, in so far as they arrange relationships to a remote, but not entirely extinguished primal object, a sonorous divine thing-in-itself. Without this connection to the intimate absolute, human expressive speech would be divorced from any transcendent cause or referent and fall prey to self-referentially closed linguistic play. According to the schema of psychoanalysis and the love/truth parade, however, the inexpressible truth is only revealed to a pre-linguistic subject. Whether this subject paradoxically refuses to have learned to read, write and speak, like mystics and ecstatics, or the analysands plunge into reading, writing and singing all the more vigorously in order to say the unsayable, this is merely a choice of strategy against the background of the same model. Which is why the ideal patient makes an effort to reach for the great lost using the refined methods of speech and writing, while the ideal cult participant devotes himself to the revelation of noise in the real presence of the loudspeaker truck. That no psychoanalytical treatment would ultimately be possible without an orientation of the desiring subject around a psychological thing-in-itself—one could also say around an illiterate transcendence—is demonstrated by Julia Kristeva in a lucid series of reflections:

In the radius of a sound juggernaut: the 1998 Berlin Love Parade

The obsession with the primal object, the object to be conveyed, assumes a certain appropriateness (imperfect, to be
sure) to be considered possible between the sign and not the
referent but the nonverbal experience of the referent in the
interaction with the other. I am able to name truly. The Being
that extends beyond me—including the being of affect—may
decide that its expression is suitable or nearly suitable. The
wager of conveyability is also a wager that the primal object
can be mastered [...]. Metaphysics, and its obsession with

conveyability, is a discourse of the pain that is stated and relieved on account of that very statement. It is possible to be unaware of, to deny the orial Thing, it is possible to be unaware of pain to the benefit of signs that are written out or playful, without innerness and without truth. The advantage of those civilizations that operate on the basis of such a model is that they are able to mark the immersion of the subject within the cosmos, its mystical immanence with the world. But, as a Chinese friend recognized, such a culture is without means for facing the onset of pain. Is that lack an advantage or a weakness?

Westerners, on the other hand, are convinced they can convey the mother […], but in order to […] betray her, transpose her, be free of her. Such melancholy persons triumph over the sadness at being separated from the loved object through an unbelievable effort to master signs in order to have them correspond to primal, unnameable, traumatic experiences.

Even more so and finally the belief in conveyability ("mother is nameable, God is unnameable") leads to a strongly individualized discourse, avoiding stereotypes and clichés, as well as to the profusion of personal styles. But in that very practice we end up with the perfect *betrayal* of the unique and in-itself Thing (*the Res divina*): if all the fashions of naming it are allowable, does not the Thing postulated in itself become dissolved in the thousand and one ways of naming it? The posited conveyability ends up with a multiplicity of possible conveyances. The Western subject, as potential melancholy being, having become a relentless conveyor, ends up a confirmed gambler or potential atheist. The initial belief in conveyance becomes changed into a belief in stylistic performance for which the near side of the text, its other, primal as it may be, is less important than the success of the text itself.[20]

Even if all problems of representation and self-reference were to be solved, the questions of absorption, participation and immanence would not even have been touched on.

Excursus 9

Where Lacan Starts to Go Wrong

The immediately problematic imago-oriented perspective of psychoanalytical relationship theories was taken to its extreme by Jacques Lacan in his legendary theorem of the "mirror stage as formative of the ego function"[21] published in 1949. Lacan assumes an early childhood sensibility that is always already cursed with the impossibility of tolerating itself. For Lacan, every infant is shattered by incurable states of inner destruction. Psychosis is its truth and reality, inescapable and present from the start. It plunges into the world, powerless and betrayed, as the body that has already been cut to pieces and can scarcely hold its fragments together. The truth would be that this dismemberment would precede totality, and that a primal psychosis would have the first say everywhere. For a being so thoroughly dissociated and stewing in its own forlornness, the sight of its own clearly defined image over there in the mirror—if we go along with the analyst's suggestions for a moment—would surely be very edifying, as the subject could finally, in the imaginary Yonder, see itself *for the first time* as a complete form without ruptures or blemishes. The self-image in the mirror would come into play here as the liberator from an unbearable sense of self.

Only the image over there in the mirror space would prove to me, against my evident sense of self, that I am not a monster but a shapely child within the beautiful boundaries of its organic form. Recognizing oneself in the mirror with the thought "that's me" would then mean: smiling at the picture that has suddenly flashed up, taking its integrity as a message of salvation and ascending with the joy of liberation to an imaginary heaven of the complete image in which it would never again have to make concede to the previous real and true disunity. Finally the *infans* could leave behind its humiliating dismemberment and raging impotence; it would suddenly be able to float out through the mirror glass, newly invulnerable, into the visual space and enter the kingdom of a delusional integrity like a transfigured hero— radiantly saved from the wretched primary condition to which it believes it will now never have to return, assuming that the dream shield of the incorruptible image ego can eliminate all later disturbances. Then ego development would always inevitably begin with a redemptive self-misjudgment: the imaginary apparition out there—my image as an intact, whole, saving one—would take me out of the imageless hell of my sensed early life, if I now accepted *it* radically at my side, and make the wonderfully deceptive promise that I would always be able to live towards this image, as if under the protection of an illusion. My illusory image of myself out there in visibility—in the imaginary or the transfigured visual realm—would, through its well-formed wholeness, be a gospel written purely for me; a promise that anticipates me and consolidates me. As soon as I had taken it up into myself, it would lie at the bottom of my self as the good news of my resurrection from early destruction. My image, my primal delusion, my guardian angel, my delirium.

It can easily be shown that this most famous early theorem from the body of Lacanian doctrines is as brilliant as it is ill-conceived—established on the basis of willful and pathos-laden misinterpretations of the early dyadic communication between the child and its augmenter-companion, which, aside from its prenatal supplementation media is usually the mother. For the child's own mirror image cannot as such add anything to the child's "self"-findings that has not long since been set up within it at the level of vocal, tactile, interfacial and emotional games of resonance and their inner sediments. Before each encounter with its own mirror image, a non-neglected *infans* "knows" very well and very precisely what it means to be an unscathed life inside a carrying-containing dual. In a sufficiently well-formed biune mental structure, pictorial self-perception occurs in the child—which occasionally notes its reflection in a glass, metallic or watery medium—as an exhilarating, curiosity-inducing additional layer of perception on top of an already dense, encouraging web of resonance experiences; by no means does the image in the mirror appear as the *first* and all-surpassing information about its own ability to be whole; at most, it makes an initial reference to its own appearance as a coherent body among coherent bodies in the real visual space, but this integral being-an-image-body means almost nothing alongside the pre-imaginary, non-eidetic certainties of sensual-emotional dual integrity. A child that grows up in a sufficiently good continuum has long since been adequately informed through other sources of the reasons for its containedness in a fulfillment form. Its interest in coherence is more or less satisfied long *before* receiving the mirror-eidetic information. The sight of its mirror image does not acquaint it with any radically new possibility of happiness and being that is based exclusively in the visual-imaginary realm. Apart from that, one must take into account that—as already observed[22]—most European households did not possess mirrors until the nineteenth century, which means that the simplest culture-historical consideration already makes Lacan's theorem, which behaves like some transhistorically valid anthropological dogma, seem unfounded.

If, admittedly, the resonance game between the child and its augmenting other is burdened with instances of ambivalence, neglect and sadism, the child will naturally develop a tendency to cling to the thin moments of positive augmentative experience—whether precarious kindnesses by its reference persons, autoerotic dreams of withdrawal, or identifications with the invulnerable heroes of fairy tales and myths. Whether the early sight of their own mirror images genuinely helps psychotic children on the threshold between the baby and toddler phases to achieve imaginary resurrections through visually assisted phantasms of integrity has not been empirically established at all. At any rate, the exceptional situation elevated to the norm by Lacan, in which the incipient subject tumbles out of itself and into the picture in order to escape the imbalance it senses in its own fragmented skin and become something deceptively whole in the world of images, only constitutes—should it ever acquire casuistic reality—a pathological extreme. It could only have a place in life within impoverished family structures, and in milieus with a tendency towards chronic neglect of infants. For every ego formation that took place in this way via a flight to the visual illusion of intactness, one could indeed predict that paranoid instability that Lacan, based on his self-analysis, wrongly sought to present as a general characteristic of the psyche in the cultures of all periods. If it were genuinely the case that one could always find a self-blinding imaginary element of this type at the bottom of a self, it would at least explain why the subject in a Lacanian universe only finds wellbeing, or at least order, in the symbolic. Only submission to the symbolic law can save the subject from a constitutive psychosis. But what is that if not the continuation of Catholicism by ostensibly psychoanalytical means? Certainly no one will suspect injuries from all sides with such feverish prescience as a subject that has made its ability to be whole dependent on the protection of fantastically extravagant glossy images of its own ego; but anyone who claimed that basal ego formations in the imaginary are, according to this mode, the universal rule would be underpinning the first extravagance with a second. This would mean placing psychology itself in the service of psychosis. Lacan surrendered early on to a dogmatic belief in primal psychosis whose motifs stemmed not from psychoanalytical interests but from crypto-Catholic, surrealistic and para-philosophical ones. In its tendency and tone, Lacan's remarkable theorem of the mirror stage is a parody of the Gnostic doctrine of liberation through self-knowledge; using a problematic model, he replaces original sin with original deception, yet without ever making it clear whether this deception should be conserved or overcome. In all cases, it is supposedly their initial self-misjudgment that provided the subjects with such indispensable, yet also disastrous illusions of themselves— Lacan occasionally spoke of the "orthopedic" function of the primary illusion. So who could survive mentally intact without the spine of self-deception—and who is supposed to have an interest in breaking that of the subject? At the same time, however, the deception is meant to be just that: an illusion which must be seen through, in so far as it holds temptations that endanger the self. To know or not to know oneself—that is the question. So much the worse for those who were never met by the credible image of their own ability to be whole, coming from a supposedly imaginary realm—let alone from a real love.

CHAPTER 8

Closer to Me Than I Am Myself

A Theological Preparation for the Theory of the Shared Inside

We must set forth the ontological Constitution of inhood [*Inheit*] itself. [...]

What is meant by "*Being-in*"? [...] Being-in [...] is a state of Dasein's Being [...].

— Martin Heidegger, *Being and Time*, p. 79

"What is this 'in'?" Agathe asked emphatically. Ulrich shrugged his shoulders and then gave a few indications. [...]

"Perhaps the psychoanalytic legend that the human soul strives to get back to the tender protection of the intrauterine condition before birth is a misunderstanding of the 'in,' perhaps not. Perhaps 'in' is the presumed descent of all life from God. But perhaps the explanation is also simply to be found in psychology; for every affect bears within it the claim of totality to rule alone and, as it were, form the 'in' in which everything else is immersed."

— Robert Musil, *The Man Without Qualities*, p. 1497

So where are we when we are in a small inside? In what way can a world, despite its opening towards the immeasurable, be an intimately divided round world? Where are those who come into the world when they are in bipolar intimate spheres or bubbles? On our path through some of the folds and turns in the human-forming microcosms of interlocked interiority, seven layers of an answer to this question have so far taken shape.

We are in a microsphere whenever we are

— *firstly* in the intercordial space

— *secondly* in the interfacial sphere

— *thirdly* in the field of "magical" binding forces and hypnotic effects of closeness

— *fourthly* in immanence, that is to say in the interior of the absolute mother and its postnatal metaphorizations

— *fifthly* in the co-dyad, or the placental doubling and its successors

— *sixthly* in the care of the irremovable companion and its metamorphoses

— *seventhly* in the resonant space of the welcoming maternal voice and its messianic- evangelistic-artistic duplications.

It will be noted that this list is missing the inter-genital relationship and the inter-manual connection, as if to suggest that coitus and handshakes are excluded from the intimate-spheric field. In truth, the two gestures are fairly peripheral from the perspective of microspheric analysis, even if they—especially the sexual one—represent intimate relationships that are prototypical for everyday consciousness. Sexuality in particular, even though it occasionally releases suggestive intimate experiences, has no intimate light of its own, any more than the encounter between warriors on the inside of a *Ring* creates intimate-spherically relevant contacts in and of itself. If *de facto* intimacy comes into play here, it is only through the transference of closeness relationships from real intimate scenes of the kind listed above to genital or athletic duels and duals. Such transferences distinguish human sexuality from that among animals. While animals can content themselves with slotting their reproductive organs together for intercourse, that same quandary motivates humans to produce an increase in intimacy. This can only be drawn from the reservoir of transferable closeness memories from elsewhere—extending to the Tristan embrace, in which the lovers both enact their return into the original womb in the shape of the other. Nothing shows more clearly that humans are condemned to intimate surrealism than the fact that most of the time, even their genital interactions have to be arranged on a virtual inner-world stage.

At first glance, the variants of intimacy relationships treated here only share a single formal quality: they never separate the subject from its environment, nor do they place it in confrontation with something that is present in concrete form or faces it as a state of affairs; rather, they integrate it into an encompassing situation and take it up into a space of relationships with two or more locations, where the ego side only represents one pole. Hence the common thread in this septernity would, if the term were permitted and current, be its "structuring" through *inhood*. This neologism, which surfaced like an apparition in Heidegger's early work,[1] expresses, oddly enough, the fact that the subject or Dasein can only be *there* if it is contained, surrounded, encompassed, disclosed, breathed-upon, resounded-through, attuned and addressed. Before a Dasein assumes the character of being-in-the-world, it already has the constitution of being-in. Having admitted this, it seems justified to demand that heterogeneous statements about intimate-spheric enclosedness and openness be brought together in an overarching pattern. The aim is thus a theory of existential spaciousness—or, differently put: a theory of inter-intelligence or the stay in animation spheres. This principle of the intimate relationship space should make it clear why a life is always a life-in-the-midst-of-lives.[2] Being-in, then, should be conceived as the togetherness of something with something in something. We are therefore asking—we shall repeat the thesis— about what is known in current terminology as a "media theory." What are media theories but suggestions of ways to explain the how and the whereby of the connection between different exis-tents in a shared ether?

Looking around in search of models for such an undertaking, one is pulled *nolens volens* into the broad field of the Old Euro-pean theological tradition. It is above all the Greek, and even more the Latin Church Fathers and Doctors who, in their trea-tises on the Trinity, their mystical theologies and their doctrines of the two interlocking natures of the God-man, occupied them-selves with the question of how to think the containedness of conceived and created natures *in* the one God, as well as God's relationship with Himself. It was inevitable that these branches of dogmatics would become a school of reflection on the *being* of intimate relationships. While it is characteristic of modern thought that it begins with Dasein's being-in-the-world or the system's being-in-its-environment, it is the *proprium* of Christian monotheism, and even more of philosophical monotheism, that it must begin with the being-in-God of all things and souls.[3] As the all-pervading God, who is beyond all finite localizations, cannot be anywhere other than everywhere *in Himself,*[4] there seems to be no alternative to being-in for theonomic thought. God is in Himself and the world is in God—so where could the slightest remainder of that which is be located, if not in the circle of influence of this absolute In? One cannot seriously speak of externality in a world that is God's work and extension. Nonetheless, the totalized inside of God is provoked by a disruptive outside whose theologically correct title is "creation after the fall." For where are the people who live in sin, or willfulness, or freedom if not outside, so to speak—albeit in a licensed externality that, because creatureliness should never be able to deny the connection to the originator entirely? And where if not out there below should a savior look for the fallen souls that are to be led home?

The emergency for the theological question of the In, then, is triggered by two logically disturbing relationships: firstly, the problematic one between God and the human soul, of which it is initially far from clear how it could continue to be *in God* or with Him after the Fall; and secondly, God's eccentric-intimate relationships with Himself, which, in the light of His self-exit in the guise of the savior, encouraged the most pensive of investigations. So how, and in what sense, could one say that humans—or the human soul—are still contained in God, even in their fallen state? And how, and in what sense, should we henceforth think of God, after His incarnation and Pentecostal outpouring, as seamlessly contained in Himself? These two questions triggered two mighty waves of theological reflection on the conditions of being-one and being-in: the Christian era identifies itself by the urge to reflect on God and space in fundamental-theoretical terms; it is the golden age of subtle topologies dealing with places in the non-where. For if God were the absolute vessel, how thick would its walls be? How was it possible to go forth to the outside from within Him? Why did He not want to take everything He had created back into Himself unconditionally? And by what mediation might lost things possibly return home? While the question as to the relationship between God and the soul is mostly answered in the mode of biunity theories, the question as to the nature of God's self-inhabitation finds its answer primarily through Trinitarian doctrines.

For the present spherology, these discourses are not interesting for their religious claims or their dogmatic willfulness; we are not visiting them as attractions from intellectual history. They are only of legitimate concern to us to the extent that, until recently, they had a virtually unchallenged monopoly on funda-mental intimacy-logical reflection. Only Platonic erotology had been able, in contemporary adaptations, to break the predomi-nance of Christian theology in the field of the theory of intimate connections. Anyone wanting to learn more closely about the spirit of closeness and more intimately about the spirit of inti-macy before the advent of modern depth psychologies in the eighteenth century inevitably had to turn to the most withdrawn regions of the theological tradition. In this tradition, as far as the more esoteric aspects of God-soul relationships were concerned, mystical transmission was almost the sole authority; anyone interested in the inner life of the so richly and enigmatically self-referential life of God had to tackle the daunting massif of Trinitarian speculation. It is in these still rather inaccessible areas that the patinated treasures of a premodern knowledge of pri-mary relationships lie stored. Much of what preoccupies modern psychologists and sociologists concerning the concepts of inter-subjectivity and inter-intelligence is prefigured in the theological discourses that, in thousand-year-old serenity, deal with the intertwined co-subjectivity of the God-soul dyad and the co-intelligence, cooperation and condilection of the intra-godly Trinity. Thus, if the concern is to deal with participatory phenomena and structures of constitutive being-in-each-other and being-with-each-other at a fundamental-conceptual level, parts of theological tradition can become a surprisingly informative source for the free spirit. It is in theological surrealism, as will be shown, that the first spheric realism lies hidden. Only through its reconstruction can we sufficiently clarify what immanence actually means.

This applies first and foremost to the field of God-soul relationships. Whoever attempts to comprehend the language games of mystical theology about the soul's reentry into the divine sphere is immediately faced with a subtle web of statements about de-objectified interconnections. For if one asks the reason for the possible mutual attention between God and the soul, one is faced with an unfathomable openness to relationships deeper than any other inclinations of kinship or sympathy that can normally be assumed between people or beings. The nature of the bond between them cannot in any way be explained by *a posteriori* affections or halfway meetings. It may be true of human love, in a certain sense, that it does not exist at all until it occurs. What precedes human love are—viewed from the perspective of individualistic modernity—two lonelinesses that are uprooted through encounter. So one could apply Alain Badiou's statement about the late Beckett's meditation on love: "The encounter is founding of the Two as such."[5] As far as God and the soul are concerned, they do not face each other like parties or business people who see a common benefit in occasional coalitions; nor do they merely form an amorous couple occasionally—depending on the coincidence of encounter—consumed by passion. If an intimate reaction occurs between them, it is by no means simply a result of what psychoanalysis—with a phrase of limited wisdom—calls a "choice of object." If God and the soul are connected, it is due to an interpersonal free radical older than any partner search or secondary acquaintance. And if their relationship at times seems a passionate one, this is only because there is, under certain circumstances, a resonance between them so radical that it cannot possibly be attributed merely to the empirical contact of each with the other. The fundamental resonance, however, if it were to be recognized as an initial or constitutive one—how should we conceive of it, when it is initially and usually "in the world," and consequently located in a place that is characterized—vaguely put—by a certain distance from the transcendental pole? How should one interpret the ability of God and the soul to belong together and to be affected by each other, when it is beyond doubt that they cannot be unadulteratedly connected, let alone identical, in the status quo? Did the incident in paradise not open up a primally painful chasm of estrangement between them? Certainly, religious sermons have always insisted tirelessly that a re-encounter is still possible between the two estranged poles, that this is indeed the epitome of all that is worth seeking and finding for the soul, and that God is only waiting to lead the alienated soul back to Himself. But such an immersion of the soul in a renewed familiarity with its lost great other can never develop from a mere chance acquaintance. Nor will the soul take God back "to itself," any more than God can simply take the soul with him; for where would each of the two be at home separately, outside of their encounter? If they become acquainted, it is through the soul's realization that it has long known the thing it is getting to know again; implicit in such knowing is the fact that long ago, each took the other along with itself, in a sense, or was taken along by the other. Hence they have, in a very unclear fashion, already been inserted into each other, as they could not have made each other's reacquaintance if they had not previously become estranged, yet could not have been estranged if they had not known each other from time immemorial. ("I certainly have seen his face somewhere," Dostoyevsky has his heroine Nastasya Fillippovna say of Prince Myshkin, the idiot, after their *first* meeting.)[6] Their fitting-together encompasses the oldest openness towards each other as well as the primordial rift. Because the rift makes the relationship possible and recognizable as such in the first place, however, the truth about the overall situation can seemingly only come to light afterwards—and, to put it more sharply, afterwards from the outset. The always-already must appear in the posterior, while in the coincidental, that which has always been valid asserts itself with delayed force. The epitome of these postponements is salvation history, in so far as it deals with God's economy—his attempts to rectify soul losses after the fact. God and the soul get to know each other because they already know each other, but their knowing is molded from early on—or even from the start?—by a tendency towards misjudgment that manifests itself as resistance, jealousy, estrangement and indifference.

It is Saint Augustine who, in his *Confessions*, developed the dialectics of recognition from misjudgment in model-like escalations.[7] Although church historians do not place Augustine within the mystical tradition in the stricter sense, he can certainly be considered the great logician of intimacy in Western theology. This is demonstrated outstandingly in Books I and X of the *Confessions*, as well as those books of his cryptic magnum opus *De trinitate* which deal with the accessibility of God through his traces within the soul (especially Books VIII–XIV). In their manner of writing, the *Confessions* in particular constitute an epochal document of intimistic speech. Through their form— that of a monumental narrative prayer with inserted dissertations—they produce a paradoxical intimate situation *coram publico*: what Augustine tells his God during a form of auricular *confession* in a tone of agonized self-renunciation is simultaneously a literary and a psychagogic act before an ecclesiastical public. The author relies on the established speech forms of prayer and confession, which have played a part in structuring the theo-psychological space since the days of early Christianity. The glorifying prayer seeks to replace the subaltern praise of the Lord with jubilation, while the confession seeks to outdo the forced admission through a facilitated escape to the utterance of truth; both speech forms are thus destined to form a sort of "unshakable foundation" for truthful speech of the Christian type. Christian language analysis is guided by the assumption that the revealing force of confessional speech extends deeper than the forced disclosure of the truth through slave torture at trials in ancient times.[8] In the matter of bringing the truth to light, the religious confession seems more productive than the forced juridical one, as it can already be uttered in the hope of forthcoming mercy; under torture, however, the motive of concealing or distorting one's own deeds or those of others can never be eliminated lastingly and with the inner agreement of the confessed offender. Whoever can withstand the pain of torture can deny to the end, and seal their lips permanently in an act of resistance against the cruel interrogators. In the religious confession, on the other hand, lying would be nonsensical, as the very idea of the confessio hinges on realizing the advantage of telling the truth. The reward for confession is that whoever speaks the truth comes "into the truth":[9] this is precisely what begins the intimacy-logical drama that lends Augustinian thought its lively modulation. For after the switch to the "true religion," truth can no longer be considered merely a property of statements and speech; truth should form the In in which all speaking and life seeks to be immersed.[10] The benchmark of whether a confessing sinner is "truly opening" himself is the pain of confession, which moves, authenticates and purifies him and separates him from his past. Confession traces the escape route to blatancy, as it were: it gives the Greek idea of truth—*aletheia*, or unconcealedness—a Christian turn, and thus a dialogic one; now the true word appears on the human side as the admission, and on God's side as revelation. What revelation and admission have in common is that each, in its own way, effects the *a posteriori* (in Christian terms: gracious) conciliatory reopening of a lost entrance to the inside of the other part. This leads to the repetition of tragic catharsis by Christian means; it need hardly be said that with the truth game of the religious confession, a prototype of Old European psychotherapeutics entered the historical stage.

In his *Confessions*, Augustine drew the most radical conclusions from the equally suggestive and presuppositional model that whoever ventures to speak the truth about himself must already "be in the truth." That an individual *wants* to declare the truth about its turn towards the truth gives a first indication of its being-in in the truth; and the fact that the declarer *can* say what he is required to say amounts to an irrefutable truth or a divine judgment via the quill. According to the model, the declaration of guilt before God and the church audience would be doomed to failure had God Himself not foreseen, approved of, inspired and caused it. Hence the impossibility of telling the untruth is already ordained in exemplary confessional speech. Just as a prophet could not lie in the moment of inspiration, an author who accuses himself of sinning in Augustine's manner cannot fall short of the truth. By positing himself as the sub-author in God's directing of language, he effectively states that his confessions have been put into his mouth by the highest authority: through his illuminated bishop, the creator of all things puts salvifically important additions to His previous self-declarations in writing. "Sub-author" is an analytical term for what is usually called an apostle: for an apostle is anyone who speaks or writes as a representative of the absolute author.[11] Consistently with this, Augustine speaks as a therapeutic apostle in the account of his resistance to God. The *Confessions* can be read convincingly as an *ex cathedra* medical history; they deal with the curability of unbelief in God—through God. In this manner, the Bishop of Hippo Regius manages discreetly to subvert the difference between human confession of sins and divine revelation; his admissions provoke a continuation of revelation by other means. Whoever tells in such a fashion of their own unsaved life, meanwhile overcome through grace, is writing evangelistic apocrypha—additional good news of the possibility of converting those who resist the primary good news; in this way too, the Holy Scripture continues itself as the success story of its own dissemination.[12]

Being-in here denotes a situation in the stream of true language: whoever speaks in it includes their own speech in the divine main text in such a way that (as far as possible) no external remainder is left. In the *vita christiana*, however, the concern is not simply to fit one's own words into the spreading of the Lord's word; one's entire existence is meant to be remolded from a willful one to one that is contained *in God*. Certainly, with a willful person of Augustine's rank, the victim of willfulness is significant: as discreetly and clearly as possible, the *Confessions* make it known that on this one occasion, the reduction of a genius to an apostle succeeded with God's help. For Augustine, his own conversion is therefore of epochal exemplary value. He himself is the antiquity that converted to Christianity; he is antiquity as an unholy genius and an agent of a spiritless society that has disintegrated into atoms of ambition and greed. In addition, however, as the co-inventor of a new God-sphere that promises the infinite to countless people, he is already the Christian era. As a witness to this difference, Augustine puts on record in his *Confessions* that heathen egotistical externality has been overcome through a spheric wonder—through the organized inner world of salvation manifested in the God-man and organized by His apostolic successors, which manifests itself in a new way in the midst of this externalized power reality.

The once-rebellious soul drawn back into God must later, according to Augustine, account to itself for the fact that it had already been seen through and incorporated into a divine economy at every moment of its seemingly independent development. Now it admits to finding happiness under the all-pervading, constant observation of its great other.

And even if I would not confess to You, what could be hidden in me, O Lord, from you to whose eyes the deepest depth of man's conscience (*abyssus humanae conscientiae*) lies bare? I should only be hiding You from myself, not myself from You. But now that my groaning is witness that I am displeasing to myself, You shine unto me and I delight in You and love You and yearn for You, so that I am ashamed of what I am and renounce myself and choose You and please neither You nor myself save in you (*et nec mihi nec tibi placeam nisi de te*). To You then, O Lord, I am laid bare for what I am. [...] For whatever good I utter to men, You have heard from me before I utter it; and whatever good You hear from me, You have first spoken to me.[13]

Just as Augustine here provides a classic articulation of his own transparency for the absolute intelligence and his role as a medium for the great other's transmission of truth, he elsewhere expresses his existential interconnection with the all-encompassing in formulations that present the relationship with God as being-there[14]-in-an-encompassing-and-pervasive entity:

But how can I call unto my God, my God and Lord? For in calling unto Him, I am calling Him to me: and what room is there in me for my God (*et quis locus est in me, in quo veniat in me deus meus?*), the God who made heaven and earth? Is there anything in me, O God, that can contain You (*capiat te*)? All heaven and earth cannot contain You for You made them, and me in them. Yet, since nothing that is could exist without You, You must in some way be in all that is: [therefore also in me, since I am]. And if You are already in me, since otherwise I should not be, why do I cry to You to enter into me? [...]

> Thus, O God, I should be nothing, utterly nothing, unless You were in me—or rather unless I were in You, *of whom and by whom and in whom are all things* (Romans 11:36). So it is, Lord; so it is. Where do I call You to come to, since I am in You? Or where else are You that You can come to me? Where shall I go, beyond the bounds of heaven and earth, that God may come to me, since He has said: *Heaven and earth do I fill* (Jeremiah 23:24).[15]

This thought movement shows a finite consciousness in the tendency to give up itself in favor of the infinite. Here Augustine follows the paths of Greek metaphysics, which suggests to ephemeral life that it perish within eternal substance. If God is the truth and the truth is substance, then the unstable subjectivity of individuals—if they are serious about the truth—must break away from itself and escape from its inessential and illusory state into the essential and real. Who can deny that a large number of Christian theologies were always in more or less explicit agreement with this basic principle of substance metaphysics? Where metaphysical concepts dominate, the search for truth is understood as a run-up to the conversion from nothing to being, or in Christian terms, as the striving from death in the illusion to life in the truth. The Latin tradition refers to this self-salvaging into substance as transcending—a word that is spoken of too little if one considers that it made history in Old European thought and feeling. Thinking in terms of transcendence, as Christian metaphysics too, organizes the escape of inane existence to the good reason. It characterizes the ingenuity of Augustinian theology that it began by balancing out the inescapable metaphysical emancipation from oneself with God's accommodation of the seemingly null self. Augustine forces the illuminated soul to immerse itself in its own complexity in order to uncover within it the traces of the God who is thrice folded into Himself. The null subject's exit from itself and its overstepping into substance are requited, or rewarded, with an entry of the substance into the subject, which is henceforth essentially used to become acquainted with God through the creature and to hold onto this acquaintance. In this manner, subjectivity or the "inner human," as Augustine calls it—now elevated to a carrier of God's trace—is afforded uncommonly great dignity. The human spirit may roam through the universe of created things at all levels, but it will never find what it is searching for outside. If God is to be found, it is only after the searcher has turned inwards. In his own mental faculties the successful searcher experiences a reflection of what he is looking for.

> See now how great a space I have covered in my memory, in search of Thee, O Lord; and I have not found Thee outside it. For I find nothing concerning Thee but what I have remembered from the time I first learned of Thee. From that time, I have never forgotten Thee. For where I found truth, there I found my God, who is Truth itself, and this I have not forgotten from the time I first learned it. Thus from the time I learned of Thee, Thou hast remained in my memory (*manes in memoria mea*), and there do I find Thee, when I turn my mind to thee and find delight in Thee (*in te*).[16]
>
> But where in my memory do you abide, Lord, where in my memory do You abide? What resting-place (*cubile*) have You claimed as Your own, what sanctuary built for Yourself? You have paid this honor to my memory, that You deign to

abide in it; but I now come to consider in what part of it You abide.[17]

And indeed why do I seek in what place of my memory You dwell (*habites*) as though there were places in my memory? Certain I am that You dwell in it, because I remember You since the time I first learned of You (*ex quo te didici*), and because I find You in it when I remember You.[18]

Where then did I find You to learn of You, save in Yourself, above myself (*in te, supra me*)? Place there is none, we go this way and that, and place there is none.[19]

Late have I loved thee, O Beauty so ancient and so new; late have I loved thee! For behold Thou wert within me, and I outside […]. Thou wert with me and I was not with Thee.[20]

Now it becomes clear why the soul that seeks to clarify its relationship with God inherently requires time to do so. Though God's connection to the soul is transhistorical, the soul's connection to God is temporal or historical in so far as history, from the Christian perspective, is the affair between the finite and the infinite.[21] In this affair, the decisive event always occurs late on. The soul is fortunate if it is fortunate late on; being fortunate late on means learning to love the right thing properly, just in time. At the center of genuinely historical events, thus understood, stands the precarious retrieval of the souls from their self-inflicted externality. In Augustine, the affair character of the relationship between the soul and God is marked by the reference to *learning of* him.[22] This, as shown above, refers to a knowledge that cannot be an entirely posterior one; if the soul gets to know God again, this is a coincidence with nothing coincidental about it; its progress uncovers the *a priori* interconnection between the two.

The gathering of knowledge—which initially means Augustine's conversion and bible study—necessarily deepens insight into an original self-knowledge that extends back to before the affair, that is to say before the estrangement and its reversal. In his interpretation of this primal acquaintance, Augustine lays his Catholic cards on the table: if the soul goes back into its outermost extreme, it does not—as it demands in metaphysical transcendence—achieve its complete self-negation in substance; rather, it only climbs up to that mysterious place where—despite being held in the most intimate containedness—it began to set itself apart from God in non-violent difference: we are referring to the moment of creation and the breath of life that turned the clay creature into a human.[23] Augustine always cultivated the gentle primal differentiation of the soul from God's totality with the greatest discretion, never allowing himself to be seduced into statements that would inevitably have put him in an awkward position. He made a wide berth around the mystery of the soul's pregnancy in God, and he barely ever spoke affirmatively of a *unio*. The only certainty for him is that the soul's differentiation from God was a process of creation in which identity and difference both receive their due; the biblical catchword for this balance is the image of God. Orthodox and Catholic, Augustine clings to the doctrine of the soul's creatureliness. For him there is no longer any question of sharing that Neoplatonic and Gnostic exuberance which seeks to give the spirit soul the same age and value as God. In relation to the epitome of the spirit, God, the individual soul is in Christian terms indisputably the younger one, though its juniority does not impair the intimate bond of kinship; even as created and younger, the soul is still spirit from spirit. Before the start of the estranging affair—that is, before the egotistical revolt and its miserogenic trace of violence—there is no *a priori* sufficient reason why the younger should have become estranged from the older. In his interpretations of Genesis, Augustine therefore places great value on the successful primary coexistence in paradise—for it is meant to prove that the creation of humans is something that was not doomed to failure from the start. Without the honeymoon of the creation morning, after all, the exclusion of the individual soul from God would itself have been a disaster of the creator God's making, and the creation as such would prove an inescapable trap for the soul. That would compromise the creator, however, and a savior could only come into play as the non-identical one; only He, the completely other, would know what the soul requires for its salvation. Orthodoxy must turn away in horror from such Gnosticizing atrocities. If all is to be as it Catholically should, one must insist on a joyful primal acquaintance between the created soul and its creator. Only then does the fatal affair explain the rest—Adam's wanton fall into hubris and his era, also known as world history (which is balanced out by the counter-time, namely salvation-historical time). If this primal acquaintance is renewed, the soul can sink back to its place beyond all physical places in the certainty that the great other inheres in it more deeply than it does itself: *interior intimo meo.*[24]

One can see that in the theo-psychology and theo-eroticism from the time of the Latin Fathers, an analytics of being-in was formulated that showed no lack of complexity or explicitness. If there was a way to develop the Augustinian logic of intimacy further, then only by radicalizing its already fully crystallized structures. Above all, this concerns the hot spot in the Augustinian field of intimacy—the latently current relation of primal acquaintance between God and the soul. It is easy to understand why the interpretation of this relation held a latent heterodox potential, and equally that this had to be released once genuinely mystical temperaments undertook attempts to radicalize the God-soul relation to the point of pre-relative unions. This ascetic-theoretical spectacle unfolded—usually in discreet forms—behind the dense curtain of Christian metaphysics, of which Martin Buber, among others, showed at the start of the twentieth century that it is mirrored in the mystical testimonies of the other monotheistic traditions, as well as the ecstatic disciplines of world cultures.[25] Only occasionally, especially at the trials of heretics, was this curtain lifted to give the audience a glimpse of battles in the non-sensory realm. In mystical literature, the analytics of being-in developed into an exercise in biunity that brought forth virtuosos of its own. It was under mystical-theological patronage that thinking in reciprocal interconnections first grew into that highly explicit form which still lends such documents an enthralling nimbus of relevance today—even if one cannot say for what they are relevant. If countless modern readers found the body of mystical literature not simply vaguely fascinating, but actually meaningful, it was probably because in its dark clarity, the mystical text emits a conceptual and visual potential for which no comparable substitute has been found so far: we mean a theory of that strong relationship which can only be understood as bi- or co-subjectivity—in our terminology, a microspheric dual or elliptical bubble.

That the connection to something of the same kind is not something produced afterwards or additionally between monadic substances or lonely individuals, but for some beings the very mode of being: this is a thought that precisely the philosophically conditioned intelligences could not initially understand. It had to be worked out from the forbidding material of fundamental concepts in Greek-Old European thought in a laborious and hazardous exercise. If it were still possible to claim a cunning of reason in intellectual history, one could say it was at work when the aim was to assert, with the aid of mystical and Trinitarian theologies, the idea of the strong relationship against the prevailing grammar of the Western culture of rationality—and hence against the fixation on substances and essentialities that had driven the European process of reason since the ancient Greeks. Even today, despite dialectical, functionalist, cybernetic and media-philosophical revolutions in our way of thinking, the cause of the strong relationship is by no means won; in the current human sciences, the idea of constitutive resonance is still as much in need of explanation as the affair between God and the soul in mystical theology once was. It is precisely in modernity, not least where it seeks to be profound or radical, that the dogma of a primary human loneliness is propagated more triumphantly than ever. It is no mere coincidence that in today's common parlance, what one terms a relationship is something that takes place between individuals who have met by chance and who, while still frequenting each other, are already practicing how to do without each other some day. The mystical task, on the other hand, was to understand the relationship not as posterior and fortuitous, but rather fundamental and immemorial. If religious mysticism had had an anthropological mandate, it would have been to explain in general terms why individuals are not primarily defined by inaccessibility to others. If mysticism were to speak in a moral voice, its demand would be: warm up your individual life past its melting point—and do what you wish. If the soul thaws, who could doubt its inclination and aptitude to celebrate and work with others?

To grasp the meaning of this insight, it will be advantageous for the free spirit to emancipate itself from the anti-Christian affect of recent centuries as a tenseness that is no longer necessary. Anyone seeking to reconstruct basic communional and communitary experiences needs to be free of anti-religious reflexes. Did early Christianity not find its strength precisely in basic communal experiences? Their self-interpretation urged a new theory of the spirit, one that would articulate why humans are able to be together in animated communes. In Paul's doctrine of the spirit, especially his statement that God's love is poured out into our hearts through the Holy Spirit, which is given to us (Romans 5:5), the principle of a solidarizing unifying power is given its classical formulation. Admittedly it primarily concerns the access of souls to their own kind; it is a long way from the pneumatic enthusiasm of early Christian communal experiences to the pretension of some medieval mystics to break through the barrier between God and the individual soul entirely.

As far as the mystical dual in the stricter sense is concerned, there is an immeasurable body of literature in which, with a wealth of impoverished words, the soul's intimate advances to God are developed to the point of a complete dissolution of boundaries and unification. If one encounters almost without exception, in language-critical terms, stereotypes and variations in this field, it is because in the Christian-Old European space—as in the Islamic—the final stages of the affair between God and the soul

The outside view of being-in: the angel's arrow and the rays from above combine in a synergy of penetration. Lorenzo Bernini, *The Ecstasy of Saint Teresa*, Santa Maria della Vittoria, Rome

are under a Neoplatonic monopoly, however occult the connection to this source might be. Whichever documents one opens, among the most diverse authors' names and the most colorful classifications of direction and origin, there is a single model that succeeds in reaching the mystical finale; the Neoplatonic mode of reading becomes inevitable, even where authors miss their own dependence on the Plotinic model and readers are deceived through the anonymity of the source. The thoughts expressed by innumerable authors in countless documents in a tone of passionate declaration endlessly reproduce the same sequence of primal scenes and ending scenes that the soul must go through

on its way back into the One. Looking at the mystical movements of medieval Europe, one has to note that the most
arousing thoughts of one's own are foreign thoughts which use
our heads. So even if medieval theology faculties had the true
doctrine firmly under their control, the most talented still
studied—it is hard to say how—at a Plotinic tele-academy[26] that
disseminated late Greek knowledge about salvation and the
ascent of the soul under Christian pseudonyms.

As one document among countless others, we shall quote a
passage from *The Mirror of Simple Souls*, a work written shortly
before 1285 and condemned as heretical, by the Beguine Marguerite Porete, who was born around 1255 near the northern
French town of Valenciennes and burnt at the stake as a heretic on
June 1, 1310 on the Place de Grève in Paris. Her book shows—in
a marked anti-ecclesiastical tone—the search for an unmediated
consummation of biune union between the soul and God.

> This Soul, says Love, has six wings like the Seraphim. She no
> longer wants anything which comes by a mediary. This is the
> proper being of the Seraphim: there is no mediary between
> their love and the divine Love. They always possess newness
> without a mediary, and so also for this soul: for the soul does
> not seek divine knowledge among the masters of this age, but
> in truly despising the world and herself. Great God, how great
> a difference there is between a gift from a lover to a beloved
> through a mediary and a gift that is between the lovers
> without a mediary![27]

It is clear that the rejection of a mediary between the communion partners must ultimately eliminate any third entity. Thus

the gift can neither have a bearer nor remain a material offering; it is absorbed into the self-gift of the giver. Marguerite Porete speaks at length about the necessity for the soul on the way to simplicity to annihilate itself to the point where its particularity no longer obstructs the gift of the divine self-giver. Her aim is that in future, through this great change of subject, the will of God shall will for her and through her:

> And thus the Soul removes herself from this will, and the will is separated from the Soul and dissolves itself, and [the will] gives and renders itself to God, whence it was first taken, without retaining anything of its own in order to fulfill the perfect Divine Will, which cannot be fulfilled in the Soul without such a gift, so that the Soul might not have warfare of deficiency. [...] Now she is All, and so she is Nothing, for her Beloved makes her One.[28]

It is conspicuous how, in Marguerite's text, the theo-erotic bipolar resonance figures are increasingly surpassed by the metaphysical urge to become one. This urge is so powerful in the self-willed Beguine that it wastes little time with the usual degrees and steps of ascent; Marguerite Porete has no interest in the drawn-out stages of the itineraries, where the soul's path to God is detailed in a wholesomely roundabout form. She is, in a sense, already at her goal from the start, and if the mystical exercise could normally only be carried out correctly as the patient elaboration of an impatient haste, speed itself becomes an agent of illumination in the case of this illuminated author. The impossible task has scarcely been uttered before its completion is announced. What unleashes mystical individualism is the end of the speed limit for self-enjoyment in God; thus the dual structure of the affair between God and the soul is also infringed upon and subsequently bypassed. The Neoplatonic ambition to exit the dual entirely in order to be subsumed under the One would ultimately, if it became the standard, suffocate the love play of the interwoven partners—were it not for the fact that the mystic's unfettered verbal elan ensures, through an opposing effect, that the affair still continues expressively and loquaciously even at the apex of its completion. At the climax of the relationship, the soul declares its peculiar unrelatedness; it now claims to have ascended to a space of immanence preceding all difference:

> All things are one for her, without a why, and she is nothing in a One of this sort. Thus the Soul has nothing more to do for God than God does for her. Why? Because He is, and she is not. She retains nothing more of herself in nothingness, because He is sufficient of Himself, that is, because He is and she is not. Thus she is stripped of all things because she is without existence, where she was before she was. She has from God what He has, and she is what God is through the transformation of love, in that point in which she was before she flowed from the Goodness of God.[29]

Like countless related documents, Marguerite Porete's resolutely Neoplatonic account demonstrates the high price of conquering the language of unconditional love or the primordial relationship. The soul's absolute belonging to God, and both to each other, could only be stated at a price, namely if the soul's pole of relation made room, through self-annihilation, for the great other to enter it. With this, the very thing that was meant to make the relationship a radical one destroys it. Where there were two, one of them must now leave; where there was a soul, God is to become everything. The idea of mutual inhabitation, of which Augustine was able to speak in a rich instrumentation, sinks into the background when confronted with the overheated Neoplatonic model of union. In exchange for this loss of reciprocity, the chance is taken to date the intimacy between God and the soul back to pre-creation regions. Consequently, at least on the semantic surface of mystical confession, the subject's attraction to self-sacrifice in favor of substance inevitably becomes dominant. What was supposed to be a mystical wedding seemingly becomes the self-burial of the subject in substance. But are our ears deceiving us? Does the ear-pricking opening of a great speech on the strong relationship end with this pitifully paradoxical revocation "In God I am nothing, and God can have no relationship with nothing"? Indeed: when it comes to the only correct wording, the schema of transcendence steals the word from the tip of the tongue of the concern of resonance—just as well-rehearsed language routines lend false tongues to the unsaid as it wells up. Under the predominance of the metaphysical code, the new words for the strong relationship sprout only hesitantly, like some unheard-of foreign language. What must be expressed semantically using the figure of self-annihilation, however—the radical participation in the great other and the stimulated interweaving with its being—permits the most impetuous self-release of the new speech event in the poetics of the mystical text and its performative unfolding: uttering formulas of abdication, Porete progresses to a state of the most penetrating intensity. She makes herself a privileged resonant body of her radiant other. Naturally God is the One in all everywhere, but here He irrupts into an individual voice, formulating Himself through its vibrations. At least, that is what this voice is presently claiming. Who could distinguish between the voices now! Who is something, who is nothing? The reader of the mystical text can say this much: instead of reaching the inside of God through a silent withdrawal, the de-selfed subject plunges into the most daring of performances, as if the unutterable one somehow needed to be uttered through it, assisted by the martial law of movedness. We know of Marguerite Porete that she sometimes traveled through the country like a show-woman, reciting from her mirror of souls in front of highly diverse audiences. The Neoplatonic diva managed to prove to her contemporaries that the enjoyment of God—which was simultaneously the first legitimized form of self-enjoyment—can liberate itself from church walls and churchmen; Marguerite Porete is one of the mystical mothers of liberality. Would this make mysticism be the matrix for performance art? Would performance then be the impulse that releases the subject? Would the subject be the manifest side of biune movedness? Would movedness be an emergence from the shared? And God an expressionist through the woman?

Suggestions of this genre can be relativized and inspected through a sideways glance at an example from medieval Iranian mystical theology. Even in the dogmatic milieu of Islam, Neoplatonic impulses had manifold offshoots, both orthodox and subversive ones, and brought forth a rich world of forms of biunity-mystical asceticisms and language games. In this context too, one question became especially pressing for the mystical protagonists: how can the word of God be staged in a presentist fashion? And here also, the executioner pushed his way into the foreground as the most important critic of the theater of God. Among the most impressive actors in the Islamic theodrama is the poet-theologian Shahab al-Din Yahya Suhrawardi, also known as Suhrawardi Maqtul, "The Murdered," born in 1155 in the northwest Iranian province of Zanjan. At the instigation of orthodox legal scholars, who accused him of questioning the privileged prophetological status of Mohammed, he was executed on Saladin's orders on July 29, 1191 in Aleppo. In Iranian tradition, the memory of Suhrawardi, whose followers also call him Sohrevardi Shahid, "The Martyr," is preserved as *Shaikh al-Ishraq*, which is conventionally translated as "Master of Illumination"; as Henry Corbin has shown, however, a more accurate description of the "philosophy of illumination" would be the "doctrine of the rising of light in the Orient." In Suhrawardi's teachings one sees a confluence of principles from Koranic theology and Neoplatonic arguments, as well as traces of the ancient Persian theosophy of light. We shall cite the ninth chapter from "The Language of the Ants" [*Lughat-i-Muran*], a twelve-part sequence of short symbolic tales:

All the stars and constellations spoke to Idris—peace be upon him. He asked the moon: "Why does your light decrease sometimes and increase at others?" She replied: "Know you! that my body is black, but polished and clear and I have no light. But when I am opposite to the sun, in proportion to the opposition an amount of his light appears in the mirror of my body; as the figures of the other bodies appear in the mirror. When I come to the utmost encountering I progress from the nadir of the new moon to the zenith of the full moon." Idris inquired of her: "How much is his friendship with you?" She replied: "To such an extent that whenever I look at myself at the time of encountering I see the sun, because the image of the sunlight is manifest in me, since all the smoothness of my surface and the polish of my face is fixed for accepting his light. So every time when I look at myself, I see the sun. Do you not see that if a mirror is placed before the sun, the figure of the sun appears in it? If by Divine decree the mirror had eyes and looked at itself when it is before the sun, it would not have seen but the sun, in spite of its being iron. It would have said 'I am the sun,' because it would not have seen in itself anything except the sun. If it says 'I am the Truth' or 'Glory be to me! How great is my glory' its excuse must be accepted; even the blasphemy 'wherefrom I came near, verily, you are me.'"[30]

Using conventional poetic images, Suhrawardi's didactic tale presents the known thought figures of Neoplatonic speculations on biunity, muted in Islam-typical fashion by references to the categorical distance between God and all other beings. This tendency towards subordination comes to light sufficiently clearly, in what initially seem irreversible gradations, in the images of the sun and the moon; not without reason is Islam, in keeping with its name, a religion of subjugation in the ancient ontological style. In its exuberance, however, the moon is subversively granted the license to think itself the sun, as long as it simply respects the original relationship that gives the first light primacy over its reflections. Thus the second element is not only connected to the first by participation in reflection; it also has an original right to exuberant communication with the origin itself. Through its pictorial character, Arab mystical poetry seems more deeply infused with dual-erotic resonance knowledge than any other—

the only work in the Judeo-Christian tradition that is comparable to Arab theo-poetics in this respect would be the Song of
Songs—but this poetic speech is also controlled by the unre-
lenting monarchy of substance, which is overdetermined by the
monarchy of Allah. Islamic theology is constrained even more
strictly than Christian theology to reject the soul's pretensions to
equal worth with the Highest; by pushing the one God and the
one substance further away in subservient superelevations,
however, the Islamic language of devotion stirs the theo-erotic
embers. Blissful yearning takes care of the rest; and last of all the
inflamed souls, desiring light, know how to go about forcing
their dissolution in the fiery substance. What the moon cannot
do through its discrete position in relation to the sun, the but-
terfly will achieve in the flame. The death-seeking moth
represents the spirit of exaggeration that brings literature and
emergency close together. Suhrawardi's flight around the fire
becomes audible in the two quotations from the sayings of the
Sufi martyr al-Hallaj (858–922), who is said to have beaten the
"drum of unity." With the notorious proclamation of *ana'l-
haqq*—"I am the truth"—and the final statement of our parable,
Suhrawardi adopts two of the most successful and incendiary
theo-erotic phrases. In his doctrine of angels—which we shall
not examine here—Suhrawardi found a way to bring the relationship between the soul and God into equilibrium in an
intermediate region: human souls are not simply immediate to
God, even if they strive back to their origin in His direction; they
possessed preexistence in the angel world; they split, for whatever
reasons, into two parts, of which one remains close to God on
high while the other descends to the "fortress of the body."[31] The
worldly part, unhappy with its lot, searches for its other half and

must seek to unite with it again to regain completeness. With these mythical figures, which transfer Plato's tale of the first humans to the angelic sphere, Suhrawardi cancels the fatal suction of substance monism, making space for images that are suitable for the never-ending task of developing the original augmentation by creating ever new forms and symbols. The sublime idea of *henosis* or *unio* may have established and spread the philosophical prestige of mystical Neoplatonism; its angelology is far more fruitful in psychological terms, however, because it formulated—without making concessions to the ambiguous unionistic references to annihilation—the creatively forward-looking, original augmentability of the soul in images, if not in words. It testifies to the symbol-demanding force of productive separateness, which manifests itself as a primordial duality. Its traces can be seen not only in the Islamic hemisphere, but also the Christian. Angelology is one of the historically indispensable means of access to the theory of medial things.[32] Media theory, for its part, opens up perspectives on an anthropology beyond the individualistic semblance.

As far as mystical theology in the Latin West is concerned, it reached its culmination in the work of Nicholas of Cusa (1401–1464). In his work, we find penetrating analyses on the question of how to envisage the being-in of finite intelligences in the infinite intelligence of God—a turn in which we justifiably see a didactic transformation of the question of the soul's relationship with God. We are essentially prepared, broadly at least, for any adequate elucidation of this relationship through the Augustine-animated Platonizing discourse on God's being-aware within those who recognize Him and the sublation of the

Rogier van der Weyden, *Image of the Archer: The All-Seeing*

knower in the known; nonetheless, Nicholas of Cusa enriched this basic figure with nuances that can be seen as explicit gains for the theory of the strong relationship. It is especially in his treatise *On the Vision of God* (*De visione Dei*) from 1453 that the Cusan adds to the known repertoire of statements about the intertwinement of God and the soul with a number of unforgettable pictorial and argumentative aspects. This applies not least to the splendid analogy of the painting that opens the treatise. Nicholas speaks about recent examples of portrait art that give the observer the feeling of being looked at by them in a very particular way, wherever one happens to be standing. If one can believe the text, the author enclosed one such painting as an object of devotional exercise when he sent his dissertation to the monks at the Abbey of Tegernsee in Bavaria.

> I am sending, to your charity, a painting that I was able to acquire containing an all-seeing image, which I call an icon of God.
>
> Hang this up some place, perhaps on a north wall. And you brothers stand around it, equally distant from it, and gaze at it. And each of you will experience that from whatever place one observes it the face will seem to regard him alone. [...] Next, let the brother who was in the east place himself in the west, and he will experience the gaze as fastened on him there just as it was before in the east. Since he knows that the icon is fixed and unchanged, he will marvel at the changing (*mutatio*) of its unchangeable gaze. [...] He will marvel at how its gaze was moved, although it remains motionless (*immobilius movebatur*), and his imagination will not be able to grasp how it is moved in the same manner with someone coming forth to meet him from the opposite direction. [...] He will experience

that the immobile face is moved toward the east in such a way that it is also moved simultaneously toward the west, that it is moved toward the north in such a way that it is also moved to the south, that it is moved toward a single place in such a way that it is also moved simultaneously toward all places, and that it beholds a single movement in such a way that it beholds all movements simultaneously.

And while the brother observes how this gaze deserts no one, he will see that it takes diligent care of each, just as if it cared only for the one on whom its gaze seems to rest and for no other, and to such an extent that the one whom it regards cannot conceive that it should care for another (*quod curam alterius agat*). He will also see that it has the same very diligent concern for the least creature (*minimae creaturae*) as for the greatest (*quasi maximae*), and for the whole universe.[33]

What is notable about the analogy is that it transports us to an interfacial or, more precisely, an interocular scene. One can admire the artful daring with which Nicholas bridges the chasm between the universalist and individualist theological motifs. How could a summary and aspecific God for all simultaneously be an intimate God for each and every person? Only a logically and existentially convincing answer to this question could provide the theological foundation for a religion that simultaneously inspires imperiality and intimacy. The painted portrait with the living, wandering eyes is an excellent representation of a God who, even as He pantocratically oversees all of humanity, only actually turns to each individual. Here we see a God of intensity whose outpouring of power is as present in the minimum as it is in the maximum. God cannot love the whole of mankind any more than a single human being (just as, according to a similarly constructed proposition by Wittgenstein, the whole earth cannot be in greater distress than *one* soul).[34] The reference to the presence of the maximum in the minimum lends a sharper logical profile to the familiar idea that God distinguishes the individual soul by being-in inside it. Certainly the metaphor of the portrait with the static yet wandering eyes cannot be developed further beyond the exterior encounter between the subject and its circumspect observer. As it presents an external object, the picture on the wall remains at an unbridgeable distance from the believer. Nicholas is only concerned with placing God's eye into the individual, in a twofold sense: as my internalized constant observation by the great other and as the fluctuating inner waking of my own intelligence. The eye of God, equipped with absolute vision, is implanted in my own eye—in such a way, admittedly, that I am not blinded by its all-seeing nature, but can continue to see in my local and corporeal perspectives in the way I am able. Nicholas draws the doctrine of the portrait metaphor—the constant following of my movements by the eyes on the wall—into the soul itself: it must now envisage itself locked inside the field of view, with an absolute eyesight that calls everything into existence through its gaze, constantly encompassing and seeing through the objects of that gaze. He thus creates a wonderful plausibility for the idea that even in my inner life, I am intended and contained in the calmly following gaze of a total intelligence. However I might go from east to west with my thoughts and feelings, the eyes of the great other within me still follow me into every position in my life of thoughts and passions. In seeing, I am always seen—to such a degree that I can believe myself destined to exhaust God's entire eyesight for myself. This calling gives me a direct sense of the reason for my similarity to God, for I am factually gifted (or, in medieval terms, enfeoffed) with eyesight of my own and see an open world around me; thus I imitate God's worldview or world-espial in absolute world-immanence. From a psychological perspective: the maximum-in-minimum idea sets me apart as the only child of the absolute. Nicholas of Cusa is level-headed enough to emphasize that every single case, especially my own, is like an only-child-hood—for the God of intensity, who lacks nothing in the smallest, is equally with Himself elsewhere and everywhere, in my neighbor as much as in the universe. His being-in-me does not restrict Him to my perspective because His intensity, capable of infinite expansion as it must by its nature be, cannot be diminished even by not-being-in-me. Nonetheless, I have a valid entitlement to my own world-opening view, as if it were the only one—assuming I keep in mind that eyesight is not private property, but that my seeing is something like a branch office of God's actually infinite vision—to continue the metaphor: the view of a preferred only child of heaven. Nicholas finds a precise term for this branch connection that pinpoints the contraction of universal eyesight into my own: *contractio*. If I have functioning eyes and see a world, it is only through the contraction of seeing as such to my seeing.[35]

> Every contraction of sight exists in the absolute, because absolute sight is the contraction of contractions (*contractio contractionum*). [...] The most simple contraction, therefore, coincides with the absolute. Indeed, without contraction nothing is contracted. Thus, absolute vision exists in all sight because every contracted vision exists through absolute vision and is utterly unable to exist without it.[36]

God, then, the actual infinite viewer or the maximum view, contracts Himself into me, a minimum; now He is, and in this specific sense acts, *in me*. God's inhabitation in me should therefore not be imagined like that of Saint Jerome in his study or the genie in the bottle; its logic resembles that of a handing-over of office or investiture, where official authority is transferred from the master to the incumbent—albeit with the nuance that the latter is simultaneously the creation of the former. The nub of this enfeoffment is that my being-me itself takes on official character and my subjectivity is conceived and approved as a post in God's household. Thus God's unextended extension determines the sense of immanence or being-in in every respect. My containedness in God's magnitude can be compared to a point in an all-encompassing ball, where the point, in its way, mirrors and contains the ball.

Thus God acts as a lender of eyesight to humans—or more generally as a lender of subjectivity. Here the word "lend" can be understood both in its feudal and its bank-capitalist sense, for both fief and credit are authentic modes of giving being or awarding strength—self-contraction, in Cusan terms—which reminds us of the precondition that none are eligible to be the feudal lord or lender save the actual infinite itself. These circumstances provide the last reason for the basic figure of modernity, which is the replacement of the all-effectuating God by all-sweeping capital. Cusa's reflections show how the most stimulated minds of the early Modern Age were opening up to the adventurous and serious idea that the subject, by becoming involved through knowledge and action, works with the credit of the absolute. This is where the change of meaning from guilt to debts begins.[37] We are here touching on the formative process of the recent history of European mentality: the birth of entrepreneurial subjectivity from the spirit of the mystical duty to repay.[38]

That Nicholas of Cusa articulates being-in not only as an optician (a theo-optician, to be precise), but also as an eroticist (a theo-eroticist, to be precise), is proved by the further course of his tract on the *visio dei*, which—like some later addition to the *Confessions*—displays the spirit and approach of Augustine on every page. While metaphysical optics speaks of contracted vision, theological eroticism speaks of contracted loves. If I am a branch-eye of God in contracted vision, then in contracted loves I am a relay of divine love.[39] This also contracts to a beam that penetrates me, pours over me and privileges me, as if this love were a fountain that expresses itself as intensely in each individual jet as in its entire overflowing. In powerful formulations, Nicholas of Cusa expands the thought that I see because the absolute vision sees in me and through me into the idea that I exist and enjoy as a loving being because I am held into the world as a vessel and outlet for divine attentions and emanations.

> And what, Lord, is my life, except that embrace in which the sweetness of your love so lovingly holds me! [...] Your seeing is nothing other than your bringing to life, nothing other than your continuously imparting your sweetest love. And through this imparting of love, your seeing inflames me to the love of you, and through inflaming feeds me, and through feeding kindles my desires, and through kindling gives me to drink the dew of gladness, and through drinking infuses a fountain of life within me, and by infusing causes to increase and to endure.[40]

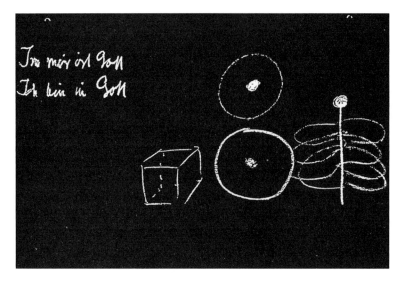

Rudolf Steiner, blackboard drawing, 1924

This passage can be read as a poem that argues in the spirit of the strong relationship; using images of a liquid communion, it articulates the existential situation of participation in a circulation of superfluity. Read in the light of the reflections above,[41] the passage offers one of the most intimate attempts of Christian speech to approach a conversation with the primal companion. It is a piece of sanguine literature in the literal sense of the word—formulated from intuition into the reality of the blood, which provides the first communion. Being-in now amounts to allowing oneself to be embraced, flowed through, nourished and cheered by the divine medium of blood, and gratefully considering and singing the praises of this embrace/flowing-through/cheering as a primal scene. One could, by way of transposition, say that consciousness-in includes perceiving that I am surrounded, carried and reached through by a force that anticipates me and flows towards me in every sense. This understanding of being-in remains integrated into a basic attitude that is religious and feudal as long as the subject aligns itself with this anticipation and this interwovenness without deviating into outraged or claustrophobic reactions. The Satanism of disgust and its small change,[42] unease, would thwart an understanding of the matter itself. In truth, the subject finds itself in a position of revolt if it ceases to view itself as a mere vassal of being; whoever invokes capital of their own and refuses to define their actions as work with the credit of the absolute becomes a rebel. But have humans, from a Catholic perspective, not always striven towards a certain independent power and felt irked by the unreasonable demand of having to be grateful for everything? Was the Modern Age not founded on the axiom that whoever begins with themselves has shaken off the burden of compulsory gratitude once and for all? How would one even envisage a non-rebellious monotheistically-based anthropology, when the race of Adam exists *toto genere* under the sign of Satan and has a part in his initial ingratitude? Has the human being, from a Christian perspective, not always been the creature that wants to reserve a part for itself? Can there be such a thing as man in non-revolt?

The answer to this, in so far as it is affirmative, articulates itself in the Christianized idea of service, which states that reintegration into the One converges with the ability to serve. In examining the question of how the independent power of humans can be placed *in* and under the power of God, Nicholas arrived at a mystical politics or a doctrine of interwoven power. It gives being-in or unconditional immanence the meaning of empowerment to isolated moments of power through the actual infinite power itself. In the first book of the dialogue *De ludo globi* [The

Game of Spheres] (1462), the learned cardinal converses with John, Duke of Bavaria in formulations of surreal clarity about a game invented by Nicholas, in which the aim is to position a ball with unequal hemispheres in the center of a target drawn on the floor.[43] They proceed to discuss the general kingship of man.

THE CARDINAL: By all means man is the small world in such a way that he also is part of the large world. [...]

JOHN: If I grasp you correctly, then it follows that the universe is one great kingdom and so also man is a kingdom, but a small one within a great kingdom as the kingdom of Bohemia is a small kingdom within the great kingdom of the Romans, or the universal empire.

THE CARDINAL: Excellent. A man is a kingdom similar to the kingdom of the universe, established in part of that universe. As long as the embryo is in the mother's womb it is not yet its own kingdom, but when the intellectual soul, which is put in the embryo in the process of creation, is created, the embryo becomes a kingdom, having its own king, and is called a man. But when the soul departs, the man and the kingdom cease to be. However, as the body was part of the universal kingdom of the large world before the advent of the soul, so also, it returns to it. Just as Bohemia was part of the Empire before it had its own king, so also it will remain if its own king is taken away. Therefore man is directly subject to his own king who rules in him, then he is subject to the kingdom of the world in an indirect way. But, when he has not yet a king or when he ceases to be, he is directly subject to the kingdom of the world. This is why nature or the world soul exercises vegetative power in the embryo as in other things having vegetative life. And this exercise of the vegetative power actually continues in certain dead men in whom the hair and nails continue to grow.[44]

So the world of power, as the exercising of ruling and producing ability, is constituted by contraction. Every human gifted with a spirit is king through the contraction of the emperor (God) into an individual dominion. As a human among humans, each individual is self-governing under the emperor, having power in its own small world through the relationship of enfeoffment or credit with the highest bestower of power. In the mode of contraction, the imperial (divine) maximum is present in the kingly (human) minimum. If the minimum is already a kingdom, however, each individual, as the ruler of the kingdom, can only be socialized in a group of royal colleagues—or a gathering of self-governing free classes. This is the prototype of a *democrazia christiana*. With shimmering arguments, the papist cardinal paves the way for the egalitarianism of the citizen-kings; it would barely take a century for civil individuals and laypersons to understand how one can claim one's earthly sovereignty as a kingly minimum under the divine maximum. From Nicholas of Cusa to Rousseau, one can follow the progress of that way of thinking which sees competent service and active subservience in any given context as the factors that enable people to be lords and legislators in their respective domains. Cusa was the first to give the thought its precise form; Ignatius of Loyola had the ingenuity to implant it in monastic politics and propagate it psychotechnically: service is the royal road to power; active subservience and independent power are one and the same; if you want to rule, you must serve. Serving means developing under a lord as energetically as if there were no lord. This is the first subject philosophy. The Modern Age follows on smoothly from the late Middle Ages in the idea that all forms of exercising power constitute vassalic service in a homogeneous divine empire that is equally intense in all its parts; thus every subject that reaches around itself in its area of the world is allowed to develop as a power minimum *sui generis*, immediate to the empire and to God. Every minimum is a minister, and every competent subjectivity is a civil servant of the absolute. This opens up the path on which businessmen, public servants, petits bourgeois and artists will be able—as previously only clerics and nobles were—to view themselves as functionaries of God; it is a path that will lead into the Reformation, democratism and entrepreneurial freedom. In democracy, admittedly, individuals will no longer claim their right and duty to power as servants of God but as owners of human rights: now humans envisage themselves as the animal entitled by nature to stake claims. The people of the Modern Age can only formulate the principle of human rights explicitly after withdrawing from the world of God and moving to the realm of nature, where, according to the Cusan, humans are only subordinate as embryos and corpses. One can see very clearly in this argument, incidentally, where the paths of the Modern Age will separate from those of the Middle Ages: while for modern people—those who think enough—view precisely the stay of the embryo or fetus in the womb as part of the archaic matrix of animation, Nicholas teaches that the child only has a vegetative status there, and does not yet belong to the realm of spirit souls. That would make the embryo's being-in-the-mother a passive prelude to spirit-animated life—and only after the allocation of spirit, that is to say after baptism, would the individual be socialized not only in nature, but also in the kingdom of God. *Mutatis mutandis*, Hegel essentially still taught the same.ₓ

It is easy to see how in doctrines of this type, the aftereffects of Platonic dualism also split the meaning of being-in. Whoever is only in nature (animated by the world soul)—even if it is the womb—is still far from the point where the Christian or idealistic mystic demands to be. It is precisely this difference, however, that has lost its validity at the end of our microspherological exposition. Passing through the sevenfold change in the meaning of being-in in the preceding chapters of this book, it has become apparent how the opposition of being-in-God and being-in-nature disappears in favor of a general logic of being-in-the-shared-space. Through the investigations of resonance with two or more poles, the particular perspectives of theological idealism and psychological materialism are recognized in their propaedeutic achievements, then succeeded and sublated in their results. If mystical theology, then, described the proximity between God and the soul in terms that the free spirit also does not forget, it is clear that its natural eye has remained as blind as that of an unborn child which has not yet learned the difference between being inside and being outside. Modern psychology, on the other hand, which has been developing outside of metaphysics for the last two centuries, is in the process of returning to nature, especially its culturally mediated form, what belongs to it in its cultural states—and this is far more than any idealism or spirit religion ever imagined. But psychology, for its part, has been unable to arrive at a concept of the strong relationship because it can no longer understand the difference between

Guercino, *Saint Augustine Meditating on the Trinity*

outside and inside from a position of naturalistically distorted externality. Our microspherology, stimulable from both sides, moves sufficiently far away from the precepts of both opponents to gain a vision that is more than the sum of two one-eyed views. Through its independence from both theological declarations and psychological discourses, the theory of spheres does theoretical justice in a new way to the self-experiences of the living being in its current tensions between inside and out-side positions. ⌄

In moving from the microspheric to the macrospheric interpre-tation of the meaning of being-in, a few remarks—however cursory—on *Trinitarian* theology are indispensable. For this discipline, in its logical structure and extension of meaning, belongs to both dimensions: microspherology, in so far as it articulates a three-part intimate relation—Father, Son, Holy spirit; and macrospherology, in so far as it identifies the "persons" of this triad as actors in a world-crossing and world-pervading theodrama. Thus Trinitarian discourses treat both the smallest bubble and the largest orb, the densest and the widest interior. We will give an inkling of why, from the start, Trinitarian theology could only advance as a theory of the strong relationship, and *eo ipso* as the doctrine of a living orb.

In an early stage of this problem process, the Greek Fathers, especially from the Cappadocians onwards, invented a new form of meditation on surreal interpersonality. Their purpose was initially to reformulate the New Testament statements, especially those by John, about the singular relationship between Jesus and God in the spirit of Greek ontotheology. This task amounted to squaring the circle—or rather, circling the ellipse—for basic Greek terminology was not ready to formulate communions on equal footing between several parties in the only substance. At this point, however, early Christianity, which had begun to consolidate itself theologically and mission-politically, could not retreat even a single step: when John wrote "Anyone who has seen me has seen the Father" (14:9), "Believe me when I say that I am in the Father and the Father is in me" (14:11), or "the Holy

Spirit, whom the Father will send in my name, will teach you all things" (14:26), this was the announcement of a program that grew into a thought task both inevitable and explosive for the Greek theologians and their heirs. It contained the unreasonable demand to conceive of strong relationships at the level of the One, but between three. That this could somehow succeed without a tritheistic relapse may have seemed plausible to the conventional and simple minds of late antiquity, if one assured them often enough with authority that one was three and three was one. The theologians, however, who stepped into the arena of theory, standing face to face with advanced pagan philosophers to defend the intellectual honor of their religion, realized that an abyss had opened up for orthodoxy, one that threatened to swallow the entire conception of right and wrong. One of the most powerful discursive vortexes of Old European culture formed at the interface between ancient Greek and New Testament language games. Its rotation began when the biblical talk of relationships made the Greek ontology of essence dance. Here, strangely enough, the learned patriarchs of the Byzantine world acted as the dance teachers; it was they who taught the static One the steps by which it learned to differentiate itself into eternal triplets. This rhythmicizing revolution took no less than a millennium to develop into a mature, lucid concept; it extends from the Cappadocian theologians to Thomas Aquinas, in whose doctrine of "subsistent relations" the inconceivable finally seemed to have become conceivable after all. Through carefully considered risks, Trinitarian speculation felt its way forwards into the field of relational logic—as if it had been its mission to unmask a God who could philosophically only be imagined as a light reactor and a smooth stone eternity, revealing Him as a

Juan Carreno de Miranda, *Founding of the Trinitarian Order*, oil on canvas, 1666

Detail: The classical quasi-quaternity encompasses the Trinity and the universe

bottomless well of friendliness, and to imitate Him as the true icon of the loving relationship. In this sense, Adolf von Harnack was not entirely right with his sharp-edged hypothesis that older Christian theology amounted to the gradual Hellenization of the Gospel. It was simultaneously—and more than just casually—the Jewish-inspired intersubjectification of Hellenism.

How several can exist undivided in one: this basic question of life-spheric theory initially occupied the early theologians less in its numerical and quantitative dimension than in the spatial disposition of the three in one. Here theology, through its own efforts, came under pressure to explain itself topologically. This first access to the intra-godly sphere initially displayed unmistakable nature-philosophical undertones, even if it had long since moved on to the inter-inhabitation of spiritual entities. This can be observed particularly clearly in the famous lamp analogy from the treatise *The Divine Names* by the late fifth-century Syrian monk-philosopher Pseudo-Dionysius the Areopagite. His explanations are instructive in showing the starting point of the later development, for they still interpret the possibility of the three divine persons being together entirely within a Neoplatonic framework, namely the discussion on how the many can be anchored and integrated in the one. Even Neoplatonism already knew a pathos of the differing of the different within the one, a pathos from which later references to the "reciprocal validation of the person-principles of the Trinity" would still profit.

> In a house the light from all the lamps is completely inter-penetrating, yet each is clearly distinct. There is distinction in unity and there is unity in distinction. When there are many lamps in a house there is nevertheless a single undifferentiated light and from all of them comes the one undivided brightness. I do not think that anyone would mark off the light of one lamp from another in the atmosphere which contains them all, nor could one light be seen separately from the others since all of them are completely mingled while being at the same time quite distinctive. Indeed if somebody were to carry one of the

lamps out of the house its own particular light would leave without diminishing the light of the other lamps or supplementing their brightness. As I have already explained, the total union of light, this light that is in the air and that emerges from the material substance of fire, involved no confusion and no jumbling of any parts. [...]

Theology, in dealing with what is beyond being, resorts also to differentiation. I am not referring solely to the fact that within a unity, each of the indivisible persons is grounded in an unconfused and unmixed way. I mean also that the attributes of the transcendentally divine generation are not interchangeable. The Father is the only source of that Godhead which in fact is beyond being and the Father is not a Son nor is the Son a Father. Each of the divine persons continues to possess his own praiseworthy characteristics [...].[45]

The images of Pseudo-Dionysius clearly present an intimistic version of Plato's solar metaphor. Here, Plato's sun shines *en miniature* in a strangely touching fashion, as if trifurcating via a three-armed chandelier, withdrawn from the open world into the house's interior. Because the sun—since Akhenaten and Plato a heroic symbol of the monarchy of principles—is unsuitable to represent an internal communion, or even a separation of powers in the absolute, the mystical theologian had to resort to the lamp analogy. This at least shares with the solar model the fact that it represents the central power of light—and thus denotes the original function, but can also render plausible the transition to the idea of Trinitarian differentiation. Certainly the lamps of Pseudo-Dionysius only offer a precarious analogy to intra-godly communication, for they illustrate how one should imagine the interpenetration of propagable light with other similar light, but they contribute nothing to an understanding of the interactions between the light partners. Their ability to interweave is envisaged more in line with Stoical philosophies of mixed bodies than in interpersonal terms—which is also evident in the obligatory analogies of closeness and mixture among the Greek and Latin Fathers: the being-in of the divine persons in one another—like the merging of divine and human natures in Christ—is tirelessly represented as the mixing of wine and water, or compared to the propagation of aroma and sound. Everywhere one finds the image of the glowing iron, which is presented as the interpenetration of metal substance and fire substance; it also returns several times in variations, such as images of glowing gold or coal embers. All this is meant to express a repression-free, non-hierarchical interweaving of substances in the same section of space—which can be understood quite naturally as a primitive attempt by theological speculation to approach the problem of spatial formation in the autogenous container of the intimate sphere. The physiological images of mixture reach their natural conclusion in the Platonizing light-in-light metaphors, which lead almost automatically into subtler metaphysical notions of the spirit space. These visual figures can certainly be no more than preparatory exercises to approach the interpersonal dimension of the strong relationship. If one takes Pseudo-Dionysius' lamp analogy further, however, one can at least develop the idea that the triune chandelier not only emits light outwards, but also holds the inner life of the light parties. This is most clearly suggested in the text by the negative statements, which certainly make a great deal of the fact that the Father is

Missal, MS 91, f. 121r.: The Trinity as a crowned triumvirate oval

not the Son, nor the Son the Father. This Not in God brings life or personal difference into the gleaming gray of the primal unity. The three (or six) Nots in the Trinity (Father *not* Son or Spirit; Son *not* Spirit or Father; Spirit *not* Father or Son) light the fire of relationship in the divine space. All definition is negation, Spinoza would later say; and all negation is relationship, the ancient theologians already taught.

The task, then, is to conceive of a difference that does not lead into separation, that is to say becoming-external-to-one-another; for if there is one thing in ancient theology even more pronounced than the pathos of non-mixture or non-coalescence between the divine persons, it is the pathos of their *a priori* connectedness. But how can unity still be envisaged if the tripersonal model mobilizes a maximum of centrifugal forces within it? This problem is solved through the supposition of an expressive or discharging act in God in which genuine differences appear without any cut surfaces or gaping seams. A perceptible gap, after all, would indicate that the separating externality had gained the upper hand over the continuum of belonging together.

The Greek Fathers already managed to overcome this difficulty by ascribing to the Father two gestures of self-exit that posit difference without endangering continuity: conception and breath. The third of God's expressive acts, that of making, is passed over, as it leads not to co-divine figures but sub-divine creatures—that is, to the sensual world and its inhabitants. Begetting and breathing life are viewed as productions or expositions whose products remain immanent in the producer—a circumstance for which theological acumen in the fourth century established the admirable term "procession," *ekporeusis* in Greek and *processio* in Latin. Thus God "Himself" proceeds from Himself and into the Son and the Spirit, but does not leave the shared inside in the latter form; here there is not yet any dialectic of self and externalization spanning processes of estrangement, only the seamlessly shared enjoyment of a common wealth. The intra-godly communards do not suffer any stimuli to agonal ailments of externalization and re-appropriation as a result of the processions; such phenomena only come into play in the salvation-historical dimension, where the Son has to share the agony of the world to the end.[46] Begetting and breath, then, are expressive acts with no separable result: the begetter retains the begotten (the Son) in Himself, just as the breathers (the Father *and* the Son) keep the breathed (the Spirit) in and with themselves; and even if the origin also goes outside itself in a sense, it by no means enters a state of externality in relation to itself. God's interior produces itself as a relation-workshop or an apartment in which every inhabitant is the room of the other. The intra-godly spatial demands transform the Platonic ball of light into a communional sphere. Its "inhabitants" find themselves in the logically and topologically unusual situation that their intertwinement permits an equality of extension without spatial rivalry, as well as a sharing of functions without competition for primacy—even if the patri-centric original rage of the older Trinitarian discourses, especially the Byzantine ones, tends to conceal this "egalitarian" trait. It is precisely this unbroken sharing that is prefigured through the ancient nature-philosophical images of contraction and mixture. Trinity is more than a perfectly shaken emulsion of three different liquids, however: it is meant to be no less than an *a priori* love life and an original inter-intelligence superior to the world. The inside of the living orb can be described with this formula: three times one equals three times everything.

The doctrine of uni-trinitas, then, provided the first coherent articulation of the idea of the strong relationship, and it emerged in unparalleled radicality on its very first appearance: if ever the idea of an *a priori* inter-"subjectivity" was taken into consideration, it was in this intertwinement of the Trinitarian persons. Now the idea of an absolute inside was established: through it, physical space is sublated in relational space—the surrealism of the persons' coinherence [*Ineinandersein*] had found its classical model. In this space, the persons no longer stand close to one another, each shining by itself, like the lamps in the room of Pseudo-Dionysius; rather, by forming the primal residential community, they make a premise pure relationship

Psalter fragment, f. 9v.: Tricephalic Trinity

Father and Son in a shared shell, touching the Spirit

The *Rothschild Canticle*: The woven band joining the Trinity gradually changes from images of personal closeness into geometric-ontological rotation figures—the peak of medieval ontography. The sequence of pictures in the canticle depicting the Trinity comprises 24 stations.

or vault a first love sphere around themselves. Here the rules are: first the love interior, then physics; first the union of three, then their historical household. Only in this order can the relationship between the absolute trio and its outside world be grasped. That is why theologians place such value on conceiving of the coinherence of the triune without any in-between to separate them.

The learned monk John of Damascus (c. 676–749) made a number of decisive points in his much-noted treatise *An Exact Exposition of the Orthodox Faith*, which became a reference work for the Latin scholastics from the late twelfth century onwards. Here he defended the absolute synchronicity—or syn-achronicity—of the hypostases or persons:

> Accordingly, it is impious to say that time intervened in the begetting of the Son and that the Son came into existence after the Father.[47]

Any interval of time would indicate a triumph of the external over the primary being-inside-with-themselves of the divine persons. At the same time, their radically relational intertwinement creates the possibility of doing away with the objectionable numerical paradox of the one that is supposed to be three:

> Thus, when I think of one of the Persons (*hypostasis*), I know that He is perfect God, a perfect substance (*ousia*), but when I put them together and combine them, I know one perfect God. For the Godhead is not compounded, but is one perfect, indivisible, and uncompounded being in three perfect beings.[48]

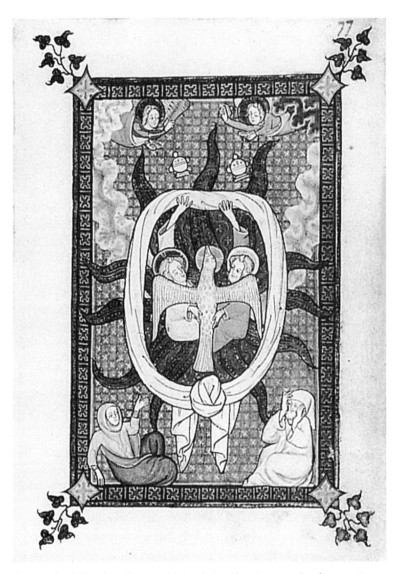

Be not afraid, Matthias Grünewald, Isenheim Altarpiece, inside of outer wing

This argument, which had already been rehearsed by the Cappadocian Fathers in the fourth century, would remain current until Cusa: it still returns in his text *On Learned Ignorance* in the formula *maximum est unum*. It seems as if the perfection argument was the early form of a naïve attempt to bridge the gap between theology and the mathematics of infinite magnitudes, for three times one is certainly not one, but three; viewed thus, the Trinitarian dogma would be mathematically absurd. But three times infinity is infinity; now the dogma makes mathematical sense.[49] The infinite is imagined in the figure of the all-encompassing orb, in which externality simply cannot appear. This model now simultaneously guarantees the absolute intimacy and reciprocal immanence of the divine persons. A letter written by Basil of Caesarea (329–379) to his brother Gregory of Nyssa formulates the rejection of external differences in the divine inner sphere:

> And through whatever processes of thought you reach a conception of the majesty of any one of the three persons of the Blessed Trinity [...] you will arrive invariably at the Father and Son and Holy Spirit, and gaze upon their glory, since there is no interval between Father and Son and Holy Spirit in which the intellect will walk in a void. The reason is that there is nothing which intrudes itself between these persons, and that beyond the divine nature there is nothing which subsists that could really divide it from itself by the interposition of some outside thing, and that there is no void, in the form of an interspace in which there is no subsistence, between the three Persons, which could cause the inner harmony of the divine essence to gape open by breaking the continuity through the insertion of this void.[50]

The divine persons are tied into quasi-Borromean rings from a continuous woven band

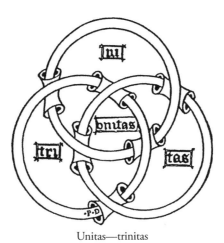

Unitas—trinitas

It should not be surprising that the internal coherence of the unified three could only be imagined with the aid of explicit or implicit circular and spherical models. Gregory of Nyssa, at any rate, knew that the unbroken nature of the intra-godly relationships could not be envisaged without a rotational concept:

> Do you see the circulation of glory through the same cyclical movements? The Son is glorified by the Spirit; the Father is glorified by the Son. And reciprocally, the Son receives His glory from the Father and the Only Begotten becomes the glory of the Spirit.[51]

With arguments of this type, the ancient theologians achieved something that even modern sociologists, when they have attempted it, have not yet been able to repeat: they arrived at a completely de-physicalized concept of person space. With this, the meaning of In was freed from all forms of container-oriented thought once and for all.[52] If Father, Son and Spirit

The fiery hyper-knot sinks into the center of a circle announcing the advent of the world

could still be localized, it was only in the housing they provide for one another. Thus the topological surrealism of religion entered its learned phase.

John of Damascus reintroduced the word *perichoresis* to describe the strangely placeless yet self-locating coexistence of the divine persons; its meaning in ancient Greek probably resembled "dancing around something" or "being whirled around in a circle."[53] By elevating this old word of movement to a technical term—denoting coinherence, intertwinement, interpenetration—he performed one of the most brilliant terminological creations in the Western history of ideas. One senses something scarcely thinkable or unthought in the word—which is evident not least in the fact that even theologians, to say nothing of philosophers, are only rarely familiar with it; and when they are, their understanding of it is usually inadequate. Whoever imagines perichoresis as the coinherence of inseparably connected elements is not wrong, yet is still far from grasping its essence. This strange term represents no less than the challenging idea that the persons cannot be localized in external spaces borrowed from physics, but that the place in which they are located is itself created through their interrelationship. By housing one another, the divine relational beings, the hypostases or persons, open the space they inhabit together and in which they call one another into existence, pervade and acknowledge one another. God's privilege, then, is to be in a place for which room is only made through relationships between the inhabitants and the co-inhabitants within itself. This is so difficult for trivial spatial thought to grasp that one would have to be someone entirely entangled in love stories—but under no circumstances a modern-age subject—to have an intimation of its meaning.

The tripersonal structure of God is covered by the Neoplatonic orb of emanation. The feet of the Father and Son remain visible at the edges, along with the Spirit's wings at the top

[…] three persons […] united without confusion and distinct without separation, which is beyond understanding.[54]

The abiding and resting of the Persons in one another (*perichoresis*) is not in such a manner that they coalesce or become confused […].[55]

In such a case of a residential community in the absolute, the question is where it sets itself up and how it divides itself into the different household duties. John of Damascus has the answer to this question too; in Chapter 13 of *An Exact Exposition of the Orthodox Faith*, he writes:

Place is physical, being the limits of the thing containing within which the thing contained is contained. The air, for example, contains and the body is contained, but not all of the containing air is the place of the contained body, but only those limits of the containing air which are adjacent to the contained body. And this is necessarily so, because the thing containing is not in the thing contained.

However, there is also an intellectual place where the intellectual and incorporeal nature is thought of as being and where it actually is. There it is present and acts; and it is not physically contained, but spiritually, because it has no form to permit it to be physically contained. Now, God […] is not in a place. For He, who fills all things and is over all things and Himself encompasses all things, is His own place. However, God is also said to be in a place; and this place where God is said to be is there where His operation is plainly visible. Now, He does pervade all things without becoming mixed with them, and to all things He communicates His operation in

The cosmic spherogenesis of God at the moment of completion. The persons are reabsorbed by the structures

accordance with the fitness and receptivity of each in accordance with their purity of nature and will, I mean to say. For the immaterial things are purer than the material and the virtuous more pure than such as are partisan to evil. Thus, the place where God is said to be is that which experiences His operation and grace to a greater extent. For this reason, heaven is His Throne [...]. The Church, too, is called the place of God, because we have set it apart for His glorification [...]. In the same way, those places in which His operation is plainly visible to us, whether it is realized in the flesh or out of the flesh, are called places of God.[56]

Therefore, places of God—in non-theological terms, places of co-subjectivity or co-existence or solidarity—are not things that simply exist in the external space. They only come about as sites of activity of persons living together *a priori* or *in a strong relationship*. Hence the answer to the question "Where?" in this case is: in one another. Perichoresis means that the milieu of the persons is entirely the relationship itself. The persons contained in one another in the shared space locate themselves in such a way that they illuminate and pervade and surround one another, without being harmed by the clarity of their difference. One could say that they are as invisible as air to one another—but an air in which they lie for one another; each one inhales and exhales what the others are—the perfect conspiration; each breaks forth from Himself into the others—the perfect protuberance. They provide neighborhood for one another—the perfect being-surrounded. Thus the Christian God—together with the Platonic universe—would be the only being with magnitude, but no surroundings, because He

The Trinitarian rosette shines forth once more

Himself supplies the Around in which He self-referentially acts out His multi-related nature. So this God would perhaps not be worldless, but certainly environment-less.[57]

Whoever began to exist as this God does would not have to start with being-in-the-world; for pure relationships would already constitute a world before the world. External conditions would never be the first data, and even the world as a whole would not be given any earlier than the complicity between those initially united; no thing could be given separately for itself; every gift would always already, and always only, be an addition to the relationship. That the totality of conditions known as "world" can exist at all is itself only a consequence of the primal gift of belonging-to-one-another. Theologians called this—with reference to the third person, who acts *a priori* as the *copula* or the spirit of community—the *donum dei*. The gift that gives the relationship is—to use an ominous modern term— immanence. Someone lives immanently if they know how to remain (*manens*) in the inside (*in*) for which the strong relationship makes room. It would be a misconstrual of this inhabitation and remaining in one another, however, if one simply took it as a calm state—as the later Latin translation of *perichoresis* into *circuminsessio*, a sort of mutual sitting-in, suggests. The earlier Latin version of this artificial word, *circumincessio*, emphasizes the dynamic character of the interpersonal relations, and was sometimes also equated with a mutual pushing forward or storming into one another.[58] This word highlights with greater psychological realism—assuming that psychology is not out of place among divine persons—the invasive sense of the influx of each into the others.

Apocalypse of the Trinitarian sphere as a symbol of cosmo-personalism

The characteristic of living together or in one another in the strong sense or *a priori* does not only belong to the intra-godly persons, but also manifests itself, in a sense, in human associations of persons. Families and peoples in their historical reproductions create and inaugurate the place in which their kin can learn to be themselves by distinguishing themselves from their ancestors and descendants. It is therefore significant that the emergence of the Son from the Father, theologically termed begetting, is the sensitive point in the intra-godly game. For what is Trinitarian theology other than the most sublime form of a generational theory? The Victorine Richard—whom medievalists consider one of the subtlest thinkers of the twelfth century—stated this in an explicit analogy:

> For a (human) person proceeds from another person, in some cases only directly, in some cases only indirectly and in some cases directly and indirectly at once. Jacob, like Isaac, proceeded from the substance of Abraham; but the procession of the one occurred only indirectly, while that of the other occurred only directly. For only through Isaac's mediation did Jacob spring from Abraham's loins [...]. Consequently, in human nature the procession of the persons encompasses three distinct modes. —And even if this nature seems very far from the unique and most excellent nature of God, there is nonetheless a certain resemblance [...].[59]

The cohabitation of younger and older persons causes a constant regeneration of the place in which the different parties practice being in and proceeding from one another. Because tribes and peoples can be devastated by traumatizing magic and political pestilence, however—and in such ways that their distant descendants will still stumble over the ills of their ancestors—monitoring or adjusting the procession from the Father to the Son through the Spirit is simultaneously an indispensable critical theory of the generational process. The Spirit—that is, the life-giving knowledge and mutual love between the older and the younger—is the norm of mental transference from one generation to the next. Aside from that, the Spirit—in the view of theologians—must not be identified simply as the grandson of the Father; then the Son would move up to the paternal position and the grandson, as a second-degree son, would be back-to-back with His grandfather. Then great-grandchildren would also come into view, creating a leak in the triad and breaking it up into an inexorable sequence of further begettings. In intra-Trinitarian fashion, the Spirit is meant to complete the liaison between Father and Son—and its breathing by the Father *and* the Son seals the absolute conclusion of the internal processions. A transition to a fourth party would be impossible in this immanence.[60] The number four would be the start of a chain reaction of processions from God: it would send the generational reactor out of control, and the first cause could no longer repeat itself identically, or at least sufficiently similarly, in the effects it would have on more distant degrees. This would potentially and actually cause a degeneration of intra-godly events; externality would triumph over the vigorously self-differentiating inside; God's process would become monstrous, and his capacity to communicate with Himself in forms of strong relation could no longer curb the tendency towards processions into the dissimilar. In the central Trinitarian process, consequently, the breathed person, who guarantees unity and similarity between the first, the second and itself, must form the final part. The Spirit, understood as *amor*, *condilectio*, *copula* and *connexio*, ensures that begetting causes a beneficial difference which remains in the continuum and does not lead to estrangement or degeneration.

In the generational processes of peoples, however, this rule is chronically violated; here, offspring very often means a degenerative continuation of the chain of life—the failed generation is an unpleasant begetting. It breaks open fatal gaps between the age groups; the earlier and later generations genuinely become alien or monstrous to one another. With reference to the distorting and de-animating actual procreations, the old church was entirely right to break away from the peoples and their forced union in the Roman Empire through a pneumatic secession, establishing a new regenerative generational process in a pneumatic or baptismatic people. The generations of the church members are spiritual generations that set themselves apart from the biological-cultural generations. Idealistically put, the children of the Christian people would be the descendants of a spiritual stream of love that seeks to act as a corrective for an inadequate empirical form of parental love. This is simultaneously the critical sense of early Christian chastity: better to produce no offspring than failed offspring. While the history of actual generations over the last millennia is largely the history of unwelcome humans, the history of spiritual generations keeps itself on the right track as the strength to welcome to being, in the name of a superhuman authority, individuals who are ill-greeted by humans. Christianity would never have survived forty generations or two millennia without performing its latent function, that of a sewage treatment plant for generativity, with some degree of success. This function has increasingly slipped out of its grasp since the birth of modern civil societies, however, and nation-state society, with its educational system and its therapeutic subcultures, has largely emancipated itself from the inspiratory services of the Christian churches. The generative processes in modern social systems have become too complex for religious authorities to play more than a marginal role in them. The institutional churches themselves, both the reformed and the Roman, have meanwhile taken on more of a subcultural character; they have primarily become filtering systems for their own offspring, and have forfeited their task of moderating the amorous processions in natural societies. To most people today, their welcomes seem more like disinvitations, and the general crisis of fatherhood has deprived the *patres* of most of the authority their office once held. Modern political mothering agencies have long had far better material and medial resources than the churches; the rest is self-referentiality. On a subsidized stage, it is not easy for a pantomime of childlessness and contempt for daughters to stay on the program. Even the fall of Rome occurs twice, it seems, and here—as elsewhere—the first time is a tragedy, the second a farce.[61]

At its medieval zenith, Trinitarian theology had led—as we have attempted to show through perspectival abbreviations—to the discovery of a language for the *strong relationship*. The partners of the immanent Trinity produce, harbor and surround themselves in such close reciprocity that their intertwinement exceeds all external conditions. Here one can see the reward for absurdity: for the first time, being-in-relation can be addressed as an absolute place. Whoever lives in such total relationships as, according to the Trinity-logical depiction, the Father, Son and Spirit do is, in a newly clarified sense, unconditionally inside. Being-in means *existing*—or, as medieval authors strangely yet understandably say with the same intention, *inexisting*—that is, in a sphere which is originally opened by internal relationships.[62] In spherological terms, speculation on the Trinity is informative primarily because it developed the phantasm of never-being-able-to-fall-out-of-the-inside-position to its ultimate conclusion. It is inspired by a fanaticism of immanence for which there is simply not meant to be any outside. In this respect, Trinitarian theology acts as a logical application form for membership in an absolute inner world on the model of the exemplary three: by declaring my allegiance to the *deus unitrius*, I apply for admission to a community that rests on indestructible immanence. And yet, this intimate community too is constituted like a group that owes most of its cohesion to external compulsion. Perhaps the curia's teacherly statements on the Trinity sound increasingly mechanical because, with the establishment of the great theological sums, the intellectual tension began to disappear from the Trinitarian motif and the hour of the confessional administrators had come. At the Council of Florence in 1442, in the papal bull on the union of the Catholic Church with the Copts and Ethiopians, the coinherence of the divine persons was only referred to in conceptually empty officialese:

> Because of this unity the Father is entire in the Son, entire in the Holy Spirit; the Son is entire in the Father, entire in the Holy Spirit, the Holy Spirit is entire in the Father, entire in the Son. No one either excels another in eternity, or exceeds in magnitude, or is superior in power.[63]

Whoever declares this joins a faith with a communional phantasm of inseparability in effect at its center. The price of this phantasm's formulation is that whoever does not profess the same is ejected from the communion; it is no coincidence that the passage quoted is followed by pages of lists detailing heretical teachings whose originators and followers are anathematized and cursed.[64]

It is clear from this how all attempts to elevate microspheric intimate structures—of which the Christian Trinity may be the most sublime formulation—to the norm or the central icon for large communities involve a high psychopolitical risk: if inclusion fails, the non-integrable face the threat of elimination. The primal ecclesiogenic fantasy of stretching an intimate bubble to the size of the world may give the faithful hope that one day, everything they now encounter as a hostile and self-centered outside will be disarmed and incorporated into their own circle of life; experiences of communal enthusiasm and solidarity also have a natural tendency to overflow, and the passing on of spiritual and caritative advantages need not always result in harmful expansionism.

Nonetheless, the Christian politics of love communities displays a paradox that can only be illuminated through fundamental spherological research. The attempt to draw the outside world comprehensively into the bubble leads to errors of format that will be discussed. What Ernst Bloch called the "spirit of utopia" gives the greatest possible format error its official title: for nothing misjudges the autonomous laws of micro- and macrospheres alike as much as the attempt to turn the whole dark, overpopulated world into a transparent and homogeneous home for all without further ado.

The large spheres will be addressed in the second volume of this book. It will set out to show how being-in on a small scale returns as a political and cosmic relationship through specific mechanisms of transference. If there is one aspect of Bloch's messianic motifs that can accompany us in this transition, it is above all his idea of exodus. Its light reveals how the ecstatic animals emerging from microspheres behave when, through their ability to transfer spaces, they cross over to the larger and largest scale.

Excursus 10

Matris in gremio [65]

A Mariological Cricket

Unpleasant begetting—this key phrase demands a commentary.[66] The Old European clerical and monastic system would be unimaginable without a severe anti-reproductive affect. Lotario de Segni (c. 1160–1216), head of the Catholic Church from 1198 as Pope Innocent III, struggles to contain his righteous nausea when he imagines the nourishment of the child in the womb:

> But notice what food the fetus is fed in the womb: with menstrual blood of course, which ceases in the woman after conception so that with it the fetus is fed inside the woman. This blood is said to be so detestable and unclean that "on contact with it crops do not germinate, orchards wither, plants die, trees drop their fruit; if dogs eat of it, they are transported into madness.[67]

How should one imagine the incarnation of God under such auspices? Mary's conception of the God-man as a virgin only fulfills half of the purity regulations; considering the usual infernal menu inside the mother, it is clear that Jesus must also be kept on a different diet *in gremio*. In Question 13 of the third book of *Summa Theologica*, Thomas Aquinas considers whether it would have been better if the body of Christ, like that of Eve, had been miraculously formed from that of man. Why did he have to take upon Himself that macabre procedure of formation through maternal blood? If He had to be born of woman, was it really necessary to be born of woman's blood too, not after the familiar model of removing a rib? Thomas reflects that the body of Christ should be formed, down to the last detail, in exactly the same way as those of other humans:

> But other men's bodies are not formed from the purest blood but from the semen and menstrual blood. Therefore it seems that neither was Christ's body conceived of the purest blood of the Virgin.[68]

But without a blood distinct *toto caelo* from the common, gruesome menstrua, the formation of the God-man's body is fundamentally unjustifiable. Thomas does concede—less crudely than Lotario—that even among ordinary women, embryos are probably formed from a somewhat better blood than the menstrual; but even this better would have been inadequate to produce Christ's body, as it tends to become impure through mixture with the man's semen. The Jesuan communion with the mother, by contrast, had to take place in the medium of a blood that deserved to be termed especially chaste and pure:

> [...] this blood was brought together in the Virgin's womb and fashioned into a child by the operation of the Holy

Ghost. Therefore is Christ's body said to be *formed of the most chaste and purest blood of the Virgin.*[69]

It can scarcely be viewed as a coincidence that it was John of Damascus, creator of the principle of perichoresis, who made a particularly important contribution to the debate on maternal blood. In truth, the blood of Mary, even without resorting to prenatal psychology and nobject theory, is a very media-theoretically special juice. In the medieval view, children grew in the womb somehow through a coagulation or concrescence of the mother's blood; hence the material of the fetus, if not its form, consisted of pure mother material. So then the body of Christ too, as a sculpture made of uniquely pure blood, would be intimately intertwined with the maternal substance through a material perichoresis. Mary's blood is in the Son, and the Son, formed from blood, is in the mother's blood.

And Hence, it is rightly and truly that we call holy Mary the Mother of God[70] [...]. In this the Mother of God, in a manner surpassing the course of nature, made It possible for the Fashioner to be fashioned and for the God and Creator of the universe to become man and deify the human nature which He had assumed.[71]

John of Damascus took the idea of the mother-son relationship's perichoretic nature to its most extreme conclusion in a delirious passage from his *Sermons on the Assumption.* Because perichoresis always implies the priority of the relationship over the external place, or because the relationship itself supplies the place in which the intertwined are located, it follows that the body of Mary cannot be buried in the usual fashion after death. To do so would be to permit—even if only

Vierge ouvrante, late 14th century, Musée Cluny, Paris

temporarily, until the Resurrection—the earth to become a barrier between the united persons. In order to defend the mother-son perichoresis *in extremis* too, John conceives the death of Mary as a mystery play of homecoming, letting the dying mother say to her son:

> I give my body to Thee, not to the earth. Guard that which Thou wert pleased to inhabit and to preserve in virginity. Take to Thyself me that wherever Thou art, the fruit of my womb, there I too may be. I am impelled to Thee who didst descend to me.[72]

After her death, the Apostles carry the transfigured body of the Mother of God to a celestial burial place from where, on the third day, it will ascend to heaven.

> The bosom of the earth was no fitting receptacle for the Lord's dwelling-place, the living source of cleansing water, the corn of heavenly bread, the sacred vine of divine wine, the evergreen and fruitful olive-branch of God's mercy. [...] It was meet that she, who had sheltered God the Word in her own womb, should inhabit the tabernacles of her Son. And as our Lord said it behoved Him to be concerned with His Father's business, so it behoved His mother that she should dwell in the courts of her Son.[73]

The *proprium* of interweaving or contraction theology thus consists not in giving mortal individuals the prospect of an eternal life or favorable rebirths, as non-Christian religions have in numerous cases. The sense of the divine lovers' co-inhabitation is rather to protect the strong relationship from its negation through death. Thus the lovers, even if they die after one another, die into one another; hence they die without touching the hard ground of any outside. If the primacy of the inside is firmly established, the absolute intimate sphere even puts the greatest force of externalization, death, in its place. With the assumption of the Mother of Christ into the tabernacle of the transfigured Son, it seems that the path is open for all those to follow who, through faith, succeed in becoming interwoven with the Son. What applies to postmortal union, however, is also true for perichoreses during life. Within certain limits, all human cohabitation in spaces of closeness is perichoretic, for the basic law of the soul space and the micro-social space is the overlapping of individuals into individuals.

One could interpret the assumptionist Marian deliria as the archetype of the psychoanalytical idea that the descendants always become the crypts of their parents. What reason is there not to admit that Mary may have found eternal rest in her great son, as in a secret tomb? Perhaps only this: in ordinary children, according to human experience, the unfulfilled lives of fathers and mothers are laid to eternal unrest.

On Ecstatic Immanence

Mystical theology and the Trinitarian system provide insight into the constitution of personal life, which is marked by dense interweaving; in these micro-universes of God's intimacy with Himself and human intimacy with God, everything is disposed towards interdependence. By virtue of its perichoretic character, this theology is fundamentally medial; it lives in the element of strong relationships. Their symbolic form is communion as a mode of being, a transaction and a sacrament. The classical theories of strong relationships therefore have no place for the idea of the self-determined individual; someone studying the old texts may have the impression of reading anticipatory criticisms of the Modern Age from premodern times and retrospective criticisms of modernity from postmodernity. If one wanted to design societies on the model of the icon of the Trinity, the result would be vigorously perichoretic social forms along the spectrum of communes, communitarisms, communisms—from the *communio sanctorum* to the idea of the homogeneous outsideless world state as the final communal structure—as recently dreamed up by the media theorist Marshall McLuhan in his pentecostal phantasms of the electronic global village.

In *Being and Time*, by contrast, Heidegger contemplates derelict forms of existential perichoresis. When he writes of Dasein as being-with that "Being-in is *Being-with* others,"[1] one could have the impression that he has in mind a positive theory of the original communality of Dasein. And a little later, when he states in his analysis of the "they" [*das Man*] that "Everyone is the other, and no one is himself,"[2] the catastrophe of the strong relationship idea becomes manifest. How theology can perish— it is clear to see in this passage. The Trinitarian sphere has fallen to earth, and there discovers itself as factual existence in the world. Everyone is the other, and no one is himself: this could almost be applicable to the persons of the Trinity, and yet it is only valid for the mutually entangled and individually lost socialized humans.

Sartre demonstrated how far the implications of this state-ment extend in *Closed Doors*, where a trinity of inauthentic people spend eternity together in hellish intertwinement. Here each becomes the sadistic cognizant of the other's sham life. But hell is only really other people when everyone gazes coldly at one another in their contemptuous mode of being.

Heidegger refrains from such escalations in his "they" analysis. He speaks—not without a certain proud difference—of the communal intimate swamps where daily coexistence takes place as an unassuming being-outside-oneself. If everyone is the other and no one themselves, a gray perichoresis comes into view that makes communional optimism, Catholic and non-Catholic alike, come to nothing. Living in one another in ecstatic immanence: that is not only the privilege of the holiest three; it is enough to be a modern, mass-medial person of the male or female variety in order to blur into one another in gray communions. Heidegger's "they" reveals the other true icon of intimate interweaving; it brings into view the imprecise interwoven life of the many and the general commitment to averageness. And yet, even in this derelict, confused, talked-to-death Dasein, there is still an inextinguishable sacred remainder. For even in the most banal existence, there is a togetherness with others that is as antecedent and immemorial as only the seamless coinherence of Father, Son and Holy Spirit. Someone is somehow close to someone else at some time. One can always reckon with some others from the start, even if their number, status and mindset remain unclear.

> These Others, moreover, are not *definite* Others. On the contrary, any Other can represent them. What is decisive is just that inconspicuous domination by Others which has already been taken over unawares from Dasein as Being-with. One belongs to the Others oneself and enhances their power.[3]

Thus the miracle of the strong relationship continues inconscpicuously in the "they"; fallen from all high heavens, the "they" is still grounded in a place specific only to itself. If Saint John of Damascus could declare that God is His own place, the same can be said of the "they" in the midst of its own kind. In the most vulgar group, the collective stuck together with its place, the unconditional inside is present in as real a fashion as it is among the divine hypostases, who harbor and glorify one another. The light of the In shines even for the self lost in busyness. Everyday existence, because it is in the world, is always blessed with an ecstatic intimacy, even if it is too sluggish to have any notion thereof. Whoever is in the world inhabits a place in which, by virtue of the In's structure, the strong relationship has always already asserted its claim. Dasein is itself a place, one that is disclosed through the mutual inhabitation of those confusedly existing in a state of being-there-with. This place has always opened up, even if the horizon is only illuminated by the average, the medial or the vulgar. Just as the mystic is concerned with his being-in-God, Dasein in the mode of the "they" is eager to be subsumed by the inconspicuous, the absent-minded and the non-ascertainable. Even the approximate life ascends to a heaven, albeit a low one; prominent figures meet in the heaven of the "they." While the mystic has relinquished his will so that God wills in him, for him and through him, the "they" always finds a way not to have been the one who did it; where someone did something, no one did it.

> Everyone is the other, and no one is himself. The "they" [...]
> is the "nobody" to whom every Dasein has already surrendered
> itself in Being-among-one-another.[4]

In the light of the preceding remarks, we can now better explain wherein the magic of *Being and Time*, which goes beyond all merely philosophical attraction, lies. If the book, for all its bleakness, captivates our thought, it is above all because it repeats the deepest ideas of Christian Gnosis in a perfect antonym. The perichoresis of the Gospel of John—I am in the Father and the Father is in me—and the perichoresis of Heidegger—no one is themselves and all are among one another—articulate themselves according to the same model, even if they produce entirely different results. If these statements differ in their scope, it is because John speaks for an intimacy that proclaims itself the mode of being of the heavenly, whereas

Heidegger's analysis describes an existence [*Existenz*] that has disintegrated into the vulgar medial public realm. John's statement conveys a microspheric message that posits an immeasurable asymmetry between inside and outside; it is accompanied by the invitation to cross over from the death-laden outside to the living inside. Heidegger's assertion, on the other hand, has a macrospheric meaning, for it parodies the result of average socialization in mediatized mass societies: the "they" is the inhabitant of the macro-world that pays the price for the symbolic and material comfort of its life form by letting itself be sucked towards the general emptying of the inner world. Its inside has turned completely into the outside; the externalities themselves are now its soul. How, then, could one conceive of a transition from being-"they" to an authentic being-oneself?

John of Damascus taught that places of God are those in which one can experience His operation, physically or spiritually; by contrast, any ordinarily God-forsaken point in the outside can become a place of the authentic self in which the "they" surrenders entirely to its abandonment. Though we are created to have an inner life, we must embrace empty and external things in the absence of appropriate augmentation; for themselves, the last humans have become the external ones. Even their intelligence is now sought in the neurological outside, in a biological apparatus, the brain, that eludes its owner on all sides.

Heidegger too, if read correctly, no longer invites us—despite Augustinian assonances—to seek the truth in the inner person; instead, he calls upon us to become involved with the monstrousness of the external. His village is a site of the immense. Like all mouthpieces of the truth, he calls out to the bystanders to come—yet here, coming no longer means entering a divine intimate sphere, but rather going out into an ecstatic provisionality.

Thus the meaning of In changes once more; in the face of the globalization wars and technological departures that lent the twentieth century its character, being-in means this: inhabiting the monstrous.[5] Kant taught that the question humans ask to assure themselves of their place in the world should be: "What can we hope for?" After the un-groundings of the twentieth century, we know that the question should rather be: "Where are we when we are in the monstrous?"

Notes

Introduction

1. *De stella nova in pede Serpentarii*, 1606, quoted in Alexandre Koyré, *From the Closed World to the Infinite Universe* (Baltimore: Johns Hopkins Press, 1957), p. 47.

2. Alexandre Koyré has pointed out that this famous statement does not express Pascal's own feelings, but is formulated out of empathy for the worldview of the *libertin*, the godless free spirit, who gazes out into a cosmos with neither firmament nor meaning. Cf. Koyré, op. cit., p. 49.

3. The line is taken from an untitled poem (trans.).

4. Cf. *Spheres II*, Excursus 5, "On the Meaning of the Unspoken Word: The Orb Is Dead."

5. Regarding the concepts of *continens/contentum* (encompassing/encompassed), cf. Giordano Bruno, *Zwiegespräche vom unendlichen All und den Welten* [Dialogues On the Infinite Universe and Worlds; original title *De l'infinito universo et Mondi*], ed. Ludwig Kuhlenbeck (Darmstadt: Wissenschaftliche Buchgesellschaft, 1983), p. 32. The concept-historical point of interest lies in the fact that the modern word 'continent' refers to the connections between parts of the ground, whereas the classical *continens* denotes the outermost layer of the heavens. Curiously enough, the modern term for the ground is the 'encompassing,' although it has been known since Columbus and Magellan that the oceans are the encompassing element in the global earth context, while the so-called continents are encompassed. Anglo-American authors refer, with justified irony, to the Old European discourses as symptoms of "continental thought."

6. Friedrich Nietzsche, *The Gay Science* (trans. Josefine Nauckhoff, Adrian Del Caro (Cambridge University Press, 2001)), p. 120.

7. Augustine, *Confessions*, trans. Francis Joseph Sheed & ed. Michael P. Foley (Indianapolis, IN: Hackett, 2006), p. 4.

8. "According to the rules of art" (trans.).

9. The New International Version is used for all biblical quotations (trans.).

10. Cf. Terry Landau, *About Faces* (New York: Anchor, 1989), pp. 193ff.

11. In the Kabbalistic tradition, God's trick was interpreted not so much pneumatically as graphematically: as a cosmogonic script. Arcane technology thus means following on from the primordial script. The medieval golem legend directly combines the motif of the ceramic creation of man with that of animation through the divine letter. See Moshe Idel, *Golem: Jewish Magical and Mystical Traditions on the Artificial Anthropoid* (New York: SUNY Press, 1990). Gotthard Günther developed a reflection-theoretical reformulation of the problematic of creation in his essay "Schöpfung, Reflexion und Geschichte" [Creation, Reflection and History], in which he outlines a metaphysics of the unfinished world; history is understood as a dimension of incompletion that invites further productions on the basis of previous ones. "… one has finally (very late) begun to comprehend that history is the phenomenon that results when man maps his own subjectivity contrapuntally onto the natural materiality of reality." (In *Beiträge zur Grundlegung einer operationsfähigen Dialektik*, vol. 3 [Hamburg: Meiner, 1980], pp. 14–56; here p. 19.)

12. Augustine, *Confessions*, p. 192 (Book X, V [7]).

13. Cf. Dietrich Mahnke, *Leibnizens Synthese von Universalmathematik und Individualmetaphysik* (Halle: Niemeyer, 1925), p. 418.

14. Cf. P.S., *Der starke Grund, zusammen zu sein. Erinnerungen an die Erfindung des Volkes* (Frankfurt: Suhrkamp, 1998). In this lecture, the title formulation is restricted to the psychopolitical formation of populations in modern nation-states. Here, in the spherological context, the formula is assigned its true theoretical format.

15. Like Heidegger, Sloterdijk here plays on the literal meaning of *Dasein* ("existence") as "being-there." It should be noted that as *Dasein* is also a conventional, i.e. non-Heideggerian word in German, it is sometimes translated here as "existence" rather than "Dasein." Where Sloterdijk uses it in a Heideggerian sense without directly referring to Heidegger, the German term has been added in square parentheses, while for specifically Heidegger-related uses, the German word has been retained in keeping with translation conventions (trans.).

16. Cf. *Spheres II*, Excursus 2, "Merdocracy. The Immune Paradox of Settled Cultures."

17. Cf. Thomas Macho, *Todesmetaphern. Zur Logik der Grenzerfahrung* (Frankfurt: Suhrkamp, 1987), pp. 195–200 and 408–426. "We do not experience *death*, but we do experience the *dead*. *Death* is not revealed to us in the experience of the *dead*; we only experience the *resistance* offered by the *dead* in their pure presence." (p. 195) Analogously, Emmanuel Lévinas writes: "However, it is not my non-being that causes anxiety, but that of the loved one […] What we call, by a somewhat corrupted term, love, is *par excellence* the fact that the death of the other affects me more than my own." (*God, Death and Time* [Palo Alto: Stanford University Press], p. 105.)

18. For a spherological theory of mourning cf. *Spheres II*, Chapter 1, "Dawn of Distant Closeness: The Thanatological Space, Paranoia and Peace in the Realm."

19. Hints at an argument that the unfolded field must have five poles are to be found below in Chapter 6, "Soul Partitions. Angels—Twins—Doubles," pp. 413f.

20. Franz Kafka, "Leopards in the Temple," in *Parables and Paradoxes*, ed. Nahum N. Glatzer (New York: Schocken, 1961), p. 93.

21. Cf. Armin Prinz, "Medizinanthropologische Überlegungen zum Bevölkerungsrückgang bei den Azande Zentralafrikas," in *Curare, Zeitschrift für Ethnomedizin*, vol. 9, 3 & 4 (1986), pp. 257ff. The author developed the hypothesis that since the seizure of their land by the Europeans, the Azande have been going through the *psychogenous death of their people*. For exogenously inexplicable reasons, their population has shrunk from c. 2 million in 1900 to a little over 500,000, with a visible tendency towards further decline.

22. For a theory of cultural synthesis through stress co-operations, cf. the significant study by Heiner Mühlmann, *The Nature of Cultures: A Blueprint for a Theory of Culture Genetics*, trans. Robert Payne (Vienna & New York: Springer, 1996).

23. Cf. Peter Daniel, *ZAUN. Normen als Zaun um das jüdische Volk. Zum Phänomen der Zeitüberdauer des Judentums* (Vienna: Edition Splitter, 1995). The author places most emphasis on the people-stabilizing effect of the ritual boundary vis-à-vis other cultures, while we would speak less of a fence [*Zaun*] than a tent effect: it is the internal existence in the text-supported tent of the ethnosphere that keeps Israel in shape as an inspiration community throughout the generations.

24. One should perhaps be aware that the word *Unding*, though normally referring to something absurd or monstrous (the prefix *Un-* is often employed in this manner), has the literal meaning of "un-thing" (trans.).

25. The German word for the amniotic sac, *Fruchtblase*, literally means "fruit bubble." This connects it explicitly to all other mentions of bubbles (trans.).

26. "Et ita tota theologia in circulo posita dicitur." *Nicholas of Cusa's Dialectical Mysticism: Text, Translation, and Interpretive Study of De visione dei*, ed. & trans. Jasper Hopkins (Minneapolis: Arthur J. Banning Press, 1985), p. 122.

27. We shall explain in Chapters 4 and 5 of *Spheres II* why it cannot be any other way.

28. Rainer Maria Rilke, Eighth Duino Elegy: "How happy are those tiny creatures who / *continue* in the womb which gave them life. / Happy the gnat: even its nuptial dance / is danced within the womb. Womb is all things. / Look at the birds, at their half-certainty, / who seem to fly with one wing in each world / as if they were the souls escaping from / Etruscan dead... from one who shares a box / with his own effigy, at liberty, / reposing on the lid. And how perplexed / must any womb-born creature feel, who is / obliged to fly thin air. As if in panic / fear they flitter through that sky..." *Duino Elegies*, trans. Stephen Cohn (Evanston, IL: Northwestern University Press, 1998), pp. 67ff.

29. Cf. *Spheres II*, Chapter 5, "Deus sive sphaera. On the Deeds and the Suffering of the Other Center."

30. Cf. *Spheres II*, Chapter 6, "Anti-Spheres: Explorations in the Infernal Space."

31. Cf. *Spheres II*, Chapter 7, "How the True Spheric Center Has Long-Range Effects through Pure Media: On the Metaphysics of Telecommunication."

32. Cf. *Spheres II*, Chapter 8, "The Last Orb: A Philosophical History of Terrestrial Globalization."

33. The original text contains a play on words: *der Sache auf den Grund gehen* means "to get to the bottom of the matter," but the author replaces *Grund* with *Un-Grund*, combining the meaning of the conventional expression with an invocation of Jakob Boehme's concept of the *Ungrund*, the unfathomable origin and foundation of being (trans).

34. Cf. Wolfgang Welsch, *Vernunft: Die zeitgenössische Vernunftkritik und das Konzept der transversalen Vernunft* (Frankfurt: Suhrkamp, 1996).

35. Concerning spheropoiesis through the fireplace and the thought figure of "thermic socialism," cf. *Spheres II*, Chapter 2, "Vascular Memories: The Reason for Solidarity in the Inclusive Form."

36. Gaston Bachelard, *La Terre et les rêveries du repos* (Paris: J. Corti, 1948; reprint 1988), p. 151.

37. Heidegger's theorem of existential place is examined more closely below in Excursus 4, "'In Dasein There Lies an Essential Tendency towards Closeness.'"

38. Friedrich Wilhelm Heubach, *Das bedingte Leben. Entwurf zu einer Theorie der psycho-logischen Gegenständlichkeit der Dinge. Ein Beitrag zur Psychologie des Alltags* (Munich: Fink, 1987), p. 163.

39. The German word for "I" [*ich*] is the same as Freud's "ego" [*das Ich*], while the word for "it" [*es*] corresponds to the "id" [*das Es*]; though the Freudian terms have usually been chosen elsewhere, it was decided in this case that they are used in their conventional pronominal sense rather than their psychoanalytical one. It is nonetheless worth bearing this overlap in mind, not least because the ordinary meaning is still visible whenever these words are used in German (trans.).

40. This does not preclude elegant combinations between advanced theories and demonological language games; cf. Arthur Kroker, *The Possessed Individual: Technology and the French Postmodern* (New York: New World Perspectives, 1992), especially the foreword, pp. 1–3: "virtual reality is what the possessed individual is possessed by."

41. Cf. Chapter 7, "The Siren Stage: On the First Sonospheric Alliance."

42. Bachelard, op. cit., pp. 124 & 150.

Chapter 1

1. Vol. 1, p. 168, quoted in Heinrich Schipperges, *Die Welt des Herzens. Sinnbild, Organ und Mitte des Menschen* (Frankfurt: Knecht, 1989), pp. 63f.

2. Cf. Guido Rappe, "*Kokoro*—Versuch einer Annäherung an des Verständnis des Herzens in Japan," in *Das Herz im Kulturvergleich*, ed. Georg Berkemer & Guido Rappe (Berlin: Akademie, 1996), pp. 41–69, and Karlfried Graf Dürckheim, *Hara: The Vital Center of Man*, trans S. M. Kospoth & E. R. Healey (Rochester, VT: Inner Traditions, 2004).

3. Cf. Paul-Emile Victor, *Boréal* (Paris: Grasset, 1938).

4. The first and ninth stories of the fourth day.

5. Cf. Jacques Attali, *L'ordre cannibale: Vie et mort de la médecine* (Paris: Grasset, 1979), esp. pp. 21–36.

6. Raymond of Capua, *The Life of St. Catherine of Siena*, trans. George Lamb (New Providence, NJ: P. J. Kenedy & Sons, 1960), pp. 164f.

7. The word *Intimzone* can also be used to mean "genital area" (trans.).

8. We recall Daniel Paul Schreber's account, in his *Memoirs of my Nervous Illness*, of how he was penetrated by divine "rays" and temporarily believed that he no longer possessed any lungs.

9. Raymond of Capua, *The Life of St. Catherine of Siena*, p. 148.

10. Marsilio Ficino, *Commentary on Plato's Symposium on Love*, trans. Sears Reynolds Jayne (Putnam, CT: Spring Publications, 1985), p. 161.

11. Concerning Plato's studies in radiation, cf. *Spheres II*, Chapter 5, "Deus sive sphaera" and Chapter 7, "How the Pure Means Enables the Spheric Center to Have Long-Distance Effects."

12. Ioan P. Couliano's treatment of this is still incomparable in *Eros and Magic in the Renaissance: With a Foreword by Mircea Eliade*, trans. Margaret Cook (Chicago & London: Chicago University Press, 1987). Couliano develops the principle that what was called magic in the early Modern Age was intended by the respective authors simply as applied general eroticism.

13. This theoretical tradition reached an unknown and overlooked peak in Giordano Bruno's texts *De Magia* (On Magic) and *De vinculis in genere* (A General Account of Bonding), which were not published in English until 1998: Giordano Bruno, *Cause, Principle and Unity, and Essays on Magic*, ed. & trans. Robert de Lucca and Richard J. Blackwell (Cambridge University Press, 1998), pp. 103–176. Cf. also in this volume: Chapter 3, "Humans in the Magic Circle: On the Intellectual History of the Fascination with Closeness," esp. pp. 212ff.

14. Henri F. Ellenberger offered impressive resistance to this forgetfulness in his classic study *The Discovery of the Unconscious: the History and Evolution of Dynamic Psychiatry* (New York: Basic Books, 1981), especially in his account of Mesmer and his successors. We will refresh our memory of the magnetopathic formation of the psychology of the unconscious in the chapter after next.

15. Cf Manfred Frank, "Steinherz und Geldseele. Ein Motiv im Kontext," in *Das kalte Herz. Texte der Romantik* (Frankfurt: Insel, 1978), pp. 253–387.

16. Julien Offray De La Mettrie, *Man a Machine* (La Salle, IL: Open Court, 1943), pp. 129f.

17. Cf. Richard von Dülmen, *Theater des Schreckens. Gerichtspraxis und Strafrituale in der frühen Neuzeit* (Munich: C. H. Beck, 1985).

18. Cf. von Dülmen, pp. 128f.

19. Concerning the role of the heart in Aztec culture, cf. Georg Berkemer, "Das Herz im aztekischen Opfer," in *Das Herz im Kulturvergleich*, pp. 23–29.

20. Regarding the concept of position spatiality and its constitutive role in the modern conception of the world, cf. *Spheres II*, Chapter 8, "The Last Orb: A Philosophical History of Terrestrial Globalization," as well as the necessary references to the explication of the term in Hermann Schmitz' *System of Philosophy*.

21. La Mettrie, *Man a Machine*, p. 128.

22. Cf. Eric Alliez, "Deleuze's Virtual Philosophy," in *The Signature of the World, Or, What Is Deleuze and Guattari's Philosophy?*, trans. Eliot Ross Albert & Alberto Toscano (London & New York: Continuum, 2004).

Chapter 2

1. Michel Foucault, "The Thought of the Outside," in *Essential Works of Michel Foucault, 1954–1984, vol. 2: Aesthetics, Method and Epistemology*, ed. James D. Faubion (New York: The New Press, 1998) p. 162.

2. Cf. Chapter 1, "Heart Operation, Or: On the Eucharistic Excess," pp. 100ff.

3. Cf. Chapter 7, "The Siren Stage: On the First Sonospheric Alliance."

4. Plato, *Symposium and Phaedrus*, trans. Benjamin Jowett (Mineola, NY: Dover, 1995), p. 65 (251, a–b).

5. Cf. Giuseppe Basile, "La Cappella degli Scrovegni e la cultura di Giotto," in *Giotto, La Cappella degli Scrovegni a cura di G. B.* (Milan: Electa, 1992), p. 13.

6. Jacobus de Voragine, *The Golden Legend: Readings on the Saints*, trans. William Granger Ryan, vol. 2 (Princeton University Press, 1995), p. 151.

7. Ibid., p. 152.

8. Rudolf Kassner, *Physiognomik* (Wiesbaden: Insel, 1951), p. 182.

9. Pavel Florensky, *Iconostasis*, trans. Donald Sheehan & Olga Andrejev (Cresswood, NY: St. Vladimir's Seminary Press, 2000), p. 67.

10. Information about the imagologies of Islam can be found in the writings of the French Islamic scholar Henry Corbin, especially *The Man of Light in Iranian Sufism*, trans. Nancy Pearson (New Lebanon, NY: Omega Publications, 1994).

11. Cf. Boris Groys, *Kunst-Kommentare* (Vienna: Passagen, 1998), pp. 119f.

12. For documents of this clarification process, cf. in particular Gottfried Boehm, *Bildnis und Individuum. Über den Ursprung der Portrait-Malerei in der italienischen Renaissance* (Munich: Prestel, 1985); Hans Belting, *Bild und Kult. Eine Geschichte des Bildes vor dem Zeitalter der Kunst* (Munich: C. H. Beck, 1990); and Jean-Jacques Courtine & Claudine Haroche, *Histoire du visage. Exprimer et taire ses émotions* (XVI–XIX siècle) (Paris: Rivages, 1988).

13. In one of the most significant attempts at a philosophy of the face in recent years—"Vision und Visage. Überlegungen zu einer Fazinationsgeschichte der Medien," in Wolfgang Müller-Funk & Hans Ulrich Reck (eds), *Inszenierte Imagination. Beiträge zu einer historischen Anthropologie der Medien* (Vienna & New York: Springer, 1996), pp. 87–108—Thomas Macho emphasizes that to be worthy of depiction, a face must *eo ipso* be that of a dead person: an ancestor, a past ruler or God. Against this background, the Jesuan *Ecco homo* would then mean: "Recognize in this living man the one who will become God after his killing."

14. As far as we know, this term was coined by Gilles Deleuze and Félix Guattari, who outline a theory of the historically contingent *visagéité* of European individuals in Chapter 7 of *A Thousand Plateaus*, trans. Brian Massumi (London & New York: Continuum, 2004), pp. 185–211.

15. In Heidegger's sense of *Lichtung* (trans.).

16. Deleuze & Guattari, *A Thousand Plateaus*, p. 196.

17. The—in our opinion—correct counter-thesis to Deleuze/Guattari is posited by Françoise Frontisi-Ducroux in her book *Du masque au visage. Aspects de l'identité en Grèce ancienne* (Paris: Flammarion, 1995), p. 21: "The face is undoubtedly a universal reality, perhaps even an invariant. In all climates and all societies, whatever the nature of their culture, people always have what we call a face. It is not certain, however, that all languages have a specific term for it."

18. Cf. Rudolf Bilz, "Über das emotionale Partizipieren. Ein Beitrag zum Problem des Menschen in seiner Umwelt," in *Die unbewältigte Vergangenheit des*

Menschengeschlechts. Beiträge zu einer Paläoanthropologie (Frankfurt: Suhrkamp, 1967), pp. 39–73.

19. Cf. Gilles Deleuze, *Expressionism in Philosophy: Spinoza*, trans. Martin Joughin (New York: Zone Books, 1990).

20. A particularly good example is Hermann Timm; in his book *Von Angesicht zu Angesicht. Sprachmorphische Anthropologie* (Gütersloh: Mohn, 1992), influenced by Lavater, Rudolf Kassner and Max Picard, he attempts to satisfy his theological interest in "facial epiphany" directly. The flamboyantly witty dissertation of his student Klaas Huizing, *Das erlesene Gesicht. Vorschule einer physiognomischen Theologie* (Gütersloh: Mohn, 1992), pursues a similar line. Both books offer typical Munich examples of the theological turn in phenomenological thought; they demonstrate an alliance for the underestimation of the difficulties faced by a historico-anthropologically founded theory of faciality. One can gain further insight into these difficulties from Deleuze/Guattari (cf. note 14) and Macho (cf. note 13).

21. Johann Caspar Lavater, *Physiognomische Fragmente*, vols. 1–4 (Winterthur: Steiner, 1775–78), vol. 1, p. 159.

22. The phrase "worldless openness to the world" [*weltlose Weltoffenheit*], coined by Thomas Macho in his essay "Musik und Politik in der Moderne," in *Die Wiener Schule und das Hakenkreuz*, ed. Otto Kolleritsch (Vienna: Universal Edition, 1990), p. 134, was also taken as a basis for my text "Ist die Welt verneinbar? Über den Geist Indiens und die abendländische Gnosis" in the book *Weltfremdheit* (Frankfurt: Suhrkamp, 1994), pp. 212–266.

23. Cf. Jean-Paul Sartre, *Baudelaire*, trans. Martin Turnell (New York: New Directions, 1967), p. 16.

24. Cf. *Spheres II*, Chapter 7, "How the True Spheric Center Has Long-Range Effects through Pure Media: On the Metaphysics of Telecommunication."

25. Concerning the Greek understanding of faciality, cf. Françoise Frontisi-Ducroux, *Du masque au visage*.

26. A description of this theorem can be found in Excursus 9, "Where Lacan Starts to Go Wrong," pp. 533–538.

27. Cf. Thomas Macho, "Vision und Visage."

Chapter 3

1. Cf. Béla Grunberger, *Narziss und Anubis. Die Psychoanalyse jenseits der Triebtheorie* (Stuttgart: Verlag Internationale Psychoanalyse, 1988), vol. 2, pp. 189–205, where the term "monad" stands for the "extrojected uterus" in which the newborn exists in closest community with its mother. It lives "in a kind of virtual space [...] that I call the *monad*. The monad is an immaterial womb that nonetheless functions like a real one" (ibid., p. 192).

2. Marsilio Ficino, *Commentary on Plato's Symposium on Love*, pp. 160f.

3. Ibid., p. 164.

4. Cf. Emmanuel Lévinas, *Totality and Infinity: An Essay on Exteriority*, trans. Alphonso Lingis (Dordrecht: Kluwer Academic Publishers, 1979). In the section "Filiality and Fraternity," he writes: "The son resumes the unicity of the father and yet remains exterior to the father: the son is a unique son. Not by number; each son of the father is the unique son, the chosen son. [...] The paternal *eros* first invests the unicity of the son; his ego qua filial commences not in enjoyment but in election" (p. 279). This ethics of the father's child reads like the original psychoanalysis minus the theory of neuroses.

5. *Giordano Bruno*, ed. Elisabeth von Samsonow (Munich: dtv, 1999), pp. 115–228. The English translation in *Cause, Principle and Unity* is based on a different version of the text, so the page numbers from the German edition have been retained here (trans.).

6. Concerning the motif of the "other shore" in this "American studies of wishes," cf. *Spheres II*, Chapter 8, "The Last Orb: A Philosophical History of Terrestrial Globalization."

7. Cf. René Girard, *A Theater of Envy: William Shakespeare* (Oxford & New York: Oxford University Press, 2000).

8. In the sense of being possessed (trans.).

9. To pin down the bloom of the first depth-psychological classicism with symbolic dates, one could take Mesmer's move from Vienna to Paris in 1778 as the beginning and 1856, the year in which the final sum of magnetopathic traditions, Carl Gustav Carus' *Über Lebensmagnetismus und die magischen Wirkungen überhaupt* was published, as the end.

10. Quoted in Emil Schneider, *Der animale Magnetismus. Seine Geschichte und seine Beziehungen zur Heilkunst* (Zurich: Lampert, 1950), pp. 338–347.

11. Immanuel Kant, "On the Power of the Mind to Master Its Morbid Feelings by Sheer Resolution. A letter in reply to Privy Councillor and Professor Hufeland," in *The Conflict of the Faculties*, trans. Mary J. Gregor (Lincoln & London: University of Nebraska Press, 1992), pp. 175–181.

12. Cf. by that author "Ideen und Erfahrungen über den thierischen Magnetismus," in *Jahrbücher der Medicin als Wissenschaft* 2 (1806), pp. 3–46.

13. Cf. by that author *Versuch, die scheinbare Magie des thierischen Magnetismus aus physiologischen und psychischen Gesetzen zu erklären* (Stuttgart & Tübingen: J. G. Cotta'sche Buchhandlung, 1816), as well as *Mysterien des inneren Lebens. Hegels Ansichten über den thierischen Magnetismus. Ansichten und Gegenansichten von Strauss und Fichte* (Tübingen: Guttenberg, 1830).

14. Cf. *Gesammelte Schriften zur philosophischen Anthropologie*, ed. Franz Hoffmann (Leipzig, 1853; reprint Aalen: Scientia, 1987).

15. *Vierzig Sätze aus einer religiösen Erotik* (Munich: Georg Franz, 1831), p. 185.

16. Georg Wilhelm Friedrich Hegel, *Lectures on the Philosophy of Spirit 1827–8*, trans. Robert R. Williams (Oxford & New York: Oxford University Press, 2007), pp. 124–139.

17. Arthur Schopenhauer, *On the Fourfold Root of the Principle of Sufficient Reason, and on the Will in Nature; Two Essays*, trans. Madame Karl Hillebrand (New York: Cosimo, 2007), p. 332.

18. Concerning Balzac's esoteric spherology, cf. Ernst Robert Curtius, *Balzac* (Bonn: Friedrich Cohen, 1923), pp. 37–72; also Burkhart Steinwachs, "Die Bedeutung des Mesmerismus für den französischen Roman um 1830," in *Franz Anton Mesmer und der Mesmerismus*, ed. Gereon Wolters (Constance: Universitätsverlag Konstanz, 1988), pp. 107ff.

19. Thus the heading of Chapter 3 of Hufeland's *Ueber Sympathie* (Weimar, 1811), pp. 45–142.

20. Hegel, *Lectures on the Philosophy of Spirit 1827–8*, pp. 126f.

21. With his vitalistic outlook, Hufeland stands in the tradition of idealistic and early Romantic natural religion. Hölderlin provided a classical formulation of its principle in Diotima's meditation on death from the novel *Hyperion, or, The Hermit in Greece*: "—if I become a plant, would that be so great a loss?—I shall be. How should I be lost from the sphere of life, in which eternal love, common to all, holds all natures together?

[…] We die that we may live. […] Natures live together, like lovers […]" (*Hyperion and Selected Poems*, ed. Eric L. Santner [New York: Continuum, 1990], p. 123).

22. Nietzsche, *The Gay Science*, p. 110.

23. Cf. *Tagebuch über den animalischen Magnetismus*, in *Johann Gottlieb Fichtes nachgelassene Werke*, ed. I. H. Fichte (βonn: Adolph Marcus, 1835), vol. 3, p. 331.

24. For information on the period in which Berlin, after Vienna and Paris, had become the third capital of the magnetopathic movement, cf. Walter Artelt, *Der Mesmerismus in Berlin* (Mainz: Verlag der Akademie der Wissenschaften und der Literatur, 1965).

25. Cf. the reproduction of Wolfart's baquet, p. 229.

26. The course of the inquiry is described by Henri F. Ellenberger in *The Discovery of the Unconscious*, pp. 65ff., and in greater detail in Emil Schneider, *Der animale Magnetismus*, pp. 202ff. Schneider also discusses (pp. 211–232) the suppressed special report by the commission member Jussieu, who had reached a positive assessment of Mesmer's methods.

27. Schopenhauer, *On the Fourfold Root of the Principle of Sufficient Reason, and on the Will in Nature; Two Essays*, p. 358.

28. Thus the critic of magnetism Johann Stieglitz, Royal Great British court physician in Hanover, in his pamphlet *Über den tierischen Magnetismus* (Hanover, 1814).

29. Concerning the complex of "political magnetism" and Hoffmann's Napoleon experience, cf. Rüdiger Safranski, *E. T. A. Hoffmann. Das Leben eines skeptischen Phantasten* (Munich & Vienna: Hauser, 1984), pp. 294–310.

30. Friedrich Gundolf, "Das Bild Georges, 1910," in Gundolf, *Beiträge zur Literatur- und Geistesgeschichte*, ed. Victor A. Schmitz & Fritz Martini (Heidelberg: L. Schneider, 1980), pp. 140 & 147f.

31. A reference to the German folk song "Die Gedanken sind frei" (trans.).

32. Fichte, *Tagebuch über den animalischen Magnetismus*, p. 315.

33. In her study *Das Zweite Gesicht. Übernatürliche Phänomene in der Psychoanalyse* (Stuttgart: Klett-Cotta, 1995), Elisabeth Laborde-Nottale outlines a history of the interrelations between clairvoyance and psychopathology (pp. 91–105), mentioning aspects of non-verbal fusionary communication.

34. Cf. below, Excursus 8, "Illiterate Truths: A Note on Oral Fundamentalism," pp. 531ff.

Chapter 4

1. Cf. Max Raphael, *Wiedergeburtsmagie in der Altsteinzeit. Zur Geschichte der Religion und religiöser Symbole*, ed. Shirley Chesney & Ilse Hirschfeld (Frankfurt: S. Fischer, 1979).

2. Cf. Carl Schmitt, *The Nomos of the Earth*, trans. G. L. Ulmen (New York: Telos, 2003), pp. 67–79, especially the section "Nomos as a Fundamental Process of Apportioning Space" (pp. 78f.).

3. The pre-metaphysical attitude is described impressively by Hans Peter Duerr in his central theological work *Sedna oder Die Liebe zum Leben* (Frankfurt: Suhrkamp, 1985).

4. Cf. Jean-Paul Sartre, *Being and Nothingness: An Essay on Phenomenological Ontology* (London: Routledge, 1969), p. 613: "The obscenity of the feminine sex [i.e. sexual organs] is that of everything which 'gapes open.' It is an appeal to being as all holes are."

5. The reasons that mystical monisms have nonetheless remained the exception rather than the rule in the course of discursive history are firstly the stupidity of philosophers, which the profane rarely imagine, and secondly the high homosexual factor of resistance among the wiser representatives of the profession.

6. Concerning the motif of "being in truth," cf. below, Chapter 8, "Closer to Me Than I Am Myself: A Theological Preparation for the Theory of the Shared Inside," pp. 539ff.

7. One can see how it is possible to pass by this entirely, not least under the pretext of presenting a cultural history of the feminine, by reading Barbara G. Walker's more irritating than useful *Woman's Encyclopedia of Myths and Secrets* (New York: Harper Collins, 1983) in the hope of learning something about keywords such as birth, fetus, initiation, placenta, return, search, separation, vulva, etc.

8. This imagery is developed extensively in Erich Neumann's book *The Great Mother: An Analysis of the Archetype*, trans. Ralph Manheim (Princeton University Press, 1983), a work whose wealth of material at least compensates for its reliance on absurd consciousness-historical concepts and completely false basic culture-historical assumptions.

9. Hans Peter Duerr, *Der Mythos vom Zivilisationsprozess, vol. 2: Intimität* (Frankfurt: Suhrkamp, 1990).

10. Thomas Macho, "Zeichen aus der Dunkelheit. Notizen zu einer Theorie der Psychose," in *Wahnwelten im Zusammenstoss. Die Psychose als Spiegel der Zeit*, ed. Rudolf Heinz, Dietmar Kamper & Ulrich Sonnemann (Berlin: Akademie, 1993), pp. 223–240.

11. Cf. Pope Innocent III, *De miseria condicionis humane*, trans. Robert E. Lewis (Athens, GA: University of Georgia Press, 1978), p. 100: "But notice what food the fetus is fed in the womb: with menstrual blood of course, which ceases in the woman after conception so that with it the fetus is fed inside the woman." Cf. also Excursus 10, "*Matris in gremio*: A Mariological Cricket," pp. 619ff.

12. *Vom Dialog. Studien über den Ursprung der menschlichen Kommunikation und ihrer Rolle in der Persönlichkeitsbildung* (Stuttgart: Klett, 1976).

13. Cf. the author's essay "Wo sind wir, wenn wir Musik hören?," in *Weltfremdheit*, pp. 294–325. There the question in the title [Where are we when we listen to music?] is answered with two localizing formulas: firstly the dynamic "in the way there and in the way back," and later the harmonical "in resonance."

14. This shares certain aspects with my reflections on music in the modern mass media and tonal populism in "Technologie und Weltmanagement. Über die Rolle der Informationsmedien in der Synchronweltgesellschaft," in *Medien-Zeit. Drei gegenswartsdiagnostische Versuche* (Stuttgart: Cantz, 1993), pp. 67–105, esp. pp. 99ff.; cf also below, Excursus 8, "Illiterate Truths: A Note on Oral Fundamentalism," pp. 521ff.

15. Macho, "Zeichen aus der Dunkelheit," p. 237.

16. Cf. Michael Hauskeller, *Atmosphären erleben. Philosophische Untersuchungen zur Sinneswahrnehmung* (Berlin: Akademie, 1995), in particular Chapter III/2, "Der Gehörraum," pp. 102ff.

17. Freud's own remarks in the context of analyzing fear and hysterical breathlessness are not suitable as the foundation for a psychological theory of breath due to their limited scope; cf. *Studienausgabe*, vol. 6: *Hysterie und Atemnot* (Frankfurt: S. Fischer, 1982), pp. 30ff., 46, 149f., 231, 273.

18. The first quotable statement on the subject would appear to be a fairly recent one: Jean-Louis Tristani, *Le stade du respir* (Paris: Editions de Minuit, 1978). As the title indicates, the author aims for a revision of psychoanalytical stage theory through the introduction of an independent breath stage.

19. Cf. Kristofer Marinus Schipper, *The Taoist Body*, trans. Karen C. Duval (Berkeley & Los Angeles: University of California Press, 1993), p. 119.

20. Cf. ibid., pp. 120 & 237f.

21. *Kan-lu*, "sweet dew," is the Chinese name for ambrosia. Compare *Tao Te Ching*, Chapter 32: "When heaven and earth unite, sweet dew will fall." (Note from original text.)

22. Ibid., pp. 120f.

23. Tradition has it that Confucius was also born from a hollow plum tree. Cf. Schipper, ibid., p. 238.

24. Epistula Apostolorum 13:14.

25. Ronald David Laing, *The Facts of Life* (New York: Pantheon, 1976), p. 36.

26. A woman says: "My father was *there* but he was never around." (Note from original text.)

27. "As far as I can make out, there is never anything but womb... It is failure to recognize the world as womb which is the cause of our misery, in large part." Henry Miller, "The Enormous Womb," in *The Wisdom of the Heart* (New York: New Directions, 1960), p. 94. (Note from original text.)

28. Cf. Heinrich Zimmer, *Maya—der indische Mythos* (Frankfurt: Insel, 1978), pp. 42f.

29. Salomo Friedlaender, *Schöpferische Indifferenz*, second edition (Munich: Georg Müller, 1926), p. 22.

30. Ibid., p. 352.

31. Béla Grunberger, *Narziss und Anubis*, vol. 2, p. 207.

32. On fetal psychoacoustics cf. Chapter 7, "The Siren Stage: On the First Sonospheric Alliance," especially pp. 477ff.

33. Ernst Bloch, *A Philosophy of the Future* (New York: Herder & Herder, 1970), p. 1.

34. *Werkausgabe*, vol. 15 (Frankfurt: Suhrkamp, 1985), p. 13.

35. Eduard von Hartmann, *The Philosophy of the Unconscious*, vol. 3, William C. Coupland (London: Routledge, 2001 [reprint]).

36. Cf. Martin Heidegger, "What Is Metaphysics," in *Basic Writings*, ed. D. F. Krell (London: Routledge, 1978), p. 105.

37. Martin Heidegger, *Being and Time*, trans. John Macquarrie & Edward Robinson (Oxford: Blackwell, 1978), p. 140.

38. The word translated here as "admission" is *Einräumung*, whose literal meaning is an assignment of space [*Raum*]; this creates an ambivalence between the literal and figurative meaning in the phrase "admission of space" [*Einräumung des Raums*]. In the translation of *Sein und Zeit* cited here, the term is rendered as "giving space" or "making room" (trans.).

39. Heidegger, *Being and Time*, pp. 79f.

40. The word for "casing" [*Gehäuse*] is directly related to that for "house" [*Haus*] (trans.).

41. Heidegger, *Being and Time*, p. 84.

42. In his analytics of place, Aristotle already provided a marvellously explicit attempt to address the problem of an "existential" topology, even if the being of "something in something" precisely could not interest him in existential terms. The fourth book of his *Physics* contains the following exposition of the eightfold sense of "in":
"Next, we had better come to understand in how many ways we use the expression 'One thing is in another.'
"First, there is the sense in which we say that a finger is *incorporated* in a hand and, in general, that a part is incorporated in a whole. Second, we also say that a whole *consists in* its parts, in the sense that there is no such thing as a whole over and above its parts. Third, we say that 'man' *falls within* 'animal' and, in general, that a species falls within a genus. Fourth, we also say that a genus is *included in* a species and, in general, that any part of the species is included in the definition of the species. Fifth, we say that health *inheres in* hot and cold things and, in general, that form inheres in matter. Sixth, we say that the affairs of Greece are *in the power of* the Persian king and, in general, that things are in the power of their original agent of change. Seventh, we say that things are *centered* in their good and, in general, their end or purpose. Finally, the most fundamental sense is when we say that something is *contained in* a vessel and, in general, in a place.
"It is not easy to decide whether something can be in itself, or whether nothing can, in which case everything is either nowhere or in something other than itself." (Aristotle, *Physics*, trans. Robin Waterfield [Oxford & New York: Oxford University Press, 1996], p. 83.)

43. Heidegger, *Being and Time*, p. 89.

44. This is the case in Heidegger's most important Freiburg lecture, "Grundbegriffe der Metaphysik. Welt—Endlichkeit—Einsamkeit," given in the winter semester of 1929–1930, *Gesamtausgabe* vols. 29–30, ed. Friedrich-Wilhelm von Hermann, second edition (Frankfurt: Klostermann, 1992). The title given on the department notice board had contained "isolation" [*Vereinzelung*] instead of "loneliness" [*Einsamkeit*].

45. The word is used here in the sense of the divine nature embodied in individual beings (trans.).

Chapter 5

1. [What shall I do without Eurydice? Where shall I go without my love?]

2. Béla Grunberger, *Narziss und Anubis*, vol. 2, p. 195.

3. Ibid., p. 196.

4. Cf. Sartre, *Being and Nothingness*, pp. 605–615.

5. Ibid., p. 609.

6. Sloterdijk's formulation *Mit-Gefühl* (feeling-with) is a play on the literal meaning of *Mitgefühl*, "sympathy" (note that the English word is simply the same in Greek), to incorporate his concept of the With (trans.).

7. Cf. Chapter 6, "Soul Partitions. Angels—Twins—Doubles," pp. 413f.

8. Hildegard of Bingen, *Scivias*, trans. Columba Hart & Jane Bishop (Mahwah, NJ: Paulist Press, 1990), pp. 116–124.

9. The word "crossing" is here used in its architectural sense, referring to the square space (often decorated) at the junction of the four arms of traditional cruciform churches (trans.).

10. Hildegard of Bingen, *Scivias*, p. 67.

11. Cf. also Excursus 10, "*Matris in gremio*: A Mariological Cricket," pp. 619ff.

12. One German word for the placenta, and the one used in this sentence, is *Mutterkuchen*, "mother cake" (trans.).

13. Cf. Jacques Gélis, *History of Childbirth: Fertility, Pregnancy and Birth in Early Modern Europe*, trans. Rosemary Morris (Cambridge: Polity, 1991), Chapter 12, "The Placenta: Double of the Child," pp. 165–172.

14. Cf. Françoise Loux, *Das Kind und sein Körper in der Volksmedizin. Eine historisch-ethnographische Studie* (Stuttgart, Klett-Cotta, 1980), p. 118.

15. Cf. Gélis, op. cit., p. 170.

16. Concerning the following, cf. Reimar Hartge, "Zur Geburtshilfe und Säuglings-fürsorge im Spiegel der Geschichte Afrikas," in *Curare, Zeitschrift für Ethnomedizin*, special issue 1/1983, pp. 95–108.

17. This culture-historical connection makes it especially interesting to note what Harold Bloom observes in his study on the latest American national theosophy, what he calls "American Orphism": that its central symbols are the flag and the fetus. Cf. Harold Bloom, *The American Religion: The Emergence of the Post-Christian Nation* (New York: Simon & Schuster, 1992), p. 45: "The flag and the fetus together sybolize the American Religion, the partly concealed but scarcely repressed national faith."

18. Some translations have "bundle of life" instead of "bundle of the living" (trans.).

19. Curiously enough, it was Rousseau of all people who most clearly informed Tzvetan Todorov's attempt to establish a Euro-communitarian ethics. Cf. *Life in Common: An Essay in General Anthropology*, translated by Katherine & Lucy Golsan (Lincoln: University of Nebraska Press, 2001).

20. The term "loneliness technique" (*Einsamkeitstechnik*) was, to the best of our knowledge, introduced by Thomas Macho in a lecture on the cultural history of the withdrawal from culture entitled "Ideen der Einsamkeit" and given during the winter semester of 1995–1996 at the Humbolt University in Berlin.

21. That the child *in utero* is not an immediate part of the mother, but rather lives in an intermediate world of its own together with the placental double, has—among other things—dramatic immunological implications. Recent studies seem to have shown that among pregnant women who were HIV positive, the illness was only transmitted to the child in 30% of the cases, while the majority profit, in a scarcely comprehensible manner, from a form of placental guardian angel. From a gyneco-logical-obstetric perspective, it remains unclear whether the placenta should be viewed as an organ of the mother or the child; there is increasing evidence to suggest the latter, however.

22. Rilke, *Sonnets to Orpheus*, trans. David Young (Middletown, CT: Wesleyan University Press, 1987), p. 81.

23. Cf. Excursus 2, "Nobjects and Un-Relationships," pp. 291ff.

24. Cf. Boris Cyrulnik, *Sous le signe du lien: Une histoire naturelle de l'attachment* (Paris: Hachette, 1989).

25. Concerning the complex of precarious cooperation with the status quo, cf. Sloterdijk. "Was heisst: sich übernehmen? Versuch über die Bejahung," in *Weltfremdheit*, pp. 267–293, esp. pp. 286ff.

26. In his parallel life stories, Plutarch presented 23 biographical pairs, including Pericles/Fabius Maximus, Alcibiades/Coriolanus, Pyrrhus/Marius, Alexander/Caesar, Dion/Brutus.

27. Cf. Thomas Macho, "Himmlisches Geflügel—Beobachtungen zu einer Motivgeschichte der Engel," in Cathrin Pichler (ed.), *:Engel :Engel. Legenden der Gegenwart* (Vienna & New York: Springer, 1997), pp. 83–100.

28. Andy Warhol, *The Philosophy of Andy Warhol: From A to B and Back Again* (New York: Harcourt Brace Jovanovich, 1975), p. 26.

29. Cf. Heinz Mode, *Fabeltiere und Dämonen in der Kunst. Die fantastische Welt der Mischwesen* (Stuttgart: Kohlhammer, 1974), p. 52.

30. Malcolm Godwin, *Angels: An Endangered Species* (New York: Simon & Schuster, 1990), pp. 62f.

31. See Chapter 3, "Humans in the Magic Circle: On the Intellectual History of the Fascination with Closeness," pp. 207ff.

32. Ellenberger, *The Discovery of the Unconscious*, p. 71. Cf. the picture of the magic elm, p. 408.

33. Franz Kafka, *The Blue Octavo Notebooks*, ed. Max Brod, trans. Ernst Kaiser & Eithne Wilkins (Cambridge, MA: Exact Change, 1991), p. 94.

34. Ibid., p. 96. One could, by way of experiment, map this exclamation by Kafka onto the final lines of Rilke's *The Notebooks of Malte Laurids Brigge*: "He was now terribly difficult to love, and he felt that only One was capable of it. But He did not yet want to." (Rilke, *The Notebooks of Malte Laurids Brigge*, trans. Burton Pike [Champaign & London: Dalkey Archive Press, 2008], p. 191.)

Chapter 6

1. *Basic Writings of Saint Thomas Aquinas*, vol. 1: *God and the Order of Creation*, ed. Anton C. Pegis (Indianoplis: Hackett, 1997), p. 499.

2. Gaston Bachelard, *The Poetics of Space*, trans. M. Jolas (Boston: Beacon Press, 1994), p. xxxvii.

3. Michel Serres, *Atlas* (Paris: Flammarion, 1997).

4. Censorinus, *The Birthday Book*, trans. Holt. N. Parker (Chicago & London: Chicago University Press 2007), pp. 4f.

5. "In the presence of the people" (trans.).

6. Cf. Hegel, *Lectures on the Philosophy of Spirit 1827–8*, p. 126, as well as Chapter 3, p. 207ff above (passage ending in note 20).

7. The figure *cogitor ergo sum* first appears, as far as we know, in Franz von Baader's metaphysics of knowledge: *cogitor a Deo, ergo cogito, ergo sum*. Cf. *Werke*, 16 vols. (Leipzig: Verlag des literarischen Instituts, 1851–60), vol. 1, pp. 370 & 395, and vol. 12, pp. 238 & 324. The Christian theologian of history and language philosopher Eugen Rosenstock-Huessy drew on related motifs to develop a processual metaphysics of mentioned and named existence. Cf. *Die Sprache des Menschengeschlechts. Eine leibhafte Grammatik in vier Teilen* (Heidelberg: L. Schneider, 1963–64); also *Spheres II*, Chapter 7, "How the True Spheric Center Has Long-Range Effects through Pure Media: On the Metaphysics of Telecommunication."

8. Kant provides the technical formation of this axiom of potential self-augmentation through self-observation in his theorem of transcendental apperception; cf. *Critique of Pure Reason*, trans. John Miller Dow Meiklejohn (New York: Barnes & Noble, 2004), p. 100. In his study "Himmlisches Geflügel," p. 94, Thomas Macho refers to the "self-guardian-angel-like" quality of the Kantian "I think" and Fichte's "intellectual observation." For a meditation-philosophical, "Eastern" version of the self-observation postulate, cf. the work of the spiritual teacher Jiddu Krishnamurti.

9. Cf. Dieter Lenzen, *Vaterschaft. Vom Patriarchat zur Alimentation* (Reinbek: Rowohlt, 1991); on the concept of susciptive fatherhood among the Romans, see pp. 91ff.

10. In a related fashion, Guy de Maupassant's tale "The Horla" (*le hors là*, "the outside there") describes the infection of a house in Normandy with a demon brought over from distant South America. Michel Serres developed the space-philosophical implications of this story in an inspired interpretation: cf. *Atlas*, pp. 61–85.

11. Cf. Bernard Lafont & Henri de Saint-Blanquat, "Figures de notre absence," in *Le réveil des anges, messagers des peurs et des consolations* (*Collection Mutations* no. 162), ed. Olivier Abel (Paris: Editions Autrement, 1996), p. 92.

12. Cf. Ioan P. Culianu, *Out of this world: otherworldly journeys from Gilgamesh to Albert Einstein*, trans. (Boston, Shambhala, 1991), pp. 50ff.

13. The second-century revelatory treatise *The Shepherd of Hermas* features a transposition of the two-genius doctrine into a Christian context: "There are two angels with a man, one of righteousness and one of wickedness. […] Trust the angel of righteousness. But from the angel of wickedness stand aloof […]" Quoted in Alfons Heilmann & Heinrich Kraft (eds.), *Texte der Kirchenväter*, 5 vols. (Munich: Kösel, 1963–66), vol. 1, pp. 254f.

14. Petrus Abaelardus, "In Annuntiatone Beatae Virginis," from *Lauda Sion*, ed. & trans. Karl Simrock (Stuttgart: J. G. Cotta'sche Buchhandlung, 1868). It should be noted, incidentally, that the command "Be not afraid!" does not here articulate the usual *tremendum* aspect of encounters between humans and the numinous realm, but must rather be understood as an expression of the precarious cognitive relationship between the subject and its informant.

15. *Basic Writings of Saint Thomas Aquinas*, vol. 1: *God and the Order of Creation,* pp. 509–537.

16. *The Sayings of the Desert Fathers*, trans. Benedicta Ward (Kalamazoo, MI: Cistercian Publications, 1975), pp. 1f.

17. Cf. Jean-Louis Chrétien, "La connaissance angélique," in *Le réveil des anges*, pp. 138f.

18. In German, the word *Autismus* is not only used in the strict clinical sense, but also to refer more generally to self-absorbed or oblivious behavior (trans.).

19. Iain Gardner & Samuel N. C. Lieu (eds.), *Manichean Texts from the Roman Empire* (Cambridge University Press, 2004), pp. 47 & 75.

20. Ibid., p. 49.

21. *Die Gnosis*, vol. 3: *Der Manichäismus*, ed. & trans. Alexander Böhlig (Zurich & Munich: Artemis, 1980), p. 78.

22. Ibid., p. 80.

23. Cf. Otto Rank, *The Double: A Psychoanalytic Study*, trans. & ed. Harry Tucker, Jr. (Chapel Hill, NC: University of North Carolina Press, 1971), pp. 69 & 71.

24. Concerning the modification of prophetic subject structure into an "apostolic pact," cf. *Spheres II*, Chapter 7, "How the True Spheric Center Has Long-Range Effects through Pure Media: On the Metaphysics of Telecommunication."

25. Ibid.

26. Cf. Marjorie Wallace, *The Silent Twins* (London: Chatto & Windus, 1986).

27. I attempted to show in my music-philosophical study "Wo sind wir, wenn wir Musik hören?" (*Weltfremdheit*, pp. 294–325, especially pp. 294–325) how it is possible to reject this mortifying educational demand in favor of a perturbable subject form that "trembles" to the end.

28. This word was introduced into psychoanalytical terminology by C. G. Jung in 1911, in his text *Symbols of Transformation*—initially as a discrete instrument for determining internalized relationships, than as an ideologically agglutinated psycho-ontological category.

29. Earlier on (in the final section of Chapter 2, "Between Faces," pp. 139ff.) we presented arguments supporting the theory that mirrors only appeared in the time of advanced civilizations as media of self-relation among the wealthy, powerful and wise (in the middle of the first century BC), and that it was only in the nineteenth century, together with the establishment of literacy and hygiene, that the use of mirrors became widespread among modern populations. In this point, Lacan's argument of a supposedly constitutive, pre-social "mirror stage" displays a media- and technology-historical weakness. Whether one could reformulate Lacan's hypothesis with reference to watery reflections or the shadow of the *infans* is more than uncertain; what is clear is that semantic deception is going on if the mother's eye is presented as an organic "mirror" given at all times.

30. Cf. *The Stories of Vladimir Nabokov* (New York: Vintage, 1997), pp. 612–618. The American surgeon William P. Pancoast wrote a sensational account of the separation of the Siamese twins Chang and Eng, who died in 1874.

31. Ibid., p. 615.

32. Ibid., p. 617.

33. Ibid., p. 613.

34. Ibid.

35. Ibid., p. 614.

36. Robert Musil, *The Man Without Qualities*, trans. Sophie Wilkins & Burton Pike (New York: Vintage, 1996), pp. 984f.

37. *Poems and Ballads of Goethe*, trans. W. Edmondstoune Aytoun and Theodore Martin (New York: Delisser & Procter, 1859), p. 215.

38. The classic model of religious "mourning" is provided by Saint Augustine in Book IV of his *Confessions*; see *Spheres II*, Chapter 1, "Dawn of Distant Closeness: The Thanatological Space, Paranoia and Peace in the Realm."

39. Andy Warhol, *The Philosophy of Andy Warhol*, pp. 26f.

40. Sigmund Freud, "Mourning and Melancholia," in *The Standard Edition of the Complete Psychological Works of Sigmund Freud*, ed. & trans. James Strachey et al., 24 vols. (London: Hogarth, 1953–1974), vol. 14, p. 245.

41. Ibid., p. 249.

42. Ibid.

43. Cf. above, Excursus 2, pp. 291ff.

44. Concerning signs of being, cf. *Spheres II*, Chapter 7, "How the True Spheric Center Has Long-Range Effects through Pure Media: On the Metaphysics of Telecommunication."

45. We owe the term "angeletic" to Rafael Capurro; concerning the history of the concept of *angelia*, cf. Capurro, "On the Genealogy of Information," in Klaus Kornwachs & Konstantin Jacoby (eds.), *Information: New Questions to a Multidisciplinary Concept* (Berlin: Akademie, 1996), pp. 259–270.

46. Only Herman Melville, if anyone, could claim to have anticipated—in his 1856 tale *Bartleby*—the shift from angeletics to idiotics that Dostoyevsky's novel of 1868/1869 then spectacularly completed.

47. Nietzsche, *The Anti-Christ, Ecce homo, Twilight of the idols, and Other Writings*, trans. Judith Norman (Cambridge University Press, 2005), p. 28.

48. Ibid., p. 27.

49. Fyodor Dostoyevsky, *The Idiot*, trans. Constance Garnett (Mineola, NY: Dover, 2003), p. 74.

Chapter 7

1. Henri Michaux, *Selected Writings: The Space Within*, trans. Richard Ellmann (New York: New Directions, 1990), p. 67.

2. Augustine, *Confessions*, p. 4.

3. There is a play on words here, as the word for "receptivity," *Empfänglichkeit*, is etymologically connected to *Empfängnis*, meaning (natal) "conception."

4. All instances of the word "movedness" correspond here to *Ergriffenheit*, meaning a state of being emotionally moved, rather than Heidegger's *Bewegtheit*. The verb *ergreifen* also has the more literal meaning "to seize or grab," which certainly comes into play here (trans.).

5. *The Odyssey of Homer: A New Verse Translation*, trans. Allen Mandelbaum (Berkeley & Los Angeles: University of California Press, 1990), pp. 248f.

6. Homer's use of dual verb forms indicates two Sirens; later accounts, as in the *Argonautica* of Apollonius Rhodius, mention three or four figures and even supply their names: Thelxiope, beguiler of the heart; Thelxinoë, beguiler of the senses; Molpe, she who dances while singing; and Aglaope, she of the magnificent voice. Other Siren tercets also include such names as Aglaopheme, the magnificently famous, and Ligeia, she of the shrill voice.

7. *The Odyssey of Homer*, pp. 249f.

8. A reference to the aria "Nessun dorma" from Puccini's *Turandot*, popularized by Luciano Pavarotti.

9. Jean Paul, *Titan: A Romance*, trans. Charles Timothy Brooks, vol. 1 (London: Trübner, 1863), pp. 6f.

10. Cf. the words of Odysseus to his comrades about the wise Circe's advice: "The prophecies of Circe are not meant for one or two of us."

11. "I bring you tidings of great joy" (trans.).

12. Cf. Chapter 2, "Between Faces: On the Appearance of the Interfacial Sphere of Intimacy," pp. 139f.

13. Cf. Alfred Tomatis, *Klangwelt Mutterleib. Die Anfänge der Kommunikation zwischen Mutter und Kind* (Munich: Kösel, 1994), p. 179.

14. The word for "bondage" or "obedience," *Hörigkeit*, is connected to *hören*, meaning "to hear, listen or obey." The sequence of "bondage," "acuteness of hearing" and "hardness of hearing" thus appears in German as three variations on the same theme: *Hörigkeit*, *Hellhörigkeit* and *Schwerhörigkeit* (trans.).

15. Nicolas Malebranche, *The Search after Truth*, ed. & trans. Thomas M. Lennon & Paul J. Olscamp (Cambridge University Press, 1997), p. 113.

16. Ibid., pp. 115f.

17. "Keys" in the musical sense (trans.).

18. Concerning the motifs of the wall and wall-lessness, cf. *Spheres II*, Chapter 2, "Vascular Memories: The Reason for Solidarity in the Inclusive Form."

19. We owe this formulation [originally *Ton-Götter*] to Andreas Leo Findeisen (Institute of Cultural Philosophy and Media Theory at the Vienna Academy of Fine Arts).

20. Julia Kristeva, *Black Sun: Depression and Melancholia*, trans. Leon S. Roudiez (New York: Columbia University Press, 1989), pp. 67f.

21. Jacques Lacan, "The Mirror Stage as Formative of the Function of the I," in *Écrits: A Selection*, trans. Alan Sheridan (London: Routledge, 2001) pp. 1–6. In keeping with standard usage, the "I" of the English translation's title has been rendered here as "ego" (trans.).

22. Cf. the final section of Chapter 2, "Between Faces," pp. 139ff.

Chapter 8

1. Heidegger, *Being and Time*, p. 79; cf. also above, Excursus 4, "'In Dasein There Lies an Essential Tendency towards Closeness.'"

2. Gilles Deleuze took a step towards the clarification of this matter in his final text "Immanence: A Life," in *Pure Immanence: Essays on a Life*, trans. Anne Boyman (New York: Zone Books, 2001) pp. 25–34.

3. In so far as biblical theology teaches a withdrawn or separate God, the immanence *in* Him of all that exists is modified into something that occurs *under* God, *with reference to* God or *on the edge of* God, though never fully *outside* God. In a sense,

classical theology was the first *analysis situs*, for all locations in that which exists constitute situations in relation to the absolute center. Radical ontology is therefore possible only as situology—and nowhere is this fact manifested more clearly than in Heidegger's early thought; cf. Excursus 4, "'In Dasein There Lies an Essential Tendency towards Closeness,'" p. 333, as well as the final connecting chapter "On Ecstatic Immanence," pp. 625ff.

4. In the view of classical metaphysics, that is to say absolute situology, God is the unity of being-with-oneself and being-outside-oneself—a trait that can also be ascribed to finite existence [*Dasein*] if, in agreement with Heidegger, one understands it as insistent *and* ecstatic.

5. Alain Badiou, *Conditions*, trans. Steven Corcoran (London & New York: Continuum, 2008), p. 276. It is clear that this is not our own view, as Badiou's claim makes excessive concessions to the ideology of prior loneliness.

6. Dostoyevsky, *The Idiot*, p. 101.

7. The words translated here as "recognition" and "misjudgment" are *Wiedererkennen* and *Verkennung*, both based on *kennen*, "to know" (trans.).

8. Cf. Page DuBois, *Torture and Truth* (London: Routledge, 1991).

9. Concerning the motif of "being-in-the-truth" or the return to the "womb of truth," cf. Chapter 4, "The Retreat Within the Mother," pp. 269f.

10. Cf. Nicholas of Cusa, "Dialogue on the Hidden God": "For outside truth there is no truth [...] Therefore, truth is not found outside truth neither in some way nor in something else" (*extra veritatem non est veritas [...] Non reperitur igitur veritas extra veritam nec aliter nec in alio*), in *Selected Spititual Writings*, trans. H. Lawrence Bond (Mahwah, NJ: Paulist Press, 1997), p. 210.

11. For a macrospherological interpretation of apostleship, cf. *Spheres II*, Chapter 7, "How the True Spheric Center Has Long-Range Effects through Pure Media: On the Metaphysics of Telecommunication."

12. Concerning the phenomenon of religious history as a continuation of the evangelistic process through apostolic history, cf. Chapter 6, note 24.

13. Augustine, *Confessions*, p. 189 (Book X, II [2]). The formula *in te*, "in You," frequently used by Augustine, refers more to the topological or situological structure of the ego-God relationship; in the passage *nec mihi nec tibi placeam nisi de te*, on the other hand, the phrase *de te* emphasizes the relationship with one's own ego

in dynamic terms as an international relationship within the relationship to God: if I am something to myself, it is because I am something to You.

14. Here the author uses *Da-Sein* rather than *Dasein*; cf. Introduction, "The Allies; or, The Breathed Commune," note 15 (trans.).

15. Ibid., p. 4 (Book I, II [2]).

16. Ibid., p. 209 (Book X, XXIV).

17. Ibid. (Book X, XXV).

18. Ibid., p. 210 (Book X, XXV).

19. Ibid. (Book X, XXVI).

20. Ibid. (Book X, XXVII).

21. If this were the place to repeat the theological deduction of temporality, the difference between theodrama (God's process with the world) and affair (the soul's process with God) would need to be developed; for our purposes it is sufficient to foreground the aspect of the affair.

22. The original word *Kennenlernen* means "to become acquainted with"; it is translated differently here because in the German, it refers to the preceding quotation from Augustine, where the Latin *didici* is rendered as *kennen lernte* in the German translation used by the author, but as "learned of" in the English translation used here. It is also worth noting, that the literal meaning of *kennenlernen* is "to learn to know" (trans.).

23. Cf. the passage on theotechnics in the Introduction, pp. 31–45.

24. *Confessions* III, VI (11): "You were more inward than the most inward place of my heart and loftier than the highest" (*Tu autem eras interior intimo meo et superior summo meo*). This highest claim of Christian topological surrealism is explained with reference to its architecture-historical preconditions in *Spheres II*, Chapter 3: "Arks, City Walls, World Borders, Immune Systems: On the Ontology of the Walled Space." Here the comparative sense of the inside emerges in the light of palace architecture in the Persian Empire: the inward is that which, in a system of nested spaces, lies not simply *intus*, "inside," but *interior*, "further inside."

25. Cf. Martin Buber, *Ecstatic Confessions*, trans. Esther Cameron (Syracuse, NY: Syracuse University Press, 1996).

26. A reference to the "SWR Teleakademie," a television series produced by the SWR (Southwest German Broadcasting) featuring presentations by university lectures on different scientific, cultural and social topics (trans.).

27. Marguerite Porete, *The Mirror of Simple Souls*, trans. Ellen L. Babinsky (Mahwah, NJ: Paulist Press, 1993), p. 83.

28. Ibid., pp. 192f.

29. Ibid., p. 218.

30. Shihabuddin Suhrawerdi Maqtul [Shahab al-Din Suhrawardi], *Three Treatises on Mysticism*, ed. & trans. Otto Spies & S. K. Khatak (Bonn: Selbstverlag des Orientalischen Seminars der Universität Bonn, 1935), pp. 25f.

31. Cf. Seyyed Hossein Nasr, *Three Muslim Sages: Avicenna, Suhrawadi, Ibn 'Arabi* (Cambridge, MA: Harvard University Press, 1964), p. 76.

32. Alongside Christology, prophetology, pneumatology and onto-semiology, or the doctrine of signs of being (meaning philosophical aesthetics).

33. Nicholas of Cusa, *Selected Spiritual Writings*, pp. 235ff.

34. Ludwig Wittgenstein, *Culture and Value*, trans. Peter Winch (Oxford: Blackwell, 1980), p. 52.

35. In the original, the author comments here on the shortcomings of the German translation, which renders Cusa's *contractio* as *Verschränkung*, which normally means "interweaving or folding"; these remarks have been omitted (trans.).

36. Nicholas of Cusa, *Selected Spiritual Writings*, p. 238.

37. The German word for "guilt" is *Schuld* and "debts" are *Schulden*, with the verb *schulden* meaning "to owe" (trans.).

38. Concerning the modernization of guilt, cf. *Spheres II*, Chapter 8, "The Last Orb: A Philosophical History of Terrestrial Globalization."

39. Although the author uses *verschränkt* [interwoven] rather than *zusammengezogen* [contracted] in these two sentences, he does so with reference to Cusa's *contractio* and its inadequate German translation (see note 35 above), which is why it is translated here as "contracted."

40. Nicholas of Cusa, *Selected Spiritual Writings*, p. 240.

41. Especially Chapters 5 and 6.

42. *Kleine Münze*, literally "small coin" or "small change," is a term from German copyright law, referring to the minimal unit of creative work subject to copyright protection (trans.).

43. Cf. *Spheres II*, Chapter 5, "Deus sive sphaera. On the Deeds and the Suffering of the Other Center."

44. Nicholas of Cusa, *De ludo globi*, trans. Pauline Moffitt Watts (New York: Abaris Books, 1986), p. 75.

45. Pseudo-Dionysius (Areopagita), "The Divine Names," in *The Complete Works*, trans. Colm Luibheid & Paul Rorem (Mahwah, NJ: Paulist Press, 1987), pp. 61f.

46. Cf. Blaise Pascal, *Thoughts*, trans. W. F. Trotter (New York: Cosimo, 2007), p. 180: "Jesus will be in agony even to the end of the world."

47. Saint John of Damascus, *Writings*, trans. Frederic H. Chase (New York: Fathers of the Church, Inc., 1958), p. 178.

48. Ibid., pp. 195f.

49. Cf. Albert Menne, "Mengenlehre und Trinität," in *Münchener Theologische Zeitschrift* 8 (1957), pp. 180ff.

50. Letter 38, written c. 370, in Saint Basil, *The Letters*, trans. Roy J. Deferrari (London: Heinemann, 1926), vol. 1, p. 209.

51. Adv. Maced. GNO, III/I, 109, quoted in Giulio Maspero, *Trinity and man: Gregory of Nyssa's Ad Ablabium* (Leiden & Boston: Brill, 2007), p. 176.

52. In *Das seltsame Problem der Weltgesellschaft. Eine Neubrandenburger Vorlesung* (Opladen: Westdeutscher Verlag, 1997), Peter Fuchs provides a brilliant introduction to sociological systems theory—emphasizing the non-spatial character of "society"—conveying the impression of attempting to approach a "perichoretic" sociology, i.e. a theory of society without drawing on images of spatial containers.

53. Cf. Anaxagoras of Clazomenae, *Fragments and Testimonia: A Text and Translation with Notes and Essays*, ed. & trans. Patricia Curd (Toronto/Buffalo/London: University of Toronto Press, 2007), p. 25 (Fragment B12): "This revolution

(*perichoresis*) caused them (the mixed qualities) to separate off. The dense is being separated off from the rare, and the warm from the cold, and the bright from the dark, and the dry from the moist."

54. Saint John of Damascus, "An Exact Exposition of the Orthodox Faith," in *Writings*, p. 177.

55. Ibid., p. 202.

56. Ibid., p. 197f.

57. The last few lines of this paragraph play extensively with the prefix *um-*, denoting the meaning of "around": *Umgeben-Sein* [being-surrounded], *Umfang* [magnitude], *Umwelt* [environment], *das Um* [the Around], and finally the pairing of *weltlos* [worldless] and *umweltlos* [environment-less] (trans.).

58. Cf. Cyril of Alexandria, *In Johannis Evangelium I, 5*. Migne PG, 73, 81; quoted in *Encyclopédie Théologique*, vol. C, p. 880.

59. Richard of Saint Victor, *De trinitate*, V, 6.

60. Cf. Richard of Saint Victor, *La trinité: Texte latin*, ed. Gaston Salet, S.J. (Paris: Les Editions du Cerf, 1959), pp. 342 & 351ff.: *quarta in trinitate persona locum habere non possit*. Immanuel Kant's listless remark that it makes no difference whether an apprentice of faith believes that God comprises three persons or ten, as this difference has no effect on his behavior, merely shows that Kant had no idea of the difference between an ethics of following rules and an ethics of communional existence. A ten-person godhead would always be monstrous, either because persons 4 to 10, if equal, would simply be serially added or, if unequal, would set off a procession into the God-unlike. Cf. *The Conflict of the Faculties*, p. 67.

61. "Hegel says somewhere that great historic facts and personages recur twice. He forgot to add: 'Once as tragedy, and again as farce.'" Karl Marx, *The Eighteenth Brumaire of Louis Bonaparte*, trans. D. D. L. (New York & Berlin: Mondial, 2005), p. 1.

62. Cf. Peter Stemmer, "Perichorese. Zur Geschichte eines Begriffs," in *Archiv für Begriffsgeschichte* XXVII (1983), pp. 24–32.

63. Denzinger, 1331; after Fulgentius of Ruspe.

64. Denzinger, 1332–1333, 1336, 1339–1346.

65. "In the mother's lap" (trans.).

66. Cf. above, p. 613.

67. Pope Innocent III, *De miseria condicionis humane*, trans. Robert E. Lewis (Athens, GA: University of Georgia Press, 1978), p. 100.

68. St. Thomas Aquinas, *Summa Theologica* (New York: Cosimo, 2007), vol. 4, p. 2182f.

69. Ibid., p. 2183.

70. The original word is *Theotokos*, literally "birthgiver of God" (trans.).

71. Saint John of Damascus, "An Exact Exposition of the Orthodox Faith," in *Writings*, pp. 294f.

72. St. John Damascene, "Sermon II," in *On Holy Images, Followed by Three Sermons on the Assumption*, trans. Mary H. Allies (London: Thomas Baker, 1898), p. 186.

73. Ibid., p. 191.

Transition

1. Heidegger, *Being and Time*, p. 155.

2. Ibid., p. 165.

3. Ibid., p. 164.

4. Ibid., pp. 165f.

5. The uses of "the monstrous" here and in the closing question correspond in the original to *das Ungeheure*, and should be taken less in the sense of "atrocious" or "horrible" than "immense" or "unfathomable" (trans.).

PHOTOGRAPHIC CREDITS